WORLD® AIR POWER
JOURNAL

Aerospace Publishing Ltd
AIRtime Publishing Inc.

Published quarterly by
Aerospace Publishing Ltd
179 Dalling Road
London W6 0ES
UK

ISSN 0959-7050

Aerospace ISBN 1 874023 66 2
                (softback)
                1 874023 67 0
                (hardback)
Airtime ISBN   1-880588-07-2
                (hardback)

Published under licence in USA and
Canada by AIRtime Publishing Inc.,
USA

Editorial Offices:
WORLD AIR POWER JOURNAL
Aerospace Publishing Ltd
3A Brackenbury Road
London W6 0BE   UK

Publisher: Stan Morse
Managing Editor: David Donald
Editor: Jon Lake
Associate Editor: Robert Hewson
Sub Editor: Karen Leverington
Editorial Assistant: Tim Senior

Origination and printing by
   Imago Publishing Ltd
Printed in Singapore

Europe Correspondent:
   Paul Jackson
Washington Correspondent:
   Robert F. Dorr
USA West Coast Correspondent:
   René J. Francillon
Asia Correspondent:
   Pushpindar Singh
Canada Correspondent:
   Jeff Rankin-Lowe

The editors of WORLD AIR
POWER JOURNAL welcome
photographs for possible publication,
but cannot accept any responsibility for
loss or damage to unsolicited material.

The publishers gratefully acknowledge
the assistance given by the following
people:

Joe W. Stout of Lockheed Martin
Tactical Aircraft Systems for his
assistance in compiling the *Lockheed
Martin F-16 Operators*.

Lt Col Brian C. Rogers and Don
Logan for their help with the B-1B
article.

Lt Col Alcantara, Capt Libreros and the
staff of the Ejercito del Aire public
relations office, 111 Escuadron, Lt Col
Sebastia (Operations Group CO of Ala
11), Spanish army and navy public
relations offices, Portuguese Madrid
embassy Air Attaché, Lt Col Carvahlo,
J.M. Sales, J. Valero, J. Matute and
Federico Wichi for their inestimable
contributions to the *Air Power Analysis*
articles on Portugal (this volume) and
Spain (previous volume).

**World Air Power Journal is
published quarterly and is
available by subscription and
from many fine book and hobby
stores.**

**SUBSCRIPTION AND BACK
NUMBERS:**

**UK and World (except USA and
Canada) write to:**
Aerospace Publishing Ltd
FREEPOST
PO Box 2822
London
W6 0BR
UK

**(No stamp required if posted in
the UK)**

USA and Canada, write to:
AIRtime Publishing Inc.
Subscription Dept
120 East Avenue
Norwalk
CT 06851, USA
(203) 838-7979
Toll-free order number in USA:
1 800 359-3003

**Prevailing subscription rates are
as follows:**
Softbound edition for 1 year:
     $58.00
Softbound edition for 2 years:
     $108.00
**Softbound back numbers
(subject to availability) are
$19.00 each. All rates are for
delivery within mainland USA,
Alaska and Hawaii. Canadian
and overseas prices available
upon request. American Express,
Discover Card, MasterCard and
Visa accepted. When ordering
please include your card
number, expiration date and
signature.**

Publisher, North America:
   Mel Williams
Subscription Director:
   Linda DeAngelis
Retail Sales Director:
   Jill Brooks
**Charter Member Services
Manager:**
   Janie Munroe

WORLD AIR POWER JOURNAL ®

CONTENTS

Military Aviation Review

International

UK demands new management techniques to curtail Eurofighter costs

In its latest Parliamentary report, the UK's National Audit Office has blamed 'cumbersome and bureaucratic' management arrangements for the continuing delays in the four-nation Eurofighter 2000 project. Delays have now extended to three years, and there is a seven-year UK cost escalation of £2.2 billion. According to the NAO, Eurofighter programme costs have risen by 23 per cent in real terms since the project started in 1987. Latest estimates are that the UK share of EF 2000 R&D will total £3.54 billion at 1993-94 values, against earlier projections of £2.88 billion.

Britain's R&D share, for which £3.919 billion in funding has already been approved for completion of development in September 2002, seems little changed from the previous NAO reports. Production estimates for the 250 EF 2000s required by the RAF, however, appear to have been revised upwards to around £10.96 billion.

The total UK Eurofighter cost of £14.9 billion represents a cost for each aircraft of £59.6 million, compared with the original total of £12.7 billion and within the revised overall four-nation budget approaching £34 billion. The NAO claims there must be added £104 million which the RAF will be forced to spend to keep its ageing Jaguars and limited-capability Tornado F.Mk 3 interceptors in service until EF 2000 deliveries start in January 2000.

As the main cause of the programme delays the NAO pinpoints the work-sharing arrangements between the four partner nations, which is designed to distribute contracts according to the number of aircraft required, and to spread technology rather than achieve best value for money. Other delays were caused, said the NAO, by doubts over Germany's continued involvement. The significant monetary cost to the UK of Germany's indecision and obstruction has not been revealed, however. More stretch-outs resulted from Germany's goalpost-changing and failure to ratify decisions promptly. Approval is still needed for the increased costs resulting from these delays, while 'significant' technical risks still remain. UK MoD Chief Scientist Peter Ewins told the NAO that these delays posed the greatest risk to Eurofighter's viability, and called for management and time-keeping improvements to be implemented before production commitments were made. Latest reports suggest that in order to meet even the revised delivery timetables now under discussion, the EF 2000 will be delivered to the RAF in three different versions. The interim, reduced-capability aircraft will come first, and second-level aircraft will be retrofitted to the full standard in service.

Air reinforcements for UNPROFOR

New NATO units recently sent to reinforce the UN's Operation Deny Flight over Bosnia have included eight Tornado ECR electronic combat reconnaissance fighters from the German Luftwaffe's JBG 32 at Lechfeld, in Bavaria. This represents the first overseas combat deployment of German military units since 1945. Operating from Piacenza, in Italy, the German Tornados use their Texas Instruments emitter location systems over Bosnia to pin-point hostile SAM systems threatening NATO air patrols, against which they can each release up to four AGM-88A HARMs for SEAD roles. The aircraft are also equipped with horizon-to-horizon IR imaging linescanner systems for round-the-clock reconnaissance in most weather conditions.

Apart from SA-7, SA-14 and SA-16 shoulder-launched SAMs, plus SA-2, SA-6, SA-9 and SA-13 medium-range air defence missiles, Bosnian Serb forces have been threatening to attack NATO strike aircraft with eight batteries of Fakel SA-10B 'Grumble' or S-300 Patriot-type SAMs, with 32 launchers and 128 missiles. This advanced air defence system has already been exported to such countries as Bulgaria and Ukraine, and SA-10 missile canisters were among new equipment displayed by rival Croatian forces in a Zagreb military parade earlier in 1995.

The German contingent in Italy also includes six Piacenza-based Tornados of Aufklärungsgeschwader (AG) 51 reconnaissance wing from Schleswig-Jagel, carrying ex-German navy camera and sensor pods. Operational and logistic support is provided by two Marine-flieger Dassault Atlantic 'Peace Peek' Sigint aircraft, plus 12 Transall C.160D transports. Total cost of the German UNPROFOR deployment was quoted by Defence Minister Volker Ruehe as about DM345 million ($246 million), requiring equivalent cuts in other defence budget items.

Among RAF units operating over Bosnia, 12 Harrier GR.Mk 7s of No. 4 Sqn from Laarbruch formally relieved the Jaguars which had been operating on Operation Deny Flight from Gioia del Colle in Italy on 1 August. Jaguars from the three Coltishall squadrons have accumulated over 5,000 hours of flight operations from Gioia del Colle in support of the UN Protection Force in the former Yugoslavia over the past two years. The 5,000th hour was flown by a Jaguar of No. 6 Sqn. After their relief by Harriers, the Jaguars flew home, but two flew back out to Italy soon after; they were recently-modified GR.Mk 1B versions with GEC-Marconi's thermal imaging and laser designation (TIALD) system to allow the aircraft to self-designate and deliver precision-guided munitions, or to designate for other PGM/LGB-carrying aircraft.

Left: The final call (almost) for the Mirage F1C in Armée de l'Air service came on 20 June 1995 with the disbandment of EC 3/12 'Cornouaille'. A handful of F1Cs remain with EC 4/33 in Djibouti, and as trainers with EC 3/33.

Above and below: EC 3/12's component squadrons were 1e Escadrille 'Scorpions' and 2e Escadrille 'Bull Mastiffs'. To commemorate the unit's disbandment, Mirage F1C 10/12-ZD was painted up with each squadron's markings on either side.

The RAF's UNPROFOR contingent was further reinforced in August by the arrival of four Chinook HC.Mk 1 heavy-lift helicopters at Ploce, on the Croatian coast. These are on detachment from No. 7 Sqn at Odiham, in support of the UN Rapid Reaction Force.

Large-scale US forces in the area have been reinforced by four General Atomic Tier 2 Predator medium-altitude UAVs deployed for reconnaissance missions over Bosnia from Gjader air base in Albania. Predator is claimed to be the first UAV fitted with a (Westinghouse) synthetic aperture radar, as well as colour video and FLIR, giving it day/night and all-weather operating capabilities. It also incorporates a Ku-band satellite communications capability, for video down-links.

Unfortunately, the Predator (P008) making the first operational surveillance flight over Bosnia with the new Ku-band satellite link on 11 August was lost nine hours into its mission. Since it was involved in low-altitude imagery roles, it may have been shot down by ground fire, although possible engine problems have not been ruled out. 'Anomalous engine behaviour' was also encountered – again, possibly due to ground fire – with another Albania-based Predator

(P002), which the ground operators then steered into high ground to destroy when the UAV appeared unlikely to regain its base. These losses left only Predators P001 and P003 in Albania, both fitted with just UHF links, but an additional Ku-band-equipped example (P009) was delivered on 12 August to continue operations after an investigatory grounding.

French revenge strike in Bosnia?

Press reports in Paris claimed that a covert air strike was made by a French Mirage 2000D on 23 July with a single 1000-kg LGB against a house owned by 'a close relative' of the Bosnian Serb leader Radovan Karadzic, in Pale. The strike was allegedly ordered by President Chirac in retaliation for the killing of two French officers by Bosnian Serb forces on the previous day.

The Mirage 2000 was said to have flown in close formation with a Mirage IVP (or alternatively a pair of IVPs) on an authorised mid-day reconnaissance mission. They flew over Bosnia, from Mont-de-Marsan, at about 10,000 ft (3281 m), the Mirage 2000 in close

formation to avoid radar detection by UN or Serb forces. While these allegations were flatly denied by French government sources, Defence Minister Millon's response was more ambivalent. He said that if the reports were true, "it would obviously be part of an appropriate response to the logic of war chosen by the Serbs."

Admitting that an operation of this type was "just about feasible", a NATO Allied Forces Southern Europe spokesman in Naples said he was unaware of a French request to fly a reconnaissance mission at that time. Two US and two Spanish aircraft were then in the area, although not in the immediate vicinity of Pale. President Chirac, then on an official visit to Dakar, added to the mystery by confirming that he had ordered retaliation for the officers' deaths in Bosnia, "which had been carried out."

NATO battlefield surveillance plans

Northrop Grumman's E-8C J-STARS is a strong contender for NATO's new battlefield reconnaissance aircraft requirement.

NATO has still to decide between a fixed-wing or helicopter platform for its battlefield sensors, and is evaluating the French HORIZON concept involving an AS 532 Cougar with a ventral Thomson-CSF radar scanner and associated equipment, as well as Alenia's similar AB.412 Creso, among other projects.

Nine European companies, including British Aerospace, DASA, Alenia, Fokker and MATRA, plus avionics manufacturers, are teaming with Northrop Grumman for its NATO J-STARS submission. For economy, this continues to rely on used Boeing 707s although with new powerplants such as the CFM56. A programme cost of $4.7 billion for 18 J-STARS-type aircraft is estimated by Northrop Grumman to be about $2.3 billion cheaper than using similar avionics in Airbus A340-200s.

Twenty J-STARS costing $5-7 billion are planned for the USAF as a follow-on to three development aircraft now completing flight tests. Three former Canadian CC-137s (707-347Cs) have recently been bought for $6.8 million by the USAF's Electronic Systems Center at Hanscom AFB, for E-8C conversion.

Europe

CROATIA:

Air force units in action

Some of the 30 or so MiG-21bis and MiG-23s of the Croatian air force obtained from Russia and Slovakia took part in last summer's recapture of the Krajina enclave. They were used in ground-attack roles against Serbian forces, as well as for strikes against Udbina airfield and a communications centre in Gracac. Support was also provided by a dozen or more Mil Mi-8s and a similar number of AT-6-armed Mi-24D/Vs. Croatia is also reported to have obtained GD Stinger and Shorts Blowpipe infantry SAMs – the latter from Chile. Croatia is known to operate large quantities of other SAMs, including S-75 modifications of SA-2 'Guidelines' and SA-10 'Grumbles'.

CZECH REPUBLIC:

MiG-21 upgrade dispute

Defence Minister Vilem Holan has authorised the modernisation early next year of a two-seat MiG-21U combat trainer in addition to the original MiG-21MF demonstrator, a move that defies a parliamentary ruling in June vetoing previously approved funding of some $135 million for this programme. Parliament was originally in favour of Czech air force proposals to upgrade 24 of its MiG-21s in the current five-year defence plans. The chairman of the defence and security committee said in 1994 that it would be inappropriate to allocate such large financial resources to modernise relatively old fighters at a

time when they are facing budget shortfalls serious enough to hamper maintaining a credible operational capability.

Holan maintained that the air force was entitled to evaluate the upgraded aircraft, after which the committee would be invited to reconsider the situation. No contractor had yet been selected, although Aero Vodochody had teamed up with Israel's Elbit Industries, as its export L-39 partner, to promote the latter's MiG-21 upgrade programme. Also in contention was the Lahav Division of Israel Aircraft Industries in conjunction with the state-owned overhaul and maintenance companies of Letecky Opravny Kbely (LOK) and Letecky Opravny Malesice (LOM) in Prague.

FRANCE:

IIR MICA makes a hit

After prolonged development in its initial form with a Dassault Electronique AD4A active radar-homing head, MATRA's medium-range (over 60-km/32-nm) MICA AAM recently completed its first air launch with a SOFRADIR imaging infra-red guidance system. Released from a Mirage 2000, the IIR MICA scored a direct hit against an Aérospatiale CT.22 drone without data-linked target update information. MATRA claims this was achieved at a range greater than any IR-guided AAM in service in the Western world. With a launch weight of only about 110 kg (242 lb), the compact MICA is being developed for use with the Mirage 2000-5, and later the Rafale. More than 2,000 have already been ordered by France, Qatar and Taiwan. IIR MICA development is scheduled for completion in 1997.

To celebrate the 50th anniversary of CEAM (Centre d'Expériences Aériennes Militaires) one of its resident Mirage 2000s adopted this commemorative scheme.

Below: Another participant at the July birthday for CEAM, at Mont-de-Marsan, was this based EC 5/330 'Cote d'Argent' Mirage F1C. EC 5/330 is proud to be a 'tiger squadron'.

Paveway II LGB kits ordered by France

Five hundred GBU-12 Paveway II laser-guided bomb kits costing $28.7 million have been ordered from Texas Instruments by the French government, following qualification trials by a Mirage F1CT at Cazaux. Options are also included for an additional 1,000 GBU-12 kits for initial use by the two Armée de l'Air Mirage F1CT squadrons

(EC 1/30 and 3/30) deployed for service over Bosnia from their base at Colmar-Meyenheim.

The GBU-12 kits comprise nose-mounted laser-homing and guide-vane units, plus rear flip-out fins. They will be fitted to about 500 227-kg (500-lb) Mk 82 HE bombs transferred to France from Germany as part of the latter country's Gulf War aid. The Paveway II system combines a limited stand-off delivery capability with an

Nancy-based EC 01.003 'Navarre' (EC 1/3) is now operational with the Mirage 2000D conventional strike aircraft. This example carries Magic 550 AAMs along with AS30L ASMs.

accuracy of 3-10 m (9.8-33 ft), but is not readily adaptable to the standard French 250-kg (551-lb) HE bomb with an SFA-MATRA retarding tail.

MATRA LGBs are also in French air force (AA) service, but the Paveway II system is being considered for use by its Jaguars and Mirage 2000Ds, as well as Aéronavale Super Etendards. TI GBU-10H systems are also used on 2,000-lb BLU-109 Mk 84 hardened HE bombs by the Dutch and other NATO air forces, while the RNAF and Britain's MoD have recently placed additional orders for TI's GBU-24 Paveway III kits.

AS30L for Super Etendard

The Délégation Générale pour l'Armement has ordered an unspecified number of Aérospatiale AS30L laser-guided ASMs at a cost of FFr43 million ($9 million). They are intended for the Aéronavale's 52 Dassault Super Etendards, which are now beginning to re-enter service after undergoing an extensive upgrade programme at the navy's Cuers workshops.

More naval Falcons

Five Dassault Falcon 50s have been ordered by the Aéronavale for SAR roles, fitted with Thomson-CSF radar and other specialised equipment. They will supplement the same number of smaller Falcon 20 Gardians operated by the navy since 1984 for similar duties. The Falcon 20s have been used by Escadrilles de Servitude 9S and 12S for patrol, general support and SAR in the Pacific, including logistic participation in the French nuclear test programme.

GERMANY:

Naval Lynx shortfalls

Delays in the four-nation NH-90 utility/ASW helicopter programme, which France's post-Mitterrand government is insisting must be drastically recosted, is causing problems for the Marineflieger in equipping its expanding frigate fleet. The German navy had been relying on deliveries of 38 NFH-90 versions from 2000 to begin replacing its 17 surviving shipborne Westland Sea Lynx Mk 88s. NFH-90 cannot now follow on until 2004 at the earliest.

Purchase of seven Super Lynx is therefore planned at an early stage, together with the upgrade of the current

Above: ET 61, based at Orléans, became fully operational with the Transall C.160 in 1970. It currently possesses one C-130 Hercules and two C.160 squadrons.

Below: Mirage 2000C no. 1 has spent most of its flying career with the Brétigny-sur-Orge-based Centre d'Essais en Vol (CEV), and in July 1995 it chalked up its 1,000th flight.

Lynx fleet to approximately similar standards with revised avionics and a maximum take-off weight increased to 11,300 lb (5126 kg). Work has started at Westland on a Lynx life-extension programme to extend service up to 2035. The programme includes the introduction of new, stronger and longer-lifed tie-bars, which link the rotor head and blades, to absorb drag and torsional loads.

HUNGARY:

New fighters sought

Sweden's JAS 39 Gripen is claimed to be a front-runner for a requirement for an initial batch of 30 new multi-role fighters to replace ageing MiG-23s and Su-22s. The Gripens are in competition with the Mirage 2000-5 and the F-16. Negotiations for the Gripen have been in progress for some time, but last summer's US State Department policy change sanctioning the release of advanced weapons to certain countries in Eastern Europe, including Hungary, brought the F-16 into contention. The MiG-29M is also an outside-chance

contender now that completion of development has been funded. It is likely to be offered at a very low price, perhaps in settlement of existing debts.

Options are reportedly now available to Hungary from the US for surplus USAF F-16s, or for the undelivered Pakistani F-16A/Bs, or for new production F-16C/Ds. The USAF is anxious to unload up to 350 stored air defence-optimised F-16A/Bs through its Coalition Force Enhancement programme so that it can use the money to help fund new F-16C/Ds, but Hungary is said to be more interested in the multi-role capabilities of the F-16C/D or JAS 39 Gripen. The USAF has now been cleared to provide detailed and classified briefings on the F-16C/D, including price and availability, to the governments of Poland, the Czech Republic and Hungary.

Air force fighters grounded

Hungary's 11 Su-22M-3 'Fitters' and two surviving Su-22U trainers, as well as 22 of its MiG-29 'Fulcrum-A' fighters and six Mi-29UB trainers, were briefly grounded last summer following several

incidents and accidents with both types. Su-22s were cleared for flight clearance in late June following examination of the 'Fitter' fleet after an engine fire on take-off destroyed an Su-22U on 25 May. Foreign object ingestion damage to three Klimov RD-33 engines, which grounded the 'Fulcrum' fleet in July, was traced to loose rivets from the auxiliary suck-in intake louvres above the wingroots. These open to maintain the required airflow during take-off and landing when the main intake grilles are automatically lowered – to prevent foreign object ingestion.

More German aircraft transfers expected

Earlier transfers of 20 former East German Aero L-39ZO Albatros jet trainers to the Hungarian air force by the Bonn government are to be followed by the similar supply of surplus ex-GDR Mil Mi-24 'Hinds'. Some 39 ex-NVA Mi-24Ds and 12 of the newer cannon-armed Mi-24Ps have been in storage since German reunification, although about a dozen are believed to have been transferred to Poland. Twelve Mi-24s are also reported to be included in a current $500 million arms transfer package from Russia to Bulgaria.

ITALY:

First Tornado F.Mk 3s delivered

Formal hand-over of the first of 24 RAF Tornado F.Mk 3s on long-term lease to the Italian air force (AMI) took place at Coningsby in July. The Tornados will function as a stop-gap pending initial deliveries in about 2002 of Italy's EF 2000s, now reduced from 130 to around 110. All 24 F.Mk 3s, starting with ZE832 (now reserialled MM7202), are being modified at Italy's expense to full operational Gulf War standards with Type AA GEC-Marconi Avionics AI-24 Foxhunter radar updates, Have Quick II secure communications radios, night-vision goggles, RHWR and chaff/flare dispensers.

Tornado fighter conversion, including training for the first AMI rear-seat weapons systems operators, all but one of whom are pilots, has been undertaken by No. 56 (Reserve) Sqn at Coningsby. This unit is also providing three RAF exchange and liaison officers to assist with further conversion training and standardisation on the initial AMI F.Mk 3 unit, which received its first aircraft on 5 July. The first AMI squadron – 12° Gruppo of 36° Stormo (wing) – was due to get 12 F.Mk 3s to replace its Lockheed F-104ASA Starfighters at Gioia del Colle in southern Italy by the end of 1995. The remaining 12 Tornado ADVs will be delivered between January and July 1997 and will be operated by 21°

Gruppo of 53⁰ Stormo from Cameri. The ADV squadrons will have a handful of MB339s to allow the backseaters to maintain their flying currency before they transition to the front seat after three years. These young officers will then be prime contenders to go on to the Eurofighter, since they will have more radar-handling and BVR experience than any other Italian pilots.

Under the 18 March 1994 MoU between Britain and Italy for the lease agreement, the 24 aircraft will remain RAF property and theoretically subject to recall at any time, if required. The RAF has adequate resources to maintain six Tornado fighter squadrons and an OCU, and also to meet its commitments to provide the AMI with the training, technical and logistic support throughout the lease period.

LATVIA:

More transports required

Two Antonov An-24 'Coke' and two An-26 'Curl' twin-turboprop transports are being sought by the Latvian Air Defence Force (APAS) to supplement two former-East German Let L-410UVP-Ts acquired from Bonn in 1993. Latvia needs more air transport capacity to support its share of the joint Baltic infantry battalion, formed earlier this year with Estonia and Lithuania. APAS also has a requirement for six surplus Aero L-39s.

NETHERLANDS:

New tanker system

Two Royal Netherlands air force McDonnell Douglas DC-10-30CFs (c/n 46956/985, T-235/264) are using a new and advanced Remote Aerial Refuelling Operation (RARO) system. The aircraft have been modified as boom-equipped air tankers with optional underwing hose/drogue pods to KDC-10 standard. Developed by MDD at Santa Ana, CA, this replaces the ventral boom-operator's position in USAF KC-10As and Boeing KC-135Rs with three-dimensional operator displays and controls located aft of the flight deck. The system uses remote TV/IR sensors with a 180° viewing arc of the area aft of the tanker.

The palletised RARO's system console can be removed to provide added space in the aircraft cabin during cargo or passenger-carrying missions. It can also be installed in DC-10-30 or MD-11 versions not equipped with the wide cargo door. Advantages claimed for the RARO system over direct-vision boom control include enhanced night vision, improved visibility in poor weather conditions, and better depth perception because of the sensors' stereoscopic and IR capabilities.

Following initial delivery in the autumn of 1995, the KLu's KDC-10s are being operated alongside the two C-130H-30s (c/n 5273/75, G-273/275) and four twin-turboprop Fokker 60 Utilities (c/n 20321/24/27/29, U-01 to 04) in No. 334 Transport Squadron

Right: The Tornados, of AG 51 (formally MFG-1 aircraft) have joined the German Deny Flight detachment at Piacenza. This aircraft is carrying an MBB/Aeritalia camera/IRLS recce pod.

Below: This former Interflug Tu-154M now serves as the Luftwaffe's Open Skies aircraft and, as such, made the first (publicly acknowledged) 'spy' flight over the USA in August 1995.

at Eindhoven. Its nine long-serving Fokker F27M Troopships are now being offered for sale by the Dutch government.

POLAND:

Western fighters evaluated

The Polish air force (PWL) plans to replace rather than upgrade some 220 MiG-21s from about 1998 onwards with an initial batch of 100 or so new multi-role fighters, and has invited possible contenders to participate in a fly-in presentation at the Air Force College at Deblin towards the end of August. Attendance was expected from such types as the Dassault Rafale and Mirage 2000-5, JAS 39 Gripen, F-16, and the MiG-29M, Sukhoi Su-27 and Su-35.

The F-16, in all current production variants, has only recently been cleared by the US State Department for sale to Poland, which has been offered surplus USAF F-16A/Bs at advantageous prices. The PWL, however, is mainly interested in new F-16C/Ds, with associated licence-production participation. The weakness of the F-16 for Poland is that it does not have a modern, viable BVR missile, since the AIM-120 AMRAAM is unlikely to be cleared for export to the former Warsaw Pact nation. MiG-MAPO has offered to upgrade Poland's existing MiG-29s to MiG-29SD standards with dual target engagement capability and the RVV-AE R-77 'Adder' AAM. A production licence for the more advanced MiG-29M has reportedly been offered to Poland, but that country has been attempting to break away from its traditional Russian/Eastern Bloc military procurement policies.

That this policy is not absolute is reflected by PWL interest in the new Czech Garret 124-powered Aero Vodochody L-159. The aircraft is intended for light attack and possible

lead-in fighter training roles, with a proposed trade-off against procurement by the Prague government of WSK/PZL Swidnik W-3W Huzar combat helicopters. These would supplement 24 Mi-24s in current Czech service. L-159 procurement is now apparently preferred by the PWL to indigenous development of a light attack aircraft, such as the proposed twin-turbofan PZL 230 Skorpion.

RUSSIA:

MiG-29 sets height record

The FAI has revealed that it has ratified a new Class C1H (turbojet landplane with a take-off weight between 12000 and 16000 kg) world altitude record without payload, of 27460 m (90,092 ft). This was set on 26 April 1995 by Roman Taskaev, Mikoyan's Chief Test Pilot, in a MiG-29 powered by a pair of standard RD-33 engines, rated at 81.39 kN (18,298 lb) each. He flew the aircraft from the test centre at Akhtubinsk, referred to in the FAI documentation as Jasmine. Mikoyan have failed to publicise this achievement, leading many to wonder why the record attempt was made at all. The record was previously held by a Lockheed SR-71 at 25929.031 m (85,069 ft), and had been set on 28 July 1976.

MiG-31 development stalled

Funding problems have brought to a virtual standstill two development programmes for the MiG-31 long-range Mach 2.35 air defence fighter. Flight-testing of the upgraded MiG-31M, which started in 1987, has been virtually completed at the VVS Akhtubinsk service trials centre, but production preparations were halted in late 1992 in the absence of further financial support. At least eight prototypes have been built at the

Sokol plant in Nizhni Novgorod, one crashing on 9 August 1991 at Zhukhovskii after an aileron control failure. They incorporate leading-edge wingroot extensions plus modified S-800 Zaslon-M ('Flash Dance') electronically-scanning phased-array radar and avionics to operate with the active radar homing Vympel R-37 and shorter range R-77 AAM-AE (AA-12 'Adder').

Having produced about 200 MiG-31s to date, Sokol has been upgrading earlier versions to a lower MiG-31B standard, by installing A-723 LORAN/Omega-compatible long-range navigation systems and improved radar software. Work has reportedly stopped on the slightly simplified MiG-31E development of this variant designed for export, with no overseas customers confirmed to date.

Aircraft losses listed from Chechnya operations

In seven months of operations in Chechnya, the Russian air forces (VVS) and Army Aviation have reportedly lost at least two Sukhoi Su-25 'Frogfoot' ground-attack aircraft, four Mi-24 and six Mi-8 helicopters to Chechen ground fire. This included SA-7, SA-14 and SA-16 infantry SAMs, as well as ZSU-23-4 Shilka and other AAA weapons, which also inflicted substantial damage on another 12 VVS aircraft and a number of helicopters. Russian aircraft of all types allegedly destroyed virtually the entire Chechen air force of 250 aircraft – mostly Aero L-29 and L-39s – and helicopters on the ground at three main airfields.

MiG-AT export interest

While the outcome of Russia's military jet trainer contest between the MiG-AT and Yak-130 awaits the conclusion of flight trials, sales presentations have been made to several interested potential export customers, including Australia, India, South Korea, South Africa and Thailand. According to MiG-MAPO, after July meetings between South African Defence Minister Joe Modise and his Russian opposite number Pavel Grachev, there is "a strong chance" that the SAAF could be an early customer for the MiG-AT. The SAAF's frequently grounded and dwindling Aermacchi/Atlas MB.326 fleet is due for replacement by 1998. Earlier this year, satisfactory financial arrangements

This TIALD-lookalike sensor pod was undergoing tests with a WTD-61 RF-4E at Schleswig-Jagel (home of AG 51 and its reconnaissance-tasked Tornados) during May 1995.

Mi-28 in helicopter fly-off

Sweden's Army Flying Service (Armeflyget) has reportedly arranged to lease two McDonnell Douglas Helicopters AH-64A Apache and two of the four Mi-28 'Havoc' prototype attack helicopters for month-long fly-offs in August and October. These were scheduled to be held mainly at the Swedish army's Boden firing range with US and Russian test crews, accompanied by three Swedish pilots trained on each type, and were to include 75-100 hours of tactical and weapons flying by day and night.

The Swedish army needs 20 new attack helicopters by the turn of the century to replace a similar number of Heli-TOW-armed MBB BO 105CB operated for anti-tank roles since 1986-87. This is the first time that Sweden has shown interest in possibly acquiring military equipment from the former Soviet bloc.

for the MIG-AT's Larzac turbofans had still not been finalised, with SNECMA's funding demands described in Russia as 'economically unfeasible'.

Yak-130 changes planned

Development plans revealed by Yakovlev and Aermacchi for their joint all-through jet trainer project, shown in prototype form at 1995's Paris air show, indicate that the production Yak/AEM-130 will be slightly scaled down in size compared with the current Yak-130D demonstrator. Aermacchi considered that its relatively low wing-loading would make it too easy to fly, and less suited for its newly-required secondary ground-attack role. The production version will therefore incorporate a reduction in span from 36.9 ft (11.25 m) to 34.12 ft (10.4 m), accompanied by a decrease in wing area to 253 sq ft (23.5 m²).

Production Yak-130s will also have a shorter and shallower fuselage, with a length of 36.9 ft (11.24 m) instead of 40.7 ft (12.4 m), although of a similar profile. They will have a more down-swept nose for a better forward view, and a pointed rear tailcone profile instead of the Yak-130D's deeper boat-tail, accompanied by a shorter wheel base. Another change will be from the prototype's twin 4,850-lb (21.58-kN) Povazske Strojarnye DV-2 turbofans to similarly-rated DV-2S versions with full-authority digital engine control (FADEC) and operating life improvements developed in conjunction with Klimov and TsIAM in Russia as the RD-35.

According to Aermacchi, the Russian air force (VVS) has given a commitment to order an initial batch of 150-200 Yak-130s, and the necessary develop-

ment funding has been allocated by the Defence Ministry in Moscow in its 1995 budget. When authorised, this will facilitate the planned construction of three pre-production Yak/AEM-130s as the first of the scaled-down versions.

SWEDEN:

Gripen progress and roll-out

Saab Military Aircraft has recently delivered the 10th JAS 39 Gripen (c/n 39.103 to 39.112) from the initial production batch of 30 to the Swedish Materiel Administration (FMV) for SAF operation. More than 1,870 flights from 2,200 required for military certification had then been completed by the five prototypes and first two production aircraft built. Around 90 per cent of all flight-test requirements had been verified, together with 75 per cent of avionics development.

High Alpha and spin-testing remained to be completed for full flight envelope clearance, which will also include cross-wind operation from the narrow Swedish motorway airstrips. Flight

testing was completed in May after 30 sorties of the new P11 edition of the JAS 39's FCS software, which is the first to incorporate non-linear phase-recovery systems to eliminate previous problems of pilot-induced oscillations (PIO) that caused the loss of two Gripens.

Eleven built-in filters now limit stick deflection when the control surfaces for pitch, roll and yaw approach their maximum angular velocities. The filters also instantly detect a change in stick deflection, and stop the ongoing control surface movement, which responds instantly to the new command inputs with no phase delay.

The eighth production Gripen (39.108) was the first to fly, on 11 April, with a new lower pivot-point control column and a modified grip known as the LP stick. This same aircraft was the first to incorporate Ericsson's new D80E computer, with the M11 software edition controlling all functions for the same company's PS 05A fire-control radar. Integration is next being planned of the AIM-120.

Further upgrading is programmed of the Martin Marietta SA11 FCS computer for second production-batch Gripens, including the 14 JAS 39Bs, to increase their growth potential and reduce weight. Batch 2 Gripens will also have second-generation PP12 display processors of approximately 50 per cent less weight and volume. Roll-out of the prototype JAS 39B (39.800) occurred on 29 September 1995, to be followed by an initial flight in the first half of 1996.

Above: The Italian Tornado force, which recently celebrated it 100,000th flying hour, has now been joined by the first of its 24 former-RAF Tornado F.Mk 3s. The first of 12 aircraft destined for 12º Gruppo, 36º Stormo arrived at Gioia-del-Colle on 6 July 1995.

Italian Atlantics are undergoing a progressive systems upgrade that adds a comprehensive EW/ESM capability to the aircraft. The most obvious outward sign of this is a large dorsal antenna.

G IVs acquired for Sigint roles

Delivery was scheduled from August to the Swedish air force of two more Gulfstream G IV twin-turbofan long-range transports. Designated Tp 102Bs by the SAF, these are being equipped in Sweden with TRW Sigint systems and will replace the venerable twin-jet Tp 85 Caravelle IIIs operated for many years by F16M from Malmen. They will also supplement a Tp 102 transport (c/n 1014) flown since late 1992 by F16 from Stockholm/Broma.

TURKEY:

Boeing tanker lease

Two USAF KC-135As have been delivered to the Turkish air force (THK) through an FMS lease programme, pending completion of a $315 million upgrade of seven similar aircraft to KC-135R standards for Turkey from 1997 onwards.

More Cougars ordered

Having taken delivery in July of the first two of an initial $253 million batch of 20 Eurocopter AS 532UL Cougars ordered in September 1993, Turkish army aviation is now buying 30 more through a $370 million contract. Delivery started in April of 19 Mil Mi-17 utility helicopters ordered by the Turkish government from Russia for about $65 million.

UNITED KINGDOM:

AH-64D Apaches for the Army Air Corps

Recently-appointed Defence Secretary Michael Portillo announced on 13 July 1995 that the Army Air Corps is finally getting McDonnell Douglas Apaches to meet its SR(A) 428 attack helicopter requirement, although almost 50 per cent fewer airframes than it first wanted.

The first of the Dutch air force's two KDC-10s (T-264) made its maiden flight on 31 July, for two hours and 30 minutes. It was delivered to No. 334 Squadron in August.

The original programme for 127 helicopters had long been scaled down by defence budget cuts to 91, the minimum to meet the AAC's requirements. These would have equipped four 16-aircraft first-line Apache squadrons, with 27 used for training, in reserve or on maintenance, but the final order proved to be for only 67 aircraft. The Apache was selected in preference to the short-listed BAe-backed Eurocopter Tiger and GEC/Bell Cobra Venom.

All the Apaches will be AH-64D versions within the original £2.5 billion programme cost ceiling. They feature greatly improved all-weather tactical and combat capabilities resulting from installation of mast-mounted Westinghouse millimetre-wave fire-control radars and associated equipment. This contrasts with the recent Dutch order for 30 AH-64Ds, which includes only a small and unconfirmed number of Longbow units.

Unlike the Dutch, the AAC will not receive any US Army AH-64As on loan for lead-in training pending initial AH-64D deliveries. UK Apaches will equip two first-line AAC squadrons in 1998-99, plus another two units of six helicopters each, with the remaining 23 in reserve. Until then, the AAC will continue to rely on its TOW-armed Westland Lynx force for anti-tank and attack helicopter roles and for training. AAC Director Major General Simon Lytle has not ruled out the prospect of acquiring some relatively low-cost surplus US Army AH-64As at a later stage to restore Britain's Apache force to somewhere near its original strength requirements.

Although the MoD's SR(A) 428 requirement specified off-the-shelf procurement, the Westland-built AH-64Ds will be uniquely re-engined with Rolls-Royce RTM322 turboshafts in place of the standard 1,900-shp (1425-kW) GE T700-701Cs. This will allow commonality with RAF EH101s and RN Merlin helicopters, which Rolls-Royce claims will produce life-cycle cost savings of 30 per cent in terms of maintenance and support. With an initial take-off rating of 2,100 shp (1566 kW), the RTM322 also has a significant growth potential, to at least 3,000 shp (2237 kW), to meet projected helicopter upgrade programmes.

Portillo told Parliament that the total British content of the AAC's AH-64Ds is around 50 per cent. This will be achieved through the RTM322s, together with Westland's £800 million workshare and Shorts' participation in IIR- and RF-guided Hellfire anti-tank missiles (and Starstreak, if it can be adapted as an AAM) production. The UK, he added, was also assured of a 100 per cent offset return on the full overseas content value of the AH-64D contracts, which would further guarantee at least 3,000 British job opportunities in nearly 180 companies. The UK order increased total Apache sales to 992, with many more in the pipeline.

Right: The two Dutch KDC-10s are both ex-Martinair DC-10-30CFs. Both have been fitted with a boom and RARO (Remote Aerial Refuelling Operator) system, whereby the boom is controlled, with the aid of TV cameras. Crews have been trained at Seymour Johnson AFB.

RAF upgrade plans

In a recent review of RAF equipment plans, the Chief of Air Staff, Air Chief Marshal Sir Michael Graydon, said that Harrier GR.Mk 7s and T.Mk 10s would be adapted to operate with GEC-Marconi Avionics TIALD systems. This follows a similar £10 million programme for 10 Jaguar GR.Mk 1Bs and two two-seat T.Mk 2Bs. Sir Michael said that relatively low-cost technical enhancements such as integrated inertial platforms, satellite GPS, miniaturised millimetric radar and imaging infra-red would allow precision weapons delivery in all weather conditions.

According to the CAS, measures are under consideration to counter the increasing obsolescence of the RAF's Nimrod fleet through the £1 billion SR(A) 420 Replacement Maritime Patrol Aircraft programme. These include Boeing mission systems in up to 25 BAe-refurbished Nimrods; a GEC-Marconi Avionics mission system in 25 new Lockheed P-3Cs; a Loral ASIC mission system in refurbished P-3Cs; or Dassault avionics in upgraded (Allison AE2100-powered) Atlantique ATL3s. A modified Rockwell-BBN AAP-400 advanced acoustic processing system is being flown in an RAF Nimrod MR.Mk 2 in connection with US submissions for the SR(A) 420 programme.

Deliveries are anticipated in late 2000 of the RAF's first Eurofighters, the advanced multi-role capabilities of which would be crucial to maintain the RAF's operational capabilities. These would also require a medium-range AAM for the critical BVR dimension, for which requests for information (through SRA 1239) had been issued to industry.

Other new weapon requirements included a conventionally armed stand-off missile (for SRA 1236), an anti-armour missile (SRA 1238), and a low-level LGB (SRA 1242).

Airbus tanker trials

An RAF Tornado and a Hawk from the Defence Test and Evaluation Organisation at Boscombe Down have recently taken part in simulated air refuelling exercises with an Airbus A310 flown from the British Aerospace factory airfield at Filton, near Bristol. Both RAF aircraft flew in close formation with the A310 to assess the slipstream effects of its advanced high-lift wing with potential wing refuelling pods, plus those from engine exhausts and wingtip vortices. The assessment contributed to Airbus plans to market multi-role tanker transport (MRTT) versions of its wide-bodied aircraft.

British Aerospace, Airbus, Aérospatiale and DASA have been jointly working on an MRTT programme for some time. The RAF wants to replace its VC10 tanker fleet from about 2005, with French air force KC-135F replacements following a few years later. At the moment, RAF tanker requirements are not included in the UK's plans to acquire 40-50 Future Large Aircraft as second-batch C-130K replacements, and Airbus estimates that the MRTT programme could involve substantial numbers of new and used aircraft over the next decade.

Briefings from Lockheed

Following US DoD clearance, presentations were made earlier this year to the RAF by Lockheed Martin on the U-2S and the proposed F-117B derivative of the projected A/F-117X (formerly F-117N) technology demonstrator which is currently on offer to the US Navy. Thirty-six GE F118-101-powered U-2Ss will be delivered to the USAF by 1998. Briefings on the aircraft were apparently unconnected with the MoD's still-to-be-fulfilled joint services SR(LA) 925 requirement for an airborne battlefield surveillance and stand-off radar system. The RAF has had a long-term interest in the U-2, which several of its pilots have flown operationally, and the presentations appear to be related to possible special applications for up to 12.

Three RAF pilots have also undertaken exchange postings with F-117 units, and Lockheed is understood to have proposed the F-117B as an option for the MoD's SR(A) 425 programme for a Tornado IDS replacement. A radical development of the original F-117 to meet the specification of the USN's now-cancelled A/F-X carrier attack fighter requirement, the A/F-117X and its land-based F-117B version would retain the original basic fuselage shape. Leading-edge sweep would be reduced from 67.5° to 42° and wing-folding introduced, in conjunction with a span increase to 65 ft (19.8 m) and additional F-22-type stabilator surfaces. Low-observable afterburning would also be added to the F404s, and MTOW increased from the F-117's (approximate) 52,910 lb (24000 kg) to 73,259 lb (33230 kg), including 5,000 lb (2268 kg) of internal stores. Engineering and manufacturing development costs are estimated at about $3 billion, and programme unit costs based on 255 A/F-117Xs for the USN and 120 F-117Bs for the USAF as $65.7 and $63 million, respectively.

Middle East

EGYPT:

SeaSprite requirement doubled

FMS negotiations have been reported with the US for a second batch of 10 remanufactured Kaman SH-2G ASW helicopters for the Egyptian navy. Like Egypt's first 10 SH-2Gs, ordered in mid-1994 and scheduled for delivery in 1997-98, these will be completely overhauled and upgraded from surplus USN SH-2Fs. They will be fitted with new General Electric T700-GE-401 turboshafts, AlliedSignal AQS-18A dipping sonar and associated equipment, at a cost of more than $100 million.

ISRAEL:

Aircraft disposals

The IDF/AF is planning to withdraw some of its older military aircraft and is reportedly inviting tenders for some of the surviving McDonnell Douglas F-4E Phantoms from 210 originally received, and the remainder of 36 Hughes 500MD Defender scout helicopters. Some 54 of the IDF/AF's F-4Es are scheduled for transfer to Turkey, apparently through an FMS resale programme.

KUWAIT:

Black Hawk purchase planned

Congressional notifications to the Pentagon of planned FMS contracts have recently included the proposed sale to Kuwait of 16 Sikorsky UH-60L Black Hawk helicopters equipped for anti-tank and assault roles. The planned $460 million contract includes spare GE T700 turboshaft engines, 11,500 Hydra rockets, 38 Rockwell Hellfire ATM launchers and 500 Hellfire anti-tank missiles, as well as night vision systems and support equipment.

In July 1995 1 PLM dispatched two MiG-29s and two MiG-29UBs as part of a squadron exchange with EC 2 at Dijon. The deployment was supported by one of the Cracow-based 13 PLT Antonov An-26s, currently on lease to LOT.

This programme appears to be an alternative to an earlier Kuwaiti plan to acquire 16 MDH AH-64A Apache attack helicopters. That plan has reportedly been put off for the moment, pending US release of the Longbow radar-equipped AH-64D version to the Middle East. AH-64D production is due to start in March 1996, with a substantial backlog of US Army, Dutch and UK orders, but clearance for wider exports is not expected before 2000. In the meantime, Kuwait will use its Hellfire-armed Black Hawks to gain initial experience with clear-weather anti-tank and airborne assault roles.

Southern Asia

INDIA:

Naval Harrier upgrade plans

Indian navy negotiations with British Aerospace to upgrade the remaining Indian navy fleet foundered on cost grounds in late 1994. Twenty-two Sea Harrier FRS.Mk 51s would have been upgraded to F/A.2 standard with GEC-Marconi Blue Vixen multi-mode pulse-Doppler radar and other new avionics. A navalised indigenous Light Combat Aircraft was suggested as an alternative. This remains an increasingly long-term option, but the navy shows continued interest in a lower-cost upgrade for its surviving FRS.Mk 51s, 24 of which remain from original deliveries from 1983.

BAe has therefore since joined with Israel Aircraft Industries in proposing a compromise modernisation with mainly IAI equipment and systems. These include an Elta Electronics EL/M 2032 pulse-Doppler radar, integration with the BAe medium-range ASRAAM, and an Elta 8240-based EW suite, plus cockpit and other improvements.

Structural improvements and engine modifications would also help to extend the service lives of the navy's FRS.Mk 51s to 2010, for an estimated programme cost of about $100 million.

Similar upgrade improvements are required by the Indian navy's four two-seat Harrier T.Mk 60 V/STOL trainers, which the Indian government is interested in replacing with a similar number of retired and refurbished RAF T.Mk 4s or USAF TAV-8As in AMARC storage. In the US, EER Systems was invited to submit a tender by 15 July for upgrading the TAV-8As, which were available from US Marine Corps storage for about $2 million.

Long-standing navy interest in the possible purchase of Russia's surplus 38000-tonne V/STOL carrier *Admiral Gorshkov* has been abandoned, according to the commander-in-chief of India's Eastern Naval Command, Vice Admiral Premveer Das. India now favours building its own new mini-carrier, he added, for which initial finance has already been allocated. A short-term lease of the *Admiral Gorshkov* might be considered, pending completion of the new Indian carrier by 2000.

Su-30MK reconsidered

Earlier in 1995, the Indian air force turned down a mid-1994 offer from Russia's Irkutsk Aircraft Production Association for the supply of 20-30 Sukhoi Su-30MK multi-role combat

Left: The air arm (15th Brigade) of the Slovenian Territorial Defence Force displayed its newly acquired, ex-US Army PC-9s at the national air show held in Portoroz on 8 July. Three aircraft are in service, of which S5-DSL/180 'Skofja Loka', and S5-DPI/182 'Piran' are seen here. The third example is S5-DPT/181. The PC-9s are used by former-JRV fast-jet pilots to keep current, until Slovenia's arms embargo is lifted and combat aircraft can be acquired.

Below left: This Bell 206B S5-HKM was newly delivered in December 1994. The Jet Ranger has adopted the name 'Kralj Matjaz' (King Mathias) a hero of legend, who sleeps beneath the Slovenian alps.

Below: The Slovenska Teritorijalna Obrana has acquired five Bell 412s from Bell-Canada (S5-HGC, HGO, HKR, HMB and HNM) in addition to the three 412HPs (S5-HAB, HAD and HAE) already in use. Aircraft are generally named after towns and carry the shield of that town. The 412s are used for 'fire-fighting and SAR'. S5-HMB is named 'Maribor'.

aircraft. The IAF has since reopened negotiations on this equipment, with a high-level delegation visiting Moscow in August 1995 to discuss a possible $600 million arms procurement package. The Indian air force is particularly interested in the 2,158-nm (4000-km) range capability of the Su-30 on internal fuel, plus provision for air refuelling, and in its promised wide range of precision-guided and other weapons plus datalink systems for joint targeting with other aircraft. The Su-30 is also being considered for licence-production in India as a follow-on to the MiG-27.

PAKISTAN:

Mirage 2000-5 interest

Pakistan has finally accepted that the US veto on the supply of 28 more F-16A/B Fighting Falcons is not going to be lifted by the present Washington administration. The veto was imposed in 1990 because of Pakistan's nuclear weapons programmes, and froze the $658 million F-16 deliveries. The PAF is now looking elsewhere for new combat aircraft. First choice as an alternative was reportedly the multi-role Sukhoi Su-35, but extensive negotiations with the Russians were apparently broken off following pressure from India, which is Moscow's major military export customer.

A Pakistani order for the more expensive Dassault Mirage 2000-5s is now being finalised, following credit facilities established in Paris for the $950 million contract for the purchase of three French Agosta A90 submarines by the Pakistan navy. Against an original requirement for 44 new combat aircraft, the PAF is expected to be able to fund only about 24 Mirage 2000-5s. These will have an estimated cost of about FFr5 billion ($1.02 billion) including equipment and weapons, notably MATRA MICA medium-range AAMs. Negotiations for the new Mirages have been confirmed in both France and Pakistan, although no contract has yet been signed.

Far East

CHINA:

Ballistic missile tests alert

Alarm was expressed in the ASEAN area concerning an announcement by the People's Republic of China of two series of ballistic missile tests over the East China Sea, into a circular area with an 18-km (10-nm) radius, some 130 km (70 nm) north of mainland Taiwan. After the Ministry of Communications in Beijing had warned shipping and aircraft to stay out of this area, the week-long trials from 21 July involved the launch of six CSS-6/DF-15 or M-9 SSMs from Le Ping, in Jianxi Province, over a reported range of almost 500 km (270 nm). The second series was for a period of 10 days in August.

The Islamabad government is asking for the return of its F-16 payments to help pay for the Mirages, but since these were from FMS funding they may not be released by Washington, despite a recommendation to the contrary from President Clinton. As the instigator of the amendment resulting in the US veto on further arms supplies to Pakistan, Senator Pressler has proposed that 11 of the PAF's new F-16s, which have been in storage since completion, should be sold through FMS programmes to the Philippines, and the remaining 17 to Taiwan.

President Clinton has proposed that other embargoed US military equipment worth around $370 million, including three Lockheed P-3C Orion ASW patrol aircraft, Bell AH-1 attack helicopters, Harpoon, Stinger and TOW missiles, plus $17 million worth of spares, should be released to Pakistan despite its nuclear programme. Congressional approval for this measure is still awaited.

Mirage radar upgrade

Finmeccanica's FIAR subsidiary in Italy has received a contract for 35 Grifo M3 lightweight and compact multi-mode pulse-Doppler I-band fire-control radars to upgrade Pakistani Mirage IIIs or 5s. About 100 Grifo 7 radars had previously been ordered by the PAF for installation in its Chengdu F-7P Airguard fighters, and the new order more than doubles total FIAR sales of this equipment, in addition to options for 100 more. The Grifo L has been selected for installation in the 72 ITEC F124-powered Aero L-159 as ordered by the Czech air force, and the Grifo F is being installed in Singapore's upgraded Northrop F-5E/Fs.

The tests were generally interpreted to be an indication of increased tension between Beijing and Taiwan following the Taiwanese president's earlier visit to the US, as well as a reminder of Taiwan's vulnerability to attacks from weapons of this kind. China is reported to have in current service at least 175 silo-based long-range ICBMs, plus shorter-range Dong Feng DF-11, DF-21 and DF-25 mobile ballistic missiles. On 30 May a test launch was reported of China's new DF-31 mobile nuclear intercontinental ballistic missile, with a range of up to 8000 km (4,317 nm).

Tu-154s used for electronic warfare

Two Tupolev Tu-154Ms have been modified in China for electronic warfare with extra avionics, possibly with Israeli assistance. Fitted with extra antennas and radomes, these aircraft

Despite the F7 markings on its nose, this AJS 37 carries the badge of 1 divisionen, F10. It was the first AJS 37 delivered to this Viggen squadron. F10's two other squadrons both fly the J 35J Draken – the last front-line Drakens in Swedish service.

have been observed with similar types at the Nan Yuan weapons and equipment research centre near Beijing.

JAPAN:

FY 1996 aircraft procurement plans

Appropriations requested by the Japanese Defence Agency for the Self-Defence Forces in the proposed Y4,723 billion ($54 billion) FY1996 defence budget for 85 new aircraft comprised 42 for the JASDF, 27 for the JGSDF and 17 for the JMSDF. JASDF requirements include, for the first time, 12 Mitsubishi FS-X fighters, five two-seat Mitsubishi/MDD F-15DJs, 15 Kawasaki T-4 advanced trainers, three Gulfstream U-4 utility transports, four Raytheon U-125A light jet transports for SAR, and three Mitsubishi/ Sikorsky UH-60J Black Hawk helicopters. The FS-X remains the JASDF's priority programme but cost escalation to an estimated $100 million or more per aircraft is expected to reduce the 130 originally planned to about 70, to equip three squadrons.

JGSDF requirements were listed as seven Kawasaki/MDH OH-6D, 10 Fuji/Bell UH-1J, five UH-60J, two Kawasaki/Boeing CH-47J Chinook, and two Fuji/Bell AH-1S Super Cobra helicopters. JMSDF requests comprised a Kawasaki/Lockheed UP-3D Orion EW training aircraft, eight SH-60J ASW SeaHawk and two UH-60J SAR, plus one Sikorsky MH-53J mine counter-measures helicopters. Some difficulties were expected in meeting these requirements, especially as the initial budget proposals were later voted to increase by only 2.9 per cent instead of the 4.1 per cent demanded by the Liberal Democratic element of the three-party ruling coalition.

Longer-term JMSDF requirements for inclusion in the next five-year defence plan could include up to five BAe/MDD Harrier T.Mk 10s. These would be equipped for electronic warfare training to supplement four similarly-modified Learjet U-36As, and operated from a 5000-tonne auxiliary aviation support vessel for offshore operations over longer ranges.

PHILIPPINES:

New aircraft requirements

A new government-approved Ps15 billion ($580 million) five-year procurement programme gives priority to the acquisition of 18 multi-role combat

Above: For the August VJ-Day commemorations, No. 4 FTS supplied 20 black Hawks in a stylish '50' formation. For the practice all available Hawks were used, regardless of colour.

Left: Bulldogs have become the latest type to adopt the RAF's 'training black' scheme. This Bulldog T.Mk 1 from the CFS, at Cranwell, has been further decorated as a display aircraft.

Below: The AWC/SAOEU is firmly established at Boscombe Down, with a fleet of Harrier GR.Mk 7s and T.Mk 4s, Jaguar GR.Mk 1Bs and Tornado GR.Mk 1/A/Bs. Sadly, one of the GR.Mk 7s (the aircraft seen here, ZG475/U) was lost on 1 June, in a crash which claimed the life of the pilot – the CO of the AWC.

aircraft for the air force. Ex-USAF F-16A/Bs are apparently favoured for this plan, which also includes six light naval attack aircraft and six maritime patrollers, three medium-range SAR helicopters, and an Elint type. The air force's five or so remaining F-5As were due to be supplemented in August by three from South Korea.

THAILAND:

F-15s and AIM-120 sought

Active radar-homing BVR AAMs have been introduced following the delivery of 18 MiG-29s to Malaysia, and Vietnam's acquisition of up to 20 Sukhoi Su-27s. The Thai government now perceives with extra urgency its requirement for a third squadron of correspondingly-equipped new high-performance combat aircraft.

Washington has offered Thailand more F-16s, or eight F/A-18 Hornets, to supplement the RTAF's 36 F-16A/Bs. The Thai government is apparently more interested in acquiring the more potent F-15 armed with active radar-guided AIM-120 AMRAAMs. The US State Department originally showed little enthusiasm for releasing either of these systems to Thailand, but was expected to waive its objections in late August. This clears the way for the anticipated acquisition of AMRAAM by Australia and Singapore, among others in the Pacific area.

Evaluations of other combat aircraft, including the Dassault Mirage 2000-5, MiG-29 and Sukhoi Su-27/35, have also been made by the RTAF, which was originally expected to select its new fighter in June 1995. A decision was deferred until after the national elections, resulting in the appointment of a new civilian coalition government with expected changes in defence policies and procurement.

A-7 deliveries begin

Deliveries started in July 1995 to the Royal Thai navy of its first fighters, the

first two of four refurbished ex-US TA-7E Corsair II combat trainers. They were ordered in 1992. These are being followed by the other TA-7Es, plus 14 single-seat A-7E strike fighters at the rate of two per month, and three purchased for spares. The aircraft will undertake maritime operations from U-Tapao naval air base, which accommodates RTN maritime patrol, transport and helicopter squadrons.

Light transport orders

A recent Thai government order for three Dornier Do 228 twin turboprop transports from Daimler-Benz Aerospace (DASA) for coast guard roles will double the Royal Thai navy inventory of this type. Two 29-seat BAe Jetstream 41 light twin-turboprop transports recently ordered by the Royal Thai army will have convertible VIP interiors. The first will arrive in November 1995, and the second a year later.

VIETNAM:

Su-27 order doubled

With deliveries of its first six Su-27s now underway, the Vietnamese air force has ordered a second batch of six Su-27s for $200 million. This represents a programme unit cost of around $33.33 million, which matches repeated claims to this effect by Sukhoi General Designer Mikhail Simonov.

Australasia

AUSTRALIA:

Replacement trainer field narrows

In August, the Australian government ruled out Dassault's submission of the twin-turbofan Alpha Jet ATS for the RAAF's Project Air 5367 requirement for 35-45 new lead-in fighter trainers costing around $A1 billion ($735 million). The move was in protest over French plans to resume another eight subterranean nuclear test explosions in the Pacific. Earlier, Italy's proposals for the Spey-powered AMX-T had also been eliminated by the RAAF, on the grounds of its size and complexity, as had the smaller AlliedSignal F124-powered and Elbit-equipped Aero

L-59F. This leaves the Aermacchi MB.339FD, BAe Hawk 100 and the navalised McDonnell Douglas T-45 Goshawk as the final contenders.

A request for tender for the new trainers, required to replace 27 rewinged Aermacchi MB.326Hs in current RAAF service, was expected to be issued in September and to be followed by final selection early in 1996. Deliveries of the first 12 new trainers, which would have secondary light ground-attack roles, are required by January 2000, when the MB.326Hs are due for retirement.

The Australian government has reserved its position at the moment on the participation in parallel military helicopter procurement programmes of Eurocopter, in which France is an equal partner with Germany. These involve 24-50 replacements for Australian Army Aviation's 40 or so Bell 206B-1 Kalkadoon LOHs, and up to 30 ship-based ASW helicopters, in conjunction with New Zealand, for the two countries' new ANZAC frigates. Potential contenders have been listed as the Eurocopter AS 565SA, Kaman SH-2G, Sikorsky S-76N and Westland Super Lynx.

Army Nomad doubts

Following another accident to a civil-registered example, and continued aerodynamic and structural problems, the Australian Army Aviation Corps has withdrawen its fleet of 22 or so Nomad light turboprop utility twins and recommended its disposal. Originally developed by the Government Aircraft Factories, which became Aerospace Technologies of Australia, a dozen unsold Nomads and two demonstrators were bought from AsTA storage by the government for issue to the AAAC (five N-22 and four stretched N-24A versions) and RAAF

(three, including an N-24) in 1987. In 1993 the AAC received another five surplus civil N-22s and a similar number of N-24s, while several others had been transferred, increasing the total Defence Force inventory to 27.

From total production of about 170, 18 N-22B/Ls were delivered to the Indonesian navy and 12 N-22Bs to the Philippine air force; 22 N-22Bs have been operated by the Royal Thai air force, together with five N-24As by the RTN. Structural problems with the tailplane and ailerons have contributed to at least 10 fatal Nomad crashes, plus another 15 or so less serious accidents, resulting in severe operating restrictions imposed by the Australian CAA and the grounding its fleet by the AAC in November 1994. Replacements are now being evaluated, both for these and the 14 Pilatus Turbo Porters withdrawn from AAAC service in October 1992.

Africa

SOUTH AFRICA:

Transalls back into service

Nine Transall C.160Z twin-turboprop medium-range transports will be returned to service with German help. They were previously operated alongside the C-130Bs of No. 28 Sqn of the South African air force until their 1993 withdrawal on economy grounds. DASA has recently reached agreement with South Africa's Denel arms group on a joint refurbishment and upgrade package for the SAAF's Rolls-Royce Tyne-powered C.160s, which may also involve Aérospatiale and SNECMA in France.

The South African government is expected to accept a US offer of four surplus Lockheed C-130B Hercules from long-term USAF storage, as part of recent new defence agreements. These would supplement seven similar C-130Bs which have been in SAAF service with No. 28 Sqn since November 1962. The US has also offered South Africa several ex-USN Lockheed P-3 maritime patrol aircraft, to supplement the SAAF's local Douglas C-47TP turboprop conversions now entering service for similar roles.

South Africa to play another ACE

Atlas Aviation subsidiary of the Denel group is going ahead with a second prototype of its all-composite evaluator (ACE). This is despite the crash landing of the first prototype on 14 February and despite current deliveries of the first of 60 Pilatus PC-7 Mk II turboprop trainers ordered by the SAAF. ACE 2

is largely unchanged from the original prototype, apart from replacement of its 750-shp 562-kW) Pratt & Whitney Canada PT6A-25C turboprop by the bigger PT6A-68C flat-rated at 1,200 shp (900 kW). This gives a useful increase in all-round performance, including a maximum sea level speed of 290 kt (537 km/h), or 310 kt (575k m/h) at 5,000 ft (1524 m), where the sustained turn rate is 24° per second; an initial climb of 4,450 ft/min (22.6 m/sec); and a service ceiling of 41,000 ft (12497 m), attainable with cabin pressurisation.

PC-7 deliveries were expected to result in the SAAF completing its last pilot training course on its veteran T-6G Harvard piston-engined trainers in November, after which all 97 aircraft are being released in batches for sale to eagerly-waiting civil warbird enthusiasts. Despite more than 50 years of service, and increasing difficulties with spares, the SAAF Harvards have been maintained in pristine condition, and will be trickled onto the market in small numbers. They are thus expected to fetch top prices, probably of at least £60 -£75,000 each.

Above right: Seen at AMARC, Davis-Monthan AFB, in early April was this Douglas A-4M (160045/50), part of the initial batch of seven Skyhawks being readied for transfer to Argentina. It was announced in August that the overhaul contract for all the Argentine-bound J52 Skyhawk engines had been awarded to Miami-based Greenwich Air Services, for a three-year period.

Right: The Argentine Army's 23 OV-1D Mohawks are operational at Campo de Mayo AFB, with Escuadrón de Aviación de Exploración y Reconocimiento 601. Delivered between December 1992 and November 1994, they will soon be joined by a second batch of OV-1s.

South America

ARGENTINA:

A-4C/P Skyhawks retired

The last surviving MDD A-4C and A-4P Skyhawks, some of which had been in service with the V Brigada Aérea since 1966, were scheduled for retirement by the end of 1995. Several were veterans of the Falklands War. The type's operations had been severely restricted following a fatal crash on 10 March 1995. Their withdrawal will leave V Air Brigade without combat equipment until delivery of the first of 36 ex-US Marine Corps A-4Ms currently in desert storage in Arizona. The aircraft will be refurbished and retrofitted in two batches of 18 each, the first at Lockheed Martin Air Services, Ontario, CA, and the second at the Area Material Cordoba facility of FMA

(Fabrica Militar de Aviones). The retrofit package includes Westinghouse AN/APG-66 multi-mode radar, new navigation-attack system, a HUD (head-up display), and liquid crystal displays. Delivery of the modernised aircraft will begin in 1997.

More Mohawks for Army Aviation

Further US military aid to Argentina includes the FMS supply of another 11 ex-US Army Grumman OV-1D Mohawk ground-attack aircraft. These will supplement 23 OV-1Ds now flying with the army's Escuadrón de Aviación de Exploración y Reconocimiento at Campo de Mayo, plus two more for spares, from deliveries between December 1992 and November 1994.

Argentine Army HueyCobra plans

Argentine Army Aviation is to form its first dedicated anti-tank helicopter unit from early 1996, with the scheduled arrival from the US through FMS sources of six to eight ex-US Army Bell HueyCobra attack helicopters. The exact version had not been specified by the end of 1995, but was likely to be drawn from the US Army's inventory of some 300 older AH-1E, P or S Cobra gunships. They were expected to be preceded in late 1995 by another six ex-US Army UH-1H utility helicopters for Argentine Army Aviation.

New helicopters for the coast guard

A $26.9 million contract has been signed with Eurocopter by the Prefectura Naval Argentina for the purchase of two AS 365N2 Dauphin civil utility helicopters for SAR and coastal patrol roles. The contract also includes the upgrade of the PNA's two surviving SA 330L Pumas with new avionics, special mission equipment and engine overhauls. PNA fixed-wing equipment now comprises only five CASA C.212-300 Patrulleros, following disposal of its three remaining Short Skyvans to a European operator.

Joint naval aviation training planned with Brazil

Naval aviation aircrew training with Brazil is now going ahead following annual cross-operational exercises held since 1993 by Argentina naval (CANA) Dassault Super Etendards and Grumman S-2E Trackers from the Brazilian carrier Nacl (A.11) *Minas Gerais*. The programme will involve fixed-wing pilots from both countries being trained in Argentina, and rotary-wing students in Brazil.

The first two Brazilian navy fixed-wing pilots are already training on the Beech T-34C-1 Turbo Mentors of CANA's Escuela de Aviación Naval at the Base Aéronaval Punto Indeo. Argentine naval students are due to start their courses in 1996 with the Forca Aéronaval da Marinha do Brasil's (FAMB) Esquadrão de Instrucão (HT-1) on Bell 206B JetRanger IIIs in Rio de Janeiro. Joint helicopter training is assisted by the fact that both navies operate the Eurocopter AS 355F2/AS 555 Ecureuil and Sikorsky SH-3D.

BRAZIL:

EMB-326H for ALX roles

EMBRAER was awarded a $50 million FSD contract on 18 August 1995 for an uprated version of its EMB-326H Super Tucano. The aircraft was originally designed and proposed with Northrop for the US JPATS primary trainer requirement, and now for the Brazilian air force's (FAB) ALX light ground-attack aircraft requirement. While the Super Tucano ALX will apparently retain the Pratt & Whitney Canada PT6A-68 turboprop fitted to the two prototype EMB-326Hs, it would be uprated to about 1,600 shp (1200 kW) instead of developing its thermal limited maximum power of around 1,344 shp (1008 kW).

For anti-guerrilla, drug-smuggling interdiction and border patrol duties, a single-seat EMB-326H/ALX would be equipped with an advanced nav/attack system including a central mission computer, INS/GPS, HUD, and provision for night-vision goggles, to facilitate precision delivery of up to 2,500 lb (1134 kg) of a wide range of weapons. The aircraft would have a maximum take-off weight of 10,140 lb (4871 kg), with clearance for operation from unpaved airstrips.

A two-seat version would also be produced for armament and tactical combat training as AT-26 Xavante (licence-built M.B. 326) replacements, and would comprise up to 40 per cent of the overall requirement for 100 aircraft. A prototype of each ALX version is being built over a 30-month period, and production of both variants is planned from mid-1998, when FAB funding is approved.

Above: The Canadair Challenger fulfils several diverse roles for the Canadian Armed Forces, including EW training and maritime patrol. This is one of No. 434 Squadron's ('Bluenoses') standard EW-configured CE-144s.

Left: Canada's long-serving Boeing 707 transports (CC-137s) have been disposed of to the USAF's J-STARS programme and replaced by the CC-150 Polaris (Airbus A310-300).

North America

CANADA:

CT-133 upgrade planned

Defence economies have resulted in the government decision to sell 60 27-year old Canadair/Northrop CF-5s now serving as lead-in fighter trainers. Some 39 had been upgraded by Bristol Aerospace through a $C79 ($US53) million contract. Canada's Air Command is now planning a similar upgrade for its 45 remaining 43-year old Canadair/Lockheed CT-133 Silver Star jet trainers to do the same job. Prototype modifications for the upgraded CT-133 have already been made by Kelowna Flightcraft, BC. They are less extensive than those for the CF-5s, but include new avionics and digital nav systems, TACAN, IFF and improved cockpit equipment.

No fatigue problems have apparently been encountered by the CT-133s, still powered by the even older but still reliable Rolls-Royce Nene 10 centrifugal-flow turbojet. Programme costs to upgrade 35 CT-133s, with options on another 10, are estimated at only about $C45 million ($US32.8) million. Ten of the CT-133s from 14 currently operated by No. 414 EW Sqn from Comox, NS, would be fitted with additional systems for EW training. EW training, plus fleet support and target-towing, is also undertaken by a similar number of Silver Stars of No. 434 Squadron at Shearwater.

No contractor has yet been selected for the upgrade programme, although the first refurbished CT-133 is due for delivery in mid-1996. The CAF expects these aircraft to continue flying until about 2015, when they will have recorded 63 years of service.

Helicopter requirements revived

Following the late 1993 cancellation of a $C4.8 billion ($US3.3 billion) order for 43 EH101 ASW and SAR helicopters by the incoming Liberal government on the grounds of excess cost, requests for proposals for 47 similar rotorcraft are being invited before the end of 1995 by the Canadian Defence Department. The most urgent requirement is for 15 medium-lift SAR helicopters to replace half a dozen CAC Vertol 107 (CH-113) Labrador and a similar number of CH-113A Voyageur versions by January 2001. Some 32 ASW types are also needed soon afterwards to replace the current Sikorsky CH-124A/B Sea Kings, within an overall budget for the 47 helicopters of $C2 billion ($US1.46 billion).

Remarkably, Westland and Agusta are now prepared to meet these requirements within the 50 per cent lower specified price ceiling, with a simplified export version of the military EH101 known as the AW320 or Cormorant 100. The companies have written off most of the development and production investment costs from 22 RAF and 44 RN orders. Mission systems equipment would also be Merlin-based and off-the-shelf, rather than the originally specified Canadian fit.

Other expected contenders include the Boeing CH-47D, mainly for the SAR roles; Eurocopter Canada AS 532 Cougar 2; Russia's low-cost Kamov Ka-32 with Western avionics and systems integrated by MacDonald Dettwiler &

Associates in British Colombia; and the Sikorsky S-70B Seahawk with Loral Canada missions systems, favourite for the ASW requirement. Contract award is expected in late 1996 or early 1997, for deliveries from 2000, and a two-type solution has not been ruled out.

UNITED STATES:

RC-135 re-engine programme

The Air Force is to re-engine its fleet of RC-135s operated by the 55th Wing at Offutt AFB, NE with the GE/SNECMA F108-CF-100 (CFM56) turbofan. The House Permanent Select Committee on Intelligence recently voted the necessary funding to enable the long-overdue programme to proceed, although no timescale has been announced. The fitment of new engines will take place at the same time as the RC-135s receive a major overhaul.

The 55th Wg presently operates four different versions, consisting of two RC-135Ss (61-2662/2663), a pair of RC-135Us (64-14847, 14849), seven RC-135Vs (64-14841/14846 and 14848), and six RC-135Ws (62-4131, 4132, 4134, 4135, 4138 and 4139). The RC-135Us (Combat Sent) and the RC-135V/Ws (Rivet Joint) are dedicated to specific Sigint-gathering tasks, with regular overseas deployments to Kadena AB, Okinawa, Riyadh, Saudi Arabia and RAF Mildenhall, UK. The new fuel-efficient engines will reduce operating costs considerably, as well as easing take-off at some of the desert operating locations.

The RC-135S (Cobra Ball) spent the majority of its service career stationed at Eielson AFB, AK until all RC-135s were centralised at Offutt AFB. The duties of Cobra Ball were largely eliminated when the Soviet Union all but stopped conducting tests of intercontinental ballistic missiles. The US Army favours a modification programme whereby the RC-135S could be employed to detect the launch of 'Scud' missiles. At present, the two aircraft are at Offutt AFB with occasional deployments to ply their unique trade.

Additional budget funding for FY96

Despite turning down an offer from Lockheed Martin and McDonnell Douglas of additional F-16C/Ds and F-15Es at a fixed unit price, Congress has voted funds to enable defence spending to be increased on these and other aircraft types. The Republican-led Congress has allocated the money even though federal spending has largely been reduced to help address the deficit. The Clinton administration had requested $257.6 billion, with the

House National Security Committee adding almost $10 billion in June, a figure subsequently trimmed to $264.7 billion by the Senate Armed Services Committee (SASC).

A sum of $553 million was approved by the House for the acquisition of long lead items needed for construction of B-2 bombers beyond the 20 currently budgeted. However, the SASC declined to add any funding to the project, with the money held in abeyance while the bomber situation is sorted.

Both the Senate panel and the full House approved the request for $2.6 billion for eight C-17s and other strategic airlifters for the 1996 budget despite the uncertainty of the Globemaster III's future. An additional sum of $70 million was added to acquire one non-developmental airlift aircraft, should the Department of Defense pursue that option.

Research and development of the F-22 fighter was boosted by the allocation of the full $2.1 billion as requested. To enable the USAF to operate at a force structure equivalent to 20 fighter wings, a further $425 million was allocated by the House to purchase six F-15Es and six F-16Cs, although the SASC did not authorise funding for these aircraft. It remains to be seen if the SASC or the House will triumph with their spending programmes.

Edwards confirmed as SR-71A operating base

The Air Force has confirmed that Edwards AFB, CA will be the stateside operating location for the two SR-71As which are in the process of being returned to service. The operation will be administered by the 9th Reconnaissance Wing at Beale AFB, CA with an operating location arrangement established at Edwards to function in the same manner as the U-2s stationed at RAF Fairford in the UK.

The first two aircraft to be overhauled prior to being returned to service are 64-17967 and 17971. The latter aircraft performed its first flight on 26 April following rework, which was a few days ahead of schedule, with formal handover taking place on 28 June. The delivery of the second aircraft was delayed slightly until mid-August as it has been fitted with a datalink.

The project could have been cancelled due to the budget being withdrawn,

but in the end the money for operations for the remainder of FY 1995 (which continues until the end of September) was made available. The programme to return two SR-71s to operational service seems certain to be funded for FY 1996, enabling a third aircraft to be refurbished. It is currently in store at Palmdale and could be returned to service within four months of the money being approved. The announcement would also indicate that the necessary finances will be budgeted for the three aircraft to be flown operationally during 1996.

Following completion of the overhaul, the SR-71s have been assigned to the 9th RW, although they remained at Palmdale until 1 September when they were transferred to nearby Edwards AFB. Once the aircraft are in residence at Edwards, the Air Force can begin to conduct overseas deployments as required.

The second SR-71 is currently undergoing overhaul and will be fitted with a Unisys air-to-ground datalink similar to that installed in the U-2. The first SR-71 lacks this equipment but will have it installed at a later date. The system enables digital inputs from the Loral advanced synthetic aperture radar system (ASARS-1) to be accepted, along with digital and analog Elint inputs from the electromagnetic reconnaissance system. Data obtained can either be downlinked in real time or recorded for later analysis once the aircraft has landed. Previously, the intelligence was gathered by sensors which could only be downloaded for analysis following the return of the SR-71 to its operating base.

The first SR-71 conducted its initial test flight on 26 April following refurbishment, during which it was flown to Mach 0.94. A second high-speed test sortie one month later enabled the aircraft to be flown to Mach 3.3 at an altitude of 81,000 ft (24690 m). This was just short of the absolute speed record established by the type in July 1976. The second SR-71 performed its maiden flight in early August.

Reports from Mildenhall suggest one of the two SR-71 barns had seen activity during the summer of 1995 in readiness for possible operations.

C-17 evaluation

McDonnell Douglas has completed durability testing on the C-17 Globemaster II, completing the final require-

ment for the full-scale engineering development phase of the programme. The C-17 static test airframe completed 60,000 simulated hours of flight, the equivalent of two design lifetimes, on 11 July 1995. Airframe loads simulating 25 different mission profiles were evaluated. Changes made during the testing were the result of cracks found in fuselage bulkheads numbers 2 and 5. In addition to modifications to the test article to strengthen the components, changes were made to existing aircraft at McDonnell Douglas' Tulsa, OK facility.

On 27 June 1995, C-17s successfully dropped 55 tons of heavy cargo and 204 paratroopers to demonstrate the aircraft's ability to meet the US Army's brigade airdrop requirement. The demonstration, called a 'slice', was to have four C-17s drop a 20-ton M551 Sheridan light tank, a five-ton 155-mm howitzer, and nine five-ton HMMWV 'Humvee' vehicles. A drogue parachute malfunctioned, preventing the second aircraft from dropping the howitzer and two 'Humvees'.

During July 1995 the C-17 undertook the most demanding test of its operational capabilities when the 17th Airlift Squadron at Charleston AFB, SC began a 30-day reliability, maintainability and availability evaluation (RM&AE) under the scrutiny of the Air Force, McDonnell Douglas and government officials. The RM&AE was literally the make or break time for the C-17, with the future of US military transport dependent upon the events of the 30 days. The 12 aircraft of the 17th AS were subjected to all manner of intense operational requirements to simulate those likely to be encountered during wartime. The results of the evaluation will be used in the decision of the Defense Acquisition Board when it meets in November 1995 to determine if the C-17 will continue to be purchased. Defense Secretary William Perry recently stated that buying more than the 40 C-17s planned depends upon lower production costs, higher production efficiency, and funding being made available beyond 2000.

The evaluation began on 7 July. The first phase of the exercise was held over 23 days devoted to simulating peacetime conditions, with routine airlift operations conducted from home base to six locations. The primary overseas destination was RAF Mildenhall, while other sorties commenced from Dover AFB, DE. Joint US Army and Air Force training missions were also con-

ducted from Pope AFB, NC. These missions included the aerial delivery of heavy equipment and paratroops as well as short field landings at austere sites and auxiliary airfields in the vicinity of Charleston. Many of the sorties involved air refuelling to extend range.

The last seven days of the evaluation were conducted during early August, with the squadron performing under simulated wartime conditions and enacting a multi-regional scenario. Whereas the first phase was conducted at a normal pace with aircraft and crews being permitted peacetime-level rest from flight duties, the second phase stipulated swift turnarounds at destinations. The week was also to include two 'surge' days to simulate the commencement of a conflict whereby a large volume of equipment was to be moved to forward operating locations. During two days of this period, the fleet was scheduled to average approximately 16 flying hours per aircraft. Apart from operating from Charleston AFB, the C-17s were also to use Pope AFB to ferry their cargoes to Mildenhall, Barstow-Daggett Airport, CA and Bicycle Lake Airfield, CA to support an Army exercise at the nearby Fort Irwin National Training Center. Sorties were varied to gain the maximum training benefit and to test the crews involved, with long-range flights coupled with short-field landings involving 30-minute turnarounds during which the engines were not shut down.

Throughout the exercise the aircraft were crewed by active-duty personnel from the 437th AW as well as Air Force Reserve crews from the 315th AW. The 12 Globemasters were expected to amass 2,100 flight hours during the month, performing every kind of mission which the aircraft could be expected to accomplish during its lifetime. A total of 25 specific missions were formulated, including special assignments, strategic airlift, tactical resupply and joint air-drop training. In this way, the performance of the aircraft and its back-up systems will be evaluated fairly. Previous evaluations on other aircraft had been conducted later in their career, when the type had reached 100,000, so the C-17 RM&AE is unique.

The C-17 failed only one of 12 key test areas during the RM&AE evaluation: it gave too many 'false alarms' to maintainers – a persistent problem – but otherwise was deemed to have passed with flying colours.

McDonnell Douglas has rectified many of the problems which had beset the Globemaster from the outset. The cost of each aircraft spiralled to a staggering $300 million, although MDD will present a proposal to cut the unit price to $212. The first 32 aircraft have cost $300 million each, but by addressing every possible area, including the contract suppliers to MDD who contribute 80 per cent of the programme cost, the company has been able to prune overheads drastically. MDD has committed $100 million to improving its manufacturing process, an undertaking which has paid dividends as several

assembly processes have seen major cost reductions through redesign. This has resulted in the number of hours devoted to assemble each aircraft being cut by 28 per cent, although MDD is committed to eventually halving the process. To facilitate this, there are 150 projects at shop-floor level and another 100 in concept which collectively will speed up production. An example of this is the use of new machined landing gear pod bulkheads designed to replace the built-up versions. These are expected to save 2,100 hours of assembly work per aircraft and 8,400 installation hours, as it eliminates 1,500 parts and 16,000 fasteners. High-speed machining is also being employed to manufacture a new unitary ramp-bulkhead which was previously built up from components. This has produced considerable savings by eliminating 700 parts and 11,000 fasteners, thereby cutting 1,100 hours of assembly.

These and other initiatives are helping to trim costs and prove to the Air Force and the Pentagon's Defense Acquisition Board that the aircraft can be obtained more cheaply. Much depends on the decision to order the remaining 80 aircraft as MDD could then specify to its sub-contractors and suppliers substantial orders at much reduced costs due to long lead terms.

The DAB at its November meeting will review the C-17 based on the RE&AE and the submission from MDD to produce the aircraft more cheaply. It will also decide whether to supplement the C-17 with other non-developmental airlift aircraft. Boeing has already proposed a military variant of its 747-400F, and Lockheed Martin has offered a revised version of the Galaxy designated C-5D. The DAB has a clear-cut decision to make: whether to proceed with the planned purchase of 120 C-17s or to purchase a mix of C-17s, C-5Ds or 747-400s. Whatever the outcome, the Air Force seems certain to receive its additional

airlifters much cheaper than expected.

Deliveries to the 14th Airlift Squadron continued with the 20th C-17A 93-0604 on 19 June. 93-0604 is the first example to incorporate improved variants of the F117 engines which require less maintenance. This completes the FY 1993 order; the next example will be 94-0056, the first from FY 1994. The 21st production C-17 was delivered to the 437th AW, Charleston AFB ahead of schedule on 31 July 1995.

Production E-8C first flight

The first of 19 production E-8C J-STARS aircraft made its first flight on 16 August 1995 at Northrop Grumman's facility in Lake Charles, LA. Northrop Grumman was scheduled to test the modified Boeing 707-300 briefly before installing its electronics suite. This was the first of six low-rate production aircraft on order for the USAF which plans to order another 13, with two per year being produced. The USAF will receive a 20th Joint STARS upgraded from the present test fleet. IOC is scheduled for 1997.

RU-38A

The US Coast Guard has taken delivery of its first of three Schweizer RU-38A Twin Condor twin-engined, twin-boom quiet surveillance aircraft. Two RU-38As are being constructed by dismantling the service's pair of RG-8A single-engined powered gliders; a third is being built from scratch. The RU-38A Twin Condor (formerly the 'RG-8A Twin') is powered by two tandem 350-hp (262-kW) Teledyne Continental GIO-550 six-cylinder, air-cooled engines driving three-bladed, constant-speed propellers. The aircraft has a 64-ft (19.81-m) wing span.

The A-10 and OA-10 community is today largely an ANG/AFRes one, though, as can be seen here, ACC's 57th Fighter Wing (A-10 Fighter Weapons School) at Nellis AFB is still a significant user of the type.

First flown on 31 May 1995, the RU-38A Twin Condor will be employed at Miami on counter-drug surveillance missions. The Coast Guard wanted the twin because of its concern over reliability and endurance problems with the RG-8A.

F/A-18E/F for stand-off role

McDonnell Douglas is studying a command and control warfare version of the two-seat F/A-18F Hornet that could eventually replace the Grumman EA-6B Prowler. The proposal will make use of some of the capabilities of the Advanced Capability upgrade for the EA-6B, which the Navy cancelled. Referred to as the F-18C²W, the aircraft would use 97 per cent of F/A-18F structure and sub-systems and 70 per cent of F/A-18F avionics.

JAST: model hovers

Outdoor hover and ground effects tests have begun on an 86-per cent scale aircraft model produced by Lockheed Martin 'Skunk Works' to help reduce the technical risks associated with developing a shaft-coupled lift fan propulsion system for the Joint Advanced Strike Technology programme. The powered STOVL model, which is not capable of flying, is providing engineers with data on jet thrust, hot gas ingestion, and ground temperatures and pressures. It is fitted with an Allison lift fan system and is powered by a 23,450-lb (104.31-kN) thrust Pratt & Whitney F100-PW-200+ engine that provides both conventional thrust and shaft power to drive a lift fan. Made of steel and fibreglass, the model has a 30-ft (9.28-m) wing span and is 45 ft (13.93 m) long.

The model was scheduled to enter the NASA Ames wind tunnel in September 1995 for tests to examine its transition from hover to conventional flight. Lockheed Martin is competing against Boeing and a MDD/Northrop Grumman/BAe team to develop a flying STOVL demonstrator, with a contract to be awarded in 1996 and first flight to take place before 1999.

JPATS protest

Rockwell and Cessna filed a protest of the Joint Primary Aircraft Training System contract award to the Raytheon Mk 2 turboprop. Rockwell claims that its Ranger 2000 aircraft was found by the US government to have a

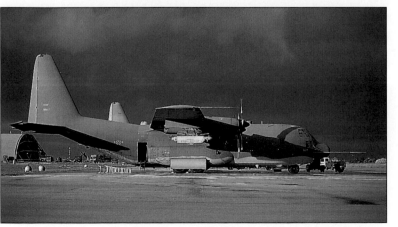

A freshly repainted 16th SOS/1st SOW AC-130H on station at Brindisi, as part of the USAF contribution to Operation Deny Flight. Note the ALQ-131 ECM pod for self-protection over Bosnia.

significantly lower life-cycle cost. Lockheed Martin withdrew its lower-level protest to the Pentagon and Northrop Grumman will not file a challenge.

Broncos to the BATF

The Bureau of Alcohol, Tobacco and Firearms (ATF) of the US Treasury Department is taking delivery of 22 ex-USMC North American OV-10D+ Bronco FAC aircraft. The ATF has been criticised for its April 1993 raid on Branch Davidians at Waco, TX. For a bargain price of $9,000 each (about £6,000), the ATF is expected to field nine airworthy OV-10s for aerial surveillance. Work on the OV-10s is being performed at Manassas, VA and Shawnee, OK.

Navy Sealift Command looking for helicopters

The US Navy's Sealift Command will lease two Kaman K-MAX helicopters for an evaluation in the autumn of 1995 of medium-lift helicopters in an airborne cargo delivery and vertical replenishment (VertRep) role. Each will have a maximum lifting capacity at sea level of 6,000 lb (2722 kg). Three pilots and three technicians will operate the aircraft from USNS *Saturn*. The K-MAX won the slot in a competition. The planned two-month evaluation will look at a replacement for the work performed today by the service's ageing fleet of Vertol CH-46 Sea Knights.

Apache developments

McDonnell Douglas has abandoned plans to sell its helicopter manufacturing facility in Mesa, AZ. In mid-1995, the company was delivering 12 AH-64As ordered by Greece, and had received several important orders. The company has confirmed an order for 12 AH-64As from Egypt in addition to 24 already ordered. Procurement of an additional dozen (bringing the total to 48) is expected in the long term. The Netherlands has selected the McDonnell Douglas AH-64D Apache over the Eurocopter PAH-2 Tiger, after also considering the Agusta A 129 and Bell AH-1W Super Cobra. Thirty AH-64Ds will be delivered from early 1998 with a stop-gap loan of 12 US Army AH-64As from 1996. The Dutch helicopters will not have Longbow radar but will have other AH-64D equipment to link them to the NATO 'digital battlefield'.

The Dutch Ministry of Defence had made known its preference for the American design in December 1994 but the final decision was not taken until 7 April 1995. A large offset package will see Dutch companies bidding for equipment sub-contracts. The helicopter

purchase is controversial in Holland, and could be undone by domestic political pressures.

F-16 force changes

The Air National Guard and Air Force Reserve have replaced many of their F-16A/B models with the F-16C/D or switched to other roles, enabling the earlier versions of the Falcon to be retired to AMARC for storage or sold to overseas customers. Fifty surplus F-16As and Bs were supplied to Israel during 1994, including aircraft drawn from AMARC and some prepared for direct delivery from the ANG squadrons themselves. By the middle of 1995 more F-16A/Bs had arrived for storage, with several nations showing interest in possible purchase.

The 31st FW at Aviano has had a number of its pilots trained to enable them to perform the role of airborne forward air control (AFAC). Training was conducted by the 355th Wing at Davis-Monthan AFB, AZ during the first half of 1995. Once fully qualified, the pilots from the 510th and 555th FS will perform AFAC missions above Bosnia to reduce the possibility of friendly fire casualties.

Several front-line units have now received their complement of ASQ-213 HARM-equipped F-16C/Ds. This targeting system provides the F-16 with a limited defence suppression capability and, while not as comprehensive as that installed in the soon-to-be-retired F-4G 'Wild Weasel', offers the Air Force a more modern and economical defence suppression platform whose capabilities will doubtless be upgraded by modification and retrofit. Units operating the version are Air Combat Command's 20th FW at Shaw AFB, SC and 389th FS/366th Wg at Mountain Home AFB, ID, USAFE's 23rd FS/52nd FW at Spangdahlem AB, Germany, and one squadron of the 35th FW at Misawa AB, Japan. Approximately 100 aircraft were due to be modified, consisting mostly of F-16C models, although some two-seat D versions have had the ASQ-213 pod fitted for test work with the 57th Test Group at Nellis AFB, NV and with the 79th Test and Evaluation Group at Eglin AFB, FL. The F-4G is still flown by the 190th FS/Idaho ANG).

At Cannon AFB the 27th FW's 74 F-111E/F 'Aardvarks' will retire from late 1995, replaced by 54 F-16C/Ds.

The 428th Fighter Squadron, which now conducts F-111 training, will inactivate.

The 162nd Fighter Group, Arizona ANG, has started exchanging its F-16A and B models for the F-16C and D. The group still had a number of F-16A/Bs during May 1995, although considerably fewer than the 72 Falcons on strength during 1994. At least 24 F-16C and D versions had been received by May 1995, many of which were transferred from the 113th and 163rd FS of the Indiana ANG. The aircraft with the Arizona ANG are mostly from FY 1984 and 1985 production, while the 113th FS had received some FY 1986 aircraft from the 149th FS/VA ANG at Richmond. The Arizona ANG F-16C/Ds have had the 'AZ' tailcode applied, which the A and B models did not display. The 162nd is also experiencing changes as a result of the rationalisation of F-16 pilot training, since it is responsible for training pilots from the Air National Guard and Air Force Reserve and from a number of overseas nations. The 162nd FG operates the International Military Training School with F-16A and B models. The group is to increase its responsibilities when the 56th FW at Luke AFB transfers to

the Arizona ANG the commitment to train all foreign pilots, apart from the Taiwanese. At the moment, Luke AFB is home to the Peace Carvin mission, responsible for training Republic of Singapore personnel, which will convert from eight F-16A/Bs to 11 F-16C/Ds from late 1995. The Netherlands air force had a dozen of its own F-16A and B models at Tucson until April 1995. These were operated in full Arizona ANG markings but with a small KLu roundel adjacent to the air intake. The Dutch training commitment will remain at Tucson, with the IMT. The 162nd FG, with the 148th, 152nd and 195th FS assigned, also parents the Air National Guard/Air Force Reserve Test Center with approximately eight F-16A, B and C versions to perform ongoing test duties.

Several active-duty and Air National Guard F-16 units are modernising, gaining or losing aircraft. The 20th FW at Shaw will gain six F-16C/D aircraft in mid-1996, while at Hill AFB the 388th FW will gain six F-16C/Ds in early 1996. One squadron of the 388th FW upgraded to FY90 Block 50s, but these were subsequentlypassed on to the 51sat Osan AB, Korea. The 4th FS later reverted to Block 40 F-16s. A number of FY 1988 F-16Cs have been transferred to the 388th FW from the 51st FS, and from the 188th FS, New Mexico ANG at Kirtland AFB.

Within the ANG F-16 community the 188th FG at Fort Smith MAP, AR will replace its 12 F-16A/B aircraft

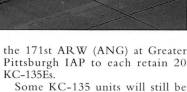

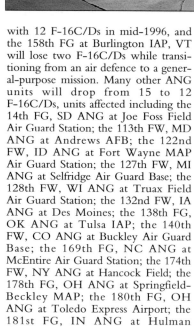

This shark-mouthed QF-4 serves alongside the other QF-4Es, QRF-4Cs and QF-106s of the 475th WEG, at Tyndall AFB. Live firings on the QF-106s is due to start in 1996, before the William Tell weapons meet.

Military Sabreliners are a dying breed. Though virtually extinct in USAF service, they soldier on with the US Navy and Marines. Seen at NAS Ft Worth, this CT-39E is an Admiral's personal transport.

with 12 F-16C/Ds in mid-1996, and the 158th FG at Burlington IAP, VT will lose two F-16C/Ds while transitioning from an air defence to a general-purpose mission. Many other ANG units will drop from 15 to 12 F-16C/Ds, units affected including the 14th FG, SD ANG at Joe Foss Field Air Guard Station; the 113th FW, MD ANG at Andrews AFB; the 122nd FW, ID ANG at Fort Wayne MAP Air Guard Station; the 127th FW, MI ANG at Selfridge Air Guard Base; the 128th FW, WI ANG at Truax Field Air Guard Station; the 132nd FW, IA ANG at Des Moines; the 138th FG, OK ANG at Tulsa IAP; the 140th FW, CO ANG at Buckley Air Guard Base; the 169th FG, NC ANG at McEntire Air Guard Station; the 174th FW, NY ANG at Hancock Field; the 178th FG, OH ANG at Springfield-Beckley MAP; the 180th FG, OH ANG at Toledo Express Airport; the 181st FG, IN ANG at Hulman Regional Airport Air Guard Station; the 183rd FG, IL ANG at Capital MAP Air Guard Station; the 185th FG, IA ANG at Sioux City MAP; the 187th FG, AL ANG at Dannelly Field; and the 192nd FG, VA ANG at Richmond IAP Air Guard Station.

At Hector Field IAP, ND the 119th FG will lose three F-16A/B Block 15 ADFs before its conversion to the F-16C, while the Puerto Rico IAP-based 156th FG will retain 12 of its 15 F-16A/B Block 15 ADFs. Other units will downsize as they trade F-16As and F-16Bs for F-16Cs and Ds, such units including the the 119th FG, ND ANG at Hector Field IAP in mid-1996. The Duluth-based 148th FG, MN ANG, and the Great Falls-based 120th FG will also transition from the air defence mission to a general purpose mission as they accept new F-16Cs, while the Klamath Falls-based 114th FS will lose its training mission together with its Block 15 F-16A/B ADFs in early 1996.

A-10 force changes

ANG A/OA-10A squadrons will be standardised at 17 aircraft each. The 103rd FG at Bradley IAP, CT, the 104th FG at Barnes MAP, MA, the

110th FG at W. K. Kellogg Regional Airport, MI, the 111th FG at Willow Grove Air Reserve Station, PA and the 175th FG at Martin State Airport, MD, will each lose one A/OA-10A. As a result of the Air Force decision to retire its F-4G Advanced 'Wild Weasels', the 124th FG at Boise Air Terminal Air Guard Station will convert from 24 F-4Gs to 17 A/OA-10As aircraft beginning in early 1996. At Davis-Monthan AFB Air Combat Command's 355th Wg will gain an additional four A-10As in late 1995.

KC-135 force changes

The Air Force is to modify an unspecified number of KC-135Rs with two wing-mounted refuelling pods each fitted with a hose and drogue system. The modification will enable the tankers to be compatible with US Navy, US Marine Corps and NATO aircraft, while at the same time retaining the ability to refuel USAF types with the flying boom. An initial contract for 33 kits was expected to be placed in August 1995, with the first aircraft due to be delivered early in FY 97. The modified tankers will be particularly

useful in supporting the United Nations peacekeeping efforts such as Operations Southern Watch over southern Iraq, Provide Comfort over northern Iraq, and Deny Flight over Bosnia-Herzegovina where NATO fighters are routinely air-refuelled to extend their operational capabilities.

The 43rd ARS at Fairchild was inactivated on 31 March when replaced by the 99th ARS which moved from Castle AFB, CA. Since January 1995 the Air Force has been using the abbreviation ARS instead of AREFS for Air Refueling Squadron. Several units scheduled to lose an aircraft will now retain their current strengths. At Phoenix Sky Harbor IAP the 161st ARG (ANG) will retain 10 KC-135Es, and will not lose one aircraft, as had been planned. Other units which will maintain 10 aircraft include the 101st ARW (ANG) at Bangor IAP, the 126th ARW at O'Hare IAP, 134th ARG (ANG) at McGhee-Tyson Airport, Knoxville, the 141st ARW (ANG) at Fairchild AFB, the 151st ARG (ANG) at Salt Lake City IAP Air Guard Station and the 190th ARG (ANG) at Forbes Field, while the cancellation of the loss of one KC-135E will allow the 108th ARW (ANG) at McGuire AFB, and

the 171st ARW (ANG) at Greater Pittsburgh IAP to each retain 20 KC-135Es.

Some KC-135 units will still be reduced in size, however, these including the 19th ARW at Robins which will lose eight KC-135Rs beginning in mid-1996, the 92nd ARW at Fairchild which will lose six KC-135Rs, and the 163rd ARG (ANG) which will replace its 10 KC-135Es with nine KC-135Rs from late 1995. The 452nd Air Mobility Wing (AFRes) at March AFB and the 927th ARW (AFRes) at Selfridge will each lose one KC-135E in late 1995. In New Hampshire, the 157th ARG at Pease Air Guard Station will gain one KC-135R in mid-1996.

CTP extended

The Companion Training Program has been extended, with T-37Bs being assigned to the 26th ARS, 366th Wing at Mountain Home AFB, ID and the 966th ACTS, 552nd ACW at Tinker AFB, OK. The CTP at Offutt AFB, NE with the 45th RS, 55th Wing has exchanged its T-38As for T-37Bs.

AFSOC changes

From late 1995, the 919th SOW at Duke Field will receive eight MC-130E Combat Talon Is, completing its transition from nine AC-130As to eight MC-130Es and four HC-130N/Ps. Four of the MC-130Es will come from the 16th SOW from mid-1996, the others from the 353rd SOG. The 353rd SOG's MC-130Es will be replaced by MC-130Hs, including some transferred from Hurlburt and Kirtland.

At Hurlburt Field the 16th SOW will gain three MH-53Js in late 1995, giving the wing 22 Enhanced Pave Low IIIs. The 16th SOW will also lose

This is one of the ex-USMC OV-10Ds allocated to the United States BATF (Bureau of Alcohol, Tobacco and Firearms). The BATF gained notoriety after the Waco/Branch Davidian siege incident in 1993 and the purpose of these overtly military aircraft remains unclear.

one MC-130H Combat Talon II. The 16th SOW will receive two AC-130Us in mid-1996, bringing the total to 12. At Kirtland the 58th SOW will gain two HH-60Gs, but will lose one MC-130H and one HC-130N/P.

USAF bomber plans

The US Air Force is planning for a total force of 181 bombers, and the service's plan makes no provision for the 20 additional Northrop Grumman B-2 Spirit 'Stealth Bombers' for which many in Washington are pushing. The Clinton administration now opposes purchase of more B-2s, but faces strong Congressional pressure for a second batch of 20.

The Pentagon's acquisition chief released a long-awaited report on 3 May 1995 concluding that more B-2s would be of little help in wartime. Emphasis should be placed instead on upgrading existing bombers and improving PGMs, the controversial report asserted. During the summer of 1995, hearings were expected on a proposal to spend $500 million in FY 1996 for parts for three B-2s in FY 1997.

The USAF chief of staff has stated that the original purchase of 20 B-2s is sufficient. In the Cold War climate of the late 1980s, the Air Force wanted 132 B-2s. In 1958, the US Air Force had 2,028 strategic bombers capable of carrying nuclear weapons on long-range missions to the Soviet Union. On 18 March 1945, the US Eighth Air Force could send 1,250 heavy bombers to Berlin on a single mission.

The USAF now perceives a stable bomber force (between now and 2014) of 66 Boeing B-52H Stratofortresses, 95 Rockwell B-1B Lancers, and 20 B-2s. The inventory currently includes 84 ACC B-52Hs, nine B-52Hs in the AFres, and one at Edwards with AMC. Five B-52Hs and six B-52Gs are in storage at Davis-Monthan. There are also 82 ACC B-1Bs and 11 ANG B-1Bs, together with two allocated to AMC at Edwards. Twelve B-2s are evenly divided between Air Combat Command and Materiel Command. This gives a current (late 1995) front-line bomber force of 192 bombers, with nine more aircraft assigned to Materiel Command.

Northrop Grumman has proposed building 20 more B-2s for $12 billion, finding a friendly reception from some Capitol Hill legislators who argue that the bomber force, as now planned, is too small.

The first Northrop Grumman GPS-Aided Munition (GAM) was dropped from a B-2 bomber at the US Navy's China Lake, CA range on 13 June 1995. The weapon uses the satellite-based global positioning system to maintain trajectory after release.

While the B-2 goes from strength to strength, the ageing B-52s face a more uncertain future. At the beginning of 1995 the 5th BW at Minot AFB, ND activated the 72nd BS as its second B-52H unit to operate alongside the 23rd BS. The unit received its full complement of aircraft transferred

The Marines remain loyal to their faithful AH-1Ws and are pressing for a major four-bladed rotor upgrade programme to keep surviving aircraft effective. These 'TV'-coded Cobras are from HMLA-167.

Right: A surprising number of A-3 Skywarriors remain flying in the hands of US civilian contract firms. This ERA-3B is flown by Raytheon from Hanscom Field, Bedford, MA.

from the 410th and 416th BW, with over 30 Stratofortresses located at Minot. However, just seven months after the squadron formed, it has been earmarked for possible inactivation with some of its aircraft planned for retirement to AMARC for storage. Grant for operations is allocated annually, with a likelihood that an allotment will only be made available for one squadron at Minot. Should this become reality, the first six B-52s would be retired between January and March 1996, with the remaining six following between April and June prior to the squadron inactivating.

The 2nd BW at Barksdale AFB, Louisiana is scheduled to retire four B-52Hs to AMARC in FY 1996, but will gain some of the functions of the 99th Wing at Ellsworth AFB, South Dakota which is slated for inactivation. The latter unit performs tactics and training courses for bomber crews, although that for the B-52 will be centralised under the 2nd BW.

The B-52 has many supporters in the House and Senate, and there is the ever-present possibility that the money for full operations for FY 1996 will be approved at the last moment, as has been the case on more than one previous e imbalance could be redressed if Barks-

dale AEB, LA transferred one of its bomber units, as it currently has one Air Force Reserve and three active-duty squadrons of B-52Hs.

A Boeing B-52H Stratofortress of the 93rd BS (AFRes), Barksdale AFB, LA, flew the firstoccasion. Should the 72nd BS be inactivated, Minot AFB will face an uncertain future as a flying facility; with just one squadron of bombers in residence, it would be a costly undertaking. Th 'global power' mission by an Air Force Reserve crew on 18 July 1995. It joined a 5th BW B-52H from Minot AFB, ND over the Atlantic for the 12-hour flight, including a simulated bomb run over northern England.

Other changes

The US Air Force plans to activate an ANG C-130 squadron with four aircraft at Boise, ID. These will be available to the National Forest Service for additional fire-fighting capability. Air Combat Command will establish a new wing at Tinker, which will begin receiving the first of its planned 17 E-8C (J-STARS) aircraft in early 1996. The previously announced loss of three E-3B/C AWACS aircraft is cancelled. The Combat Rescue School at Nellis will receive a pair of HH-60s to replace the helicopters it now borrows from other units. At Patrick AFB the 71st Rescue Squadron will gain one HC-130N/P in late 1995.

On the other side of the balance sheet, beginning in late 1995, the 97th Air Mobility Wing at Altus will lose three of its C-141B StarLifters. At Elmendorf the 3rd Wing will lose one C-12F in late 1995, while at Langley the 1st FW will lose three UH-1N 'Huey' helicopters. The previously announced allocation of three Boeing E-3B/C Sentry aircraft to the Mountain Home wing is cancelled due to the worldwide commitments of the AWACS mission.

Operation Deliberate Force

On 12 April 1993, United Nations Resolution 816 established a 'No-Fly Zone' over Bosnia. As the threat to UNPROFOR troops increased and Bosnian-Serb aggression towards the declared UN 'safe havens' became untenable, UN Resolution 836 finally sanctioned the use of NATO air power. In September 1995 the assembled NATO air forces were at last let off their leash, with devastating effect.

Sarajevo rocked with explosions and the night was lit with decoy flares dropped by NATO strike aircraft. Operation Deliberate Force had begun. For nine days NATO pounded the Bosnian Serb military in the largest demonstration of air power since the 1991 Gulf War. Peace has yet to be secured in war-torn Bosnia-Herzegovina, but the siege of the country's battered capital seems at last to have been lifted.

The trigger for the unleashing of NATO air power was a mortar attack on Sarajevo on 28 August 1995 which killed 37 civilians. Within hours NATO and the United Nations began preparations for the air strikes which would dramatically change the military balance in the former Yugoslavia.

Following the fall in July of the so-called UN 'safe areas' of Srebrenica and Zepa in eastern Bosnia, Western political leaders had resolved to use 'disproportionate air power' in response to Serb attacks on the remaining 'safe areas'. To hasten the decision-making process and response times, the powers to initiate air action were delegated to the UN Peace Force's Commander in the former Yugoslavia, Lieutenant General Bernard Janvier, and NATO's Southern European Commander-in-Chief, Admiral Leighton Smith.

During the morning of 29 August Admiral Smith had a number of telephone conversations with General Janvier and with the UN Protection Force (UNPROFOR) commander in Bosnia-Herzegovina, Lieutenant General Rupert Smith. They attempted to determine if a military response was necessary to mortar attack on the Sarajevo market, which was determined to have been fired from Serb-held territory. By the end of the day the UN and NATO high commands had agreed on the necessary action and targets.

Battle plan

At this point NATO's Southern European commander, Lieutenant General Mike Ryan, gave the 5th Allied Tactical Air Force (5 ATAF) the mission to execute Operation Deliberate Force in co-ordination with the UN's Rapid Reaction Force (RRF) positioned on Mount Igman, overlooking Sarajevo. From its Combined Air Operations Centre (CAOC) at Dal Molin AB, near Vicenza, in northern Italy, 5 ATAF air planners under the CAOC's director Major General Hal Hornburg began to move into high gear to match aircraft and weapons to targets. Contingency plans for the air campaign were already at an advanced stage

Above: Dutch forces have been active in Bosnia in the air and on the ground. A KLu F-16 detachment, drawn from a number of different squadrons, is based at Villafranca. They have flown CAP, CAS and BDA sorties, the latter with Oude Delft Orpheus reconaissance pods.

but there was little time before the first bombs were due to be dropped that night. All the details the NATO aircrews needed to conduct the air strikes were contained in 5 ATAF's air tasking messages, which were faxed by secure communications and satellite links to NATO air bases in Italy, France, Germany and Britain and to aircraft-carriers in the Adriatic Sea. The air armada was organised into a series of strike packages, which combined bomb-dropping or missile-firing aircraft with fighters, suppression of enemy air defence (SEAD) aircraft, combat search and rescue (CSAR) support and air-to-air refuelling tankers, backed up by photographic reconnaissance aircraft. Each package contained aircraft drawn from the nations participating in the NATO operation.

Above: The Mirage 2000N K-2 was the most capable of the strike assets deployed in the region by the Armée de l'Air. Unfortunately, on the first day of operations, one aircraft was shot down and the crew was not recovered.

Left: The first combat deployment of Luftwaffe aircraft outside Germany since 1945 came with the arrival of eight Tornado ECRs and six Tornado IDS at Piacenza, Italy.

Turkish F-16Cs have been an important element of Operation Deny Flight since their introduction in the area in 1994. The first unit to de deployed was 141 Filo, operating from Ghedi, Italy. They were replaced by 161 Filo in May 1994, and now 191 Filo continues to provide combat air patrols with its Sidewinder-armed aircraft.

Additional co-ordination was required with UNPROFOR's Air Operations Centre (AOCC) in Sarajevo and the RRF's Tactical Air Operations Centre (TACC) in nearby Kiseljak, to ensure UN ground troops knew exactly what was about to happen. USAF EC-130H airborne battlefield command and control centre (ABBCC) aircraft, with their extensive radio and satellite links, provided the real-time link between inbound NATO aircraft and UN forward air control (FAC) on the ground who

were to direct some of the strikes. The FACs would also call in any close air support attack aircraft if Serb artillery and mortars retaliated against UN troops around Sarajevo.

Dead-Eye Southeast

NATO aircraft started taking off late in the evening of 29 August, bound for their targets in eastern Bosnia. In this first phase of the operation, targets in the west of Bosnia were left alone. USAF KC-135 tankers were orbiting over the Adriatic near Split to refuel the first strike package of 14 SEAD and three strike aircraft (all from the USS *Roosevelt*). Armed with AGM-88 high speed anti-radiation missiles (HARMs) and Paveway laser-guided bombs, the US Marine Corps F/A-18D Hornets plus US Navy EA-6B Prowlers and Hornets had the

mission of crippling the Serbs' integrated air defence network in eastern Bosnia. Using the codename Dead-Eye Southeast, the package hit 15 targets including surface-to-air missiles (SAM) batteries, communication sites, radar networks and command bunkers. The span of the attack stretched from Neveslaje, near Mostar, up to Bijelina, near Tuzla. The main air defence control bunker on Mount Jahorina, east of Sarajevo, received a heavy pounding to prevent any co-ordinated response by the Serb SAMs or anti-aircraft guns. In the 20 minutes following midnight (all times in GMT) on 30 August, the Dead-Eye Southeast package hit home with devastating effect. Support from radar-jamming EF-111A Ravens and EC-130H Compass Call jammers blinded any radars that remained in operation.

Above: Operating from Aviano the EF-18s of the Spanish air force were deployed to the region for their SEAD capability, courtesy of the AGM-88 HARM. This EF-18A+ wears the fin badge of Grupo 12 which operated two squadrons of Hornets from Torrejon.

Right: This pair of Dutch F-16s, with squadron markings carefully removed, is carrying a warload of four AIM-9Ls, two Mk 82s and an ALQ-131 ECM pod each. Dutch F-16s will be AMRAAM equipped after a deal signed in September 1995 to acquire upwards of 200 missiles.

Right and above: The key to the Jaguar GR.Mk 1B upgrade is the GEC TIALD laser designator. Over Bosnia a pair of Jaguars is used to designate targets for LGB-carrying Harriers, which lack their own designation equipment.

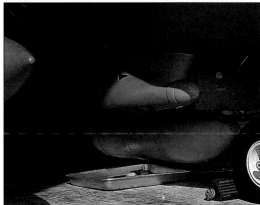

Left and above: During Operation Warden, RAF Harrier GR.Mk 7s were equipped with the primitive optical camera pods previously used by Harrier GR.Mk 3s. Over Bosnia they can carry a new optical reconnaissance pod, which is understood to be a Vinten LOROP pod similar to that previously used by the Jaguar.

Operation Deliberate Force

Orbiting over the Adriatic were USAF RC-135 Rivet Joint electronic intelligence-gathering aircraft, watching for any response from the Serb air defence radar network. Also in the air was a pair of close air support aircraft ready to respond to Serb artillery fire and a CSAR package of USAF Special Operations Command (SOC) MH-53J Pave Low helicopters and HC-130 tankers. In the event, they were not required.

Sarajevo strike cycle

One hour and 40 minutes after the Dead-Eye Southeast package had headed for home, its mission accomplished, 5 ATAF sent the first of five strike packages of the day into action over Sarajevo. Codenamed Sarajevo Strike Package Alpha, Bravo, Charlie, Delta and Echo, these packages attacked specific targets with laser-guided bombs. Each raid lasted between 20 and 30 minutes.

Television cameras filmed the first package hitting targets around Sarajevo at 02.00 on 30

Deployment to the Adriatic as part of Operation Deny Flight/Deliberate Force has provided invaluable experience for the Royal Navy's new Sea Harrier F/A-2 fleet. Squadrons and carriers have rotated at six-month (roughly) intervals.

August. Ghost-like images of F/A-18s could be seen firing decoy flares as they delivered laser-guided bombs against targets in the hills to the south of Sarajevo. Massive explosions reverberated around the city as Serb ammunition dumps took hits, along with SAM sites and command posts.

Strike package Alpha

Sarajevo Strike Package Alpha involved 10 strike and four SEAD aircraft. As dawn broke Sarajevo was shaken by the attacks of Strike Package Bravo going into action against more ammunition dumps and SAM sites. When the 14 strike and four SEAD aircraft were over the city, a pair of reconnaissance aircraft swooped over the target area to assess the damage from the first three packages of the day.

Five hours later the 12 aircraft of Strike Package Charlie pounded two ammunition dumps and storage sites near the Serb capital of Pale. A French Mirage 2000N K-2 of EC 2/3 'Champagne' was hit during the raid by an SA-7 hand-held heat-seeking SAM. The crew ejected and were captured by the Serbs, in spite of three CSAR operations being launched by NATO Special Force helicopter crews. One rescue mission came under Serb fire and the other two

were aborted due to bad weather. More Serb ammunition dumps were the target of Strike Package Delta three hours later.

During the morning two Area SEAD packages of 12 and 25 aircraft respectively were in the air to respond instantly to any SAM threats. This exercise was repeated in the afternoon with two Area SEAD packages of 19 and six aircraft on patrol. US Navy, US Marine and Spanish F/A-18 Hornets, along with US Navy EA-6B Prowlers, flew these missions.

USAF CAS

A close air support (CAS) presence was constantly maintained over Sarajevo throughout the day, to protect UN troops. This involved 60 aircraft being cycled through a patrol pattern over the city between 04.30 and 00.00. During daylight, pairs of USAF A-10As and Dutch F-16As took the brunt of this effort and on a number of occasions the 'Warthogs' fired AGM-65 laser-guided Maverick missiles. Serb artillery, mortar, anti-aircraft artillery and bunker positions were all attacked after calls for help from UN FACs. At night the AFSOC AC-130H gunships were called upon to take out any offending gun positions. Some 10,000 rounds of 30-mm, 40-mm and 105-mm ammunition were expended during 13 CAS attacks around Sarajevo on the first three days of the NATO mission.

Further reconnaissance missions to provide more photographs of bomb damage were flown at 18.30 and 19.45 by Dutch F-16A(R)s, US Navy TARPS-F-14s, French Mirage F1CAs, British Sea Harrier F/A-2 and Harrier GR.Mk 7s. Strike Package Echo, made up of two strike aircraft and three SEAD aircraft, hit another ammunition dump at 19.10. This completed the first day of Operation Deliberate Force.

Back at 5 ATAF in Vicenza, General Hornburg's planners were already at work

Above: The F-15E has again been at the forefront of air operations over Bosnia. Its PGM capability is unrivalled by any other NATO aircraft in the theatre. This 48th FW Strike Eagle is en route to its target with a load of 500-lb GBU-12 Paveway IIs.

Left: A pair of 494th FS/ 48th FW F-15Es stand ready outside an Aviano HAS, with a load of GBU-12s and AIM-120s. Aircraft from Lakenheath's 48th FW have been deployed to the region for some time, in addition to undertaking Provide Comfort missions over Iraq.

The OA-10, which the USAF seemed to be in indecent haste to rid itself of after Operation Desert Storm, has once again proved its 'low and slow' CAS credentials over Bosnia. In this role it has no equal.

preparing the air tasking message for the following day. By early evening aircraft were being prepared and crews briefed for the next day's five strike packages.

The packages again were aimed at destroying Serb ammunition bunkers and supply depots around Sarajevo and Pale. Spectacular television images showed huge mushroom clouds around the city, followed by secondary explosions. These were plum targets that were ideal for destruction from the air with precision-guided munitions.

RRF artillery on Mount Igman continued to add to the bombardment, often being called into suppress Serb anti-aircraft defences. In the afternoon of 1 September an RRF artillery observer called down gun fire on a Serb SA-7 shoulder-fired SAM team that had fired upon a NATO jet over the city.

In the early hours of 1 September, NATO suspended its operations for 48 hours to give the Serbs time to withdraw their heavy weapons from around Sarajevo. 5 ATAF planners continued their work, sending close air support, fighter, reconnaissance, SEAD and surveillance missions over Bosnia. Strike packages were kept on ground alert at Italian bases, ready to go into action at a moment's notice should a crisis develop. In spite of a few tanks being paraded in front of television cameras, NATO and the UN commands concluded that the Serbs had not complied with their demands by the 21.00 deadline on 4 September. 5 ATAF was ordered back into action.

5 ATAF back in action

In the afternoon of 5 September, General Hornburg's staff readied their strike packages again. Twenty NATO aircraft hit five targets – storage depots, ammunition dumps and a command bunker – during a 45-minute raid beginning at 11.00. Twenty minutes later 10 aircraft hit a similar set of targets. The third package of the day was launched one hour later, with 20 aircraft hitting more storage sites and command posts. An 18-aircraft strike package was in action at 14.05 but the weather closed in, cutting short the bombing for the day.

Sarajevo was the focus for these raids as ammunition dumps around the city, including one at Hadizci, were hit and the Lukovica Barracks was reduced to rubble. A number of targets in eastern Bosnia were revisited, including the Mount Jahorina bunker complex, communications sites near Tuzla, an ammuni-

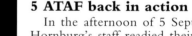

With the elimination of much of the Serbian integrated air defence system it was safe for the AC-130Hs of the 16th SOS to undertake night time gunship missions. A total of 13 sorties was flown against concealed Serbian gun emplacements.

tion dump at Visegrad and the Bosnian Serb alternative military command bunker complex at Hans Pijesak. These attacks cut telephone links between the Bosnian Serb capital Pale and the outside world. Many aircraft returned to base without dropping their bombs. Some 50 SEAD aircraft supported the strike packages during the day.

Serb lines of communications next came under attack, with the Foca highway bridge being hit and badly damaged on 6 September. Bad weather hampered NATO air attacks and it was not until the evening of that day that the weather cleared and 5 ATAF got hack into its stride.

F-16 HARM combat debut

For the next five days 5 ATAF continued to send five strike packages a day against eastern Bosnia, hitting a wide range of targets with precision-guided munitions. A high degree of accuracy was achieved and NATO's 'target sets' were soon almost exhausted. Tragedy truck on 8 September when RRF artillery fire hit a hospital while trying to neutralise a Serb SA-7 team firing at NATO aircraft over Sarajevo. An F-16 Fighting Falcon of the 23rd Fighter Squadron, equipped with the AN/ASQ-213 HARM targeting system, was called upon to fire in anger on 8 September when a Serb radar site locked onto the aircraft. The offending site was destroyed by a HARM.

Above: VMFA(AW)-533 flew 12 F/A-18Ds from Aviano. The Marines routinely use these two-seat Hornets for 'fast-FAC' missions, but this aircraft carries a load of AGM-88 HARMs and flew as part of 5 ATAF's substantial SEAD effort.

Left and below: A unique aspect of Deny Flight/Deliberate Force has been the deployment of VAQ-141s EA-6B Prowlers away from their carrier (USS Theodore Roosevelt), to a permanent home at Aviano. The Prowlers now have a lethal SEAD role, armed with AGM-88, in addition to their comprehensive ECM/jamming support capability.

Operation Deliberate Force

At 18.41 on 10 September, NATO upped the stakes by expanding the air campaign to targets in western Bosnia. Thirteen Tomahawk land–attack missiles were launched by the USS *Normandy* in the Adriatic against the Serb SA–6 SAM batteries around Banja Luka. Three strike packages were then sent into action over western Bosnia.

This opened the way for 5 ATAF aircraft to range freely over Bosnian Serb–held territory, hitting target after target. On 11 September, strike packages involving 70 strike aircraft hit six ammunition and storage depots, a number of command and control sites, and bridges.

By this time, the Serbs were getting the message that NATO and the UN meant

A sizeable international maritime patrol fleet has been assembled to undertake Operation Sharp Guard surveillance missions over the Adriatic, enforcing the UN arms embargo.

business and talks were under way to broker a lifting of the siege of Sarajevo. The last full day of air strikes was 13 September, when three strike packages containing 38 strike and SEAD

UN/NATO Bosnia Air Order of Battle August–September 1995

BASE	UNIT	No.	TYPE
CANADA			
Ancona		1	CC-130
Sigonella	405, 407, 415 Sqns	2	CP-140
FRANCE			
Cervia	EC 03/005	6	Mirage 2000C
	EC 2/3	3	Mirage 2000N K-2
	EC1/3	4	Mirage 2000D
Istrana	ER 02/033	5	Mirage F1CR
	EC 03/011	8	Jaguar
Istres	ERV 93	1	KC-135R
Avord	ED 36	1	E-3F Sentry
Vicenza	EET 11/54	1	C-160D
		1	Nord 262
Evreux	EE51	1	DC-8
Sigonella/Elmas			Atlantic
Split-Divulji	Det ALAT	6	Puma
/Kiseljak	(3RHC/4RHCM)	4	Gazelle
Ploce	5 RHC	8	Gazelle
		7	Puma
Ancona	ET 2/61	1	C-130H/H-30
Brindisi	EH 67?	3	Puma
GERMANY			
Sigonella/Elmas	MFG 3		Atlantic MPA
		2	Atlantic SIGINT
Ancona	LTG 61	1	C.160D
Piacenza	JBG 32	8	Tornado ECR
	AG 51	6	Tornado IDS
ITALY			
Ghedi	6° Stormo	8	Tornado IDS
Gioia del Colle	36° Stormo	8	Tornado IDS
NATO AIRBORNE EARLY WARNING FORCE			
Gelienkirken/		8	E-3A Sentry
Trapani/Previza			
NETHERLANDS			
Sigonella	320/321 Sqn		P-3
Villafranca	322 Sqn	13	F-16A
	306 Sqn	5	F-16A(R)
NORWAY			
Tuzla	720 Sqn	4	B.412
PORTUGAL			
Sigonella	601 Sqn		P-3P
SPAIN			
Aviano	311 Sqn	1	KC-130
	12/15 Wings	8	EF-18A+
Sigonella	221 Sqn		P-3B
Vicenza	37 Sqn	1	CASA C. 212

BASE	UNIT	No.	TYPE
TURKEY			
Ghedi	191 Filo	16	F-16C
UKRAINE			
Split		2	Mi-26
Zagreb-Pleso		3	Mi-8TV
UNITED NATIONS PEACE FORCES			
(civil contract aircraft)			
Pleso-Zagreb		2	Il-76
		1	Tu-154
		2	Yak-40
		2	Bell 212
		1	Bell 206
Skopje		1	Bell 212
		2	Bell 206
UNITED KINGDOM			
Gioia del Colle	4 Sqn	12	Harrier GR.Mk 7
	54 Sqn	2	Jaguar GR.Mk 1B
	111 Sqn	6	Tornado F.Mk 3
	39 Sqn	1	Canberra PR.Mk 9
Palermo	216 Sqn	2	Tristar
Aviano	8 Sqn	2	Sentry AEW.Mk 1
Sigonella	Kinloss Wing		Nimrod MR.Mk 2P
	51 Sqn		Nimrod R.Mk 1P
Ancona	Lyneham TW	1	Hercules C.Mk 1/3
HMS *Invincible*	800 Sqn	6	Sea Harrier F/A-2
	814 Sqn	7	Sea King HAS.Mk 6
	849 Sqn	3	Sea King AEW.Mk 2
Ploce	7 Sqn	6	Chinook HC.Mk 2
	33 Sqn	6	Puma HC.Mk 1
	3 Regt AAC	9	Lynx AH.Mk 7
		9	Lynx AH.Mk 9
		9	Gazelle AH.Mk 1
Split-Divulji	661 Sqn AAC	6	Lynx AH.Mk 7
Gornji Vakuf	845 NA Sqn	4	Sea King HC.Mk 4
Zagreb-Pleso	RAF SHF	2	Chinook HC.Mk 2
	(returned UK end Aug 95)		
UNITED STATES			
Aviano	7490th (Provisional) Wing		
	31st Fighter Wing		
	494th FS	8	F-15E
	VFMA(AW)-533	12	F/A-18D
	510th FS	24	F-16C
	555th FS	24	F-16C
	104th FG	12	O/A-10A
	42nd ACCS	4	EC-130H ABCCC
	43rd ECS	3	EC-130H Compass
Call			
	429th ECS	6	EF-111A
	(departed mid-September)		

BASE	UNIT	No.	TYPE
	23rd FS	8	F-16C HTS
	E Coy/502nd Avn Bn	16	CH-47D
	USN/USMC	5	EA-6B
(over a one month period, EA-6Bs were deployed to Aviano by VAQ-130, -141, -209, VMAQ-1 and -3)			
Ancona	37th ALS Det	1	C-130E
Sigonella	various	8	P-3C
Pisa	91st ARS	6	KC-135R
Istres	712nd ARS/999 ARS	6	KC-135R
(the 712nd were deployed in August, followed by the 999th in September)			
Bari	HC-4 Det	2	CH-53E
Brindisi	21st SOS	4	MH-53J
	67th SOS	2	HC-130
	16th SOS	4	AC-130H
Rota/Souda Bay	VQ-2	5	EP-3E
	USNR TDY Det	2	P-3C
Mildenhall	55th Wing Det		RC-135
Fairford/Cyprus	9th RW Det	3	U-2R
Capodinichino		2	C-21
Genoa	9th RS	5	KC-10
USS *Theodore Roosevelt*			
	VF-41		F-14A
	VFA-15		F/A-18C
	VFA-87		F/A-18C
	VMFA-312		F/A-18C
	VAW-124		EC-2C
	HS-3		H/SH-60F/H
	VS-24		S-3B
	VQ-6 Det D		ES-3A
USS *America*	(arrived 9 September 1995)		
	VF-102		F-14A
	VFA-82		F/A-18C
	VFA-86		F/A-18C
	VMFA-251		F/A-18C
	VAW-1234		EC-2C
	HS-11		H/SH-60F/H
	VS-32		S-3B
	VQ-6 Det A		ES-3A
Camp Able Sentry, Skopji, Macedonia			
	7/1st Av Regt	3	UH-60A

Note: Maritime patrol aircraft (MPA) are tasked for short deployment (usually two weeks) in support of Operation Sharp Guard, the NATO/WEU embargo enforcement operation aimed at the former Yugoslavia. US and Canadian MPA are on longer deployments.

aircraft hit four ammunition depots and three electronic warfare sites. The second package of the day against two ammunition storage depots was aborted when weather obscured the targets. The final bombs of the campaign were dropped just before 18.00 on 13 September on an ammunition depot. Since 30 August a total of 3,500 sorties had been flown, including 750 strike sorties against 56 targets which caused heavy damage.

As talks continued to resolve the crisis, 5 ATAF reverted to its ground alert posture with strike packages poised at Italian bases to take out more Serb ammunition depots. An intense air presence was maintained over Bosnia to search out fresh targets and to be ready to provide close air support for UN troops on the ground.

Serbian withdrawal

The Serbs were given until 22.00 on 16 September to withdraw all their heavy weapons from the Sarajevo 10-km exclusion zone. This was later extended by 72 hours after they managed to pull out only 160 of their tanks and artillery pieces.

With tension easing around Sarajevo, the UN High Commissioner for Refugees (UNHCR) humanitarian air bridge to the city was reopened on 15 September when a French air force C-130 landed, carrying the French defence minister. The next day the air bridge

Unsung participants in Deliberate Force have been the EC-130E ABCCCs of the 42nd ACCS. These airborne command posts have monitored the ever-changing battlefield and co-ordinated NATO air strikes.

got into full swing when eight aircraft landed at Sarajevo's battered airport. Ancona in Italy was the main hub for the UNHCR effort, with British, Canadian, French and USAF Hercules, as well as German C-160Ds, rejoining the airlift after its five-month shut down. The UNHCR aimed to have eight to 10 flights a day flying into Sarajevo. UNPROFOR Il-76s from Zagreb made their first flight into the city on 16 September.

The reopening of the airport was the first tangible sign that Operation Deliberate Force had persuaded the Bosnian Serbs to change their behaviour. At the same time, it emerged that Croat and Bosnian government troops were taking advantage of the damage caused to Serb forces in Bosnia by the NATO air strikes to

While VMFA(AW)-533 and its F/A-18Ds have been shore based at Aviano, VMFA-321 has gone to sea aboard the USS Theodore Roosevelt (with its F/A-18Cs). As a result, Roosevelt has three Hornet squadrons and only one Tomcat squadron.

launch a major offensive. Serb defences collapsed and with days their stronghold of Banja Luka was being threatened.

On 20 September Admiral Smith and General Janvier flew into Sarajevo to assess Serb compliance with the UN/NATO ultimatum. By now the Serbs had pulled back 250 tanks and heavy weapons, so the two NATO/UN commanders called off the air strike threat. However hostile Serb SAM sites were .attacked on 4 October before a US-brokered cease-fire came into force the next day.   **Tim Ripley**

BRIEFING

Saab (IG JAS) JAS 39B Gripen
Roll-out of the two-seat Gripen

On 29 September 1995 the first JAS 39B two-seat Gripen (39-800/58) was rolled out at Saab's Linköping home. The ceremony was presided over by Mr Bengt Halse, President and Chief Executive of Saab AB, Mr John Weston, Chairman and Managing Director of BAe Military Division, and Lieutenant General Kent Harrskog, the C-in-C of the Swedish air force. The JAS 39B roll-out is a major milestone in the Gripen project and the first significant event since Saab (and IG JAS) announced a Gripen co-production and marketing agreement with British Aerospace, at the 1995 Paris air show.

The two-seat Gripen does not carry an Sk (Skol/school) designation, like the Sk 35 Draken or Sk 37 Viggen. This is because the air force firmly views the type as a fully operational aircraft, and not merely a 'single-role' trainer. The JAS 39B is similar in most respects to the JAS 39A, apart from an obvious 0.655-m (2-ft 2-in) fuselage stretch to accommodate the second cockpit. Like the JAS 39A, the B was designed using Dassault's CATIA CAD/CAM software (the design team numbered between 150 and 200 Saab staff), so all engineering diagrams were completed on-screen, without any paper blueprints or wooden mock-ups. The B incorporates 5,200 new components and dispenses with the 27-mm gun of the single-seater. Neither is the rear cockpit equipped with a HUD – instead,

flight information is displayed on the cockpit MFDs. Internal fuel capacity is also slightly reduced.

One unique feature of the JAS 39B is its pilot's airbag, which has been added to protect the rear occupant in the event of an ejection. Sled tests revealed that the rear pilot was exposed to shards of perspex blowing backwards through the cockpit after the front seat ejected. Together with Autoliv, a leading automobile airbag manufacturer, Saab developed an airbag that sits between both pilots. During a command ejection (where the front seats ejects first) the bag inflates and deflates within milliseconds, to first protect the rear pilot and then allow him to exit the aircraft safely.

The JAS 39B is being acquired as part of the air force's Lot 2 Gripen purchase of 130 aircraft (in total). Fourteen JAS 39Bs will be delivered, budgetary restrictions having reduced this number from an optimum 25. 39-800 was rolled in for final assembly on 1 September 1994 and is scheduled to make its maiden flight during the second quarter of 1996. The second aircraft, 39-801, is now in final assembly. Assembly of the fatigue test airframe (39-71) commenced in October 1995. A 2,000-hour flight test programme is planned for the JAS 39B and the first aircraft will be handed over to the air force in 1998. Operational deliveries will follow in 1999, to the air force's first Gripen-equipped wing F7 (its

Gripen squadrons will be 2 divisionen Gustav blau and 1 divisionen Gustav rot, respectively). The AJS 37 Viggen will then be phased out of service with F7.

The next link in the chain for the JAS 39 training programme will come in spring 1996 with the delivery of the first two LORAL full-motion dome FMS (Full Mission Simulator) to F7's newly-completed training centre, at Sätenas. It is planned to eventually install a similar simulator at each Gripen wing, and perhaps one for each squadron. The FMS is an integral part of the Gripen training programme, so much so that it has been suggested that an hour in the simulator could equate to a real flying hour. This suggestion has been greeted with horror by the air force.

The JAS 39B owes its origins to a 1988 study of future training requirements for the Gripen. At that time it was proposed that a new student would complete his first year, and 125 flying hours, in the Sk 60 (GFU – basic flying training). The second year would involve 160 flying hours with an unspecified aircraft, either the BAe Hawk or an indigenous new-build trainer, the SK/NY. The third year would comprise 140 flying hours (plus 85 in the simulator), for platform and tactical training, split between the JAS 39B (30 per cent) and JAS 39A (70 per cent). The final and fourth year would see the new pilot undergoing four months advanced operational training with his new squadron, at its home base.

This programme was substantially revised with the current large-scale reduction in *ab initio* pilot training

with which the air force is now faced. All initial Gripen pilots will be experienced aircrew converting from the Viggen/Draken force. These pilots will undergo a six-month period at F7, flying the AJS 37, followed by 12 months of advanced tactical training with the JAS 39B, at their home base, with F7 instructors. The full Gripen training syllabus, as set out by F7 and TU JAS (the Gripen advanced planning and tactics group that is run by the air force) is shown in the table opposite.

Outline plans for the JAS 39B as a fully-fledged combat type exist, and the Swedish air force has spoken tentatively of an all-weather interdictor version or perhaps an ECM version. It will be a long time before these plans are realised, however.

Meanwhile, the single-seat Gripen programme continues to gather pace. By October 1995, the 24th production aircraft (39-124) had been delivered, and Lot 1 production (30 aircraft) was virtually complete. Twenty aircraft from Lot 2 are in assembly, and from 1996 JAS 39s deliveries will reach 20 per year. The test fleet of five aircraft has completed over 1,880 flights, of the 2,400 planned for the programme. 39-103/105 are still in

Prior to the unveiling of the JAS 39B, Saab took the opportunity to unveil the 24th production JAS 39A for F7, which is visible here on a raised platform, behind the two-seater. Like another JAS 39A on display outside (39-112), this aircraft wore a slightly darker grey camouflage scheme and sported a black radome, not hitherto seen on production Gripens.

The JAS 39B roll-out at Linköping was accompanied by a massive audio-visual presentation along with banks of flashing strobe lights and the precision of the Arméns Musikkår (Swedish army band). Indeed, every taste had been catered for.

With BAe participation in the JAS programme comes the opportunity for Eurofighter test pilots to fly the Gripen (though no reciprocal arrangement has been made). This special badge has been issued to the initial BAe pilot candidates.

CONVERSION TRAINING SYLLABUS JAS 39 GRIPEN

Phase	Module		Flight Hours Module	Accumulated
LOCAL WING	PHASE 0 Preparation	– Centrifuge Training – Classroom Studies – Aircraft System	1-2 Months	
CENTRALISED PHASE 1 Conversion training		AIRCRAFT CONVERSION (JAS 39B) AIRCRAFT CONVERSION (JAS 39B)	10.5 Hours	
PHASE 2 Tactical Intro		AIR to AIR STRIKE RECCE	4.2 Hours	14.7 Hours
PHASE 3 Weapon System		AIR to AIR RECCE STRIKE AIR to AIR	25.9 Hours	40.6 Hours
PHASE 4 Tactical Training		AIR to AIR STRIKE AIR to AIR	26.6 Hours	67.2 Hours

OPERATIONAL GRIPEN PILOT

Phase		Module	Flight Hours Module	Accumulated
LOCAL PHASE 5 Threat Scenario		AIR to AIR STRIKE RECCE Including ECM AIR to AIR RECCE STRIKE	26.6 Hours	94.5 Hours
PHASE 6 Applied Multi-role Tactics		SPECIAL SPECIAL SPECIAL AIR to AIR STRIKE RECCE SIMULATOR MODULE RECCE STRIKE AIR to AIR	67.2 Hours	161.7 Hours

use as ground trainers for F7, while 39-106/112 are flying regularly. The remainder of Lot 1 JAS 39As are still in the check-out phase.

The Gripen is now flying with version P.11 of the FCS software. By October 1995, P.11 had been installed in all five test aircraft and had made 200 flights. It has replaced the interim R10.2/P9.14 software installed after the August 1994 crash of 39-102 (which was then flying with version R9.13).

The Gripen is still operating under some limitations. Angle of attack continues to be limited to 20° (planned maximum is 26°), the aircraft is subject to IAS limits and spin/stall tests will not begin until early 1996 (with the black-painted 39-2). At the end of August 1995, however, the first Ericsson-developed PP12 processor (running K12.1 software) was flown in the JAS 39. The PP12 is optimised for the EP17 colour displays and is an integral part of the Lot 2 Gripen. PP12 is substantially more powerful (and lighter) than the existing PP1 and PP2 display processors and will be of particular benefit to the JAS 39B with its additional set of cockpit displays.

Both Saab and BAe are working hard on Gripen exports, for the so-called 'JAS 39X'. On 13 September 1995, the Swedish and Hungarian governments signed an MoU for economic and industrial collaboration, paving the way for a substantive evaluation of the JAS 39 by the Hungarian air force. The Hungarian press has speculated about an order for up to 60 aircraft, although Lockheed Martin has been vigor-

ously promoting the F-16 in Eastern Europe with the hopes of achieving a second 'sale of the century' co-production deal. However, speaking at the JAS 39B roll-out, the deputy-chief of Hungary's parliament stated that no other type evaluations were being undertaken, at present.

BAe is keen to offer an EJ200-powered Gripen to Saudi Arabia, as a Northrop F-5 replacement; this powerplant will replace the current Volvo RM12, which is a licence-built GE F404. The RSAF's 100 F-5s are scheduled for replacement in 1996/97 and British Aerospace's good sales record in the area, coupled with the Gripen's high-tech image, might tip the balance. Success with 'JAS 39X' may well bolster the Swedish air forces attempts to acquire a further batch (60 to 140 new-build) of improved Lot 3 JAS 39Cs. Pictures have been released already of the Gripen carrying BAe's ASRAAM, as an AIM-9L replacement, and this weapon is one of Sweden's chief requirements for the Lot 3 aircraft.

The link with BAe finds Saab and the Gripen sailing into new waters. Both partners remain confident, but as Saab's Bengt Halse said, "With the help of British Aerospace, we think we can move mountains if we have to, and I think we have to." **Robert Hewson**

All Swedish air force trainer serials are allotted in the -800 series, but the first JAS 39B carried a '58' on the tail to mark its overall position in the Gripen test fleet.

BRIEFING

McDonnell Douglas RF-4C
Photo-Phantoms bow out in style

Based on the F-4C but featuring a redesigned nose housing a camera installation, the RF-4C first took to the air on 18 May 1964. The first service examples were delivered to the 33rd TRTS at Shaw AFB, South Carolina, on 24 September 1964, and by August 1965 the type was declared operational with the 16th TRS. In October the first examples were deployed for combat duty in Southeast Asia. Replacing the RF-101 Voodoo, the RF-4C rapidly became the backbone of the tactical reconnaissance effort, although the force was gradually reassigned to Air National Guard units. ANG tactical reconnaissance squadrons which operated the type were the 106th/Alabama, 153rd/Mississippi, 160th/Alabama, 165th/Kentucky, 173rd/Nebraska, 179th/Minnesota, 190th/Idaho, 192nd/Nevada and 196th/California.

By the time of Desert Shield the force had slimmed to five squadrons, of which one (the 106th) was dispatched to Bahrain to provide tactical reconnaissance assets during the pre-war build-up. The six aircraft were modified to employ the LOROP camera. On 18 December 1990 the Alabama

Left: The 'High Rollers' operated the RF-4C for 20 years until the type's retirement in September 1995. The unit has transitioned to the C-130 for transport duties.

Above: Seen in September 1995, this aircraft carries a baggage pod marked for the 514th Test Squadron. This unit is from the Ogden ALC, which maintained the RF-4C.

guardsmen were relieved by those from the 192nd TRS from Reno, Nevada, who subsequently flew 412 Desert Shield/Storm missions. In spite of facing intense AAA and SAM defences, no RF-4s were lost, and not one mission was cancelled for technical reasons during the conflict. One aircraft crashed soon after the war ended, with both crew safely recovered.

Following Desert Storm, the RF-4C force was further drastically cut so that by the start of 1995 the Nevada squadron was the last USAF user. The 192nd RS (of the 152nd

Reconnaissance Group) had first converted to the RF-4C in July 1975, having previously operated the RF-101B. In the on-off world of which assets were to be retained by the US Air Force in its ever-changing force cutbacks, the 192nd saw its future change twice. Immediately after Desert Storm it was decreed that the RF-4C tactical reconnaissance assets were to be retained until the end of the century, overturning a previous decision that the 152nd RS would retire its Phantoms and transition to the C-130 Hercules.

Then followed the classified Pentagon study *Desert Storm Scud Campaign* into reconnaissance platforms

during the war, in which it identified aircraft equipped with radar and electro-optical sensors as providing the most timely information. In many quarters, the day of the hard print was seen as being over.

As a consequence, it was announced at the start of 1995 that the US Air Force would retire its tactical reconnaissance Phantoms, with the last aircraft to leave the inventory by 1 October. This came like a thunderbolt to the crews of the 'High Rollers' at Reno, Nevada,

The final weeks of the RF-4C saw the 'High Rollers' engaged in speed record attempts and photo-calls to ensure that the reconnaissance Phantom would not be forgotten.

who had expected to fly their RF-4Cs for at least five more years. Despite the shock, it was decided that if the Phantom was to go, then it would go in style.

With the final four aircraft (64-01014, 64-1050, 65-0832 and 65-0901) leaving for the boneyard on 27 September, the crews at Reno set out in the last few weeks to ensure that their Phantoms would remain in the history books for all to see. On 9 and 12 September the unit attempted to set a number of speed records in the classes C1I (for aircraft of 35,000 to 44,000 lb/15876 to 19958 kg weight and C1J (above 44,000 lb/19958 kg). Records were then attempted in the 15-km (9.3-mile) and 25-km (15.5-mile) straight-line and 500-km (310.7-mile) closed-circuit speed categories, followed by attempts on the 100-km (62.1-mile) and 1000-km (621-mile) closed-circuit speed figures. The record attempts were made over the Black Rock Desert, and were verified by using two downward-looking cameras, a cockpit camera and a radar recorder, using points previously marked out on the ground as reference. According to Major Rick Vandam, chief

architect of the record attempts, all previous figures were passed easily, although official FAI ratification is awaited. The four aircraft used were taken straight from the line, saying much for the capabilities of the RF-4 and its maintenance crews.

A further legacy of the 'High Rollers' will linger on in Spain. Six aircraft (64-1006, 64-1039, 65-

0823, 65-0864, 65-0876 and 65-0897) were transferred to the Spanish air force's 123 Escuadrón for continued service in the tactical reconnaissance role. **Peter R. Foster**

The colonel's wings in the camera window identify this as the 'boss-bird'. The RF-4's camera nose was easily reconfigurable with a variety of sensors.

Rockwell/MBB X-31

Above: The X-31 grew, in part, from Rockwell's 1983 SNAKE (Super-Normal Attitude Kinetic Enhancement) programme which paved the way for a super manoeuvrable aircraft design, fitted with thrust vectoring paddles.

Below: MBB's F-104CCV (Control-Configured Vehicle) programme of 1974 to 1981 was tied into Germany's future advanced agile fighter requirement for the 1990s, but its data was of great assistance to the X-31 team.

Designed to explore the post-stall area of the envelope, the X-31 is capable of extraordinary agility, using vectored thrust to overcome normal aerodynamic constraints. Extravagant claims have been made about the ways in which X-31 type agility could revolutionise air combat, and it has performed brilliantly in simulated engagements against aircraft like the F/A-18. Detractors counter-claim that any pilot who engages in such low-speed antics is almost certainly as good as dead, in the age of the BVR missile.

When the X-31 research aircraft went out of control and crashed near Edwards Air Force Base, California on its 292nd flight on 19 January 1995, German test pilot Karl Lang ejected and parachuted safely to earth. But the revolutionary X-31 project, which has been pushing back the boundaries of aviation, was as good as 'dead' even before the mishap occurred. Although the X-31 overcame design handicaps to achieve 'firsts' in a new realm of aviation – described by programme manager Colonel Michael S. Francis as the "first aircraft in history to go beyond 'Wright flight'" – it was cash, not the crash, which finished the programme.

The second prototype X-31 survives and flew at 1995's 41st Salon International de Paris. A last-minute effort to impose safety restrictions on its flight display was quashed and the X-31 proved to be the star of the show, the one aircraft which drew crowds out of Paris' chalets and into the open to gaze upward in disbelief.

To the audience it was breathtaking, as it should have been, after the routine was practised rigorously for weeks in advance. The withdrawal of funding, in today's lean financial climate, means that the X-31 is unlikely to do any more research flying, however.

The programme had the backing of both the United States and Germany. On 10 December 1994, Deputy Defence Secretary John M. Deutsch informed the German government that he was unable to secure funds to continue testing the X-31. "The money has run out," says Lieutenant Colonel Michael P. Curphey, an engineer who watched the X-31 change the way aircraft of the future will fly and fight.

Some engineers over-dramatically describe the X-31 as the first aircraft to overcome the main obstacle to aerial flight: gravity. From the Wright Flyer to the B-17 to the Boeing 777, manoeuvring an aircraft has arguably depended upon differential lift control, usually by altering camber on the wings or tailplane. In this respect, as Francis puts it, "Even an AV-8B [Harrier II] is (only) a Wright flyer with plumbing." Enter thrust vectoring (for manoeuvring, as opposed to vertical flight), which changes everything. Says Francis, "Thrust vectoring offers a lightweight, elegant escape from the shackles of 'Wright flight'."

The X-31 would never have become reality had it only offered a new way to fly, which, incidentally, it did. The X-31 went ahead because it offered a new way to fight.

The X-31 Enhanced Fighter Maneuverability (EFM) programme began with 1977 research by the German manufacturer MBB (Messerschmitt -Bolkow-Blohm), which recently changed its name to Daimler-Benz Aerospace (previously Deutch Aerospace or DASA). MBB's Wolfgang Herbst and Karl Knauer were among a generation of aerodynamacists and designers who rediscovered the long-known truth that the combat effectiveness of a fighter would be improved by the use of high turn rates coupled with low turn radii. Translation: in order to fight better, you must go quickly around a sharp corner, moving fast and using little space.

The unstable equation

To maximise turn performance it was clear that an unstable aircraft, which already tended to pitch nose-up, would turn faster and tighter than a conventional, stable aircraft. The advent of advanced fly-by-wire control systems allowed human pilots to fly aircraft whose stability could only be maintained through computers, and which would therefore be able to manoeuvre closer to what might be called the 'departure limit'. Aircraft like the British CCV Jaguar, the General Dynamics F-16 and Rockwell's unmanned HiMAT showed the potential of combining inherently unstable airframes with advanced fly-by-wire control systems. There was still a problem: most aircraft, when turning sharply, lose speed due to increasing drag and decreasing lift. As airspeed reduces and the angle

of attack of the wing increases, they become progressively more likely to stall and then to depart from controlled flight. Even an aircraft with a fly-by-wire control system will eventually stall.

If a way could be found to prevent an aircraft from departing after its wing had stalled, aerodynamacists reasoned that a new kind of fighter should be able to turn towards a target, and to point the nose at it to aim and fire, while travelling at very low speed, perhaps at less than stalling speed. Russian designers concentrated on tailoring their fighters' aerodynamics for brief forays into the post-stall area of the envelope, and to allow them to be able to briefly point their noses well off-axis in order to

achieve a snap missile shot (or to decelerate rapidly or spoil an enemy aiming solution). This is what allows the Su-27 (and perhaps more impressively the non-FBW MiG-29) to perform the Cobra and Hook manoeuvres, in which angle of attack can briefly be increased to beyond 90°. 'Angle of attack' (AoA) is the aerodynamacist's term for the angle between an aircraft's wing and its actual flight path; it is measured in degrees, or more often, in units of Alpha. At 90° AoA, an aircraft would be pointing vertically upwards, while continuing to fly along horizontally. While of some tactical significance, Cobra-type manoeuvres are extremely transient and allow only the briefest firing opportunity, while at the same time bleeding off airspeed and energy alarmingly. Some FBW-equipped Western fighters (such as the F/A-18) from the same generation have similar high-Alpha capabilities, but none have the same ability to point the nose so far off-axis.

Rewriting the rules

From the biplanes of World War I to today's F-15 Eagles, aerial victory in close combat has traditionally depended on tail-chase tactics. The pilot has to manoeuvre into the enemy's six o'clock – his tail – and blast him out of the sky with gun or missile. Modern short-range, heat-seeking missiles can lock on to an enemy fighter from any aspect, not just from the rearward-facing heat of his exhaust, and this theoretically allows a pilot to kill his opponent by pointing his aircraft nose at the enemy. In traditional fighters this still means flying directly towards the enemy, which may not always be possible,

Left and below: The X-31 and the EFM project finally took to the air on 11 October 1990. Ted Dyson made a 38-minute journey from Palmdale to NASA's Dryden Flight Test Facility (Edwards AFB), CA. Dyson was a former USAF pilot who made the maiden flight of Lockheed's second Have Blue stealth prototype, in July 1978. Dyson was forced to eject from HB 1002 in July 1979 after an in flight fire. Carl Lang, seen opposite, was the second German pilot in the project (German Ministry of Defence) and the fourth to fly the X-31. When the No. 2 aircraft flew in January 1991 the test programme accelerated considerably.

Above: After 108 flights from Palmdale, the programme moved to Edwards AFB in December 1991. It had been planned to next move to Patuxent River for US Navy 'military tests' – indeed, the entire X-31 performance specification had been written around the need to operate from 'Pax' River's runways – but budget cuts meant the X-31 never made it there.

Left: At Edwards the X-31 team relied on venerable Vought RF-8A (F8U-1P) Crusaders to act as chase planes during test flights.

since to merely pull the nose onto the target would usually result in a stall/spin-type departure. Pilots of aircraft like the MiG-29 and Su-27 merely need to get into a position where they can point their aircraft's nose briefly at the target, by performing a Cobra (known as the Hook when performed in the horizontal plane).

The X-31 advantage

By flying and manoeuvring at high Alpha, the X-31 can fly in one direction while pointing its nose in another. The Grumman X-29 research aircraft which tested a FSW (forward-swept wing) configuration was once touted as a performer at high AoA but had almost no lateral control, and hence no real agility. Other aircraft can fly at high stabilised angles of attack but cannot transition to or from these rapidly. Russian

pilots claimed to have conquered high AoA when they demonstrated the Cobra manoeuvre with the Sukhoi Su-27 'Flanker' at the 1987 Paris air show. However, the Cobra is a short-lived manoeuvre, and the Su-27 emerges from it almost devoid of energy, airspeed and ideas. When the X-31 emerges from similar manoeuvres it is still totally controllable and ready to go into another.

Antics like the Cobra are great crowd-pleasers at air shows, and do have some military application, but the ability to point the nose off-axis for more sustained periods would be more useful. The answer was clearly to design an aircraft which could point its nose (and thereby its weapons designators) towards a target, without altering its direction of flight or flight path and without going out of control,

while continuing to fly in its original direction. Such an aircraft would be able to pitch nose-up without climbing, or to yaw right or left without turning or drifting, allowing the pilot to point the nose of his aircraft at an 'off-axis' target without flying towards it, and indeed without altering his flightpath.

The ability to manoeuvre in the post-stall part of the envelope, without departing from controlled flight, was a vital goal. Around the world, aircraft companies set about designing aircraft which could manoeuvre in hitherto unknown ways, using various new technologies. These were aircraft that could fly in one direction while pointing and shooting in another, a concept known as flight path decoupling. This notion, admitted one, "made even the most experienced aerodynamicist shudder."

CCV development

Flight path decoupling inferred the application of control forces which would destabilise a traditionally designed aircraft, by simultaneously using aerodynamic control surfaces both forward and aft of the centre of lift. The use of CCV (Control-Configured Vehicle) and FBW technology was essential to maintain artificial stability while using such control inputs. CCV aircraft which explored the use of aerodynamic controls for flight path decoupling included the YF-16 CCV, the AFTI F-16, the Mitsubishi T-2 CCV, and a canard-equipped German F-104G Starfighter.

MBB forged ahead with its own work on highly agile/high-Alpha aircraft until 1982, when formal contact was made with Rockwell. To give an idea of how far MBB had progressed, the outside world gained its first glimpse of what a modern, agile combat aircraft might look like at the 1980 Hanover air show when MBB displayed a model of the TKF, the firm's proposal which helped shape today's multi-national EFA (European Fighter Aircraft). The X-31 was closely based on the original MBB proposal for the EFA, and the prototype uses the same wing unaltered, since this was optimised for low supersonic drag and maximum lift.

MBB had been working with British Aerospace on a planned Agile Combat Aircraft (ACA), but withdrew from that effort. It also

Resting in a hangar at Edwards, X-31 No. 1 sports a subtle sharkmouth on its intake cover. Throughout their lives the X-31s received little decoration beyond their basic blue and white colour scheme and a few small agency and project logos on the fuselage and tail.

worked with Saab on the Viggen RCFAM (Roll Coupled Fuselage Aiming) demonstrator which was designed to slew the nose to track a target during head-on gun attacks. In the United States, Rockwell had started working on super-manoeuvrability with the unmanned HiMAT (Highly Maneuverable Aircraft Technology) demonstrator. This primarily explored high *g* manoeuvring at very high speeds (especially in the transonic regime) through the use of an inherently unstable airframe and advanced fly-by-wire controls. At one stage Rockwell proposed using HiMAT for post-stall manoeuvring, but the benefits of doing this in an unmanned platform were held to be marginal. The company had subsequently explored producing a highly-manoeuvrable manned fighter demonstrator, but lost out when a contract was awarded instead to Grumman for its X-29 forward-swept-wing agility demonstrator. Still, Rockwell went ahead with wind-tunnel tests of what it called the SNAKE (Super-Normal Attitude Kinetic Enhancement) aircraft.

In October 1982, MBB leaders met with Rockwell and in 1983 the two companies agreed to embark on a joint programme to explore agility. At the time, the US had rigid laws on technology transfer which were viewed by both parties as an obstacle to working together, but some of these obstacles were later overcome by the Nunn-Quayle R&D initiative.

The F-15 S/MTD (STOL Maneuvering Technology Demonstrator) which flew in September 1988 had validated some of the principles behind the future X-31, although it used two-dimensional vectoring nozzles instead of paddles and involved heavier, costlier modifications. The sum of $400 million was spent to convert the S/MTD, which was a modification of an existing aircraft, while the wholly new X-31 cost just half that figure. In fairness, the S/MTD incorporated a very complex flight control and thrust vectoring system, including thrust reversing, and was, in any case, intended primarily to develop short landing capability and to develop technologies applicable to advanced fighters, but not to be an agile fighter demonstrator itself.

German/US 'X-plane' deal

In 1986, the German Ministry of Defense and the United State's Defense Advanced Research Projects Agency signed an MoU (memorandum of understanding) for the development, manufacture and flight-testing of two experimental aircraft. This bilateral arrangement between two countries – the first international 'X-plane' project – was made possible by the Nunn-Quayle amendment for international research and development which eased technology-transfer constraints and supplied both the institutional mechanism and $80 million in initial funding. The program was to be divided into four distinct phases. Phase I covered conceptual design, while Phase II covered design of the demonstrator and definition of the manufacturing approach. Phase

A basic design requirement for the X-31 was that is should incorporate as many off-the-shelf components as possible. Ultimately, 43 per cent of each X-31, or 603 items, from the engine and the canopy to the wheels and the on board computers, were obtained from stock.

III covered detail design and limited flight test, and Phase IV covered comprehensive flight testing to establish the feasability of controlled flight in the post stall region and to explore use of the aircraft in close-in Dissimilar Air Combat Training (DACT) engagements. Following in a tradition of pioneer 'X-planes', beginning with the Bell X-1 (formerly XS-1) which made the first confirmed supersonic flight on 14 October 1947, the new American-German aircraft was designated X-31 on 23 February 1987.

The X-31 differs from previous 'X-planes' in an important way. From the beginning, it was meant to demonstrate operational capability (the term was underlined in planning documents),

not merely to investigate or demonstrate technology. Early thinking focused on an X-31 which would include features of a fighter, including cannon and missile armament, external fuel and an inflight-refuelling receptacle.

International fellowship

To run the X-31 programme, the two nations created the ITO (International Test Organization), an autonomous entity which conducted flight tests. Hosted by NASA, ITO included participants from DARPA, the German Ministry of Defence, Rockwell and MBB. ITO has been hailed as a model of smooth management. The US Navy was picked

Above: The X-31 structure (by weight) comprises 51 per cent aluminium, 17 per cent graphite/epoxy, five per cent steel, five per cent titanium, four per cent aluminium/lithium, two per cent carbon/carbon, one per cent fibreglass and 15 per cent of assorted other materials.

Below: X-31 No.1 undergoes engine trials at Palmdale in 1991. Note the original DARPA titles (later changed to ARPA) and the lack of thrust vectoring paddles. Note also the configuration of the air data probe. This would be revised once real EFM tests were underway.

AoA and pitch down recovery moment from high AoΛ.

The configuration was also heavily influenced by the fact that the engine was selected before other critical features were defined. Due to cost reasons and the US Navy's role, power was to be provided by a 12,000-lb (53.38-kN) thrust General Electric F404-GE-400 turbojet, the engine used on the McDonnell F/A-18 Hornet. The powerplant was chosen so that the Navy would be a continuing source of spares. The F404 was also viewed positively because it tolerated airflow disruption remarkably well, a useful attribute for high-Alpha flight. The F404 has an established record for reliability and has performed well on twin-engined warplanes like the F/A-18 and F-117. With this engine the X-31, however, was underpowered, an issue that engineers kept returning to but never solved.

Performance goals

The performance needed in the X-31 programme obviously entailed a high thrust-to-weight ratio. Simulations indicated that the X-31 needed a sea level thrust-to-weight figure of at least 1.2:1. Studies showed that the X-31 would not achieve this figure unless its gross weight could be kept below 13,000 lb (5,896 kg). This was recognised from the beginning as a difficult challenge and one not likely to be met.

Other choices in the X-31 design resulted from the viewpoint of the partners. The Germans' focus was almost exclusively on the technological objective of controlled, post-stall flight. After thousands of simulations, they were convinced that controlled flight in this unexplored region was already a 'given' and that it was time to move ahead to tactical applications. The American participants wanted a more versatile airframe and limited supersonic capability, even though flight beyond Mach 1.0 was largely irrelevant to exploring the world of post-stall. The supersonic capability was included, as a Rockwell engineer puts it, "to give the programme credibility to the [US Air Force] 'fighter Mafia'."

The USAF largely resisted the X-31, believing that it had determined that close-quarter dogfighting was a thing of the past and that future engagements would take place beyond visual range. This thinking was reminiscent of the pre-Vietnam days when the USAF had determined that fighters no longer required guns because future engagements would be at missile ranges. The advent of all-aspect Sidewinder, the coming of age of Sparrow and, more recently, the introduction of AMRAAM has lent some credence to this argument, and the vast majority of post-Vietnam kills have been scored with missiles, many of them in BVR engagements. This has been as much due to favourable circumstances and rules of engagement. In the fog of a full-scale air war visual identification will often be necessary, and many close-range missile battles will degenerate to a visual gun fight after the merge. Many still regard the X-31's type of low-speed manoeuvrability as an expensive luxury in an air combat world where the majority of engagements take place at medium range and high subsonic speed. The argument runs that any combatant engaging in a low-speed, high-Alpha, multi-bogey fight

as DARPA's 'agent' and was charged with managerial and technical oversight of the $80 million X-31 programme. (DARPA had the 'Defense' removed from its title, becoming ARPA in 1993.)

When the MoU was signed, the design of the aircraft was far from finalised, but planners agreed on four firm goals: to provide a rapid demonstration of high-agility manoeuvring concepts; to investigate the tactical benefits of EFM technologies; to develop the design requirements and database to support future applications; and to validate a low-cost international prototyping concept. The core requirement was simple, though, to design an aircraft which would demonstrate the practicality and utility of using new technologies to allow an aircraft to use very rapid fuselage pointing to acquire and engage a target in close-in combat, beyond normal flight envelope parameters. Enhanced fighter manoeuvrability was defined as including post-stall manoeuvrability (calculated to give twice as many first shots and to triple the exchange ratio), steep descent capability (giving 75 per cent fewer losses to ground fire), and enhanced conventional agility (improving exchange ratio by 160 per

cent and giving 15 per cent fewer non-combat losses). It was also defined as allowing enhanced decoupled (roll-coupled) fuselage aiming (calculated as quadrupling exchange ratios in gun engagements), and enhanced deceleration and enhanced negative g capability (which together enhanced survivability, gave more first shots and doubled the chances of surviving a gun attack).

Defining a shape

Designing the X-31 air vehicle became both a technical and a practical obstacle, and one which entailed unhappy trade-offs. The now-familiar shape of the X-31 Enhanced Fighter Manoeuvrability demonstrator closely followed that of MBB's original TKF 90 submission. Its aerodynamic design is thus closely based on MBB's proposed configuration for the European Fighter Aircraft. The original TKF 90 wing planform, subsequently used on the X-31, was a compromise solution to competing requirements of low drag at supersonic speeds, maximum lift at corner speed, minimum induced drag at the design manoeuvre points, and a balance between relaxed stability at low

X-31 pilots

Agency	Name	Principal responsibilities
Rockwell	Ken Dyson	First flight, envelope expansion
MBB	Dietrich Seeck	Envelope expansion
Rockwell	Fred Knox	Envelope expansion, combat manoeuvring
GMoD	Karl Lang	Envelope expansion, combat manoeuvring
USMC	Major Bob Trombadore	Evaluation
USN	Cdr Al Groves	Envelope expansion, combat manoeuvring
USAF	Major Derrick Hess	Evaluation, combat manoeuvring
USAF	Lt Col Jim Wisnewski	Envelope expansion
NASA	Rogers Smith	Envelope expansion
NASA	Ed Schnieder	Combat manoeuvring
Luftwaffe	Lt Col Quirin Kim	Combat manoeuvring
USMC	Major Gus Loria	Envelope expansion, combat manoeuvring

Above: The badge worn by the X-31 pilots (this one belonged to Lieutenant Colonrl Jim Wisnewski) summed up every aspect of the project, from its international nature to its revolutionary EFM goals.

Below: The key to the X-31's manoeuvrability is its thrust vectoring system, which was developed from one first fitted to an F-14 and test flown on an F/A-18. The three paddles fitted to the X-31 are made from carbon/carbon composites.

Above: The X-31 cockpit was modified from an F/A-18's and had several unique features. Flight modes were controlled from the bank of switches beneath the HUD display. The control column had its switches reconfigured, disabling the X/Y MFD cursor control on the top right. Half way down the grip, on the left, was the (large) post-stall enable switch which activated the FCS for extreme flight conditions. The FCS used JOVIAL as its programming language, rather than the more modern ADA.

exposes himself to such danger from wild card aircraft that the outcome will depend more on luck than skill or aircraft quality. The same critics did, however, acknowledge the ability of thrust vectoring to improve high energy manoeuvrability at higher engagement speeds. At the bottom line, the question must be whether a fighter pilot can afford to ignore close-in combat capability and rely totally on BVR tactics, regardless of rules of engagement or system saturation.

Putting it togther

Although the attributes to be demonstrated by the X-31 were controversial in some quarters, the programme pushed ahead. Workshare was allocated according to the share of funding, with 75 per cent allocated to the US partner and 25 per cent to the German.

Rockwell specified requirements, designed the aerodynamic shape of the aircraft (although basing it on an existing German design), built the fuselage, canard foreplane and tailfin, and served as integrator for the X-31 system. Some 'old hands' at the Palmdale, California facility see in the broad fuselage, and especially in its aftersection which is closer to being square than rounded, the influence of an earlier North American aircraft, the F-100 Super Sabre. Rockwell used advanced composites in developing and manufacturing the X-31's canards, vertical surfaces and some access doors. The X-31 canard is not closely coupled with the wing aerodynamically. Left and right canard panels are identical and can be used on either side. The idea of cambering and twisting the panels was examined but was dropped in favour of the lower-cost uncambered panels actually

adopted. The primary function of the canards is to provide a powerful nose-down pitching control for recovery from high AoAs. Rockwell examined the possibility of using the B-1B's structural mode control vanes, but these were considerably heavier than the X-31 canard's target weight. The B-1B vane's forged spindle was used as the core of the newly designed canard, however, albeit with more material removed to save weight. Rockwell also developed an X-31 flight simulator inside a 24-ft (7.43-m) dome at Palmdale to provide realistic handling in post-stall manoeuvres.

MBB wrote the flight control laws, designed and built the wings and thrust vectoring paddles for the new aircraft, and were responsible for Post Stall performance. The wing is dry, containing no fuel (4,000 to 4,500 lb/1814 to 2268 kg of fuel are held by two tanks in the fuselage).

X-31 configuration

The cropped double-delta wing makes use of graphite epoxy skin and is joined to a fairing which covers the wing attachment fittings at the root of the wing. The cranked wing has 56.6° of leading edge sweep inboard and 45° outboard, plus leading- and trailing-edge flaps. The trailing-edge flaps are built and actuated as two separate sections on each side. These are the principal pitch and roll controls; the canard is basically a pitch recovery control but is co-ordinated with the trailing-edge flaps for secondary pitch control. The canards are programmed to remain unloaded during AoA changes, but a power approach mode can be selected, in which the canards produce lift, deflecting the elevons down and reducing approach speed by about 15 kt (27 km/h). Inboard and outboard leading-edge flap actuators are buried within the wing contour, which was thickened slightly to make this possible, but actuators for the trailing-edge flaps are mounted in two 'bathtubs' suspended beneath the wings. It proved impossible to bury these actuators and their associated control valves within the mould line.

The flying controls are actuated by a conventional stick and rudder, although longitudinal stick movement commands an angle of attack below 325 kt (585 km/h) and load factor at higher speeds. Lateral stick movement commands roll, as you would expect, but the aircraft rolls around its velocity vector (direction of flight) and not its own axis. In normal flight the velocity vector and fuselage axis are the same but, as Alpha increases, a roll around the velocity vector becomes a combination of conventional roll around the fuselage axis and yaw until, at 90° AoA, the aircraft fore and aft axis (seen in plan view) would appear to travel around the direction of flight like the hand of a demented clock.

The X-31 was required to keep its gun pipper stable on a target for at least one second to register a 'kill'. Observers tell of watching gun camera film of an F/A-18 seemingly locked in the X-31's sights, while the 'bored' X-31 pilot repeated, "bang, bang, bang, bang..."

The post-stall system is activated by a switch on the stick. A 'soft' stick stop delineates the 30° AoA boundary for normal flight, and pulling beyond this detent has no effect unless the post stall switch has been enabled. This can only occur in normal flight above 10,000 ft (3048 m), with thrust vectoring on and thrust at minimum burner or greater. The HUD can generate a display centred on the body axis or on the velocity vector.

The heart of the X-31

If a loss of lift is inevitable (by definition) at and after the stall, it became increasingly obvious that loss of control is not. The solution was to use vectored thrust to maintain control after the stall, and to provide a sufficiently powerful nose-down pitching moment to allow recovery from high-Alpha flight. A simple concept was developed in which three 'thrust vector vanes' encircling the engine exhaust would serve as a primitive vectoring nozzle. These carbon-fibre paddles were described by programme manager Colonel Francis as "the aircraft's visible technological masterpiece." The thrust vectoring system is in part a development of the yaw-producing paddle system fitted to the F-14 Tomcat spin test aircraft. To break the 'stall barrier' and achieve supermanoeuvrability, thrust can be vectored up to 15° from the normal thrust line, in any direction, vectoring thrust to replace the effect of aerodynamic controls. Rockwell's early studies showed that no more than 10° to 15° of thrust vectoring of the F404 engine maximum afterburner thrust was needed to meet planned control requirements.

Composites and construction

To increase strength and reduce weight, MBB used carbon-carbon (a high-temperature composite material) for the wing and for the paddles, forming 2 per cent of the structural weight of the aircraft. Aluminium formed 51 per cent of the aircraft, with 17 per cent graphite/epoxy, 5 per cent steel, 5 per cent titanium and 4 per cent aluminium-lithium. The motions of the paddle are controlled independently but co-ordinated by a sophisticated digital flight control system. The resultant forces are then automatically blended with those generated by the aircraft's conventional aerodynamic flight controls to achieve desired inflight performance, but without the pilot having to actually point the thrust vector himself. In the post-stall regime the pilot simply uses the stick in the normal sense in order to point the aircraft in the intended direction.

The X-31 paddles each deflect in and out of the exhaust stream to point the thrust. Together they weigh about 103 lb (47 kg), while the aft fuselage frame holding the assembly weighs 28 lb

Once the X-31 was allowed to commence its F/A-18 engagements with a neutral start and use its post-stall capability, its kill ratio shot up to 32:1. Similar scores were chalked up against NASA's own 'enhanced manoeuvrability' Hornet.

(13 kg), the support for the vectoring hardware weighs 30 lb (14 kg), and the flight control system components weigh 79 lb (36 kg), the total package adding up to an economical 240 lb (108 kg). By contrast, General Electric's AVEN (Axisymmetric Vectoring Engine Nozzle) adds about 400 lb (181 kg) to the weight of the MATV F-16, although this does achieve total, as opposed to partial, deflection of the thrust, and to a greater angle (18°). They were fitted to the aircraft some time after its first flight.

Off-the-shelf components

The two X-31 aircraft were designed, refined and built with exceedingly limited funding in a closely-managed, austere programme which could serve as a model for other experimental aircraft programs. The formal Design Approach statement had specified that the aircraft should be "designed and fabricated within a minimum time period consistent with a reasonable development risk," and using military specifications as design guides only. Flight readiness clearance procedures were streamlined by new management systems. Rockwell sought the lowest-cost components and sub-systems and used 'off-the-shelf' items wherever feasible. In order to save money and time the X-31 made use of many components actually taken from or designed and flight-cleared for other

aircraft. These included F-16 rudder pedals, landing gear, nosewheel tyres, emergency power unit and fuel pump, F-16XL leading-edge flap drives, C-130 HTTB (High Technology Test Bed) Honeywell flight control computers, V-22 actuators and trailing-edge control modules, an F-5E environmental control unit, Cessna Citation III mainwheels and brakes and mainwheel tyres from the A-7 Corsair. The flight control computers have three channels, with a fourth used as a tie-breaker. Parts were also used from the T-2C (a zero *g* fuel accumulator), and the F-20. Not all of these turned out to be wise choices. A low-cost, hydrazine-based emergency air start system developed for the Northrop F-20 Tigershark proved difficult to use, fragile, and almost impossible to maintain with spare parts. Mishaps with this subsystem caused a number of delays. "When we have a hiccough with this, it's a big problem," says Colonel Francis, since parts for the system are now difficult to locate.

The F-16's landing gear was selected after examining those of the Alpha Jet and F-5, which either did not fit or required major structural modifications to the wing.

In addition to the engine from the F/A-18 Hornet, the X-31 used the Hornet's primary electrical generators, airframe-mounted accessory gearbox, leading-edge actuators, cockpit instrumentation and windscreen and

When the X-31 arrived in Paris in 1995 its paddles started to malfunction in the unaccustomedly damp climate. Special lagging 'jackets' were hastily improvised to protect its carbon/carbon composites and intricate actuators.

canopy. The pilot of the X-31 has an F/A-18 centre stick rather than a right-hand sidestick controller like that found on the F-16 Fighting Falcon, although Colonel Francis says, "There is no best way. This is just the way it happened." The throttle also comes from the F/A-18. Forty-three per cent of the empty weight is accounted for by 600 items from other aircraft.

Most of the key items for the high-AoA flight tests were new and unique to the X-31. These included the 'floating' canard, articulating air intake lip, all-composite wing and high-temperature thrust vector blades.

Despite the efforts of some hard-headed project managers, who took ruthless decisions where necessary, the X-31 kept increasing in weight. As the weight of the X-31 escalated to almost 16,000 lb (7257 kg), reducing the thrust-to-weight ratio to about 1:1, engineers dropped the planned 'typical operational features' including radar, air-refuelling receptacle, gun, and hardpoints for supporting weapons. Instead, at the final stage of its test programme the X-31 would fly mock combat missions using simulated, 'virtual' weapons. This was an acceptable compromise but planners remained worried that the inability to carry external fuel would severely limit range and sortie duration. Typically, sortie duration of the X-31 would be 50 to 60 minutes, reducing to 35 minutes if afterburner was used.

Flight test programme

Following a roll-out ceremony in March 1990, the first X-31 (BuNo. 164584) made its first flight at Palmdale on 11 October 1990, with Rockwell chief test pilot Ken Dyson at the controls. Dyson is a retired USAF pilot who flew early tests with the Have Blue project, although it had already been decided that test pilots from both Rockwell and MBB would fly the aircraft. During the 38-minute flight, Dyson took the X-31 to 340 mph (547 km/h) and reached an altitude of 10,000 ft (3096 m). Dyson reported that the flying qualities and subsystem performance of the aircraft were as expected.

The X-31's Menasco-built main landing gear was adapted from that of an F-16. The nose gear came from a Cessna Citation and was fitted with brakes and a tyre from an A-7 Corsair.

Specification
Rockwell/MBB X-31

Type: single-seat manoeuvre research aircraft
Powerplant: one 12,000-lb (53.38-kN) thrust General Electric F404-GE-400 turbojet with three-paddled vectored exhaust
Max speed: Mach 1.08 or 717 mph (1,155 km/h) at sea level
Capability: with its ability to manoeuvre at high

angles, the X-31 can fly as slow as 30 mph (45 km/h) IAS and turn in less than 30 ft (100 m)
Ceiling: 40,000 ft (12384 m)
Range: 236 miles (380 km)
Weights: empty 11,570 lb (5248 kg); fuel 4,085 lb (1852 kg); loaded 7,100 kg (15655 lb)
Wing span: 23.83 ft (7.37 m)
Length: 43.33 ft (13.25 m)
Height: 14.58 ft (4.51 m)
Wing area: 2,045 sq ft (190 m²)

X-31 pilots have had to compete for the limited cockpit space available. To offset this, a dome simulator was installed at Rockwell's Downey, California, facility. This lead to fewer nasty surprises when taking the real machine aloft for its demanding test schedule.

Some 600 flights were planned for the X-31, to take place at Edwards and subsequently at the Naval Air Test Center, Patuxent River, Maryland over two years. The flight test programme is best understood if it is seen as having two phases: conventional flying to expand and test the aircraft envelope, followed by experimental/research test flying in the post-stall regime. After the conventional and post-stall research phases came applied research flying, using the X-31 in air-to-air engagements with conventional jet fighters.

During early flight tests, it looked as if the programme would accomplish none of its goals. Almost a year was consumed in establishing and proving the conventional envelope, which included an altitude of 40,000 ft (12384 m), a speed of Mach 0.9, and a structural load factor of 7.2 *g*. At first, the conventional envelope was defined to limit AoA to 30°. Interim limits of 30,000 ft (9144 m), Mach 0.67 (365 kt; 672 km/h) and 4 *g* were set by Navair for the very early part of the flight test programme. During

the second flight the electronic flight control computers went to reversionary modes, as a result of disagreements between the two air data sources. This happened four times during the first nine flights, largely as a result of the 1960s logic used in the software. The problem was easily cured.

Everyone connected with the programme felt it was moving too slowly. Still, there was clear progress. As tests with the paddles proceeded, the X-31 evaluated agility and handling qualities at higher AoA up to the 30° limit, including 360° rolls. Further, the X-31A was kept at these angles for increasing periods of time. The first such tests in June-July 1991 evaluated the affect of the paddles upon the exhaust stream of the aircraft under varying conditions. As steeper AoA were attained, the X-31 began a process which would persist throughout the programme, enhancing knowledge essential to combat manoeuvrability in future fighters. (Above 30° AoA, the aircraft is manoeuvred using the stick only, not using rudder pedals.)

Tests deploying an inflight spin chute using ship no. 1 began on 27 August 1991 with Rockwell's Fred Knox as pilot. Ship no. 1 was scheduled to work in the 40°-50° AoA range in September-October 1991, and then to proceed to even higher AoA manoeuvring. Following deployment of the spin chute one year into the flight-test programme, the stability benefits of canards were tested.

A sad moment for those in the X-31 programme came in October 1991 when the brilliant Wolfgang Herbst died in a crash of his

Rockwell/MBB X-31

1 Air data probe
2 Pitch and yaw vanes
3 Test instrumentation boom
4 Glass-fibre nosecone
5 Air data computers
6 Flight test instrumentation
7 Foreplane hydraulic actuator (Bendix from V-22)
8 Composite canard foreplanes
9 Foreplane pivot and spindle (from B-1B foreplane)
10 Rudder pedals (F-16)
11 Control column (F/A-18)
12 Fully shrouded instrument panel
13 HUD (F/A-18)
14 Windscreen (from F/A-18)
15 One-piece transparency (Swedlow – F/A-18)
16 Martin-Baker SJU-5/6 ejection seat
17 Throttle (F/A-18)
18 Side console panel
19 Boundary layer spill duct
20 Variable capture area intake cowl lip

21 Intake lip hydraulic actuator
22 Leading edge extension strake
23 Nose gear (Menasco), nosewheel and tyre (B. F. Goodrich), all from F-16
24 Cockpit ECS and avionics cooling system
25 Emergency air start sub-system reservoir
26 Canopy hydraulic jack
27 Avionics equipment bay, port and starboard, communications and FCS equipment, digital fly-by-wire control system
28 Wheels and brakes (B. F. Goodrich – Citation III), tyres from A-7D

29 Main undercarriage (Menasco – F-16)
30 Centre fuselage integral fuel tankage
31 Fuel feed and vent piping
32 Gravity fuel-filler for single tank
33 L-band communications antenna
34 Two-section leading-edge flap
35 Starboard navigation light
36 Starboard outboard elevon
37 Elevon tandem hydraulic actuators
38 Hydraulic reservoir
39 Air turbine starter
40 Airframe-mounted accessory equipment gearbox
41 Accessory gearbox

42 Full authority digital engine control (FADEC)
43 General Electric F404-GE-400 afterburning turbofan
44 Engine bay venting ram air intake
45 Afterburner duct
46 Position/anti-collision light
47 Fuel vent line to dump at fin trailing edge
48 Rudder
49 Rudder tandem hydraulic actuator (Bendix – V-22)

53 Thrust vectoring paddle hydraulic actuator
54 Port airbrake
55 Airbrake hydraulic jack
56 Port outboard elevon
57 Elevon tandem hydraulic actuator
58 Flaperon actuator
59 Port outboard elevon
60 Port navigation light
61 Port leading-edge flap segment

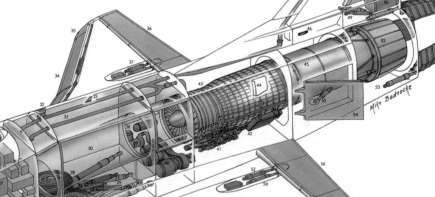

50 Brake parachute (Syndex)
51 Carbon/carbon thrust vectoring paddles (SIGRI)
52 Variable area afterburner nozzle

62 Flap rotary actuator
63 Leading-edge flap drive motor with cross-shaft to starboard side

Rockwell/MBB X-31

sub-scale Focke Wulf Fw 190 replica. There was tremendous irony in the death of this man who wanted to take flying into new realms. Herbst was a 'total aviation person' but despised showboating and saw the X-31 programme in cold, hard engineering terms. He would never have agreed to the ultimate manoeuvre by the X-31 being named after him, as, indeed, was destined to happen. Meanwhile, the X-31 flight effort forged ahead in fits and starts. Every few months, some change in the fiscal environment raised questions as to whether funding would continue.

The second aircraft

Dietrich Seeck made the first flight in the no. 2 X-31 (BuNo. 164585) at Palmdale on 19 January 1991. The aircraft initially flew without paddles, which were installed in March 1991, after the third flight. This second aircraft had made 11 flights by 1 September 1991.

The thrust vectoring paddles were left off the X-31s for the early envelope expansion flights, because they were unnecessary for conventional flying (and to prevent accidental damage). They were installed for the 10th flight of ship no. 1 on 14 February 1991 (but were not used on that flight). Actuation of the paddles was delayed because even on the ground they overloaded the flight control computer, and the software had to be rewritten. The first X-31 began using its thrust-vectoring paddles for the first time during a test flight on 31 May 1991. During this one-hour flight, pilot Dietrich Seeck moved the paddles up to 15° at altitudes from 10,000-40,000 ft (3096-12384 m). Soon thereafter, Rockwell test pilot Fred Knox flew the X-31 to 54° AoA. This 'manoeuvre milestone' was deemed the last event in the first phase of flying.

Phase one of the X-31 flight test programme had a fairly simple goal: to push, and thus define, the envelope of the aeroplane's performance in conventional flying. The X-31 people who call this 'Wright flight' argued that the second stage of the flight test programme represented the most revolutionary development since the historic Wilbur and Orville Wright hop on 17 December 1903.

The X-31 programme always faced insecurities, fiscal and otherwise. At one point, "the flight safety community wanted to baby-step us," says Francis. Threatened with bureaucratic obstacles to moving the X-31 from conventional to post-stall flight, the colonel put together an off-site meeting at Lancaster, California (adjacent to Edwards) in March 1992 to address safety concerns and establish milestones for the planned programme.

If recurring threats to funding could be kept at bay, the second, or post-stall, phase of X-31 flying was to follow a gradual, logical course toward more difficult and, thus, more dramatic, manoeuvres. This phase had four parts. Part one was to maintain steady flight at maximum AoA (70°). Part two was to roll the aircraft around its velocity vector. Part three was 'dynamic entry' (described below) and part four an incredible achievement called the Herbst manoeuvre.

The first 108 test flights in the X-31 programme were made at Palmdale, but the facility was too small and not well enough equipped to host the more advanced phases. NASA's Ames-Dryden facility at Edwards was made available on short notice on attractive economic terms. On 21 December 1991, the two X-31s flew from Palmdale to Edwards – the only time the two aircraft ever flew together. As

much as four months later, ITO was still saying that a period of flying at Ames Dryden would be followed by 'military tests' at Patuxent River, something the US Navy very much wanted. Later, it was determined that the cost of moving to Patuxent outweighed the benefits.

After a considerable hiatus for minor technical fixes, the X-31 resumed flying on 23 April 1992 when Lang took the second ship aloft for a one-hour routine check of aircraft systems. The X-31's study of post-stall manoeuvring began in the summer of 1992, examining unsteady external aerodynamic phenomena, inlet and engine effects, control authority schemes, and pilot orientation issues.

70° up

The first X-31 reached its design 70° AoA for the first time during a series of flights on 18 September 1992. Test pilots Commander Al Grove, Seeck and Rogers Smith explored the range of 31° to 70° AoA during three flights that day. The second goal in 'phase two' was attempted in November 1992. Now that the X-31 had demonstrated stability at high AoA, it was time to show agility at high Alpha. The objective was to roll the aircraft around its velocity vector. Fred Knox accomplished this by achieving 360° of roll while holding the aircraft at 70° AoA. The X-31 was now boldly entering a regime that no aircraft had entered before.

The third step in 'phase two' was to achieve 'dynamic entry', the term for transitioning rapidly into low-speed, high-AoA post-stall from high speed at low AoA. This may be achieved in a split-S manoeuvre. USAF Lieutenant Colonel Jim Wisnewski attempted 'dynamic entry' on 25 November 1992, and achieved the unique feat of losing control of the aircraft for the only time in the entire flight test programme. To put this in perspective, MiG-29 and Su-27 pilots were regularly demonstrating dynamic entries into high AoA flight at air show heights at Farnborough and Paris shows.

The X-31's wing was derived from MBB's EFA research. The double-delta was swept to 56.6° on the inboard leading-edge and 45° on the outboard section. Leading- and trailing-edge flaps are fitted, the latter providing primary pitch recovery.

The X-31's canards are lightly loaded and not highly coupled with the wing. Early studies looked at fitting the B-1B's structural mode control vanes as canards, but these were too heavy. In the event only the B-1B's forged spindle was incorporated in the X-31 design.

Wisnewski went into the manoeuvre and the X-31 'departed', the modern term for a classic stall/spin departure from controlled flight. He regained control of the aircraft not by using an academic spin recovery (centralise controls, simultaneously apply full anti-spin rudder and forward stick), but via the time-honoured and traditional method, namely taking his hands off the controls and letting the X-31 right itself.

Following the departure incident, minor changes were made to the X-31 to improve its post-stall controllability. Vortex-generating strakes were added to the nose and thrust vector vane travel was increased from 26° to 35° inward (previously, it had been impossible for the vanes to hit each other; now, only software prevented this). Changes were made to the flight controls to make them more responsive. With these changes, Wisnewski achieved a successful 'dynamic entry' in February 1993.

The Herbst manoeuvre

The fourth and final goal in 'phase two' was the ultimate manoeuvre in post-stall flying, named after Herbst. Now, the X-31 made not only a 'dynamic entry' but a 'dynamic exit' at high speed. In the post-stall realm, the X-31 stayed at 70° AoA and accomplished a 180° reversal of heading. At the completion of the manoeuvre the X-31 was going in the opposite direction and used its thrust-to-weight ratio to get out of post-stall.

As with much of the flying by the X-31 in its new realm, the Herbst manoeuvre cannot be fully appreciated until it is seen: no number of printed words will convey the image of a jet aircraft inscribing an enormous circle in the sky while pointed in a different direction. At one juncture in the Herbst manoeuvre, the X-31 has its tailpipe pointed upward and forward in its direction of travel and its nose pointed downward and to the rear.

Subsequently, the X-31 developed new, rapid 'nose pointing' manoeuvres. In 1993 and 1994, up until the loss of the no. 1 aeroplane, the X-31 continued to push back the envelope of fighter manoeuvrability. The aircraft proved that it can fly and fight at virtually any angle.

Helmet-mounted displays

Once having accomplished everything in its 'baseline' programme, the X-31 was employed in research efforts which were not part of the original plan. This began in late 1992 with tests of helmet-mounted displays (HMDs). To solve the problem of 'own ship situational awareness' which keeps fighter pilots flicking their gaze from the instrument panel to the sky, the X-31 was flown with HMDs which provide 'own ship symbology' right in front of the pilot's eyes.

Three HMD designs were tried. The first, a German design, was too heavy and cumbersome and was discarded early. Next came the I-NITES helmet and display, which had been developed for night vision work but offered a stereo capability applicable for day use.

Phase IV of the X-31 programme (flight testing) originally called for 18 initial air worthiness flights, 80 conventional envelope flights, 200 flights in a post-stall envelope, 80 optimisation and tactics development flights and 40 tactical evaluation flights, between May 1990 and April 1992. This schedule was much modified and the aircraft never actually reached Patuxent River.

The X-31 crossed the Atlantic for the 1995 Paris Air Salon courtesy of an AMC C-5. It was never part of the plan that the aircraft would leave the United States but the surviving X-31 was partially disassembled and taken to the show without any major hitches.

I-NITES performed well but the helmet was deemed too heavy and to have its centre of gravity too far forward, and there was concern for the safety of a pilot who might have to eject with the helmet on. The third HMD unit was the GEC Marconi Viper helmet which offered the same capability but which was monocular, not binocular. This flying confirmed the HMD as an effective substitute for, and an improvement over, a head-up display.

Air-to-air 'combat' with the X-31 began with a Basic Fighter Maneuver Phase (BFM) starting in the summer of 1993 at Ames-Dryden and ending in October 1993. A standard US Navy F/A-18, configured with two pylons and centreline drop tank, which was deemed to have approximately the same conventional performance as the X-31, was chosen as a 'co-operative adversary'. A far better adversary (or, in the terminology of scientific experiment, a 'control')

would have been another X-31 employed in conventional flying. The two X-31s had flown together on only one occasion, and usually one was 'down' to provide support for the other.

In conventional battle, the standard F/A-18 Hornet, which itself is among the most agile of current fighters, defeated the X-31 twice for each loss, thereby racking up a 2:1 ratio against the X-31. But when the X-31 went into post-stall flight, everything changed. Since an AIM-9L Sidewinder cannot be launched at high AoA, all battles were fought with guns. Many people believe that the post-stall advantages of an X-31-type aircraft will be squandered until the US military develops an off-boresight, high-AoA missile, like the already-deployed Russian R-73 (AA-11 'Archer'), while there are others who argue that development funds spent on such a weapon would reap greater benefits than the pursuit of aircraft supermanoeuvrability. Still other experts believe that the pursuit of close-in manoeuvring performance is irrelevant, and that all future engagements will be won or lost at beyond visual range (BVR). Generations of pilots have been brought up on the dictum 'Speed is Life', and regard the conservation of energy as their most important priority. Even though the X-31's generous thrust-to-weight ratio allows rapid acceleration, there is a residue of concern about deliberately slowing down into the post-stall corner of the envelope.

Gunfighter

To avoid any charge of inflating the data, the X-31's simulated gun had to be on target for one full second to receive credit for a kill. When the X-31 began the fight from a 'neutral start' (both aircraft having equal chance to prevail) and went into post-stall, it achieved a 32:1 kill ratio against the F/A-18. When the X-31 was handicapped with a 'defensive start' (the F/A-18 beginning with advantages in speed, height, position or surprise), the ratio dropped to 3:1.

The BFM phase was replaced on 5 November 1993 with CIC (Close-in Combat) in which the opposing fighter was no longer 'co-operative' and the initial manoeuvre intention was no longer pre-briefed by pilots. Luftwaffe Major Quirin Kim and US Navy Commander Al Groves launched the CIC effort against NASA's 'enhanced manoeuvrability' F/A-18A Hornet, substituted for the standard Navy Hornet. Now, the other side did slightly better: the X-31 won 77 out of 94 engagements, lost 10, and tied seven times. Little changed when 'invited adversaries' were put into the X-31 cockpit. Kim and USAF Major Derrick Hess, neither trained as test pilots, flew the X-31 and the F/A-18. In post-stall, the X-31 kept winning. When pitted against a standard Navy F-14 Tomcat in 20 engagements, the X-31 won 16, lost two, and tied twice.

The X-31's tail is built as a single fail-safe structure, to guard against the known buffeting loads during high angle-of-attack flight and the unknown stresses that the X-31 might encounter in post-stall flight.

On 6 January 1994, previous work performed with HMDs was combined with simulated, close-in air combat with the NASA F/A-18A. Now, the no. 2 X-31 employed an HMVAD (Helmet-Mounted Audio/Visual Display) based on the GEC Marconi Viper in mock combat, flown by Kim and Knox. The HMVAD provided the 'head up' afforded by a helmet sight plus audible tone cues to tell the pilot his angle of attack.

JAST funding

In March 1994, the Pentagon's JAST (Joint Advanced Supersonic Technology) aircraft programme coughed up extra dollars to keep the X-31 in the air and helped support the X-31's supersonic 'quasi-tailless experiment'. Previous tailless aircraft, from the Northrop X-4 of 1947 to today's Northrop B-2 Spirit bomber, are subsonic. The envelope had been opened for this test back on 24 November 1993 when Langmade the first supersonic flight in the no. 1 X-31, reaching Mach 1.08 at 37,500 ft (11610 m). Soon afterward, Lang attained Mach 1.28. Programme manager Colonel Francis says, "I wish I could simply take the tail off" for this test. Instead, "We fooled the control system into thinking the aircraft had no tail." The aerodynamic effects of the vertical tail were cancelled by forces generated by the other aerodynamic surfaces through the flight control system. "We used thrust vectoring for pitch and yaw control. We can't control roll with vectoring because the engine is on the centreline, so this had to be done aerodynamically."

The mishap which claimed an X-31 in January 1995 appears not to have roots in any flaw on the part of aircraft or pilot. The aircraft was returning from a test flight and was not employing thrust vectoring. The aircraft began a series of rapid pitching oscillations, followed by a sharp roll. Lang, a test pilot employed by the German Ministry of Defence, bailed out at 18,000 ft (5573 m) using the ship's Martin-Baker ejection seat. A NASA investigation board found that the 19 January 1995 mishap

Turning in on finals at Edwards, for one of the dry lake bed runways, this X-31 displays its three paddles to advantage. The fairings under the wing house the actuators for the trailing edges.

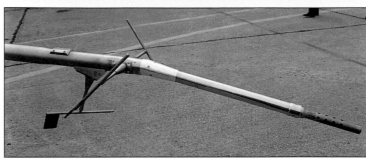

Above: The 1995 Paris air show had several star attractions, including the B-2 and V-22 Osprey, but none could quite compare with the X-31's staggering performance.

Right: The X-31's highly individualistic air data probe is off-set and angled to ensure it is unaffected by air flow, no matter what the attitude of the aircraft.

was caused by icing of the airspeed total pressure probe. The blocked probe made the airspeed read erroneously low as the aircraft descended, which caused the gains in the fly-by-wire flight control system to be too high for the actual airspeed. Eventually there was no gain margin and the aircraft went out of control.

X-31 at Paris

For its appearance in Paris, the no. 2 X-31 was carried by C-5 Galaxy from Edwards to Manching (home of its German builder) on 22 May 1995, where it was reassembled, then flown under its own power to Le Bourget airfield. Fred Knox and Quirin Kim shared the flying displays, each of which began with a dynamic entry to high-Alpha flight (70°) three-quarters of the way around a loop straight after take-off, followed by an immediate velocity vector roll through 150°.

The display went on to include the 'Mongoose' manoeuvre (in which the aircraft executes a 'hook' before slicing the nose upwards in a right-hand velocity vector roll, to

the vertical) before performing the Herbst turn. In this manoeuvre the aircraft pulls briefly to 70° AoA before relaxing to 50° for a climbing left-hand turn during which the heading changes by 150°. The routine culminated in a breathtaking manoeuvre in which the X-31 performed a high-Alpha loop (15-17°) pulling to 70° and performing 180° rolls in each direction during the recovery from the downward vertical.

The contributions of the X-31 are considerable. The aircraft was flown by 12 pilots, including the Luftwaffe's Lieutenant Colonel Quirin Kim who is not a test pilot, demonstrating that operational fliers can push the envelope in this shift. Nearly all of the fully controlled sustained manoeuvring at genuinely high angles of attack has been achieved by the X-31. Its exploration of post-stall flying has been a genuine pioneering effort. In addition, there were spin-offs: with its largely composite structure and tightly controlled programme, the X-31 has also explored low-cost ways of designing and developing future high-technology prototype/experimental aircraft. **Robert F. Dorr**

Djibouti:
France's African Outpost

A photo report by Yves Debay

Right: Sandwiched between Ethiopia, to the north and Somalia to the south, Djibouti has been in French hands since 1862. It gained independence in 1977, but France maintains a significant military presence in this strategic nation which sits at the mouth of the Red Sea. The Armée de l'Air's prime asset in Djibouti is EC 04.033 'Vexin' and its Mirage F1Cs.

Below: Supporting the troops on the ground is a job for DELALAT Pumas. The air force relies on Alouette IIIs to provide a SAR detachment for the Mirages.

Right: FFDJ (Forces Françaises de Djibouti) units are air mobile, and they can rely on the Transalls and C-130s of COTAM to move their heaviest equipment. This ET 61 Transall has just delivered an ERC-90 Sagale light tank, of the 5e RIAOM (mixed-arms overseas regiment).

Left: Today's EC 04.033 (EC 4/33), based at Ambouli, was previously EC 3/10, and flew the Mirage IIIC until 1986. It operates eight to 10 Mirage F1Cs in Djibouti today – the last F1Cs in front-line French service.

Above: Several regular French army units are based in Djibouti, along with a detachment of the French Foreign Legion and special forces on TDY. The army Pumas which support these units provide a vital 'heavy' lift capability, transporting artillery pieces and other supplies. When French troops were dispatched from Djibouti to neighbouring Somalia in 1993, their Pumas went with them, and land and air units train together constantly for rapid intervention missions.

Left: Regular visitors to Djibouti-Ambouli International Airport are some of the Aéronavale's last surviving Breguet Atlantics. Most of the first-generation Atlantics have been retired in favour of the updated Atlantique 2, but some of the older Atlantics still serve as dedicated surveillance aircraft at Djibouti, Dakar, Réunion and the French Antilles. For overland and maritime reconnaissance missions the Atlantics carry an underwing FLIR/sensor pod, similar to that carried by the German navy's aircraft.

Left: This anonymous Aéronavale Atlantic is sharing the ramp at Ambouli with a Transall and several civilian Antonov An-26s. France's FLIR-equipped Atlantics are a regular sight over the Gulf of Aden and the approaches to the Red Sea.

Below: The terrain throughout Djibouti varies widely, but the camouflage scheme on this Puma is very effective in this instance.

The 9,000-strong Djibouti National Army maintains a small Air Detachment of 270 personnel and five active aircraft. Djibouti's President has a Dassault Falcon 20 at his disposal and the only other fixed-wing aircraft in the inventory is a single (PZL) An-28 (below) obtained from Poland in 1994. It is likely that Djibouti's two Mil Mi-8s (above) and single Mi-2 (right) were also supplied by Poland. The Mi-8s were used extensively during the Affar rebellion of 1993/94, when they flew troop transport, casevac and attack missions, armed with cannon and rocket pods. The Mi-8s have also been fitted with a Chinese-built Type 63 12-round rocket launcher under the fuselage.

Rockwell
B-1B Lancer

Conceived as a strictly nuclear bomber, the B-1B
has more recently adopted a conventional mission,
although this was initially restricted to dropping
Mk 82 500-lb bombs, as demonstrated here by a
28th BW machine. Since the end of the Cold War,
the USAF has stressed this conventional mission
over and above the nuclear penetration role, while
tests are under way to clear a wider range of
conventional stores for the B-1B.

Few military aircraft requirements have been debated and reshaped as much as that for a new strategic bomber to supersede the B-52. Trailing a long string of programme acronyms behind it, the new bomber emerged as the B-1A, only to be cancelled in this form by the Carter administration. Development continued, and after yet more acronyms the aircraft resurfaced as the B-1B, a low-level penetrator of enormous potential. It has taken some time for the system to mature and for much of that potential to be released, and there are still problems with the aircraft, but in the 1990s the B-1B is without equal for its ability to deliver weapons on target, on time, in any weather ... and survive.

Above: 74-0158 was the first of three B-1A prototypes ordered on 5 June 1970, taking to the air for the first time on on 23 December 1974 with a flight crew of Charles C. Bock Jr, Col Emil Sturmthal and Richard Abrams. The flight lasted for 1 hour 18 minutes, and took the aircraft from the factory at Palmdale to the test site at Edwards.

Right: A full-scale mock-up was built by Rockwell, mostly of wood. The left wing could be swept manually, and the right side of the aircraft was largely uncovered to show internal structures and systems.

Far right: The first aircraft was unveiled to the world on 26 October 1974 at Palmdale, with suitable media fanfare. The aircraft wore Rockwell's corporate logo on the fin for the roll-out, but this had been removed by the time of the first flight.

The entry into limited service of the B-2 in 1993 inevitably stole much of the thunder and media attention that previously had surrounded the B-1. Many B-1 people were glad to escape the media's constant interest, because a lot of it had been unhelpful and damaging. Stories had inflated or distorted real or imagined shortcomings in order to create sensational stories. The truth is that today the B-1 (which is always known the 'B-One', or 'Bone' and never as the Lancer – its formal name) has settled down as the much-valued backbone of the strategic strength of the US Air Force's Air Combat Command (82 on inventory), and also as an important part of the Air National Guard (11 on strength).

With the near-collapse of strategic air power in Russia and Ukraine, the currently active force of 93 'Bones' represents the only substantial force anywhere in the world of aircraft that, with a few hours' notice, can drop bombs with pinpoint accuracy on almost any target on Earth. The 84 venerable but geriatric (if low-houred) B-52Hs are slowly fading from the scene, increasingly committed to stand-off missions. Although ACC is building up to an eventual strength of 20 B-2s, the B-1B force will continue to handle almost all the calls for strategic air power. It will also greatly expand its capabilities as faults are cured, new avionics are introduced, spares become plentiful and, in particular, as the aircraft are certified to carry and release a range of new weapons.

Background

The B-52 was developed in a great hurry in the early 1950s for service with what was then Strategic Air Command. The aircraft was expected to be progressively withdrawn from service from 1961 or 1962. The replacement was planned to be either the WS (Weapon System) 110 CPB or the WS-125 NPB. The CPB was to be a Chemically Powered Bomber, so-called because it was to burn not ordinary kerosene but higher-energy 'zip fuel' based on ethyl borane in order to cruise at Mach 3 at very high altitudes. The NPB was to be a Nuclear Powered Bomber,

slower than the CPB but with essentially unlimited range and thus able to attack any target from any direction.

In the event, the NPB was never built, the high-energy fuel was abandoned, and all that left the drawing board were two giant 2,000-mph (3220-km/h) prototype XB-70 Valkyries, the first of which flew in 1964. Undeniably impressive, these aircraft were no longer viable when it was recognised that ICBMs (intercontinental ballistic missiles) could hit fixed targets with far greater speed and reliability. Even modified as the RS-70 (reconnaissance/strike) and able to search for and attack mobile targets which could not be hit by ICBMs, their combination of great speed and high altitude no longer promised immunity to being shot down by SAMs (surface-to-air missiles).

Accordingly, throughout the 1960s the USAF and various Department of Defense agencies studied ways of following the B-52 with a new manned strategic bomber. The Convair B-58 was never in the same class. Although it had outstanding range for a Mach 2 aircraft, it relied heavily on air refuelling and even then could hit only a very few peripheral Soviet targets from the USA. Combined with high operating costs, this resulted in its withdrawal from SAC in 1970.

Another aircraft in the same class from the same Fort

Worth plant (which was by then called General Dynamics) was the FB-111A. A derivative of the F-111 tactical strike aircraft, the FB was again a Mach 2 bomber with severely limited operating radius. Defense Secretary McNamara had from the start been centred on the F-111 as a swing-wing marvel, and ordered 210 of the FB version for SAC. Rising costs eventually cut the purchase to 76, and they did nothing to meet the need for a true strategic aircraft.

Many unclassified sources are available describing the 50-plus projects proposed by 14 US aerospace firms from 1960 to fill the need for a new long-range bomber. By 1964 the requirement had been formalised as AMSA, which actually stood for Advanced Manned Strategic Aircraft and not, as some suggested, 'America's Most Studied Airplane'. In the 1960s nobody had the slightest belief that, with a lot of costly updating in structure and avionics, the B-52G and H would soldier on into the 1990s.

Despite arguments over the need, and fights on Capitol Hill over the budget, in April 1969 AMSA crystallised into a USAF programme as the B-1. RFPs (Requests for Proposals) were issued seven months later, and on 5 June 1970 Secretary of the Air Force Robert C. Seamans Jr announced that the B-1 would be built by North American Rockwell, which as North American Aviation had built the B-70. The engine award went to General Electric with an augmented turbofan designated F101-100. The vital contracts for avionics took longer to decide.

The original programme comprised two test airframes, five flight articles and 40 engines, but in 1971, when an accurate artist's impression of the B-1 was published, this was cut to one ground- and three flight-test aircraft, plus 27 engines. A fourth prototype was ordered in the FY 1976 budget (ending 30 June 1976), built virtually to production standard. Some 240 production aircraft were planned, the first to fly in October 1977, with initial operational capability with SAC scheduled for 1979.

B-1A airborne

The programme slipped slightly. First flight had been due in April 1974, but in fact the first B-1 flight article (74-0158) was rolled out from USAF Plant 42 at Palmdale, California, on 26 October of that year. It made its first flight on 23 December and landed at Edwards AFB, home of the Air Force Flight Test Center. The crew comprised Rockwell test pilot Charlie C. Bock Jr, Colonel Emil 'Ted' Sturmthal (who had flown the XB-70) and engineer Richard Abrams. The No. 3 aircraft (74-0160, the avionics testbed) flew on 26 March 1976. The second B-1 (74-0159) was initially used for static structural testing, and so did not fly until 14 June 1976. The considerably modified No. 4 aircraft (76-0174) first flew on 14 February 1979.

Like most of the precursor projects, the B-1 was a swing-wing aircraft. Aerodynamically the design was otherwise conventional, although the slim fuselage was blended smoothly into the long-chord wingroots. Each outer wing had full-span slats and slotted flaps, but no ailerons. Lateral control was effected by spoilers and differential operation of the slab tailplanes (horizontal stabilisers), which were mounted on the fin well above the fuselage. The rudder was in three sections.

The F101 turbofans were installed in twin-engine packages under the wingroots spaced far enough apart for the main landing gears to fit between them with adequate track and space to retract inwards. Each inlet was fully variable to match the different demands of take-off, subsonic flight at low altitude and Mach 2 (1,320 mph; 2125 km/h) at 50,000 ft (15240 m). The nozzles also had to be fully variable, reaching a convergent/divergent profile with maximum augmentation in Mach 2 flight.

Even though it was calculated that the B-1 would be able to soak at Mach 2 temperatures, the ruling material throughout the structure could be aluminium, just as in Concorde. Originally it had been hoped that Mach 1.2

could be sustained during low-level penetration, but this target was lowered to about 650 mph (1046 km/h), or Mach 0.85, in order to give the crew more time to identify targets. This greatly facilitated the problem of alleviating turbulence, and also enabled the proportion of aluminium alloys to be increased. Titanium was needed mainly for the highly stressed wing carry-through box linking the pivots, the inner ends of the outer wings incorporating the pivots and for some skin areas round the engines and rear fuselage.

About 150,000 lb (68 tonnes) of fuel could be housed in eight integral tanks, one in each outer wing and the rest in the fuselage. Weapons were to be carried in three 15-ft (4.6-m) fuselage bays, two ahead of and one behind the wing carry-through box. Each could house about 25,000 lb (11340 kg) of nuclear or conventional weapons, or eight AGM-69A SRAMs (Short-Range Attack Missiles) on a rotary launcher. No provision was made for defensive armament, apart from comprehensive electronic warfare systems managed by the DSO.

The OSO's tasks of navigation and weapon aiming were to be accomplished using duplicate Litton LN-15 inertial

Above: A B-1A demonstrates its terrain-following flight capability. The flight test programme proceeded cautiously during the first 15 months, when 74-0158 was the only B-1 flying. Mach 1 was passed on the seventh flight (21 April 1975).

Left: 74-0158 touches down at Edwards at the end of its inaugural flight. It was exactly a month before the aircraft flew again, on 23 January 1975. The first aircraft was the general aerodynamic and performance test vehicle.

The fuselage of a B-1A takes shape in the Palmdale factory. The position occupied by the crew escape module is filled by a representative shape for fit.

Rockwell B-1B Lancer

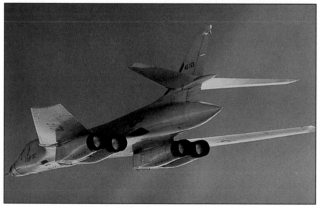

Above: A dramatic underview of aircraft No. 3 reveals the position of the FLIR turret, details of the bomb bays and also of the auxiliary louvres under the intakes.

Right: The second aircraft was initially assigned ground structural load tests, and it was actually the third to fly. With its ground trials completed, it was hastily readied for flight, joining the airborne test fleet on 14 June 1976. Here it is seen during acceleration trials, with all four F101s in full afterburner.

Below: B-1A No. 1 taxis out at Edwards for a test hop. Noteworthy are the 'elephant's ears' – the pop-out surfaces which stabilised the escape capsule. These were stowed externally flush with the fuselage sides. The No. 1 aircraft performed 79 sorties during the official B-1A testing period.

systems, a Singer-Kearfott (Teledyne Ryan in aircraft Nos 3 and 4) Doppler, Honeywell radar altimeter, Hughes FLIR (forward-looking infra-red) and two radars, a General Electric APQ-144(mod) main forward-looking set plus a Texas Instruments APQ-146 duplicated TFR (terrain-following radar) similar to that of the F-111F. Other systems were generally conventional, most ancillary power services being hydraulic. One unusual demand was that, to enable aircraft to be launched in under two minutes from a nuclear alert, hitting a large button behind the nose leg would initiate starting of all engines and alignment of the inertial platforms, and would in all respects ready the aircraft for immediate take-off.

On the whole, the B-1 flight test programme went according to plan. Numerous modifications and items of additional equipment were introduced, and throughout the programme the avionics integration contractor, Boeing Aerospace, strove to resolve problems in what was probably the most complex avionics installation ever to fly at that time. AIL Division of Cutler-Hammer, prime contractor for the defensive avionics system, also had plenty to do, but none of the original four prototypes ever carried anything remotely resembling a definitive system.

During the Phase I test programme various alternative options were studied. One was the B-52I. This was a general designation for the B-52G and B-52H force, and possibly even B-52Ds, refitted with modern engines. For example, the eight old-technology engines could be replaced by four Pratt & Whitney 2000s or Rolls-Royce 535s. This could have reduced launch time, increased range and increased reliability. A second option was the F-111G, which was a further stretched F-111 aircraft, or the further stretched FB-111H powered by two F101 engines (the same as those fitted to the B-1) and with many other changes. A third was the CMC (Cruise Missile Carrier), perhaps based on the Lockheed C-5A or Boeing 747, able to launch up to 100 precision missiles from somewhere beyond the reach of enemy defensive systems. None of these options proved attractive.

One of the B-1's major hurdles, an IOT&E (Initial Operational Test & Evaluation) that simulated SAC combat missions, was successfully passed in September 1976. The Phase I flight test programme was completed on 30 September 1976, with all test objectives met. Following completion in November of DSARC III (Defense Systems Acquisition Review Council), the DoD and USAF jointly announced on 2 December 1976 that the B-1 would go into production. Contracts had been placed for the first three aircraft and for long-lead items for Block 2 of eight, and funds were authorised for production tooling. All these funds were included in the FY78 budget of the Ford administration.

Throughout the period from his appointment in 1970, the B-1 Program Director, Major General Douglas T. Nelson, never had reason to doubt that the 240 production aircraft would be built. Although the debate over whether to stand off and launch cruise missiles or penetrate to a defended target continued, Nelson even said [of the B-1], "There is no technology in sight that can prevent it from penetrating to target."

Escalating cost

Apart from the largely unresolved question of the avionics (especially the defensive suite), the only cloud on the horizon appeared to be cost escalation. In 1970 a ballpark unit price was $40 million, and by 1972, allowing for RDT&E (research, development, test and engineering), this had reached $45.6 million. Unimpressive by today's standards, this was at that time substantially higher than the figure for any previous production aircraft. Moreover, by 1975 the unit figure had risen to (in then-year dollars) just over $70 million.

These figures clearly worried the new President, Jimmy Carter, who took office on 20 January 1977. On 30 June 1977, the last day of FY77, in his regular press conference Carter announced, "My decision is that we should not continue with deployment of the B-1, and I am directing that we discontinue plans for production of this weapons system." He expressed the view that ICBMs, SLBMs (Submarine-Launched Ballistic Missiles) and modernised B-52s armed with ALCMs (Air-Launched Cruise Missiles) would provide adequate defence capability.

The decision to cancel the B-1A was made by the new president based on principle (Carter genuinely hoped to reduce the arms races) and on cost (then, as now, the price tag on a new bomber was an easy target for those in all

areas of society who wanted resources directed elsewhere). At the time, the first steps were yet to be taken on the Advanced Technology Bomber (ATB) programme which would eventually produce the Northrop B-2 Spirit. Only later in the Carter administration did the President become fully briefed on, and fully authorise, two supersecret programmes to develop stealth aircraft – the Have Blue effort which led in due course to the Lockheed F-117 Nighthawk and the Tacit Blue programme which produced a Northrop quarter-scale bomber design inspired in part by the builder's flying wings of the 1940s. Tacit Blue and Project Senior C. J., the secret efforts which evolved into the ATB-cum-B-2, did not begin to gather momentum until after the B-1A cancellation and made little progress until President Ronald Reagan took office in January 1981. At this juncture, the Rockwell B-1A was still a cancelled project so no obvious conflict existed between B-1 and B-2 development. Reagan, however, having come into office on a strong promise to restore heavy spending on the Cold War competition with what he termed the 'Evil Empire' – the Soviet Union – was under strong pressure to restore the Rockwell B-1A bomber programme in some form. Those applying the pressure had no knowledge of the 'black' programme which would create the future B-2.

Resurrection

Despite the cancellation of the production programme, the Carter administration permitted flight testing to continue, together with many related RDT&E efforts. The greatest effort continued to be focused on the avionics, particularly the defensive system, but GE never ceased to develop the F101 engine, many other contractors kept their engineering teams intact and working on B-1 hardware, and Air Force facilities continued to give direct B-1 support. For example, wind tunnels at the Arnold Engineering Development Center in Tennessee tested ejection seat trajectories and investigated the carriage and separation of external weapons, such as the fast-maturing Boeing AGM-86B, the stretched ALCM. Never had work on a cancelled programme been so intense.

Throughout the 1970s the need to reduce the RCS (radar cross-section) of any penetrating aircraft came into ever-sharper focus. Classified test programmes proved the

feasibility of achieving dramatic reductions, by changing the shape of aircraft to minimise reflectivity in the direction of the hostile radar, by paying the most careful attention to achieving a smooth unbroken external surface without cracks or badly fitting joints, and by covering the exterior skin with RAM (radar-absorbent material), of which several varieties were giving promising results. What became known as 'stealth design' grew rapidly in importance, and in 1978 formal work began on a 'black' (highly classified) programme loosely called the ATB (Advanced Technology Bomber). Of enormous potential importance, the ATB was regarded as a relatively long-term high-risk project which in no way negated the need for a new strategic aircraft in the near term.

GD's FB-111H led to a proposed FB-111B/C which might be created by modifying existing aircraft. In early 1979 Rockwell came up with a scheme for using a modified B-1 as a 'core aircraft', to have a huge gap along the underside from crew cabin to tail. The basic aircraft was simplified for operation at Mach 0.8, with wings fixed at 25° sweep, fixed inlets and conventional lateral control by ailerons and spoilers only. To adapt the core aircraft to different roles, a choice of large assemblies could be incorporated on the assembly line. Thus, the aircraft could be completed as a near-term penetrator with SRAMs, SMCS, extra fuel and comprehensive EW equipment, or as a strategic weapons launcher with ALCMs, or as a conventional bomber carrying Mk 82 bombs or mines or even Harpoon missiles, or as an air-refuelling tanker.

The ALCMs proposed were of two new types, the Boeing AGM-86B and General Dynamics AGM-109 Tomahawk. Both had a range just over twice the 745 miles (1200 km) of AGM-86A, and their near-term availability coloured thinking on strategic aircraft. In November 1979 the DoD again looked at the prospects for what was now called an LRCA (Long-Range Combat Aircraft), to achieve IOC in 1987. The FB-111 growth versions were not well

Above left: 74-0160 was the third B-1A, but was actually the second to fly, leaving Palmdale for Edwards on 1 April 1976. The aircraft was assigned to offensive avionics, terrain-following and weapons tests. The large marking on the intake was for photographic calibration.

Above: With wings fully back, the first B-1A sweeps through the Mojave desert. One area of the design which appeared rather clumsy was the overwing fairing to accommodate the rear section of the wing as it swept back. This was considerably cleaned up in the B-1B design using a neat hinged upper flap and inflatable upper and lower seals.

SAC's bomber trio formates off the boom of a KC-135 tanker. The B-1A featured the speed performance and terrain-following ability of the FB-111 while exhibiting a load-carrying ability and range performance similar to that of the B-52.

Rockwell B-1B Lancer

A major feature of the first three B-1As was the crew escape capsule, depicted here in a four-shot sequence. The ejection sequence began with the restraint of the crew within the capsule (0.3 seconds), followed by the firing of the two 60,000-lb thrust rocket motors at 0.4 seconds. As the capsule left the aircraft the side fins and chin spoiler deployed between 0.4 and 0.7 seconds, at which time a drogue chute was deployed from the rear of the capsule. The rocket motor burned out at 1.9 seconds, and the drogue chute was disconnected at 2.5 seconds. At 2.8 seconds the pilot mortars fired to launch the three main chutes, which reached full line stretch at 4.5 seconds. As the capsule decelerated inflatable bags were deployed under the capsule to provide a soft landing, and the module was repositioned for a vertical landing after 10.6 seconds. If the ejection was initiated at ground level, the capsule would theoretically alight after 13.8 seconds. For a water landing the capsule deployed fore and aft flotation bags and a self-righting bag on top. The only time the capsule was employed the module failed to reposition under the chutes, resulting in a hard nose-first landing which killed Rockwell chief test pilot Doug Benefield.

Below: This test object provided a graphic illustration of where the capsule was located. The 'elephant's ears' would be attached to the rear stepped portion of the capsule, drooping down over the main fuselage section.

matched to the larger missiles, which had to be carried externally with little ground clearance, and not only degraded aircraft speed and range but posed undesirable risks. Rockwell, however, had already shown on paper that the B-1, in a version called SAL (Strategic ALCM Launcher), could easily carry 30 of the new missiles, on two eight-round rotary launchers and 14 externally.

During 1980 Rockwell refined its LRCA proposal. Though a minimum-change derivative of the B-1, it was significantly more capable in the stand-off ALCM mission. Among the major changes were a reduction in dash speed from about Mach 2.25 to 1.25, simplification of the engine inlets and overwing fairings, and general structural and main gear strengthening to operate at an MTO (maximum take-off) weight increased from 395,000 to 477,000 lb (180000 to 217000 kg). This increase of 82,000 lb (37000 kg) was explained as 50,000 lb (23000 kg) of additional weapons, 24,000 lb (11000 kg) of additional fuel and an air-frame 8,000 lb (3000 kg) heavier. (The weapon loads are discussed later.) Finally, by further modifying the fixed engine inlets and making extensive use of RAM, it was predicted that the LRCA's RCS could be reduced by a factor of 10; in other words, cut to one-tenth that of the B-1.

Cancellation of the production B-1 did not terminate flying of the prototypes. Less than a month after the decision was taken, on 28 July 1977, the No. 3 aircraft became the first to launch a SRAM. Released over the White Sands Missile Range at 6,000 ft (1829 m) at 500 kt (927 km/h), the missile correctly impacted a target ahead of the aircraft. This prototype was later modified with an advanced ECM system (adding a dorsal spine) and with DBS (Doppler-beam sharpening) added to the forward-looking radar. This aircraft continued flying to 15 April 1981. The second aircraft, which only began flying in June 1976, continued with No. 1 to push up the Mach scale. The first aircraft had reached Mach 2 in April 1976, and after completing its stability/control, performance and flutter tests, was placed in storage in 1978. The No. 2 prototype continued with air-loads testing and engine/inlet evaluation, and on 5 October 1978 reached Mach 2.22, the highest speed attained by any B-1. The No. 4 aircraft did not fly until 14 February 1979, long after the cancellation, and in 70 flights totalling 378 hours carried out many valuable tests on both offensive and defensive avionics before closing the prototype flight programme on 30 April 1981. The four aircraft were stored at Edwards in a near-airworthy condition, having logged 1,895 hours in 347 flights.

Strategic study

From 1979 to 1981 several defence agencies collaborated in a BPE (Bomber Penetration Evaluation). Though of necessity founded on theoretical predictions of how US hardware might perform, and with guesses as to the effectiveness of future Soviet defences, the conclusion was that the ALCM-carrying LRCA could defeat predicted Soviet defence systems into and possibly through the 1990s. This was enough to tip the scales of the hawkish Reagan administration in favour of funding a new LRCA.

On 1 June 1981 the USAF not only recommended continued RDT&E on the ATB but also announced selection of the Rockwell LRCA as its new multi-role strategic bomber. On 2 October 1981 President Reagan announced a Strategic Modernization Program, key features of which were a contract with Northrop for the development of the ATB (though this was not revealed publicly and was still known to only as few) and the procurement of 100 LRCAs for the inventory. The LRCA was to be designated B-1B, the previous prototypes being redesignated as B-1As.

The Senior C. J. contract which would lead to the future Northrop B-2 had been signed in early 1981 and was deemed highly speculative: there was no assurance that this project's exploration of 'low observables' technology would soon produce an actual bomber or that the result would fit into the USAF's plans for strategic bomber operations. In any case, only a handful of leaders – those privy to the 'black' world with compartmentalised security clearances known as SAR (special access required) – had any clue that the American aerospace industry was developing two strategic bombers at the same time. In the climate of the era – Reagan had, after all, defeated Carter the previous year and it was unthinkable to unseat a sitting president – it is unlikely that there would have been much protest, had this dual-track approach been known. The SAC plan was for a total bomber force of 340 aircraft, divided between 'penetrators' which would strike targets directly and 'standoff' aircraft which would launch missiles from a distance; the ageing B-52 was not viewed at the time as part of this combination. With the Soviet Union rapidly developing mobile, relocatable targets such as railway-borne ICBM launchers, the need for a robust force of manned nuclear bombers seemed beyond challenge. Ironically, the very foreign policy event which had decided the 1980 election, the taking of American hostages in Iran, was a better clue to the new world in which the B-1B and B-2 would evolve than was the nuclear threat of the Soviet 'Empire', although there were still 11 years of the Cold War left to survive.

On 20 January 1982 Rockwell received two major contracts. One, valued at $1,317 million, was the FSD (full-scale development) award. This required the company to complete the design of the B-1B and modify the B-1A Nos 2 and 4 prototypes and carry out a further flight test programme with these aircraft in support of the B-1B. The second, valued at $886 million, covered production tooling, construction of the first B-1B and procurement of long-lead items for the first production lots. It was not explained that almost all the tooling and long-lead items had already been paid for once, in December 1976.

Other contracts were placed for avionics, avionics integration and for the host of hardware items from suppliers. The target programme cost for the 100 aircraft was announced as $20.5 billion in 1981 dollars, or $205 million per aircraft. Recognising that a vociferous lobby in Congress, in the media and in the public would challenge the need for such an expensive aircraft, everything possible was done to keep down costs. The airframe was said to have 85 per cent commonality with the B-1A and the engine modifications were minor, while the costly OAS (offensive avionics system) was to be 90 per cent the same as that of the B-52H.

The B-1B airframe

Superficially, the B-1B has almost the same airframe as the No. 4 B-1A, but there are important differences. These included strengthening the structure so that, in theory, the aircraft can take off at weights up to 82,000 lb (37195 kg) heavier. The engine inlets were simplified, because there was no longer a requirement to exceed Mach 2, and they were further modified to reduce RCS. At first it was claimed that RCS of the B-1B was only 1.0 m² (one-tenth that of the B-1A and 1 per cent that of the B-52G), but this represented the best case, with a brand-new fresh-from-the-factory paint scheme; in 1993 it was admitted that a more accurate value for the clean aircraft is 1.45 m².

As before, the fixed inboard wing is blended into the fuselage so that it is difficult to tell where the one becomes the other. The inboard wing does not have a recognised aerofoil profile, and its highly swept leading edge is very blunt in order to accommodate a row of LRUs (line-replaceable units) and antennas forming part of the countermeasures, as described later. Nonetheless, the inboard wing generates a significant fraction of the total lift and is especially important in flight at extreme angles of attack, such as

A fourth B-1A (76-0174) was ordered to serve as a pre-production aircraft, and was configured with full avionics systems. When the B-1A was cancelled on 30 June 1977, work was well advanced on this aircraft, while the first three production machines were also taking shape. The prototype was allowed to be completed to join the BPE test programme. It first flew on 14 February 1979 and went on to fly 70 sorties during the official B-1A/BPE trials.

The four B-1As continued to fly on the Bomber Penetration Evaluation programme until April 1981. The No. 3 aircraft, shown here, retired from flying on 15 April after having flown 138 sorties for 829.4 hours, the highest of the four prototypes. By this time it had acquired the three-tone desert scheme for which the No. 4 aircraft is better known. Despite its grounding it played an important part in the B-1B programme as a ground test airframe, including trials with the B61 nuclear bomb. It was also the principal object for media and VIP tours associated with the B-1B. It was subsequently moved to Lowry AFB, Colorado to act as a ground loading trainer.

Rockwell B-1B Lancer
37th Bomb Squadron
28th Bomb Wing
Air Combat Command
Ellsworth AFB, South Dakota

Blending
The fixed inboard wing is blended into the fuselage. It does not have a recognised aerofoil profile, and its highly swept leading edge is very blunt in order to accommodate a row of DAS LRUs (line-replaceable units) and antennas. It generates a significant fraction of total lift, especially at extreme angles of attack.

The 37th Bomb Squadron was activated on 1 October 1986 as the 37th Bombardment Squadron, Heavy. It was redesignated as the 37th Bomb Squadron on 1 September 1991. The 37th BS has a black tail stripe with a yellow-gold border containing the word TIGERS in a yellow-gold maze. The 37th BS was identified by a Bengal Tiger badge.

Crew
The B-1B is manned by a crew of four, with pilot and co-pilot up-front (left and right, respectively) and with defensive systems operator and offensive systems operator behind (left and right again). As a new type, with some demanding characteristics, entry into the B-1 community was tightly controlled, and its members were something of an elite. When IOC was achieved on 1 October 1986, the minimum requirements for selection as a B-1B commander stipulated 1,800 hours' flying, including three years flying a SAC aircraft, with not less than 18 months as aircraft commander.

Today, requirements are less stringent, and with conversion of ANG aircrew to the B-1B there are ex-F-16 'Bone' pilots with no previous bomber experience. All backseaters are now being requalified as WSOs (weapon systems officers), able to sit in either the left or the right seat as the OSO or DSO. This is a major challenge, demanding intimate knowledge of, and instinctive control of, two systems of enormous complexity. It is doubtful if any aircrew in history have been required to have such capability and technical knowledge.

Colour scheme
All four B-1A prototypes were painted overall anti-flash white, although all were later repainted in the definitive B-1B strategic scheme. The third and fourth fourth B-1A wore an interim three-tone desert camouflage on its topsides, with tan, green and brown shades and with white undersides. It was originally proposed to paint production B-1Bs in a two-tone grey 'Killer Whale' scheme, with pale grey covering flash-sensitive areas such as the crew compartment and avionics bays. It was never used, and instead production B-1Bs were painted in wrap-around camouflage with dark green and dark grey on the upper surfaces and dark grey and gunship grey on the undersides. From late 1990, the USAF slowly started applying an overall gunship grey colour scheme, similar to the scheme applied to B-52Gs and B-52Hs. Radomes initially remained in dark grey.

Protective coatings
Only before it is painted does a B-1B reveal how far it is from being a conventional aluminium aircraft. Then they show various local coverings on the yellow chromate anti-corrosion primer. Grey strips at the wingroots are Teflon protective coatings over the areas that rub against the overwing fairing as the wing is swept. Darker areas are RAM, but these disappear as the finish camouflage is sprayed on.

Reliability
The poor MCR (mission-capable rate) of 55 per cent for B-1B units spurred a major Operational Readiness Assessment. This assessed the 28th BW between 1 June and 30 November 1994. The unit flew from Ellsworth at an accelerated rate and deployed a squadron to Roswell, New Mexico, to simulate flying from an austere location at wartime sortie rates. The ORA MCR fluctuated between 82.8 and 85.6 per cent, the average being about 83.8. Spare parts, equipment and people were brought in from two other units, the 7th BW and the 384th BW. General Loh said, "For the first time... we were able adequately to fund and man a unit for its mission. We showed that if you fund the B-1B to a given level of readiness, it can sustain that readiness. And if you improve the reliability, it can sustain those improved levels of readiness for the long term."

Defensive avionics

The DAS comprises the ALQ-161A and a management system designated ASQ-184. It senses enemy air defence and missile-guidance radars, identifies them from a threat library, and then jams them. The system also manages an EXCM (EXpendable CounterMeasures) system for firing chaff cartridges or IR decoy flares. Under the management of Eaton's AIL (Airborne Instrument Laboratory) Division, in partnership with Systems Command, the DAS had to be developed and put into production concurrently, in order to meet the target of IOC in 1986. This was an unrealistic approach and led to problems later. The DAS comprises an exceptional number of LRUs, all interlinked to computers via the EMUX bus. Not including the considerable weight of control units, displays and high-power cabling, they weigh about 5,500 lb (2.5 tonnes). For jamming to be effective, it has to be accomplished in microseconds, so that the enemy emitter is jammed in real time. It must be possible to receive and jam many signals in the same waveband simultaneously, constantly responding to new threats. The B-1B system proved to be flawed – when overloaded it would try to jam its own defensive emissions. This failure of the defensive avionics system to perform as advertised was latched upon by the media, who delighted in the idea of a self-jamming bomber. The basic problem was an inability to detect and counter hostile systems while ignoring any others. The system could usually detect most of the existing Soviet radars, especially if 'thin on the ground', but not newer equipment brought into service in the 1980s. In a near-panic programme in 1986-87, the Air Force schemed a considerably upgraded DAS, capable of meeting at least the original specifications. This was to be introduced in three stages, called Mod 0, Mod 1 and Mod 2, and to be completed by 1992. This proved over-ambitious and the main effort has been focused on simplifying the AL0-1.61A architecture to process signals in a reduced range of bands. This was one way of maintaining capability against the most serious known threats, both air and ground, while preventing the processors from being overloaded in a high-threat environment. These attempts were to salvage an effective capability to meet the original specification, drawn up against the Soviet defence systems of the 1980s. The revised ALQ-161 system was not expected to be able to perform against air defence threats of the 1990s. The official view remains that "The B-1B's defensive avionics will probably not achieve the level of performance called for in the original specifications for the baseline B-1B bomber in the near term, and may never achieve that level without major modification."

Tail warning

The main AN/ALQ-161A system has a discrete TWF (tail-warning function) which monitors the hemisphere behind the aircraft. Although it is part of ALQ-161A, the TWF is individually located in a radome at the aft end of the tailplane/fin fairing. It has a pulse-Doppler radar designed to detect any interceptor or missile approaching in the rear hemisphere. Threat azimuth and range are displayed and a missile warning tone is sent to each crew-member over the intercom. Multiple threats are prioritised. The EXCM can respond automatically, but the DSO has the option of manually selecting which dispensers to use, and when. There are eight dispenser locations, four on each side of the centreline recessed into the top of the fuselage above the forward stores bay. Each may be loaded with a dispenser containing either 120 chaff cartridges, to screen the aircraft from radars, or 12 flares to decoy IR-homing missiles. On being fired by the DSO, each payload follows a trajectory which is initially upwards and to one side. The rapidly blooming chaff cloud instantly decelerates to pass directly aft, but the flares arch up and away from the aircraft track. The TWF is reportedly inadequate to deal with newer generations of Soviet interceptors and missiles.

Wing

In order to attain the best performance and handling at both high and low speeds, Rockwell chose a variable-geometry 'swing wing' for the B-1B. During the 1970s and 1980s this was a fashionable solution to the conflicting requirements for minimum span/minimum area (low drag) at high speeds and for maximum span/high aspect ratio (maximum lift) at low airspeeds. Rockwell chose to pivot the wing outboard, in the fixed inboard wing sections, which were smoothly faired to the centre fuselage. These large wing/body fairings are almost entirely glass-fibre and give a smooth junction between body and wing. Even with the inboard trailing edge of the outboard wing panel cut away, part of the wing has to enter the fixed structure as sweep angle approaches the maximum. In the B-1A the aperture into which the wing slid was sealed by a complicated series of doors which were individually raised during wing sweep and then lowered tight against the wing. In the B-1B there is a simpler system with a hinged upper and fixed lower edge, both provided with an inflatable seal. The inboard leading edge of each wing terminates in a curved knuckle fairing which covers the mechanical drive and prevents any gap appearing at maximum sweep. Wing sweep was controlled by an irreversible screwjack driven by dual hydraulic motors. The four motors were tested to a push or pull of 1,000,000 lb (453600 kg), though nothing like this is needed to position the wings between their minimum and maximum settings of 15° and 67°30'. The two screwjacks are linked by a torque shaft to ensure that both wings move in unison. Each drive motor is part of a different hydraulic system, and any two systems can be lost without preventing wing sweep control. The pilot's wing sweep control lever is shaped like a wing, and is moved in the natural sense, fully back for 67.5°. The wings move at only about 1°/sec to give the FCGMS (fuel centre of gravity management system) time to pump fuel to maintain the aircraft CG within limits. With flaps extended a detent arrests the lever at 20°, and with flaps up but gear extended another detent arrests motion at 35°. Conversely, with flaps housed, as the wings rotate beyond the 20° setting an interlock shuts off power from the flap drive.

Rockwell B-1B
34th Bomb Squadron
366th Wing
Air Combat Command
US Air Force,
Ellsworth AFB, South Dakota

This compass grey painted B-1B Lancer is one of those assigned to the 'Gunfighters' of the 366th Wing, the US Air Force's rapid deployment air intervention wing. Although known as the Mountain Home Super Wing, the 366th includes assets normally based elsewhere, these being its single squadron of B-1Bs. On 4 April 1994, the 34th Bomb Squadron was activated at Ellsworth as part of the 366th Wing, having previously operated B-52Gs as part of the 366th Wing from Castle AFB, California. The replacement of the B-52G has been a welcome step, although the older aircraft had a longer range, and was compatible with the AGM-142 Have Nap (a stand-off precision attack weapon with a 1,995 lb/887-kg warhead). As of late 1995, the B-1B's only operational weapon was the conventional Mk 82 bomb. The Lancers are stationed at Ellsworth to take advantage of the infrastructure and maintenance facilities of the 28th Bomb Wing and to avoid the unnecessary expense of maintaining the B-1Bs at Mountain Home. The B-1Bs augment F-16Cs and F-15Es in the offensive role and are supported by KC-135R tankers and F-15C fighters. The wing's disparate elements exercise together on a regular basis to allow easy co-ordination in time of war. The composite wing concept was created by USAF chief of staff General Merrill A. (Tony) McPeak in the post-Desert Storm era and was put into effect at the same time that the new Air Comand Command was established, on 1 June 1992. In theory, a composite wing would be able to conduct operations with little or no support, although the concept remains controversial.

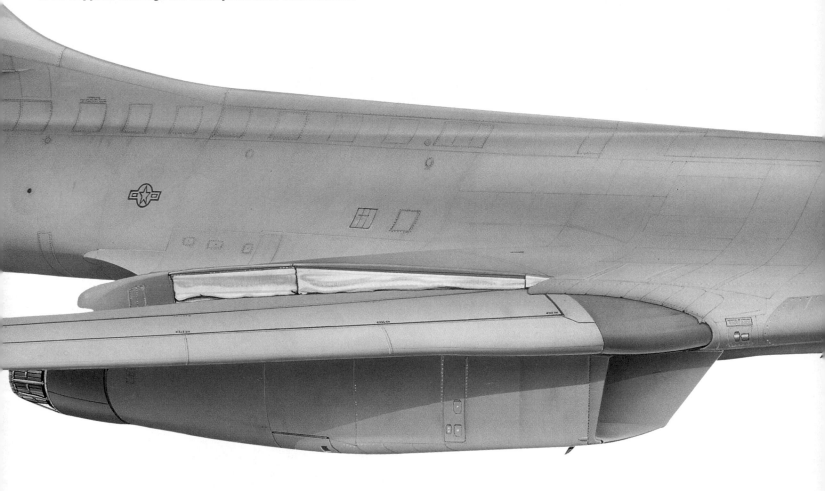

Powerplant
The B-1B is powered by four afterburning General Electric F101-GE-102 engines each rated at about 17,000 lb st (75.6 kN) dry at sea level. Turbofans with a bypass ratio of about 2, they were installed in twin-engine packages under the wingroots, spaced far enough apart for the main landing gears to fit between them with adequate space to retract inwards.The engines are each 4.6 ft (1.4 m) in diameter, weigh about 4,450 lb (2019 kg) dry, and at take-off have a mass flow of 352 lb (160 kg) per second, which with maximum augmentation gives a nominal thrust of 30,780 lb (136.92 kN). The engines were modified so that the main bleed connection was at the upper centreline, so that any engine can be installed in any of the four locations. The augmenter has sequenced fuel rings in both the core and bypass flows, and automatic ignition. Compared with the engine nozzle used by the B-1A, the 12-petal nozzle originally fitted to the B-1B was simpler and about 85 lb (39 kg) lighter, although its 'turkey feather' actuator covers have since been removed to further reduce weight and complexity. Under each fan case is a power take-off shaft linking the HP spool with an ADG (accessory drive gearbox) on which are mounted an IDG (integrated-drive generator) with a rating of 115 kVA and two hydraulic pumps which each energise a self-contained system to a cut-out pressure of 4,000 psi (276 bars). Each ADG also carries an air-turbine starter with which, using a ground air supply, all four engines can be started simultaneously. In addition, the No. 2 and No. 4 engines (the right engine in each pair) have a clutch and torque converter for a shaft connection to the nearby APU (auxiliary power unit). These two small gas turbines are mounted ahead of the main engines on the centreline of each nacelle. Both can be started on battery or ground power. They then start the starboard engine by shaft power, and then the left engine by APU bleed air. Each APU transmission shaft can also drive the recipient engine's IDG and one hydraulic pump without any need to start the associated main engine. This assists maintenance, and can also provide cooling and other services required for cockpit alert. The B-1B fleet has had some engine problems. By the 100,000-hour point there had been six F101 fan failures. GE designed completely new first-stage fan blades. As an interim measure, the first-stage retaining ring, made of 0.06-in (0.15-cm) stainless steel, was replaced by a ring made of 0.125-in (0.32-cm) Inconel 718, and new standards were introduced for acceptable first-stage damage, enforced by an inspection before each flight and a 25-hour eddy-current check.

Fuel

The fuel system is normally filled with JP-4 (MIL-T-5624), but JP-5 is an alternative. If the engines cannot be retrimmed the residual JP-5 must be replaced after one flight. Fuel not only supplies the engines and APUs but also serves as the main sink for waste heat, and controls the centre of gravity of the aircraft. The system is refuelled or defuelled through two pressure connections in the underside of the right engine nacelle. A typical refuelling rate from underground hydrants is 1,000 Imp gal (1,200 US gal; 4546 litres) per minute. Higher rates are possible when refuelling in flight via the universal aerial refuelling receptacle slipway above the nose, which is compatible with the high-speed booms of the KC-10 and KC-135. Fuel can be jettisoned through nozzles inset in the trailing edge of each wing immediately inboard of the glass-fibre tip. The eight airframe tanks contain 29,755 US gal (24,775 Imp gal; 112635 litres) or 193,403 lb (87728 kg). In addition to the inbuilt fuel system, each of the three weapon bays may be used to house a cylindrical drum tank 15.0 ft (4.5 m) long, with a capacity of 2,419 Imp gal (2,903 US gal; 10996 litres) or 18,870 lb (8559 kg). Each of these tanks is loaded empty by an MJ40 'jammer' lift truck and filled when locked in place. Thus, the total fuel internal capacity can be increased to 32,032 Imp gal (38,464 US gal; 145623 litres) or 250,013 lb (113405 kg). With cruise missiles in the lengthened intermediate bay, a smaller 91-in (231-cm) tank can be loaded into the short bay at the front. This has a capacity of 1,071 Imp gal (1,285 US gal; 4864 litres) or 8,352 lb (3788 kg). Every one of the above fuel figures can be increased by from 1 to 3 per cent by air refuelling, which enables more fuel to be pumped into each tank. The B-1B also has provision for carrying six external tanks (capacity unstated) on hardpoints adjacent to the six dual external stores pylons. These tanks can in theory be plumbed into the aircraft system and jettisoned when empty, but to date this capability has not been used. Indeed, as explained later, in the aircraft's designed low-altitude mission even the normal internal tankage cannot be fully utilised due to severe limitations on gross weight. The problem of fuel leaks was second only to the DAS in generating media scorn, though in fact the worst situation – 20 leaks per 30 aircraft per month – was one of the best rates ever achieved by a large USAF aircraft with all-integral tankage (the corresponding KC-135 figure was 55, and that for the C-141A was 70). The problem arises because in the construction of the B-1B, as in most aircraft, different pieces of metal have to be joined by fasteners. The length of joints exceeds 5 miles (8 km), and the number of rivets is 292,500. To make the airframe itself house the fuel, supplied under pressure, every joint and rivet-hole has to be sealed. In Lot II, Lot III and most Lot IV aircraft there was extensive seepage, especially from the wings and from the inter-fuselage section joints, which required either shutting off the affected tank or grounding the aircraft pending a messy resealing process. The sealing process was redesigned at aircraft 85-0086, the 46th B-1B, since when trouble has been rare. To rectify the first 45 aircraft, Rockwell contracted with the Air Force's Oklahoma City Air Logistics Center to carry out test deseal/reseal programmes at Palmdale. B-1Bs Nos 3 and 4 used PR-1750 sprayable membrane, Nos 2 and 5 used PR-1770 and Nos 6, 7 and 8 used a different technique with PR-2911 polythioether. The latter was then selected to deseal/reseal B-1Bs Nos 9-45. This has greatly improved the situation, raising the average time between leaks from the five-hour level to around 100 hours, nearing the USAF target of 130 hours. At its height, the situation required frequent washdown of the parking ramps. Today such fuel loss is extremely rare, but testing for leaks continues.

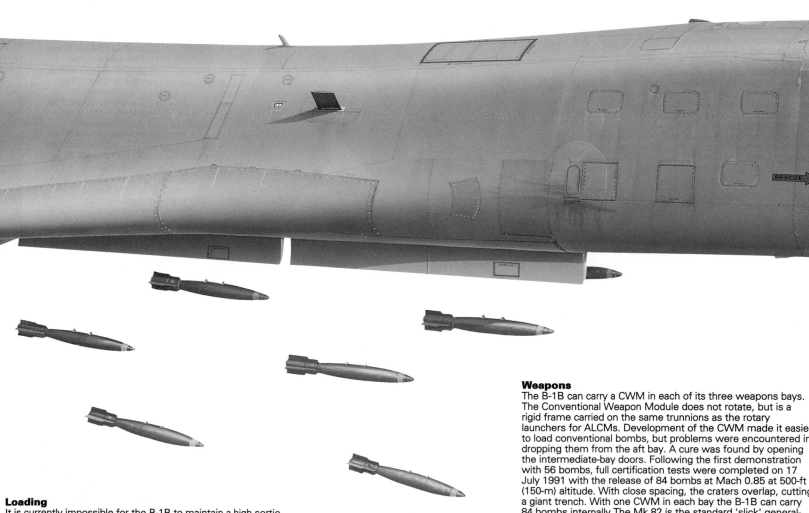

Loading

It is currently impossible for the B-1B to maintain a high sortie rate. Even at a major base the lack of a pre-load facility slows the mission rate seriously. When a B-1B returns from a mission the weapons module must be serviced while in the aircraft. First, 56 spent impulse cartridges must be removed from the ejector racks of each module. Then the area around each cartridge must be carefully scrubbed to remove sooty carbon, and fresh cartridges put in and the wiring checked. Then 28 bombs must be loaded. Loading the first bomb takes up to 40 minutes, and every subsequent bomb needs five minutes, so loading each CWM takes three hours.

Weapons

The B-1B can carry a CWM in each of its three weapons bays. The Conventional Weapon Module does not rotate, but is a rigid frame carried on the same trunnions as the rotary launchers for ALCMs. Development of the CWM made it easier to load conventional bombs, but problems were encountered in dropping them from the aft bay. A cure was found by opening the intermediate-bay doors. Following the first demonstration with 56 bombs, full certification tests were completed on 17 July 1991 with the release of 84 bombs at Mach 0.85 at 500-ft (150-m) altitude. With close spacing, the craters overlap, cutting a giant trench. With one CWM in each bay the B-1B can carry 84 bombs internally. The Mk 82 is the standard 'slick' general-purpose bomb. With the AIR (air inflatable retard) added at the tail it deploys a BSU-49/B ballute (balloon/parachute) to allow low-altitude delivery. As the bays ahead of the wing are quite near the engine inlets the bombs do not use metal arming wires and clips, which could damage the engines if ingested, but have a frangible link to pull the lanyard actuating the BSU-49/B timer actuator. The Mk 82 AIR can be fitted with a Mk 75 arming kit, comprising nose and tail fuses, which convert it into the Mk 36 AIR, a ballute-retarded mine. This can be dispensed over land or water. In the real world, today's B-1B would almost certainly go to war with a 15-ft (4.5-m) tank in the forward bay and 56 Mk 82 AIR bombs in the intermediate and aft bays.

Cockpit

The crew board the spacious modern cockpit using an electrically driven ladder incorporated in a ventral hatch behind the nose gear bay. They enter the compartment through a pressure-bearing hatch between the two rear (DSO and OSO) seats. Inside, everything is modern, airy and ergonomic, all light grey panels and beautifully designed instruments, and dominated by the large colour CRT displays which have become de rigeur in today's combat aircraft. The cockpit is big enough to accommodate two instructors as well as the crew of four, and includes a toilet and galley. The pilots' windscreens are exceptionally large but sharply raked and meet severe birdstrike specifications. Each rear crew station has a small window. These were absent from the B-1A, and backseaters sometimes felt claustrophobic. In a nuclear attack it would have been possible for the crew to attach darkening panels which reduce incoming light and other radiation to 0.003 per cent of normal. The panels are secured by push-button snaps, leaving an external field of view through 5.5-in (14-cm) portholes. Pre-cooled bleed air from the 5th and 9th stages of all four engines is fed to four air-cycle machines, each comprising a turbine driving a compressor. From here various flows of heated or cooled air pass to many parts of the aircraft. The crew compartment can be pressurised to a differential, holding the interior to a level equivalent to 8,000 ft (2438 m), at any desired temperature. Air recirculation loops cool the large avionics bays ahead of and behind the crew compartment, augmented by three liquid cooling loops which for some avionics items cool the unit directly. Waste heat is generally dumped in the fuel, which forms the prime heat sink. Various bleed or electric supplies serve the EPS (environmental protection system) which protects the forward and main side windows against ice, misting and rain, and which heats the dual pitot heads under the nose.

Specification
Rockwell B-1B

Wing: span 136 ft 8½ in (41.67 m) at minimum sweep (15°) and 78 ft 2.5 in (23.84 m) at maximum sweep (67° 30'); aspect ratio about 9.58 fully spread and 3.14 fully swept; area approximately 1,950.00 sq ft (181.16 m²)

Fuselage and tail: fuselage length 143 ft 3½ in (43.68 m); length overall 150 ft 2½ in (45.78 m); height 33 ft 7¼ in (10.24 m); tailplane span 44 ft 10 in (13.67 m); wheel track 14 ft 6 in (4.42 m); wheelbase 57 ft 6 in (17.53 m)

Powerplant: four General Electric F101-GE-102 turbofans each rated at 14,600 lb st (64.94 kN) dry and 30,780 lb st (136.92 kN) with afterburning

Weights: basic empty 182,360 lb (82840 kg); empty equipped 192,000 lb (87091 kg); maximum take-off weight given as 477,000 lb (216365 kg), but maximum taxi weight given as 470,000 lb (213192 kg); low altitude operating weight 422,000 lb (191419 kg); payload nominally 294,500 lb (133585 kg)

Fuel and load: internal fuel given as 195,000 lb (88450 kg), actually 193,405 lb (87728 kg), or 206,160 lb (93514 kg) with latest SIS/SEF FCS software; external fuel none; maximum ordnance 75,000 lb (34019 kg) carried internally and 59,000 lb (26762 kg) carried externally

Speed: maximum level speed 'clean' at high altitude about Mach 1.25 or 715 kt (823 mph; 1324 km/h); penetration speed at about 200 ft (61 m) more than 521 kt (600 mph; 965 km/h) or Mach 0.92

Range: range claimed as about 6,475 nm (7,455 miles; 12000 km) with standard fuel, but actually around 3,000 nm (3,444 miles; 5542 km) with typical weapon load

Performance: service ceiling more than 50,000 ft (15240 m)

Accommodation: four-man crew on individual McDonnell Douglas (Weber) ACES II ejection seats

SMCS vanes

The bottom rudder section is linked to small foreplanes on each side of the nose. In dense air at low level, turbulence can cause airframe fatigue and severely degrade crew performance. Rockwell developed a system called LARC (Low-Altitude Ride Control), or Softride, and later SMCS (Structural Mode Control System) in response. Accelerometers near the centre of gravity and near the nose sense lateral and vertical accelerations and send signals to the vanes and lower rudder to counter them.

Escape systems

Each of the B-1B crew-members sits on a Weber ACES II ejection seat. In the B-1A, individual seats were not used, with the crew inside a jettisonable capsule. The pressurised, air-conditioned capsule could in emergency be separated from the fuselage, steered and stabilised by small rockets and by various fins and spoilers, and lowered by three Apollo-type parachutes. Impact with the surface was cushioned by air bags, and the capsule then served as a survival shelter on land or water. In October 1974 it was announced that any future B-1s would not have an ejectable crew capsule but instead would be equipped with four ACES II ejection seats. These seats were first fitted to B-1A No. 4. On being fired, each goes through a typical routine in which an inertia reel pulls the occupant tightly into the seat, a rocket ejects the seat up through the jettisoned roof-hatch aperture, pitots sense dynamic pressure to set recovery switches to the altitude and speed, emergency oxygen is switched on, and a divergence rocket is fired to separate the seat from any others. Each crew-member has a knob with which he can set his seat to Auto or Manual ejection. The normal mode is Auto, in which either pilot can eject all four seats. They are fired with a very brief interval in a programmed sequence. Any seat not in Auto mode is instantly bypassed, the sequence going on to the next. In the Manual mode any crew-member can initiate only his own ejection.

Radar

The B-1B has a single radar, with a single antenna, which incorporates attack and terrain-following functions. The APQ-164 ORS was developed by Westinghouse from the Common Improved version of APG-66 used in the F-16. It has a fixed phased array (electronically scanned) antenna, which is mounted at an angle to reflect enemy radar emissions downwards. It can operate in any of 11 modes, and is optimised for use in single sweeps or partial sweeps to minimise both emissions and the risk of detection. Ground-map modes can thus be modified to a snapshot, in which the OSO manually aims the radar at the area of interest and fires a very brief burst, which is still sufficient to display the required map on the radar display unit or multifunction display. In many modes the radar switches constantly between different kinds of operation. For example, during TER FLW the radar automatically switches rapidly between scanning ahead, to build a profile of the approaching hostile terrain in its memory, and scanning to each side in the HRGM mode. The main operating modes are real-beam ground mapping, high-resolution ground mapping, velocity update, ground-map beacon mode, terrain following, terrain avoidance, precision position update, high-altitude calibration, rendezvous beacon mode, rendezvous mode, and weather detection. Terrain following is the standard mode over hostile territory. It provides signals to the VSDs and guidance for automatic or manual low-altitude flight. In this mode the radar looks straight ahead to a distance of 10 miles (16 km), to build a constantly changing profile of the terrain to be overflown. The TFACU (Terrain-Following Avionics Control Unit) figuratively 'draws a line' parallel to the terrain profile seen by the radar, and the aircraft flies this line. The actual distance is dialled by the pilot's clearance-plane selector. Over the sea or flat desert the scans may be several seconds apart, but in hilly terrain the scans will be in rapid succession. The software has to take into account the fact that in such terrain the aircraft is constantly banking as it follows a weaving course around and over obstructions. This means that a large obstruction, such as a cliff face, can suddenly appear as the aircraft turns towards it, possibly in a pitch-down after passing over a small obstruction. The problem is complicated by severe weather (in particular turbulent air), and by the ability of the software to command a soft ride with a gentle profile in the vertical plane, or a hard ride in which the terrain profile is followed more precisely. This can impose violent vertical accelerations.

Above: A Dyess-based B-1B lets loose a stick of retarded Mk 82 bombs, fitted with AIR tails. In late 1995 the Mk 82 was the only conventional weapon cleared for front-line use by the B-1B, although a host of other weapons was being cleared.

Right: The unloaded CWM in the bomb bay of a B-1B. This can accommodate 28 Mk 82 bombs and uses the same mountings as the old rotary launchers used by the B-1B's nuclear weapons. Reloading remains a time-consuming task, as individual ejectors have to be cleaned and reloaded.

Below: With AIR (Air Inflatable Retard) tails fitted, Mk 82s have to have noses and tails interleaved. The blue bodies of these bombs indicate that they are inert.

Left: Loading bombs individually is a time-consuming process. When it was designed, no-one realised that B-1Bs would come back to reload. They were optimised for a single-shot nuclear Armageddon in which return to base was unlikely, let alone mounting a second sortie.

Right: Loading the bombs is an exhaustive process, although it can be speeded up by assigning loading teams to all three weapons bays simultaneously. Improvements in loading procedures are urgently sought.

Rockwell B-1B Lancer

Above: The fourth aircraft differed from the first three by being fitted with standard ejection seats in place of the crew escape module, a fact denoted by the lack of 'elephant's ears'. Inflight refuelling formed an important part of the flight trials programme.

Right: The No. 4 aircraft, resplendent in its desert camouflage scheme, receives attention on the Edwards ramp. The scheme was introduced in 1980, leaving the undersurfaces in the original gloss-white. It was wearing this scheme when it appeared at the Farnborough air show in September 1982.

during a pull-up at high gross weight.

Each wing has a specially designed aerofoil profile with a thickness/chord ratio which varies between about 9 and 6 per cent depending on wing sweep. Made by Avco at Nashville, the structure is conventional aluminium alloy with two spars, 28 forged and machined ribs and one-piece integrally stiffened skins. Again the interior is sealed to act as a tank.

A single flap-shaped lever on the central console controls the slats and flaps. With the wings at 20° or less, movement aft of this lever initially controls the six Fowler flap sections on each wing. The inboard trailing edge is cut away to reduce stowage problems at maximum sweep, so at 15° sweep the inner flap section is well outboard of the over-wing fairing. The outer end likewise stops nearly 13 ft (3.9 m) from the tip, the trailing edge beyond it being fixed. Each section has its own hydraulically powered screwjack drive, but all are mechanically interlinked so that the 12 sections move together, travelling on tracks of high-strength steel. A gearbox on the cross-shaft takes the drive to another shaft ahead of the front spar to drive the seven slat sections covering the full length of each leading edge. This progressively extends the slats to a maximum of 20° for take-off and low-speed flight. For landing, the cockpit lever is pulled further back, the flaps then moving as commanded. With the lever on its stop, the flaps reach their maximum setting of 40°.

Ahead of the four outer flap sections, normally flush with the upper surface of the wing, are four sections of spoiler. Each panel has the same span and approximately the same chord as the flap section behind it. Each is driven by a dual hydraulic motor and screwjack to reach a maximum angle of 70° in about 2.7 seconds. The spoilers are discussed later.

The fuselage begins with a circular cross-section, which changes to a vertical oval and then to a rounded triangular shape governed by the blending into the wing. Almost the entire structure is 2025 or 7075 aluminium alloy, with a few longerons, a steel/titanium spine and an extraordinary

number of closely spaced frames. Discounting the radome at each end, the structure is made in five sections: forward, forward intermediate, wing carry-through, aft intermediate and aft. The nose, tail and lateral (inner leading-edge) radomes are of erosion-resistant polyimide quartz. Several areas, including the inboard pairs of spoilers, the large over-wing fairings and the wingtips, are of glass-fibre. Smaller regions are advanced composites, most of the skin of the two rear-fuselage sections and around the engine augmenters are of titanium, and before the aircraft were painted many areas were covered by patches, which showed where the skin is of RAM.

Made by Martin Marietta at Baltimore, the tail comprises a fixed fin carrying left and right tailplanes (horizontal stabilisers) and three sections of rudder. The fin is mainly aluminium and titanium, but the tailplane spindles are steel. Each tailplane power unit can drive the surfaces together from 10° leading-edge up to 25° down for control in pitch, and differentially between +/-20° for control in roll. Each rudder section can move +/-25° but, while the upper and intermediate rudders control the aircraft in yaw (for example following engine failure), the lower section is controlled by the SMCS to damp out yaw motions in turbulence. All tail surfaces are hydraulically powered and mechanically signalled, and provide both primary control and trim.

Stick control

The aircraft is flown by the pilot's and co-pilot's sticks (control columns) and pedals, which are all mechanically linked across the cockpit. The pilot's stick, on the left, is mechanically linked to the surface power units, but the co-pilot's stick drives transducers sending electrical signals to the SCAS (stability and control augmentation system) to provide FBW (fly-by-wire) control. In emergency a lever can disengage either stick, leaving the other in sole control. There is no pedal disengage, but again only the co-pilot's pedals have an electrical SCAS link.

The wing spoilers have a dual function. In the air they work with the differential tailplanes to control and trim the aircraft in roll, the inboard pair on each wing being mechanically signalled and the outer pair being FBW. A switch on each No. 4 throttle lever commands the inboard pair on each wing to act together in the speed-brake mode, their deflection varying according to switch movement. A mixer allows these surfaces to act simultaneously as speed brakes and as roll controllers. With weight on the main gears, all four spoilers on each wing can be opened to kill lift and slow the aircraft after landing.

The engine nacelles are generally similar to those of the B-1A, with structure of aluminium and titanium alloys, glass-fibre and composites. A major difference is that the inlets are fixed, and also inclined in side view. Inside the inlet an array of baffles deflect incoming radar signals and prevent them from reaching the highly reflective fan on the front of each engine. Like the inlet, these are de-iced in flight. Each nacelle contains large doors giving access to each main engine, together with inlet and exhaust doors for the APU and various ground servicing connections.

The landing gears are conventional, with footprint pressure lower than for a B-52. The nose gear, of mainly light alloy, has twin 16-in (41-cm) wheels with 35 x 11.5-16 tyres with 22-ply rating, inflated to 210 psi (14.5 bars). The twin-wheel truck is hydraulically steerable and hydraulically retracted forwards into a bay closed by twin doors and a large door behind the main leg. The leg's rearward movement is restrained by a short Y-shaped drag brace, whereas the first three B-1As had a single long brace attached ahead of the crew capsule. The main gears, of high-strength steel, have twin tandem 23.5-in (60-cm) wheels carrying 46 x 16-325 tyres of 30-ply rating inflated to 220-275 psi (15.2-19 bars). All landing gears have an emergency extension system using high-pressure nitrogen. A curious recognition feature is that the wheels of the B-1B are painted white, those of the B-1As being black.

Aircraft systems

The fuel system supplies the engines and APUs and also serves as the main heat sink, while fuel management is used to control centre of gravity. Capacities of the eight airframe tanks are:

Tank	US gal	Imp gal	litres	lb	kg
No. 1 forward fuselage	4,747	3,956	17983	30,855	13996
No. 2 forward intermediate	5,785	4,821	21896	37,606	17058
No. 3 aft intermediate	3,556	2,963	13461	23,116	10485
No. 4 aft fuselage	7,759	6,466	29371	50,435	22877
Main (wing carry-through)	3,127	2,606	11837	20,324	9219
Left wing	4,779	3,983	18090	31,065	14091
Right wing	4,779	3,983	18090	31,065	14091
Total	**29,755**	**24,775**	**112635**	**193,403**	**87728**

In addition to the inbuilt fuel system, each of the three weapon bays may be used to house a cylindrical drum tank.

The four hydraulic systems are all independent and of equal status. They are filled with non-inflammable MIL-H-5606 fluid, and are pressurised to 4,000 psi (276 bars), with a maximum flow rate per system of 52.4 Imp gal (63 US gal; 239 litres) per minute. Each system is served by a primary pump on the ADG of one engine and a secondary pump driven by that of the adjacent engine. In an alternate mode, the two APUs drive the Nos 2 and 4 ADGs, which power one pump in each system. The four systems serve to operate wing sweep, flaps/slats, spoilers, tailplanes, rudders, landing gears, weapon-bay doors, weapon rotary launchers, wheel brakes, nosewheel steering, and the ECS blower motors.

Electric power is generated by three main and one emergency IDGs, rated at 115 kVA at 230 and 400 volts, 400 Hz (cycles per second). The APUs have their own permanent-magnet generators, and are normally started by the aft battery. The batteries provide DC power, and are recharged by transformer/rectifiers. Apart from windscreen and pitot heating and entry-ladder drive, the main loads are avionic, the ALQ-161 system alone (see later) requiring over 120 kW of power in the 'all-out' jamming mode.

Once the IDGs are on-line, the system is automatically controlled and protected. There are four main buses, and the entire system is managed by the EMUX (electrical multiplexing) which requires only two twisted-wire cables to collect and condition signals from terminals throughout the aircraft and supervise all data transfer through a central computer. Among other things, the EMUX provides load management by limiting power demands to the available generating or cooling capacity. There are 16 load-management modes, of which the following seven manage power from the IDGs: ground refuel/defuel; manned alert/simul-

Bottom: When initially painted in the desert scheme the No. 4 aircraft had a black radome, but this was subsequently repainted to match the camouflage.

Below: A rear view of No. 4 during 1983 shows a B-1B-style tailcone. The aircraft was intended from the outset as a full mission avionics testbed, and continued this role during B-1B testing. When painted with the lizard scheme and fitted with the broader nose radome in the latter part of B-1B trials, there was little to distinguish this aircraft from an early B-1B apart from the overwing fairings, intakes and lack of rear cabin windows.

taneous four-engine start; one engine-driven IDG; all-up demand in normal flight; CITS (see next) ground maintenance; proximity test switch; and one IDG out or Bus Tie Controller No. 2 open, nacelle RCS vane anti-ice on.

The CITS (central integrated test system) simplifies fault detection and ground maintenance. It comprises a control/display panel in the aft crew station forward panel midway between the OSO and DSO, a computer, four DAUs (data-acquisition units) distributed in various fuselage bays, a printer and recorder. It is said to provide 95 per cent fault detection and 75 per cent fault isolation. Ground personnel access the printer to read any malfunctioning mode or LRU (electronic line-replaceable unit) and their troubleshooting is guided by specific test parameters on the recorder tape.

Crew oxygen is generated on board by an MSOGS (molecular-sieve oxygen generating system). Bleed air from the engines is cooled, dehumidified and filtered, and then passed through concentrator beds which extract nitrogen and dump it overboard. The result is product gas extremely rich in oxygen. Each crew station has its own control panel, and an oxygen bottle is provided in each seat. A backup main supply is provided by a pressurised gaseous-oxygen tank in the central avionics compartment.

Each of the four members of the B-1B crew has an ACES II ejection seat (in this case made not by McDonnell Douglas but by Weber). In Mode 1, for minimum-altitude use, the seat is separated from the occupant only 0.5 second after firing, and his parachute canopy is fully deployed only 1.0 second later. In Mode 2 the seat is first stabilised and slowed by drogue, deployed 0.03 second before firing the divergence rocket, the occupant descending on his canopy 2.5 seconds after firing. In Mode 3, for high-altitude use, the seat falls with the drogue deployed until the Mode 2 environment is met, when the sequence is continued. Each

seat incorporates a survival kit including a life raft and radio beacon.

On training missions provision is made for the crew to be accompanied by two instructors. They wear individual parachutes with the ML-4 survival kit, but sit on fixed seats. In emergency they leave their seats, pull the Bottom Bailout handle to jettison the entry door and ladder and extend the nose gear. This provides a wind break so that, at any speed up to 300 KIAS (knots indicated airspeed), they can tuck their knees to their chest, roll forward and leave headfirst through the entry hatch. Although the Bottom Bailout system successfully completed testing in January 1989, it is clearly of little use in TER FLW at 200 ft (60 m) altitude. Following the deaths of the two instructors in a crash at La Junta on 28 September 1987, the decision was taken to limit the total crew to four on any mission involving low-level flight, even though this means that each instructor has to replace one of the aircraft's regular crew.

Avionics

The B-1B avionics comprise the automatic flight-control system, the OAS (Offensive Avionics System) which also provides the functions of navigation, stores management and weapons delivery, and the DAS (Defensive Avionics System). In the B-1B there is no separate TFR; it is a mode of the main ORS (Offensive Radar System), using the same antenna.

The basic autopilot mode is to hold wings level and maintain heading. From this it is possible to engage TER FLW for low-altitude attack, as explained later. Other modes are pressure-altitude hold, airspeed hold, Mach hold, heading hold, automatic navigation, automatic approach and autothrottle. In each case the parameter is maintained at the value at the time of engagement. In the auto-nav mode, signals from the navigation and weapon delivery systems steer the aircraft, with roll limited to 30° and roll rate limited to 7°/sec.

Using the ORS an automatic landing approach can be made in any weather, even to runways without an operative Instrument Landing System. The OSO keys in the desired glideslope angle and localiser heading on his integrated keyboard and then centres the offensive radar system crosshairs on the runway touchdown reference point. Capturing the localiser engages the auto-approach mode in the roll axis, while capture of the glide/slope engages the pitch axis. From that point the landing is automatic, but with the possibility of manual override at any time. The navigation computer provides the approach trajectory, and the flight-director computer (with the other on standby) processes

what it perceives as LOC (localiser, giving direction) and G/S (glide/slope, giving height guidance) deviation signals in order to make a precise touchdown.

This is called AILA (airborne instrument landing approach) and is one of the basic modes of the twin flight-director computers. The others are manual heading, navigation, TACAN, ILS and tanker rendezvous. In each case the FDCs provide steering commands to the pilot's and co-pilot's VSDs (vertical situation displays). These are the only large electronic displays facing the pilots.

In a low-level attack the aircraft will be in the TER FLW (terrain-following) mode, in which the aircraft maintains height above the ground at a value selectable between 200 ft (61 m) and 2,000 ft (610 m) in response to pitch signals from the ORS. This mode is selected manually and then made automatic by a quick trigger movement of a switch on the pilot's or co-pilot's stick. If both ORS channels and both flight-director pitch switches are in this mode, no single failure will interrupt TER FLW, though it can be broken off at any time by squeezing the stick trigger to the first detent. Release of the trigger switch automatically inhibits manual flying, and returns TER FLW. The better the hostile radars, the lower will be the selected terrain clearance. The autopilot is configured to continue providing pitch or roll commands in the event of failure of the other axis. In TER FLW, dangerous failure of the pitch axis commands a 2.4-*g* pull-up to ensure that the aircraft will not fly into the ground ahead. This severely limits the permissible weight of the aircraft, to the extent that in a typical mission the operating radius originally could not exceed around 1,300 miles (2090 km). This is discussed later.

Automatic turns and autothrottle

When not in TER FLW the AFCS can be set to heading-hold. The desired reference heading is first dialled on either HSI (Horizontal Situation Indicator). The aircraft then flies to capture and hold this heading, using roll limited to +/-30° achieved at not more than 4°/sec. Selection of autothrottle in cruise governs engine thrust to maintain the established Mach number. If the aircraft has gear down and more than 5° flap, autothrottle maintains 0.7 units on the AoA (Angle of Attack) indicator, which is the optimum value for an automatic approach.

The OAS (Offensive Avionics System) is the third such system overseen and integrated by Boeing Military Airplane Co., its predecessors being those for the B-52G/H and B-1A. In some cases the same LRUs are used. The entire system is computer-controlled via the EMUX buses, and the chief elements comprise the inertial navigation system, Doppler, radar altimeters, gyrostabilisation, ORS, stores management, cockpit controls and displays (of which there are 34) and an avionics control-unit complex. The data bus

also links each LRU with the CITS.

Throughout the aircraft, software has been progressively debugged and updated. The central computing software for navigation and stores management and delivery was designed and written by Boeing. The PACU (Preprocessor Avionics Control Unit) formatting solution, which governs the DAS (Defensive Avionics System) and has to take account of each new hostile threat, was the responsibility of Eaton's AIL division. The ORS software was designed and written by Westinghouse. Avionics flight testing, which involved the Nos 2 and 4 B-1As, the Westinghouse BAC One-Eleven and a Lockheed C-141A, used Block 0 software. Block 2 was that delivered to SAC with the first B-1B. Block 3 incorporated cruise missile programmes. By November 1994 the software had reached Block 4.5 Merge 3, which among other things changed the programme for the aft stores bay. Tests showed that when dropped from this bay a SRAM would pitch 45° nose-down, and never recover to level flight. The new programme was triggered by a software indication that the aft bay housed SRAMs, and commanded the spoilers ahead of that bay to extend only halfway, giving a clean missile separation. At this point Block 4.7 was introduced. Block 6 was planned by 1995 to incorporate the programmes for the AGM-131A SRAM II, but this was cancelled in 1991. After 1996 Block 7 will save AFS (Avionics Flight Software) memory capacity by transferring all weapon programmes to a separate DTU (Data Transfer Unit). As each mission is planned, this DTU will be loaded with only the programmes needed for that mission.

The navigation system comprises the INS (Inertial Navigation System), DVS (Doppler Velocity Sensor), GSS (Gyro-Stabilisation System), a DR (Dead-Reckoning) system, radar altimeter and ORS. Normally the B-1B has a single Singer-Kearfott SKN2440 INS, but for special missions a second can be plugged into a waiting interface. If funding allows, all active B-1Bs might be equipped with dual systems as standard. Before each mission, the system is

On 20 January 1982 Rockwell signed a contract to proceed with B-1B testing. While Nos. 1 and 3 B-1As were used in a ground test function, Nos 2 and 4 were chosen to flight test aspects of the new variant, this pair having the lowest hours of the four-aircraft fleet. No. 2 was modified to fly again on 23 March 1983, sporting a B-1B fin logo and red and blue markings. Here it is seen undertaking refuelling trials from a 4950th Test Wing NKC-135A. No. 4 was modified after its trip to Farnborough, and took to the air again on 30 July 1984.

During the B-1B trials all of the B-1A fleet received the dark strategic scheme intended for the production bomber. No. 1 wore this scheme for ground visibility trials, subsequently being transferred to Rome ADC as a general test platform. Both flying aircraft were repainted, and it was in this scheme that No. 2 crashed on 29 August 1984, just four flights short of the end of its allotted test programme. Throughout its career, 74-0159 retained the nose instrumentation boom and the pointed tailcone, as seen here.

The angular wing/fuselage fairing identifies this aircraft as the B-1A No. 4, during the latter part of its trials for the B-1B programme. This aircraft retained the Mach 2-capable inlet system, but featured full B-1B avionics systems, including the terrain-following radar being tested here.

Above: B-1A No. 4 nudges in for a tanking, displaying the original Mach 2 intake design. This and early B-1Bs had black refuelling marks, but these were subsequently exchanged for a complicated white 'spider's web' as the black did not show up at night. The web pattern was also changed, B-1Bs reverting to the old pattern displayed here, but now worn in white.

Right: Not even a KC-10 can dwarf a B-1. Again the wingsweep fairings identify this aircraft as the No. 4 B-1A.

aligned on a surveyed spot. In emergency the aircraft can take off on stored alignment modes, and then improve navigation accuracy in flight by position fixes and other aids. In 1995 MTBF (Mean Time Between Failures) for the INS was a little over 500 hours. Future accuracy will be enhanced by adding a GPS (satellite-based Global Positioning System) receiver, though until 1991 a significant factor was that, in a nuclear war, reception on the satellite link might be disrupted by ionospheric disturbance.

The DVS (Doppler Velocity Sensor), or Doppler radar, is the Teledyne Ryan APN-230, developed from the APN-218 used in late models of B-52. It provides accurate velocity measures along lateral, longitudinal and vertical axes. The GSS (Gyro-Stabilisation System) is a free all-attitudes platform with an Earth-inductor magnetic azimuth detector. It serves as a backup (for example in permitting take-off before the INS is fully aligned) and feeds attitude and heading reference to both cockpit HSIs, the automatic flight-control system and the weapon-delivery system. The APN-224 radar altimeter is crucial in low TER FLW, and so most of its elements are duplicated. It provides a precise indication of vertical distance to the Earth's surface up to a ground clearance of 5,000 ft (1524 m).

The APQ-164 ORS was developed by Westinghouse from the Common Improved version of APG-66 used in the F-16. It has an electronically scanned antenna, which is therefore both flat and also rigidly fixed in the nose, mounted at an angle to reflect enemy radar energy downwards. It operates in any of 11 modes, with the addition that over hostile territory any emission has to be brief to minimise detection. The ground-map modes can thus be modified to a snapshot, in which the OSO manually aims the radar at the area of interest and fires a very brief burst, which is still sufficient to display the required map on the radar display unit or multifunction display. In many modes the radar switches constantly between different kinds of operation. For example, during TER FLW the radar automatically switches rapidly between scanning ahead, to build a profile of the approaching hostile terrain in its memory, and scanning to each side in the HRGM mode. The operating modes are:

RBGM: Real-beam ground map is the normal mode for surface mapping, the radar looking to left and right at a +/-45° angle off the nose, using Doppler ranging.

HRGM: High-resolution ground map is used in TER FLW attack. It combines Doppler ranging with a synthetic-aperture capability to give the same high-resolution picture as would be obtained by a radar with an antenna hundreds of feet across.

VU: Velocity update backs up the DVS to supply the INS

with precise ground velocity measures.

GMB: Over friendly territory the ground-map beacon mode interleaved with RBGM signals the precise relative position of ground beacons.

TER FLW: Terrain following is the standard mode over hostile territory. It provides signals to the VSDs and guidance for automatic or manual low-altitude flight. In this mode the radar, in between other modes such as HRGM, looks straight ahead, if line of sight permits to a distance of 10 miles (16 km), to build a constantly changing profile of the terrain to be overflown. The TFACU (Terrain-Following Avionics Control Unit) figuratively 'draws a line' parallel to the terrain profile seen by the radar but raised above it by from 200 to 2,000 ft, as noted. The actual distance is dialled by the pilot's clearance-plane selector. The software has to take into account the fact that in such terrain the aircraft is constantly banking as it follows a weaving course around and over obstructions. In TER FLW the radar checks itself at the rate of 16 'frames' per second, while the whole TF system self-checks at over 180 times per second. At the end of each frame, provided every one of over 500 input signals is correct, the two TFACUs, which are high-speed processors, send a 'valid' signal to the flight-control system. If any input is outside limits an 'invalid' signal is sent, and several of these in succession (occupying up to 0.25 sec) commands an automatic fly-up at 2.4 *g* to ensure that the aircraft avoids the ground ahead. The same fly-up signal is sent if the radar altimeter gives an indication below a predetermined tolerance band around the pre-set clearance. The fly-up signal, though essential for safety, has caused major headaches, as outlined later.

TER AVD: Terrain avoidance feeds ground clearance data to the VSDs.

PPU: Precision position update supplies precise aircraft position from a designated offset or other checkpoint. With HRGM it is the main method of aiming gravity stores.

HAC: At heights greater than the radar-altimeter limit, the high-altitude calibration mode provides a measure of vertical distance from the aircraft to the ground, which a pressure altimeter cannot do.

RB: The rendezvous beacon mode can interrogate another aircraft, designate it by the crosshair cursor on the display and track it with a continuous readout of slant range.

RM: The rendezvous mode enables the OSO to search for

and skin-paint a friendly aircraft, such as a tanker, to enable the RB mode to be used.

WD: Weather detection enables severe weather to be avoided.

Other navigation LRUs are off-the-shelf. The ARN-118 TACAN (TACtical Air Navigation) provides bearing and distance to a TACAN ground beacon up to 300 nm (555 km) distant. It shares two UHF antennas, one between the OSO/DSO roof hatches and the other under the front of the right engine nacelle. The ARN-108 ILS (Instrument Landing System) receiver has a flush antenna group above the nose. From high cruising altitude it can capture a localiser at 45 nm (83 km) and the glide slope at 15 nm (28 km). The APX-105 beacon has its antenna inside the front of the fin cap; it enhances the B-1B's radar cross-section to assist rendezvous with a tanker or other aircraft.

The communications LRUs have been repeatedly updated. The ARC-190 HF, with a nominal 5,000-mile (8045-km) range from high altitudes, has its flush antenna in the fin leading edge, with the coupler at the junction with the dorsal spine. The duplicate ARC-171 UHF for clear line-of-sight links has a small blade antenna above the fuselage and two others under the front of each engine nacelle. The

B-1B No. 1 takes shape in the Palmdale assembly facility. This aircraft was largely hand-built, and incorporated several sub-assemblies completed for the No. 5 B-1A, of which construction had been well under way when the B-1A was cancelled. Notable in this view are the escape hatches for the OSO and DSO and the large hollow pins which attached the wings to the centre section.

This is the first B-1B, 82-0001, seen in front of the Rockwell flight test shed at a ceremony. It was officially rolled out on 4 September 1984, bearing a gold '1' on the starboard side of the nose.

82-0001 first flew on 18 October 1984, treading the well-worn path from Palmdale to Edwards AFB. After a 3-hour 20-minute test flight it landed at the AFFTC to join the B-1 Combined Test Force. Here it is seen landing at Edwards with a 6510th Test Wing F-111 flying chase.

ICS-150 intercom also serves as the communications monitor. The King KY-58 secure voice line-of-sight coding/decoding radio is a late addition, operated by the co-pilot only. Another addition is the ARR-85 miniature receiver terminal, which receives secure or non-secure line-of-sight messages, and prints hard copies. A third is the ASC-19 AFSATCOM satellite receiver, with its antenna on the upper centreline just behind the crew compartment. The APX-101A IFF/SIF (Selective Identification Facility) shares the UHF-2 antennas above the fuselage and under the left nacelle.

It is remarkable that the OAS can aim gravity bombs accurately without using any optical or electro-optical sighting system. The need for accuracy was multiplied in 1991 when the conventional mission became dominant, and the nuclear mission became essentially part of history. To make life harder, the need to attack at low level remains, and in the TER FLW mode the forward-looking radar's priority is following the terrain. With present software this requires the OSO to calculate targeting information through an offset aimpoint from 30° to 60° off the nose. The INS places the crosshair cursor on the OSO's radar display unit where it thinks the aimpoint is, and the OSO then manually repositions the crosshairs to the exact point. Steering information is then transferred to the command heading marker on the pilot's horizontal-situation display. The aircraft is steered to the release point where the SMS (Stores Management System) releases the bomb(s) automatically.

Though part of the OAS, the SMS is discussed later, under the heading of 'weapons'.

Defensive avionics

Of all the B-1B's problems, perhaps the most publicly visible has concerned the DAS (Defensive Avionics System). Under the integration management of Eaton's AIL (Airborne Instrument Laboratory) Division, in partnership with Air Force Systems Command, the DAS had to be developed and put into production concurrently, in order to meet the target of IOC in 1986. This plan failed.

If the B-1B were to be used solely as a launcher for long-range cruise missiles, such as the ACM (range 1,800 nm/3336 km), there would be much less need on most missions for either the DAS or for TER FLW. It is the concept of this bomber as a penetrator that has caused much argument, and multiplied the effort needed to make it perform as advertised. The DAS comprises an exceptional number of LRUs, all interlinked via the EMUX bus. In 1995 a typical system comprised 115 LRUs.

The basic function of the DAS is to sense enemy electronic signals, especially those from air-defence and missile-guidance radars, identify them in a threat library, and then pump out high-power emissions to jam or confuse them. The system also manages an EXCM (EXpendable Counter-Measures) system for firing cartridges containing chaff to blind enemy radars, or bright flares to distract IR-homing missiles. Altogether the DAS comprises a huge system called ALQ-161A and a management system designated ASQ-184. The main 161A system is made up of the RFS/ECMS already mentioned, and also a TWF (Tail-Warning Function).

In designing such a system, the starting point is the perceived or predicted enemy threats. These cover a wide range of frequencies from about 200 MHz to 50 GHz. In traditional notation these limits extend from B-Band to K-Band, but in the B-1B system these are called Band 1 to Band 8, with almost all the emphasis on Bands 4 to 8. Thus, the RFS portion of ALQ-161A has to provide receivers able to tune in to all the possible hostile emissions, arriving from any direction. It must then record these, compare them with signals stored in a threat library, positively identify each one, assign an order of threat priority, and then command the ECMS part of the system to jam them in order of priority.

In theory, before each mission the crew have an up-to-date idea of the hostile DOB (Defensive Order of Battle). Satellite imagery and other intelligence sources provide information on the types and locations of the enemy's defence installations that might affect the mission. These

Far right: The General Electric F101-GE-102 which powers the B-1B is larger than a typical fighter engine, chiefly because the bypass ratio of around 2 requires a fan of large diameter. The core engine has a nine-stage compressor with variable stators on the first three stages, annular combuster and two turbines, the final low-pressure turbine driving the two-stage front fan. Many of the components are modular for ease of maintenance, and there are strategically placed borescope ports for rapid inspection of key areas such as blades and blade clearance.

Left: A B-1B lets rip with all four afterburners in the engine test bay. The afterburners are of the mixed-flow type, with 28 chutes channelling engine exhaust gas and a similar number ducting bypass air. A convoluted flow mixer ensures the most efficient mixing from the two sources. The flameholders are arranged radially, and light-up progresses from the inner flameholder to the outer as augmentation is increased.

include surveillance radars, missile-guidance radars, SAM batteries, gun-direction radars, interceptor air bases, interceptor vectoring (ground control of interception) transmitters, interceptor lookdown/shootdown radars, early-warning aircraft emitters, and radio communications generally. The DSO loads the predicted DOB for the mission into his DAS memory and software.

For jamming to be effective, it must be almost instantaneous; the RFS has to accomplish its tasks in microseconds, so that the enemy emitter is jammed in near real time. It must be possible to receive and jam many signals in the same waveband simultaneously, and to constantly respond to new threats. At 600 mph (965 km/h) the surface (or airborne) threats never stay the same. Because of the high power needed to jam the enemy emitters – which can be much larger and more powerful than airborne equipment – computers must allocate the available RF power to the jamming transmitters tuned to each threat so that each matches its emitted power to that needed to defeat the threat. As the surface threats can surround the aircraft, yet are constantly moving past, the transmitter antennas must be able to emit in any direction.

Again, there is no point in wasting RF power by sending it in all directions; each threat must be countered by a beam aimed as accurately as possible. Not least, there is no point in trying to make a penetrating aircraft stealthy and then making it broadcast RF power like a lighthouse, so in some circumstances the DSO may choose to override the DAS and keep it silent.

The system is naturally digital, to facilitate software control, and modular so that it can be continually altered and upgraded. Many of the LRUs are in the floor-to-roof rack-

ing in the left and right central avionics bays immediately behind the crew compartment. The rest are mainly accommodated in the left and right fuselage side fairings (which could equally be described as the inboard wing leading edge) and the rear end of the fuselage. Many of the receiver antennas are inside the blunt tail dome, sending signals to LRUs in the main wheel wells. The only antennas which project prominently are the large, almost square, blades which transmit on Band 7 from high on each side of the fuselage behind the crew compartment and on each side of the rear fuselage; smaller Band 8 blades are close alongside. All other antennas are inside electronically transparent regions of the airframe.

An early production B-1B taxis from the Rockwell facility out on to the Palmdale taxiway. Rockwell's installation is protected with a fence which rolls across the taxiway to prevent unauthorised access by vehicle or aircraft. Although a civilian airfield, Palmdale is home to major production facilities of many US aerospace giants, including the Lockheed Martin Skunk Works and Northrop Grumman. As a consequence, security is very tight.

Climatic testing was accomplished using B-1B No. 10 (84-0050) in the McKinley Laboratory at Eglin AFB, Florida. During the course of this the aircraft was subjected to temperatures from 125°F to -65°F and various precipitation conditions. A duct from the starboard jetpipes to the outside of the laboratory allowed the engines to be run.

Rockwell B-1B Lancer

It is part of ALQ-161A, but the TWF comprises equipment unrelated to the rest, and is individually located. An automatic pulse-Doppler radar designed to detect any interceptor or missile approaching in the rear hemisphere is packaged in the tailplane/fin fairing. When a threat is detected and confirmed, a signal is sent to the DSO, the threat azimuth and range are displayed on his threat-situation format, and a missile warning tone is sent to each crew-member. Multiple threats are prioritised and the most immediate are passed to the DSO in order.

The DSO then decides what action to take. If necessary the EXCM can respond automatically, but the DSO has the option of holding fire as the threat approaches, while he decides what type of EXCM to fire and from which dispensers. There are eight dispenser locations, four on each

side of the centreline recessed into the top of the fuselage above the forward stores bay. Each may be loaded with a dispenser containing either 120 chaff cartridges, to screen the aircraft from radars, or 12 flares to decoy IR-homing missiles.

Weapons

Like the B-1A, the B-1B has three internal stores bays. In the B-1A each bay had a length of 18 ft (5.49 m). This was matched to the AGM-86A, the original ALCM (Air-Launched Cruise Missile), which could be carried on specially designed rotary launchers which were also tailored to the weapon bay of the B-52. With the cancellation of the B-1A, Boeing was free to develop the increased-range AGM-86B, with a length of 20 ft 9 in (6.3 m). As this became the most important US air-launched strategic missile, Rockwell had to redesign the B-1B fuselage.

The decision was taken to leave the aft bay as it was, with a length of 15 ft (5.5 m). This is available for any weapons below that length, as described later. The forward weapons bay (the terms weapons bay and stores bay are both in common use) was redesigned so that it could be reconfigured to any of three forms. Not yet required is the single bay, with a length of 31.24 ft (9.5 m). In this configuration all six bay doors would in theory be joined together. All doors are almost flat panels of high-strength composite, opened downwards hydraulically on plain hinges to project into the airstream.

As actually built, the forward bay can have either of two configurations. In one, an intermediate bulkhead, with the spoiler, is inserted at Fuselage Station 737 (inches from ref-

It was no mistake that the B-1 was designed with a stick control rather than the traditional yoke, for compared to the B-52 the aircraft has fighter-like manoeuvrability. This is put to the full by this aircraft, venting fuel from the wingtips as it pulls g. Such agility is necessary for low-level penetration through difficult terrain.

erence station zero near the nose of the aircraft). This divides the space into two 15-ft bays, the forward bay having two pairs of doors and the intermediate bay one large pair. This configuration gives the aircraft three bays which are essentially identical. Each can be loaded with an MPL (Multi-Purpose Launcher), for up to eight nuclear weapons; a SRAM launcher, for up to eight AGM-69A missiles; a CWM (Conventional Weapon Module), for up to 28 bombs or mines; a 15-ft fuel tank; or, later in the 1990s, a new launcher configured for 10 Mk 84 conventional bombs. In about 24 hours the intermediate bulkhead can be repositioned at Fuselage Station 648. This provides an intermediate bay with four doors with a length of 22.08 ft (6.73 m). This can accommodate the CRM (CRuise-Missile) launcher and the resulting short forward bay can then be used only for a 7.5-ft tank.

It is appropriate here to describe the weapons for which the B-1B has been certified. Initially the emphasis was on nuclear weapons; indeed the first seven aircraft were at first certified to carry gravity NW only. At the time of the Gulf War in early 1991 the official view of the DoD was that the B-1B had not been certified to use conventional bombs (this was disputed by some B-1B crews). Since then, the process of qualifying the aircraft on additional weapons and stores has continued, and according to funded weapon programmes it will go on until at least 2004, as described later.

Nuclear bombs

B28: This strategic gravity bomb was introduced from 1958. Over 1,200 were produced in numerous versions, all having a parallel drum configuration with four low aspect-ratio fins, in most versions with a parachute retarder. All had a diameter of 20 in (51 cm) and a length typically of about 14.16 ft (5.18 m). Launch weights were 2,027-2,540 lb (919-1152 kg). Yields varied up to 1.45 Mt. The B-1B MPL can carry four of this class of bomb. B28s were withdrawn from 1984, and under the SALT II treaty most bombs of this type have been dismantled, although two modified versions called B28-0 and B28-1 remain available.

B61: This is a lightweight multi-purpose weapon developed from the B61-0 through B61-7 and deployed from 1968. All have a streamlined tubular shape with four small swept fins. Various versions have a parachute and/or spin rockets for stabilisation, some being cleared for external carriage at over Mach 1, and others for release from as low as 50 ft (15 m). Diameter of all variants is 13.4 in (34 cm) and length is usually 11.8 ft (3.6 m). Weights are in the range 718-825 lb (326-374 kg), and yields varied from 10-500 Kt. Of some 3,000 delivered, only the B61-1 and B61-7 remain available for use, and these weigh 740 lb (336 kg). The -7 was preferred because of its new electronic safety system and insensitive trigger explosive. Prior to the SALT II modification, the B-1B could carry up to 24 B61s internally on three MPLs.

B83: This bomb was the replacement for the B28. Compared with the B61 it is larger, having a diameter of 18.5 in (47 cm) and length of about 12.08 ft (4.45 m). The configuration is slightly more bluff than the B61, and it has three short fins spaced at 120°. Standard mass is 2,456 lb (1114 kg), and the yield is selectable to either 1 Mt or 2 Mt. Like the B61 the delivery options covered free-fall or retarded air or ground burst at heights down to 50 ft (15 m). Before

For the carriage of cruise missiles the B-1B can be reconfigured with a long intermediate weapons bay to accommodate the missiles, and six external dual-missile pylons. Aircraft No. 9 (84-0059) conducted tests with AGM-86B ALCM, while this aircraft (No. 28/85-0068) was assigned to AGM-129 ACM integration. Four ACMs can be carried on the internal rotary launcher, and 12 externally, whereas eight AGM-86Bs could be carried internally and none externally. A total of 13 jettison tests was undertaken from all stations. On the ground large bags covered the ACMs to hide their shape. The two test aircraft were fitted with redundant antennas on the spine for satellite verification of their cruise missile-carrying status.

Early B-1Bs (No. 11 in the foreground) progress along the Palmdale assembly line, nearing completion. The next step was the Automated Checkout Facility and then the paintshop. The nearest aircraft has a protective cover over the nose to contain harmful radiation when the radar was being tested.

modification the B-1B could carry up to 24 on three MPLs. The MHU-196/M munitions lift trailer could bring an MPL with eight B83s to any B-1B weapons bay and raise it into position.

Nuclear missiles

AGM-69A SRAM: Also now called SRAM A, the Short-Range Attack Missile was developed by Lockheed in the 1960s primarily to knock out hostile air-defence systems, to enable the launch aircraft to penetrate with gravity bombs. A streamlined shape with three fins at 120°, SRAM has a diameter of 17.5 in (45 cm) and length of 14 ft (4.3 m), mass at release being 2,240 lb (1016 kg). Each round is pre-programmed with inertial guidance, which the OSO can update just before release. It drops free and is immediately accelerated to high supersonic speed by the first pulse of a solid rocket motor. The missile flies on body lift, and can be steered by the fins to describe a ballistic trajectory, or follow the terrain, or even make a dogleg path. Range varies with trajectory to a maximum of about 115 miles (185 km). Near the target the second pulse of the motor

fires to give highly supersonic arrival. The W69 warhead has a yield of 170 Kt. In 1983 B-52 and FB-111 squadrons had 1,140 SRAMs. These were planned to be replaced by AGM-131A SRAM II, but following cancellation of this weapon in 1991 most of the SRAM stockpile became available for B-1B units. Up to 24 could be carried on three MPLs. No provision was made for external carriage, though the missile was qualified for such use at over Mach 1. Loading and delivery was practised with inert missiles.

AGM-86B ALCM: The Air-Launched Cruise Missile was developed by Boeing in the 1970s to carry the W80-1 common warhead with a yield of 200 Kt. It is a stretched version of the AGM-86A, and similarly has a slender fuselage with a near-triangular cross-section so that eight can fit around a CRL like the segments of a grapefruit. Body diameter is 27.3 in (69 cm), length 20 ft 9 in (6.3 m), wing span 12 ft (3.7 m) and launch weight 3,200 lb (1452 kg). After release, pivoted wings of high aspect ratio swing out from the bottom of the fuselage, a vertical fin and two downswept tailplanes are unfolded, and an air inlet is extended to serve the Williams F107 turbofan engine. Guidance is inertial, updated by terrain-contour matching. At high altitude the maximum range can be 1,500 nm (2779 km). The B-1B can carry eight on the CRL mounted in the 22.08-ft (6.7-m) intermediate bay. The AGM-86B was not designed to withstand the high dynamic pressure and intense acoustic environment of external carriage on the B-1B. Loading and release used to be practised using inert missiles of the correct mass, and during integration testing in 1987-89 two live missiles (without nuclear warheads) were launched, hitting their targets on the Utah Test and Training Range.

AGM-129A ACM: The Advanced Cruise Missile has been under development by General Dynamics since 1983. Intended as a replacement for AGM-86B, it carries the same warhead at the same speed, over similar trajectories and using similar guidance. Its advantages are an increased maximum range of 1,800 nm (3336 km), the ability to withstand external carriage at Mach 1 and, even more important, dramatically reduced radar signature, making it virtually undetectable until very close to its target. Powered by a Williams F112 turbofan, the missile has a pointed nose, forward-swept high wings and a tail with an underfin. Although it is lighter than the ALCM at 2,750 lb (1247 kg), the fact that the body has quite a large circular cross-section

The B-1B was first delivered to SAC on 7 July 1985, when the first aircraft arrived at Dyess AFB, Texas for the 96th Bomb Wing. The unit assumed nuclear alert duties on 1 October 1986, marking the true start of the B-1 as an operational aircraft.

Below: With afterburners glowing blue, a B-1 departs for a training mission. Compared to the B-52, the aerodynamic efficiency and sheer power of the B-1B have a marked effect on take-off and landing performance, allowing the B-1B to operate from many more airfields than its predecessor.

restricts carriage on the CRM to only four missiles. On the other hand, AGM-129A's ability to withstand external carriage means that the B-1B's external dual pylons can carry pairs of ACMs. Under the terms of the SALT/START treaties, not more than 12 missiles may be carried externally, so the single launchers are not used. Thus, the maximum theoretical B-1B load is 16 ACMs. Inert AGM-129A missiles have been carried internally and externally on separation/jettison tests, but at the time of writing no live launch has been made. Only one B-1B has ever been equipped with external launchers and two with the long intermediate bay.

AGM-131A SRAM II: This completely new weapon was being developed by Boeing to replace AGM-69A. Advantages included even smaller RCS, increased range, more accurate RLG (ring-laser gyro) inertial guidance (which, with other ancillaries, was packaged along a dorsal fairing) and increased shelf life. Many software integration, missile carriage and jettison tests had been completed when SRAM II was cancelled on 27 September 1991.

Conventional stores

Mk 82 AIR: In 1995 the only non-nuclear store for which the B-1B was certified was the Mk 82 AIR bomb, and its Mk 36 counterpart. The Mk 82 is the standard 'slick' (low-drag) general-purpose bomb, which on ground impact produces a crater, blast and fragmentation. With the AIR (air inflatable retard) added at the tail it deploys a BSU-49/B ballute (balloon/parachute) which causes sufficiently rapid deceleration for low-altitude delivery over a wide range of airspeeds. The B-1B can carry 84 on three CWMs, one in each weapon bay. As the bays ahead of the wing are quite near the engine inlets the bombs in this aircraft do not use metal arming wires and clips, which could

damage the engines if ingested, but a frangible link to pull the lanyard actuating the BSU-49/B timer actuator.

Mk 36 AIR: This is essentially the Mk 82 AIR fitted with a Mk 75 arming kit, comprising nose and tail fuses, which converts it into a ballute-retarded mine. This can be dispensed over land or water.

Mk 84: This is a standard low-drag general-purpose bomb, resembling the Mk 82 but scaled up to a nominal weight of 2,000 lb (907 kg). An AIR for this bomb is available, although it is normally used from medium altitude. In 1995 it was the intention to certify the B-1B to carry up to 30 (according to some documents, 24) of these bombs on up to three of a new type of CWM, which has yet to be developed.

AGM-86C ALCM: This is identical to the AGM-86B but the W80 is replaced by a unitary conventional warhead. Little has been heard of it since it was first announced, although the possibility exists of converting AGM-86Bs to this standard.

Above: Manoeuvring at low level, this grey-painted B-1 displays the large extending trailing-edge flaps which provide considerable extra lift. Also displayed is the inflatable wing/fuselage joint.

Right: The cold weather trials had not been undertaken in vain when the B-1B entered service with the 319th Bomb Wing at wintry Grand Forks. The standard support umbilicals to provide vital services on the ground can be powered by portable generators or at some bases are incorporated into the concrete ramp.

Training stores

BDU-38/B: This has the appearance, mass and ballistic properties of the B61 nuclear weapon. It enabled armourers and flight crews to practise using the software and loading, fusing, pre-arming/arming/safeing and going through release modes with the actual bomb.

BDU-46/E: This is the training version of the B83 nuclear weapon. Again, it enabled the complete process of using the live bomb to be simulated.

BDU-50 AIR: This is an inert store exactly simulating the Mk 82 AIR, and carried in the same way on the CWM. Many have been dropped with different spacing from all three bays.

BDU-33: Thanks to the PBAR (practice-bomb adapter rack) devised by the 28th Bomb Wing, the B-1B can carry four practice bombs on each MPL. These bombs are the BDU-33C/B, simulating low-drag stores, and the BDU-33D/B which has a high-drag configuration. Both are 23 in (58 cm) long and weigh about 25 lb (11 kg). On impact they emit a bright flash and a white smoke spotting charge.

Interfaces

No provision is made at present for attaching stores directly to the B-1B in the traditional manner. Instead, each store is loaded on a special interface, either internal or, rarely, external. Nuclear weapons, gravity and missile, are carried internally on rotary launchers resembling the cylinder of a revolver. The launcher is loaded on the ground and raised into the appropriate bay of the B-1B by the MHU-196/M munitions lift trailer.

Each launcher comprises a strong tubular beam rotating in a bearing at each end by which it is secured in the aircraft. Around the centre of the launcher assembly are eight stations tailored to particular types of store. These incorporate sway braces, DC electrical power supplied via a transformer/rectifier, electronic connections, software couplings, cooling connections and a lanyard coupling. At the front is a drive assembly incorporating a torque plate which engages with a hydraulic motor mounted on the front bay bulkhead. This accurately rotates the launcher to index the selected weapon for release at the 6 o'clock position. The minimum time interval between successive weapon drops is about five seconds.

It is possible to load launchers into the aircraft with any number of stores attached, but, because of limitations in the existing software, it is not yet possible to load stores of two different types on the same launcher.

MPL: The Multi-Purpose Launcher is 15 ft (5.5 m) long, and configured for six nuclear gravity bombs of types B28-0, B28-1, B61-1, B61-7 or B83. At the front is the NUC SLU (nuclear station logic unit), which is the interface unit (part of the Stores Management System) which controls weapon carriage and release. On practice missions it can carry the same number of BDU-38/B or BDU-46/E bombs, or four BDU-33C/B or D/B on PBAR interfaces.

SRAM: The SRAM launcher is also 15 ft long, and is configured for up to eight AGM-69A SRAM missiles. These are carried on ejector racks. This launcher is almost identical to the MPL except for the ancillaries at the front, which have different power supplies and missile interfaces. The latter includes the DR (decoder receiver), which is the SMS weapon interface. SRAM was a short-range weapon intended to blast a way through Warsaw Pact air defences. This task is now essentially redundant and SRAM has been withdrawn from the active USAF inventory.

CRM: The Cruise Missile Launcher was developed from the CSRL (Common Strategic Rotary Launcher) of the B-52. It is 26.5 ft (8.08 m) long, and thus cannot be carried except in the intermediate weapon bay with the intermediate bulkhead at the 648 Station. It provides interfaces for eight AGM-86B ALCMs, or the inert practice version, or four AGM-129 ACMs. It too incorporates the DR weapon interface. At present, all active B-1Bs are physically prohibited from carrying this launcher.

CWM: The Conventional Weapon Module does not rotate, but comprises a rigid frame carried on the same trunnions in the weapon bay as the rotary launchers. Under its arched roof are pivoted four arms, A1 and A2 at the front and B1 and B2 at the rear. These arms vary in length, and each can carry from three to six standard 14-in ejector racks. As the Mk 82 AIR is slightly too long to be carried in tandem nose-to-tail on these racks, the noses of the

Thundering along at low level, the B-1B is an impressive sight. Its ability to fly safely at such high speed and low altitude is the key to its survivability in the penetration role, although for its conventional mission the B-1B would also be required to operate from medium level.

B bombs are interleaved between the tails of the A bombs. The software controls the release in a timed sequence. This begins with A11, the first (lowest) bomb on arm A1, to A13. Arm A1 then swings vertical, out of the way, to permit release of B11 to B15. When B1 has swung out of the way, the sequence continues with A21-A26, B21-B26, A31-A35 and finally B31-B33. All 28 bombs can be dispensed in extremely rapid succession, provided that no bomb hangs up. A software interlock in the CONV SLU (conventional station logic unit) prevents a release signal from being sent to a higher bomb, or a higher arm, until the preceding bomb or arm has cleared. The CWM, which can also carry the Mk 36 AIR mine, is raised into the aircraft fully loaded. With one in each 15-ft bay the B-1B can carry 84 stores internally.

Mk 84: As noted, development is proceeding on a new CWM which will be configured to carry 10 Mk 84 bombs of 2,000 lb (907 kg) each. It will fit in the 15-ft size of weapon bay, but it is not yet known whether it will rotate.

The B-1B has attachment points and service connections for six dual and two single external pylons. With the correct interfaces and SMS software, these could have been used for a total of 14 of any weapons qualified for external carriage on supersonic aircraft. Under the terms of the SALT/START treaties no more than 12 nuclear weapons may be carried externally, so there was no attempt to activate the two single pylons.

External pylons

As delivered, all B-1Bs from No. 8 were equipped to carry the six dual pylons, and the first seven were later modified. In theory, each station could have been activated by adding an ACM DR (decoder receiver) linked to the SMS software, plus a PCU (pylon control unit) inside the wing near the right pivot. However, at the time of writing only one aircraft was ever fitted with external pylons. This was No. 28 (850068). The only weapons to have been carried externally were dummy AGM-129A ACMs, which on the ground were for security reasons shrouded by fabric covers. Today the B-1B has no external carriage capability. The CMIP ([Advanced] Cruise Missile Integration Program) has been cancelled, and external carriage of SRAM is considered to degrade aircraft speed unacceptably. External carriage of ACM or other weapons would degrade speed even more, but for political reasons the B-1B's nuclear capability was removed in 1991.

For the 100-aircraft B-1B programme new manufactur-

ing and testing facilities were constructed at Palmdale. In March 1982 ground was broken for a new 'Bomber building', called No. 703, on the far side of the airport, across the runways from Sites 1, 2 and 3 of Air Force Plant 42 which had manufactured the XB-70s and B-1As. In this programme, on Site 3, Rockwell was to manufacture only the B-1B forward fuselage. As these were completed they were trailered across the runways to the impressive new Building 703. Everything else came, usually by rail, from other parts of the United States.

Building 703 actually comprised three main facilities. The biggest, at 422,000 sq ft (39204 m²), was the B-1B assembly building where the incoming structures were mated. A special building of 256,000 sq ft (23782 m²) produced the electrical cable looms, EMUX wiring and many forms of pipe-runs and tubing, fed to the assembly area. Finally, a 254,000-sq ft (23597-m²) checkout building was provided to test all the aircraft systems before each B-1B took its place on the ramp for flight test and delivery. To meet the schedule with a 21-day checkout the building housed four B-1Bs at a time, tails together and noses in the corners.

The B-1B manufacturing programme was generally a textbook example of how things should be done. It ran on or ahead of time, and did not exceed budgets except on the

The elderly F-106 got a new lease of life flying chase for the B-1 flight tests from Palmdale between October 1986 and June 1990. These initially retained their ADC colour schemes with Dayglo fins (above), but were subsequently given tail logos reflecting the new task. A total of four F-106As and three F-106Bs were used as chase aircraft. The single-seaters wore blue logos (top), while the two-seaters had black (subsequently changed to red).

Rockwell B-1B Lancer

With a T-38 flying as safety chase, the first B-1B drops a BDU-46/E practice round for the B83 free-fall nuclear bomb. Some way behind the weapon is the small drogue chute which is used to extract the main retarding chute. Both this and the second aircraft were used to drop dummy B83s during the B-1B FSD programme, a total of 25 releases being accomplished from all three standard-size bays. Aircraft No. 9 (84-0049) also undertook three drops from the long intermediate bay used for cruise missile carriage.

A B-1B approaches a tanker during a practice mission over the snowy Midwest. The strategic camouflage was an extremely efficient 'light sink', consisting of FS 34086 dark green and FS 36081 dark gray disruptive camouflage on the upper surfaces and fuselage sides, with FS 36118 'Gunship Gray' replacing the dark green on the undersides.

inevitable ground of inflation. The baseline cost established by Congress in 1981 for the entire programme was $20.5 billion, and despite numerous engineering modification this was exceeded by about 14 per cent only. In 1986-88 about 4,600 Rockwell employees were wholly engaged on B-1B production, using some 167,000 tools (UK term, jigs). An indeterminate total number were employed nationwide in 5,200 suppliers.

Because the President had used the words 'as soon as possible', aircraft in early Lots were allowed to come off the assembly line deficient in various respects. For example, the first seven had no ability to carry cruise missiles. The first aircraft, 82-0001, was scheduled to fly in March 1985. It actually made its first flight on 18 October 1984, mainly because it was able to incorporate major airframe sections originally built for the never-completed B-1A No. 5. Initial delivery, of the No. 2 aircraft, took place on 7 July 1985, and the first B-1B unit achieved IOC on 1 October 1986, as related in the section on operating units. Deliveries continued at four per month until the 100th aircraft was rolled out on 20 January 1988, for delivery on 2 May 1988. The Air Force acceptance flights on every one of the 100 aircraft were flown by Major Valda J. Robbins.

Under the terms of the FSD contract, Rockwell had to support development with two modified B-1A prototypes. Though these were the most important supporting aircraft,

many others were required. The principal chase aircraft accompanying the B-1As and later B-1Bs of the CTF (Combined Test Force) at Edwards were an F-111A, three F-111Ds and an F-111E. Chase aircraft accompanying B-1Bs on production and acceptance test at Palmdale were four F-106A Delta Darts and three F-106Bs. Photo chase aircraft used on all missions involving weapon release were five F-4Cs and five F-4Es. Two F-15s fitted with radars whose waveforms simulated Soviet interceptors were used in ECM development, and the ALQ-161 DAS was first developed with an installation in a YC-141A. The Westinghouse BAC One-Eleven was the testbed for the ORS.

There was no requirement to modify the two selected B-1A supporting aircraft to simulate the B-1B engine inlets, overwing fairings or other structural changes, but they had to be extensively reworked internally. B-1A No. 2 was modified for over a year, mainly having B-1B flight-control system features incorporated. It returned to flight status on 23 March 1983, still painted white but with 'B1B Test Program' tail markings. It immediately began exploring flight stability and control, especially at the much higher weights to which the production aircraft had to be cleared. It went on to conduct many other tests, including cruise-missile integration and release.

Fatal accident

B-1A No. 2 was later repainted in B-1B strategic camouflage. On 29 August 1984, during investigation of minimum-control speeds, control of the aircraft was lost as a result of the CG migrating too far aft during manual management of the fuel tankage. There was insufficient height for recovery. The aircraft still had its ejectable crew capsule, and this was separated successfully, but failure of an explosive bolt prevented release of the parachute risers. This caused the capsule to hit the ground nose-down, in which attitude the inflatable cushions could not soften the impact. Rockwell chief engineering test pilot Doug Benefield was killed, and Major Richard Reynolds and Captain Otto Waniczek were seriously injured. This accident could not happen again, as the B-1B does not have an ejectable capsule, but its underlying cause was addressed by modifying the flight-control system, as explained in the later 'Three-stage update' section.

The B-1A No. 4 resumed flying on 30 July 1984, still in its desert camouflage scheme. Externally the main change was removal of the long dorsal spine, but internally the integration of as much as possible of the B-1B avionics systems had been a seemingly endless task. At the renewed start of flight testing it was recognised that neither the OAS nor the DAS were in any way definitive, but the planned test programme was: OAS, 135 hours; DAS, 245 hours; aircraft development, 25 hours; and adverse weather tests, 15 hours. When fully modified, and repainted, this aircraft differed visibly from a B-1B only in the engine installations, overwing fairings and absence of backseat windows.

From the outset, B-1B flight testing went well. On the first flight of No. 1 on 18 October 1984, the crew comprised Rockwell's M. L. Evenson, and Lieutenant Colonel L. B. Schroeder, Captain D. E. Hamilton and Major S. A. Henry. It was already quite a mature vehicle, and in a 3-hour 20-minute flight terminating at Edwards the crew carried out numerous avionics tests, incidentally encountering several malfunctions. Later this aircraft carried out basic flight control and flutter testing, with a nose pitot boom and power-energised flutter wands at the tips of all wing and tail surfaces. Early night air refuelling tests resulted in the boom guidance marks above the nose being repainted in white. Many other tests included a live SRAM launch from Intermediate-bay Position 5 on 16 January 1987, and release of two CWM loads totalling 56 BDU-50 AIR (Mk 82 AIR practice) bombs from the forward and intermediate bays on 14 December 1987. This aircraft could not be brought to operational standard, and so was retired as a ground weapon-loading trainer.

Only two B-1Bs were modified for CMI (Cruise-Missile Integration) testing. Aircraft No. 9 was assigned primarily to the AGM-86B ALCM, and No. 28 to the AGM-129 ACM. These were the only B-1Bs to fly with the weapon bay bulkhead positioned at station 648 to give a 22.08-ft intermediate bay. They were also the only aircraft with active hardpoints for external missile pylons. Aircraft No. 9 launched two AGM-86B missiles, on 24 November 1987 and 7 April 1989, both scoring direct hits on their Utah Test and Training Range targets. No ALCMs were carried externally. Aircraft No. 28 carried out 13 successful separation tests of inert ACMs, five from the internal CRM, three from forward pylons, three from intermediate pylons and two from aft pylons, but the entire CMI programme was cancelled before any launch of a live missile. Aircraft 28 also carried out extensive tests with AGM-131A SRAM II before this missile was cancelled in September 1991.

Aircraft Nos 1, 2 and 3 carried out test and certification of gravity NW Types B61 and B83, though of course there were no live drops. One photograph shows the BDU-46/E

(B83 simulator) impacting the ground less than four bomb-lengths from the striped post target. Following the first aircraft's demonstration with 56 BDU-50 AIR in December 1987, Aircraft 51 (85-0091) and 59 (85-0099) were used for full certification with Mk 82 AIR bombs. These tests were completed on 17 July 1991 with the release from No. 59 of 84 bombs at Mach 0.85 at 500 ft (150 m) altitude. With close spacing, the craters overlap, cutting a giant trench. It should be noted that this test took place after the 1991 Gulf War, at which time the B-1B was not certified for conventional bombing.

Among the thousands of tests of navigation and other avionics, the DAS, escape systems, special equipment, diagnostics and maintenance, extreme climatic environments and the crucial AFOTEC testing, several special flights hit the headlines. The AFOTEC (Air Force Operational Test and Evaluation Center) at Edwards is tasked with determining how a weapon system will actually perform when maintained in a realistic Air Force environment. Using No. 32 (85-0072) at Dyess AFB, the 144-mission AFOTEC programme involved two long polar navigation flights, one deployment to the western Pacific and southern hemisphere, 90 ECM missions against ground and aerial threats, and three live SRAM launches, five BDU-46/E drops, five BDU-38/B drops and four CWM tests in which 276

Following initial deliveries to Dyess, the 28th Bomb Wing was next to receive the B-1B at Ellsworth, its first aircraft arriving on 21 January 1987. Re-equipment was completed in September. Both of these wings have retained the aircraft, although the Dyess wing has renumbered from the 96th to the 7th.

Closely monitored by 6512th TW chase aircraft, the No. 1 B-1B lays a pattern of Mk 82 AIR bombs on the Edwards PIRA (Precision Impact Range Area). The B-1B can accommodate 28 Mk 82s in each bomb bay for an impressive total of 84.

To give a flavour of the period from November 1986 to early 1987, the highly respected *US News and World Report* ran a major article entitled 'The B-1 Bomber: a Flying Lemon'. The sedate *New York Times* followed with 'Debut of the Wrong Bomber', while even Ben Schemmer, Editor of *Armed Forces Journal*, headlined 'The World's First Self-jamming Bomber', without a question mark. Day by day new shortcomings were uncovered or invented. Invited to the first B-1B base, Dyess, the media studiously avoided quoting anything said by any crew-member, and instead – in the words of SAC Commander, General Jack Chain Jr – "trashed the B-1." Eventually, the USAF Chief of Staff, General Larry D. Welch, invited the Press to a unique in-depth interview; not a single article followed.

This overkill brought back memories of how Concorde was going to poison the atmosphere and tended to mask the fact that there were serious problems, some of which the media failed to unearth. One problem which surfaced very early was that in the low-level mission, which to this day is regarded as the only way anything but a B-2 can penetrate defended airspace, the B-1B was unable to fly with anything like the brochure payload. Some specialist magazines have unearthed many problems, which would have been extremely serious had the B-1B still been expected to mount very long range autonomous penetrations of the Soviet heartland, but many of which are less serious now that the aircraft is a conventional bomb truck, likely to be used over shorter distances, against less heavily defended targets.

Mission range limitation

According to the brochures, the difference between the B-1B's empty weight and maximum take-off weight is about 294,500 lb (134 tonnes), all of which apart from the weight of four men is available for fuel and weapons. In practice, the figure turned out to be about 125,000 lb (57 tonnes). Thus, with a typical load in the pre-1991 nuclear era of eight B61s and eight SRAMs, the fuel available is not 195,000 lb (88 tonnes) but a mere 78,990 lb (34 tonnes), limiting range in a practical, manoeuvring low-level mission to 1,300 miles (DoD documents appear to mean 1,300 nm; 1,496 miles; 2409 km). On an out-and-return mission this equates to an inability to hit targets further from the B-1B's base than about 700 miles (1125 km).

This figure is based on an assumed empty weight of 182,360 lb (82.7 tonnes), whereas actual aircraft weigh about 190,000 lb (86.2 tonnes), so the true radius was even shorter. It is made shorter still by the fact that low penetrations over practical landmasses have to dog-leg around obstructions, not to mention hostile defences, so a newly delivered B-1B might have found it very difficult, without air refuelling, to hit a defended target more than 500 miles (805 km) away. This figure compares with the brochure 'maximum unrefuelled range' of 6,475 nm (7,455 miles; 12000 km), which suggested an operating radius of over 3,700 miles (5954 km).

We are not comparing like with like, but the proverbial apples and oranges. Published range figures, such as 12000 km, are based on serene cruising flight along a perfect Great Circle course at high altitude. The problems are: to penetrate defended airspace the aircraft must fly at minimum height AGL for about 300 miles (480 km) before crossing the enemy frontier, and continue at this height until leaving enemy territory; throughout this low-level penetration the aircraft cannot fly in a straight line but must manoeuvre around mountains and along river valleys (and possibly make violent manoeuvres to avoid interceptors or missiles); it cannot save fuel by flying more slowly but must maintain maximum dry power, and in emergency may even have to

A refuelling close-up provides detail of the UARSSI receptacle and associated marks, pitot tube cluster and SMCS vanes. Positioning the UARSSI immediately ahead of the cockpit makes the establishment of a good contact position much easier for the pilots. The white markings give the boom operator a clear guide when refuelling at night, showing up clearly under the dim floodlighting available from the tanker fin-tip light.

BDU-50 AIR bombs were dropped.

This aircraft received the name *Polarized* because of its polar navigation mission on 14 April 1987 in which, among other things, it flew over the north-west tip of Alaska within 160 miles (257 km) of the USSR without triggering any noticeable response. In June 1987 it did well in Red Flag 87-4; a typical comment by F-15 pilots was, "Even if we locate it we can't catch it." The Pacific deployment in May 1988 was called Distant Mariner. While based at Guam the aircraft extended as far as Australia, the first major overseas deployment since B-1A No. 4 participated in the 1982 Farnborough air show.

IOC was achieved on 1 October 1986. At that time the minimum requirements for selection as a B-1B commander were stringent, including 1,800 hours, three years in a SAC aircraft, and 18 months as an aircraft commander. As related in the section describing the B-1B operators, the sheer professionalism of SAC resulted in this aircraft of unprecedented complexity having a generally encouraging introduction to combat duty. That cloaked the fact that there were very serious shortcomings.

Some of these surfaced. At a published unit cost of $283 million, quite apart from its controversial nuclear capability, this aircraft was inevitably of intense interest to the media. Not only tabloids and broadcasters, but even supposedly

The front cockpit is beautifully laid out, with all key systems falling to hand. While the necessary complications of the engine instruments and nav/comms gear are grouped in the central dashboard and between the pilots, the main display for each pilot is kept very simple to avoid overloading the pilot with information during critical portions of the mission. Both pilots have an MFD as the primary display, fighter-style stick and throttle quadrants. An overhead panel (below left) carries the controls for the aircraft systems such as environmental control, refuelling and the APU. Soviet Tu-160 crews have expressed sincere envy when faced with the B-1B cockpit.

go into afterburner to outrun enemy fighters; and, to ensure that the aircraft does not fly into the ground following failure of the terrain-following system, the software commands an immediate 2.4-*g* pull-up manoeuvre (called a fly-up) to a safe height – despite the fact that this immediately increases exposure to the enemy defences – and the aircraft must be physically able to make this fly-up.

The nub of the problem is that the lift generated by a wing cannot be increased beyond a certain limit, which depends on air density, airspeed, wing area and AoA (angle of attack, the nose-up angle at which the wing meets the oncoming air). Nothing can be done to alter air density. Wing area and lift could be increased by unsweeping the wings, but this would slow the aircraft dangerously; low penetration demands maximum sweep.

The actual speed of low penetrations might vary slightly between a training mission and 'for real', and in the latter case a higher speed would mean an even shorter range. The brochure figure is 'more than 600 mph' (521 kt; 965 km/h); various B-1B crews have spoken of 'over 550 kt' and even 'Mach One' (which is nonsense at low level). Don Logan's book *Rockwell B-1B* cites penetration speed at 500 ft as Mach 0.92. On a 15°C (59°F) day this equates to almost exactly 700 mph (608 kt; 1126 km/h). This can be accepted as the absolute limit, sustained only for short periods in favourable conditions, and certainly resulting in even further reduction in mission radius. To get an unbiased official figure, the Congressional study of B-1B performance, which was based on direct evidence from the Air Force, assumed not only a penetration speed of 650 mph (564 kt; 1046 km/h; Mach 0.85) but also 'a shorter escape from the target at 420 mph'.

The only remaining variable is AoA. Leaving the other parameters unchanged, wing lift can be increased by increasing AoA, but only up to a sharp limit. One of the first things any pilot learns is that at an AoA of around 15°-20° the airflow over the top of the wing suddenly breaks down. Instead of remaining 'attached' to the wing it eddies away in violent turbulence, and the lift suddenly slumps towards zero. This is called an aerodynamic stall, and any aircraft supported by the wing would drop like a stone. At high altitude, with most aircraft, a stall can safely be demonstrated because there is enough height to recover. In low-level penetration a stall means immediate impact with the ground.

Apart from this, the L/D (ratio of lift to drag) of a wing reaches a maximum at quite a modest AoA, such as 4°, and for best range the aircraft should not exceed this by very much. As AoA increases towards the stall the drag increases dramatically, reducing range seriously. Moreover, the available power of manoeuvre is reduced, because any manoeuvre involving a banked turn at low level increases the lift that must be generated by the wing. By definition, a 2.4-*g* fly-up demands that the AoA be increased until the lift is multiplied by 2.4. Thus, during its low-level attack, the B-1B must not weigh so much that attempting suddenly to multiply wing lift by 2.4 would immediately result in AoA

Rockwell B-1B Lancer

In the rear cabin sit the Defensive Systems Officer (port) and Offensive Systems Officer (starboard). The cabin is connected to the front cabin by a short tunnel, which provides sufficient room for one crew member to stretch out for a rest on long missions. The DSO is responsible for operating and monitoring the ALQ-131 ECM set and EXCM suite. The defences have full automatic operating facility, but can be overridden by the DSO when required. The OSO is largely responsible for working the weapon system, of which the major component is the ORS. Between the two dedicated stations is the central communications and CITS panel. The DSO usually controls the comms system, which includes a satcomms keyboard. Under current training concepts, B-1 back-cabin crew are being trained as WSOs, able to perform either DSO or OSO functions.

dinally unstable, and the pilot or autopilot would be unable to prevent a disastrous aerodynamic pitch-up. In a normal stall, caused for example by letting speed bleed off to a dangerously low value, most aircraft including the B-1B warn the pilot by the progressive onset of aerodynamic buffeting caused by the start of flow breakdown. Loss of control caused by CG moving too far aft gives no such warning until the pitch-up has gone too far for recovery. This is what happened to B-1A No. 2 on 29 August 1984.

With proper fuel management, the only other factor that could dangerously move the CG is incorrect release of weapons, and even here the fuel would have to be mismanaged for control to be lost. In general, moving the CG forward increases stability, though of course this must be trimmed out by the flight-control system moving the tailplanes. Thus, when 56 BDU-50 AIR bombs were first dropped, they all came from the front and intermediate bays. This moved the CG aft, but nowhere near the neutral point, tending to pitch the aircraft up and away from the ground.

Performance degradation

Although much could be done to improve flight control software, almost nothing can be done to improve the performance degradation caused by a dramatic increase in loaded weight. For example, at a time when the brochure ceiling of the F-111 was 'over 60,000 ft (18300 m)', the FB-111A was trashed by the media because 'with bombs on, it can't climb above Pike's Peak' (14,109 ft/4300 m). At the brochure maximum take-off weight of 477,000 lb (216 tonnes), the B-1B's optimum cruise altitude is not at 35,000 or 50,000 ft (10670 or 15240 m) but at about the same 14,000 ft level. Even at a modest 430,000 lb (195 tonnes), the refuelling altitude drops to between 10,000 and 13,000 ft (3050 and 3960 m), right 'in the weather' where turbulent clouds make a successful hook-up extremely difficult. In the real world the weight of 477,000 lb, like the range of 7,455 miles, is little more than fiction.

Early in the B-1B programme the maximum weight for low-level penetration was 360,000 lb (163 tonnes), the same as for the B-1A. Later the Air Force demanded that

going beyond the stalling angle, which would be catastrophic. Indeed, because the air might be turbulent, there must be a large safety margin. This is the crucial demand that limits the quantity of fuel and bombs a B-1B can carry. On a mission entirely over the ocean or absolutely flat desert the 2.4-*g* demand could in theory be waived, the software modified, and fuel or bomb load tripled or quadrupled.

A further complicating factor is the position of the centre of gravity. This is assumed to lie on the centreline, and the aircraft is designed so that it may be located anywhere within specified longitudinal limits. These are defined by the MAC (mean aerodynamic chord) of the wing, and typical limits might be 0.22-0.31 MAC. So long as the CG lies within these limits the aircraft can be flown safely. Traditional aircraft, such as the B-1, must never let the CG migrate too far aft, behind the neutral point (aerodynamic centre) of the wing. This would make the aircraft longitu-

this weight be increased to 440,000 lb (199 tonnes), in order to increase mission radius. In fact, this again is an unrealised target; even the original B-1A weight was not originally met. Assuming penetration at 650 mph (1050 km/h) at 1,000 ft (305 m) above sea level (e.g., TER FLW at 200 ft/60 m over ground 800 ft/245 m above sea level), the maximum TER FLW weight of the B-1B as delivered was 312,000 lb (142 tonnes), which left only the previously mentioned 125,110 lb (38134 kg) available for fuel and weapons. Assuming a load of eight B61s and eight SRAMs, and 18,300 lb (8300 kg) of recovery fuel (to meet the USAF requirement of 500 nm at fuel-efficient cruise followed by 30-minute loiter at base), this left 78,990 lb (35830 kg) of fuel for the mission, equated with a mission range of 1,330 miles (2140 km).

This situation, quite apart from the loss of the second B-1A, resulted in urgent modifications to the B-1B FCS (flight control system), and in particular to the software. A key factor in the severe limits on cruise and refuel altitudes, and on mission weight and range, was the programming of the fly-by-wire software in the SCAS (stability and control augmentation system) to counteract input demands progressively as AoA approached the safe limit. Like such systems in most modern aircraft, it continually compared the achieved AoA with the limiting value (defined not as that at which the wing stalls, but as the AoA corresponding to neutral static stability) and triggered a stick-shaker, siren and flashing warning when it reached 80 per cent of that value.

Three-stage update

The Air Force, with Rockwell and FCS contractors such as Sperry Phoenix, initiated development of three stages of FCS modifications. These were designed to maintain and if possible improve pilot feel and cueing in low-level penetration, while enabling the B-1B to approach much closer to the dangerous limiting AoA, and even to exceed it. This would dramatically increase the weights at which low-level

flight could be undertaken. The problem was determining how to do this without impairing either safety or the confidence of the crew.

The first modification was SIS1 (Stall Inhibitor System No. 1). Basically computer software, this continually (many times per second) compared the achieved AoA with the limiting value. If the measured AoA exceeded the 80 per cent margin, then, as it continued to increase, the SIS1 software would progressively send a signal to the fly-by-wire output tending to cancel the input from the stick. Thus, the pilot would have to haul back increasingly strongly, until at 95 per cent of the limit value the stick would be immovable.

Testing of SIS1 was generally trouble-free, and was completed in March 1988. Between then and June 1988 it was installed in the first 17 aircraft. At this point SIS1 was superseded by SIS2, an improved installation matched with the same hardware as SEF (Stability Enhancement Function) but giving the same performance parameters as SIS1. This was installed in the remaining 83 aircraft between March 1988 and June 1990.

SEF is a more comprehensive system, incorporating additional sensors to measure the achieved AoA and other parameters more precisely, as well as a major upgrade in software to evaluate more clearly the true limits to which the aircraft may be flown and then recover. Under certain conditions, this allows AoA to exceed the limiting value. Obviously, this is to some degree 'pushing one's luck', where there is no margin for any untoward circumstance such as sudden aerodynamic turbulence. Even a birdstrike during the fly-up could stall a wing and destroy the aircraft.

SEF testing began in March 1988. The last 83 aircraft were scheduled to be retrofitted with SIS2/SEF between March 1988 and June 1990, though software verification took a little longer before the system became fully operable. The first 17 aircraft were retrofitted between November 1988 and January 1992. An accompanying table shows the

On 20 January 1988 Rockwell rolled out the 100th and final B-1B (86-0140) from the assembly shed prior to its move to the Automated Checkout Facility. The occasion was marked with a large turnout of the company employees who had worked so hard on the aircraft throughout its production run, and featured a flypast by the 85th aircraft in company with a safety chase F-106. The date was significant: exactly six years earlier Rockwell had signed the production contract for the first B-1B Lot I aircraft.

very significant increase in fuel load made possible by this modification, which required no changes to the aircraft itself:

Weights in pounds (lb)	Basic FCS	SIS1	SIS2/SEF
Low-altitude maximum weight	312,000	342,000	422,000
Basic empty weight	182,360	182,360	182,360
Crew	900	900	900
Equipment and supplies	3,630	3,630	3,630
Weapon bay tank	-	-	1,130
Available payload	125,110	155,110	233,980
Eight SRAM	17,680	17,680	17,680
Eight B61	6,010	6,010	6,010
Support equipment	4,130	4,130	4,130
Recovery fuel	18,300	18,300	18,300
Fuel available for mission	78,990	108,990	187,860
Mission range (nm)	1,330	1,820	3,000

Despite the long prior experience with terrain-following flight in six versions of F-111, considerable difficulties were experienced in the early years of B-1B deployment. One was that the software could not handle the situation in hilly country. The software might guide the bomber over small obstructions but around large ones. The radar beam, sweeping from side to side, would 'look' up to 10 miles (16 km) ahead, but situations often arose in which the aircraft would be turned towards a large obstruction previously outside the scan limits. This was especially hard to handle when the aircraft had just passed over a smaller obstruction, and the large (and close) obstruction was detected by a fresh sweep just as the FCS was commanding the pitch-down on the far side of the small obstruction. One of the early software upgrade blocks limited the rate and magnitude of pitch-downs, and improved early detection of obstructions in turning flight.

Less serious, except to structural fatigue life and the demeanour and confidence level of the crew, were repeated unnecessary fly-ups in TER FLW. These were a plague for many years, and are still distressingly frequent. Part of the trouble is that automatic systems whose failure means death have to err very strongly on the side of being oversafe. Thus, the APQ-164 ORS software, the terrain-following avionics control unit, the radar altimeter input, the GNACU navigation computer and the central flight control computing software are all checked 16 times per second, and on every check more than 500 (nearly all harmless) fault conditions would cause an 'invalid' signal to be

sent to the FCS. Several of these in a row trigger a fly-up, an extremely firm zoom at 2.4 g sustained for 10 seconds. The expletives of the crew may be imagined.

With so many variables and possible causes, fly-ups on some training missions have been commanded every three minutes. Facetiously, one could say such a switchback ride hardly leaves time between fly-ups to make progress towards the target, besides making nonsense of the aircraft's ability to hug the terrain. The Air Force goal has always been an MTBUF (mean time between unnecessary fly-ups) of 15 minutes over all types of terrain, at any penetrating height, speed or hard/soft ride setting. ORS software Blocks 6.3 and 7.1 were intended to improve the achieved rate, but testing in spring 1988 gave no significant improvement, with the MTBUF rate still fluctuating between three and 50 minutes. By 1989 ORS Block 8.1, matched with AFS (avionics flight software) Block 4.5, did achieve something, but fleet-wide the Air Force 15-minute goal has yet to be met except in favourable circumstances.

Modified real beam mapping modes have recently been added to the APQ-164 to allow the crew to change settings and weapon parameters in flight.

The DAS nightmare

At least as serious as the shortfall in achieved range in low-altitude penetrations was the failure of the defensive avionics system to perform as advertised. This was the chief supposed 'scandal' latched upon by the media, who were delighted at the idea of a bomber that could jam its own emissions. The basic problem was inability of the massive, distributed and astronomically complex DAS, comprising ALQ-161A, ASQ-184 and the TWF (as described earlier), to detect, identify, locate and counter predicted Soviet defence systems while ignoring any others. The system could usually detect, locate and identify most of the older known Soviet air defence radars, but not a range of newer equipment brought into service in the 1980s. There were even more serious problems in the unprecedentedly ambitious system of active countermeasures, and also in the TWF intended to counter interception by fighters and air-launched missiles from the rear, which was inadequate to deal with newer generations of Soviet interceptors and missiles.

In this situation, an attacking B-1B would have either to

avoid all the threats, or find a track protected by only very sparse defences which the DAS could handle, or else destroy the threat. Destruction of ground installations is assigned to the cruise missiles, especially SRAM. These all have nuclear warheads, and there are obvious problems in setting off such explosions directly in the path of one's own aircraft, and any accompanying it.

The shortcomings had emerged progressively throughout the 1980s, as the DAS was developed. To meet the 1986 in-service demand the LRUs making up each system were produced in quantity at the same time. Thus, hardly any two B-1B bombers had identical installations, because improvements and upgrades were continually being introduced. Worse, all of these installations were in various ways deficient.

In 1986-87, the Air Force planned a considerably upgraded DAS, capable of meeting the original specifications (but ignoring the many later demands). This was to be a three stage project, to be completed by 1992. Mod 0 consisted of modifying all the aircraft installations so that all were at least to the same standard. This was an essential condition before trying to introduce improvements. In practice, it was decided to save money by not carrying out Mod 0 on 18 aircraft, which it was planned would be brought directly up to Mod 2 standard when this had been designed. The other 81 aircraft (one was lost during modification) were brought to uniform Mod 0 standard by late 1987.

Mod 1 introduced several new features, including the option of either manual or automatic jamming and operation of the TWF. It included a range of hardware changes, but the central task was to develop a new DAS software entitled Block 4.0. The Mod 1 installation was flight tested in March-June 1988. It was soon apparent that, though the Mod 1 system had 'good capabilities to identify and counter the top 10 airborne threats', it was unable to process a large number of radar signals simultaneously, as would be encountered from ground installations, even though this had (of course) been part of the original B-1B specifications. The root cause lay in the basic architecture of the processing circuits covering the eight radar bands. This is a far more difficult problem to overcome than a mere fault in individual circuits or even in a complete LRU, and solving it is still an ongoing problem.

The 1987 plan had been to design and test Mod 2 in 1988-89, and to complete installation on the fleet by 1992. By 1988 it was clear that this objective had to be abandoned, and Mod 2 was put on hold. As an interim move, as Mod 1 did effect improvements, this was deployed on the operational B-1Bs from 1990, including the 18 aircraft previously selected to go straight to Mod 2. Meanwhile, fur-

ther options were studied to try to rescue as much of the existing DAS as possible. Priority was accorded to simplifying the ALQ-161A architecture to process signals in a reduced range of bands. This gave a capability against the most serious known threats, both air and ground, while preventing the processors from becoming overloaded.

The seriousness of the situation was, and is, underlined by noting that these attempts to salvage an effective capability were in order to meet the original specification, which was drawn up against the Soviet defence systems of the 1980s. Even the revised ALQ-161 system was not expected to be able to be effective against air defence threats of the 1990s. The B-1B's defensive avionics will probably never

The B-1B was designed to be as maintainer-friendly as possible, with many systems being readily accessible. Here ground troops work on the hingeing upper wing flap mechanism, which incorporates an inflatable bag to seal any gaps when the wing is swept back.

Left: Of the various weapon bay interfaces the most important in the 1990s is the Conventional Weapons Module (CWM), which can mount up to 28 Mk 82 iron bombs on diagonal swinging supports. For cluster weapons based on the SUU-64/65 dispenser the maximum load for each CWM is 30.

A view of the Dyess flight line in 1991 shows B-1Bs of the 96th Bomb Wing. From IOC being attained in October 1986, the B-1B force took its part in the SIOP nuclear retaliation plan, with aircraft sitting on ground alert armed with B61 and B83 free-fall weapons. On 27 September 1991 the SAC forces stood down from alert, to be replaced by a slowly increasing integration into the conventional force structure.

Rockwell B-1B Lancer

achieve the performance originally required in the near term, and could only achieve that level without major modification. By October 1995, however, the 419th Test Squadron were guardedly optimistic that many problems are being solved, and that 'early problems have been overcome'. The tail-mounted pulse-Doppler warning unit has been the subject of particular improvements. The only other bright feature in the entire story is that since 1991 the countries formerly making up the Soviet Union are generally considered to have ceased to pose a serious threat, and there are at present no indications that B-1Bs will have to face their air defence systems.

A less serious and unrelated problem has been shortcomings in the RFSMS (radio-frequency signal-management system). This is tasked principally with preventing emissions from the OAS (offensive avionics system) reaching the receiving antennas of the DAS, which could classify them as powerful defensive threats. It works by requiring the DAS continually to keep sending the OAS an 'Avoid' command on all the frequencies it is jamming, so that these are not used by the OAS. As soon as the DAS ceases using that frequency it sends the OAS a 'Delete' signal, opening that frequency to the use of the OAS.

It was soon found that the OAS frequently failed to keep track of the Avoid commands, and transmitted on banned frequencies. This has been addressed by Boeing designing improved software for the OAS, especially for the APQ-164 radar. The second problem was that sometimes the DAS failed to send the Delete command, thus progressively decreasing the number of frequencies available to the OAS. DAS software Mod 1 was intended to deal with the second problem, but again, like most DAS difficulties, it is a hard nut to crack. At present, if too many Avoid commands pile up, the OAS software simply ignores them.

The B-1B suffered from fuel leaks and these were second only to the DAS in generating media scorn, though in fact at its worst the rate was 20 leaks per 30 aircraft per month. The rate was one of the best ever achieved by a large USAF aircraft with all-integral tankage (the corresponding KC-135 figure was 55, and that for the C-141A was 70).

At its height, the situation required frequent washdown of the parking ramps. Today such fuel loss is extremely rare, but testing for leaks continues. On 26 May 1989 B-1B 83-0066 happened to be at Tinker AFB, the home of Oklahoma City ALC. The refuelling crew carried out a leak test, in which the system vents are plugged and the tanks pressurised. This was satisfactory, so they then began refuelling, but omitted to remove the plugs. When about 150,000 lb (240 tonnes) of fuel had been supplied, the No. 2 (forward intermediate) tank burst, blowing an 8 x 8-ft

(2.4 x 2.4-m) gap in the upper skin and damaging five frames. Rebuilding took six months.

CITS and birdstrikes

The Central Integrated Test System fell foul of its own complexity. As explained earlier, this was intended to facilitate maintenance by drawing attention to problems and pinpointing their source. To do this, it monitors about 22,000 parameters in the basic aircraft and in the OAS and DAS, and then issues more than 10,000 different maintenance codes. During early testing as many as 350 false alarms were issued on each flight.

Part of the trouble lay in faulty sensors, wiring and other hardware shortcomings, but the chief cause lay in the software. This has been repeatedly upgraded, progressively reducing the false-alarm rate per flight from 350 to 120, to 95, and then, from 1990, to less than five. In recent years many flights have been completed with no CITS false indication, apart from the DAS. The ongoing difficulties with that system have naturally affected maintenance and fault indications regarding it.

Apart from faulty indications, a major CITE Expansion programme, as well as CEPS (CITS Expert Parameter System), have been proceeding since 1985. CEPS is a ground-based processor which supplements the inflight diagnostics with analytical rules for determining maintenance action. It has reached Phases IIIA (Boeing), IIIB (Rockwell) and IIIC (AIL). CITE Expansion addresses the major improvement in electronic miniaturisation since the early 1980s, allowing more of the possible parameters to be used in automatic fault detection and isolation.

On 28 September 1987, B-1B 84-0052 was flying at high speed at low level over the radar bomb-scoring site at La Junta, New Mexico, with its crew of four plus two instructors. It was thought that a large bird impacted the support between an engine nacelle and the wing, penetrating the wing and breaking fuel, hydraulic and electrical lines. Whether or not this was the case, fire broke out and the crew abandoned the aircraft. Neither instructor had time to egress through the bottom hatch and both were killed, as was a crew member whose seat failed. Although it is inconceivable that birdstrikes had not been considered in the B-1B design, this accident resulted in a temporary suspension of low-level training and launched an engineering evaluation of areas where severe strikes could cause critical damage.

Five such locations were identified, including the wing/nacelle junction and support structure, the base of the fin ahead of the tailplane power unit and the leading edge immediately inboard of the wing pivot. In each case pro-

Above: The pilot enjoys a far better view from the B-1B cockpit than from a B-52, making formation flying and low-level work safer. The adoption of conventional roles has vastly expanded the range of mission profiles undertaken by the B-1, and consequently improved flying skill levels. SIOP missions were strictly single-ship sorties, whereas with conventional bombing formation-holding has become an important art.

Left: Two views give an impression of the excitement of flying a large bomber at high speed and low level. One depicts using the TFR to thread through a desert mountain landscape; the other shows the aircraft thundering over the vast agricultural plains of Texas.

tective shields of hardened steel and/or Kevlar were designed, to be attached by adhesive bonding and mechanical fasteners. These were produced as kits. By February 1989 Rockwell had fitted these to 29 line aircraft, and Oklahoma City ALC to the remaining 67.

Of course, B-1Bs have suffered hundreds of birdstrikes, but few have caused problems. An exception occurred to aircraft 86-0099 on 19 September 1990. A flock of ducks was encountered during night TER FLW at high speed over Montana. A normal landing was made despite fractured windscreens, which severely impaired forward view and threatened to implode until airspeed had been allowed to bleed off.

Fire suppression and wingsweep

On 8 November 1988, B-1B 85-0063 was close to Dyess AFB when uncontrolled fire broke out above the left engines in the overwing fairing area. The crew ejected safe-

ly. There was no suggestion of a birdstrike, the cause being a fuel leak – possibly due to failure of a fuel manifold –and it at once became apparent that the same failure might have caused the previous B-1B loss by fire just over a year earlier. Urgent action was taken to prevent a recurrence.

In Phase 1, two fire-detection loops were added in each overwing fairing. Upon receiving a warning, the pilot depresses and latches that indicator, shutting off the 4-in (10-cm) main fuel pipe and the 2-in (5-cm) pipe to the nacelle pre-cooler, closing the crossfeed shutoff valves and opening the air-induction valves to ensure quick drainage of the fuel lines. In Phase 2, dams and drains were added to prevent any fuel from being ignited, and two Halon extinguisher bottles were added to discharge into the overwing fairing.

On 10 March 1986 the first aircraft delivered to SAC, 83-0065, took off on the first flight of an instructor team. The first demonstration involved flight at different sweep

angles, in the course of which the wings eventually refused to move from the 55° position. With wings at this setting, one engine shut down and the other in afterburner, fuel was taken from a KC-135A. After many tests and practice approaches a landing was made at 238 kt airspeed (252 kt, 290 mph, 467 km/h ground speed). The cause was the breakage of the interconnect cable which mechanically feeds wing angle to the control box. Unable to determine the sweep angle(s), the box locked the wings. It was found that there was no drawing or other data showing the correct routing for the cable, the surrounding duct for which had in this aircraft become kinked, causing the breakage. A standard kink-free routing was promptly designed, and all aircraft were modified.

As originally built, the first 26 B-1Bs suffered chafing and severing of electric cables when the wings entered the fuselage at the 67.5° position. Another problem encountered

Below: The B-1B has a commendably short landing run, despite the lack of thrust reversing or brake chute. While powerful Goodyear five-rotor carbon brakes are fitted, the aircraft also uses aerodynamic braking in the form of the overwing spoilers and by setting the stabilators at maximum deflection. The strong undercarriage can cope with landings at 90 per cent of maximum take-off weight.

by an early aircraft (84-0051) was that during the pre-taxi check the left wing continued to rotate forward past the 15° setting and penetrated the No. 2 fuel tank. The cause was a combination of incorrect rigging of the sweep system, a broken left gearbox quill-shaft, worn splines on the right angle-gearbox joining the drive shafts, and a damaged control shaft linking the left and right hydraulic drives.

Nose-gear and F101 fan failures

On 4 October 1989 aircraft 85-0070 suffered inflight failure of Hydraulics No. 2, losing nosewheel steering, 20 per cent of braking capacity and requiring the alternate (No. 3) system to be used for gear extension. After a conference at Dyess, inflight refuelling, two hard touch-and-gos on the main gears, and various workaround procedures, a nose-gear-up landing was made on the Shuttle runway at Edwards, with little damage. The cause was that the electrical plug supplying the nose-gear emergency (alternate) selector valve had become disconnected.

On 14 October 1990 aircraft 86-0128 was in the course of a task-packed training mission when, as engines went to MIL power to start a climb, there was a loud explosion, and the crew became aware of an orange glow. Several Master Caution lights lit, and a blue flame was seen streaming from the left side. After shutting down No. 1 engine and pressing that engine's fire push-button, a night landing was made at Pueblo, Colorado. Uncontained failure of No. 1 engine fan had caused severe local damage, including severing the forward engine mounts. The engine had broken completely away from the aircraft, fortunately without hitting anything, but the burning main fuel line damaged the tailplane and aft radome. The aircraft was ferried on three engines to Tinker (Oklahoma City ALC) with jury struts in the No. 1 engine nacelle.

Just over two months later, on 19 December 1990, aircraft 83-0071 was engaged in night touch-and-gos when, on engines going to MIL power, the crew felt a sharp jolt and again became aware of an orange glow. Engine No. 3 was shut down, and its fire button pushed. Again, the cause was uncontained fan failure.

On the following day all B-1Bs were grounded, except any on alert status. At the 100,000-hour point there had been six F101 fan failures. GE designed completely new first-stage fan blades, with part-span dampers. As an interim palliative, the first-stage retaining ring, made of 0.06-in (0.15 cm) stainless steel, was replaced by a ring made of 0.125-in (0.32-cm) Inconel 718, and severe standards were introduced for first-stage damage, checked by an inspection before each flight and an eddy-current check every 25 hours.

Above: With vortices streaming from the wingtips, a 37th BS B-1B pulls g. During the early 1990s the B-1B fleet was stripped of its exhaust nozzle actuator fairings ('turkey feathers') as part of a weight and complexity reducing programme. This was achieved at the expense of slightly increased drag.

Left: The FS 36118 gunship grey scheme began to appear in late 1990, but took some time to be applied fleet-wide. Initially the radome was left in dark grey, but subsequently a dielectric version of gunship grey was developed. Nevertheless, the nosecone and ECM tailcone do feature a subtly darker shade compared with the rest of the aircraft.

Rockwell B-1B Lancer

In a programme originally known as Accelerated Co-pilot Enrichment (ACE) and now known as Companion Trainer Program (CTP), trainer aircraft are assigned to bomb wings to provide extra flight hours without the expense of operating the mission aircraft. B-1B wings have Northrop T-38 Talons assigned, this combination comprising a 28th BW B-1B flying with a 319th BW T-38A. The Talons are painted in the same gunship grey as the mission bombers.

Early flight testing showed that the thermal anti-icing system on the engine inlets and RCS vanes was inadequate. There was little danger, but ice building up on unprotected areas and then entering the engine was requiring fan blades to be replaced. Remedial action involved prolonged investigation and test at Arnold Engineering Development Center and the NASA Lewis icing tunnel, leading to a variety of thermal, electrothermal and pneumatic answers. In 1995 a definitive solution was still being sought.

Structural problems

Despite the severe stresses imposed by fast low TER FLW flight, no dangerous airframe failure has occurred, but there have been many minor cracks. Aircraft 85-0069 was found to have a crack in the 25° shoulder (upper left) fuselage longeron at Station 928, just ahead of the wing carry-through. Fleet inspection revealed similar cracks, on either side of the aircraft, in 38 B-1Bs with over 700 hours. Most

of these aircraft had the SMCS deactivated, which significantly accelerates the onset of fatigue damage. The Air Force immediately prohibited high-speed low-level missions without the SMCS operative, and the 38 cracks were drilled to prevent them continuing, and covered with bolted light-alloy plates.

In July 1991 one of the cracks was discovered to be progressing beyond the crackstopper hole. Further inspection found either new cracks, or drilled cracks continuing to spread, in 16 aircraft. Rockwell designed a boron-epoxy cover plate which was attached to all 96 active aircraft by adhesive and bolts. This is expected to provide a fix.

Fatigue has caused cracks in other regions. The upper mount for the main landing gear primary actuator is one example, and this has been redesigned with larger dimensions, and the material has been changed from titanium to steel. Fatigue was also causing loss of vortex generators on the fin root and upper rear fuselage. The hoped-for cure is to move generators Nos 4-6 from the body to the fin and raise Nos 7-10 plus a new 11th blade around the top of the rear fuselage. Another affected item is a bellcrank in the nose-gear uplock mechanism. Failed cranks have been welded, and the unit will be redesigned.

A different airframe problem has been delamination of the very large cockpit windscreens, supplied by Pilkington and Sierracin. These are thick sandwiches of hard outer glass and structural polycarbonate, bonded by a silicone interlayer. The cause is believed to be inbuilt stress, accentuated by thermal and/or pressurisation loads. New windshields from both suppliers are on test.

Weapon and other problems

Unlike ALCM, the AGM-129A ACM has been designed from the outset for external carriage on supersonic aircraft. Thus, it was designed to accept an acoustic environment at the intense level of 162 dB (decibels). Measurements taken in low-level flight at Mach 0.85 showed acoustic levels often as high as 165 dB. This is not considered to present a problem, because there were no plans to launch ACMs except while standing off at higher altitudes at lower speeds, where noise is a small fraction of that at low level. Should it be necessary to carry the ACM in high-subsonic flight at low level, the outer pair in the rearmost row could be removed, because the 10 remaining missiles experience lower acoustic levels. With termination of nuclear-weapon training, the problem should not arise.

Development of the CWM made it much easier to load

The B-1B is currently undergoing Phase I of its CMUP (Conventional Mission Upgrade Program). To be completed by the third quarter of FY96, Phase I adds the CBU-87, CBU-89 and CBU-97 cluster munitions (based on the SUU-64/65 dispensers) to the B-1B's armoury. Until this is completed, only the Mk 82 is available, demonstrated here by this 7th Wing aircraft carrying BDU-50 AIR training stores for the 500-lb (227-kg) bomb.

conventional bombs, of which the Mk 82 AIR is the only type currently certified, but problems were encountered in dropping such bombs from the aft bay. After various investigations, including varying spoiler position, a cure was found in simply ensuring that the intermediate-bay doors are open.

An endemic problem which has very gradually eased has been shortage of spare parts, caused entirely by inadequate funding. Throughout 1987 the first two B-1B bases were able to keep flying only by cannibalisation (removing parts from one aircraft to keep another mission capable). At this time the number of such 'canns' fluctuated between 0.9 and 2.9 per sortic, and at the first base, Dyess, the mission-capable rate (including partially capable) over the period June 1987-June 1988 varied from 28.2-45.9 per cent, which are unacceptable levels. The matter is referred to in thesection 'Today and tomorrow'.

Prolonged difficulties with the electrical systems have proved difficult to pin down. In several aircraft one particular generator (alternator) has failed repeatedly, and three consecutive aircraft (Nos 47, 48 and 49) suffered frequent anomalies and local failures. On 9 February 1988 one of these, No. 48 (85-0088), even suffered total electrical failure while landing in severe winter weather. Despite the whole aircraft being 'dark', the landing was successful, but the inoperability of the electrical throttle interconnects caused problems, as did Bus No. 3 failure and lack of nose-wheel steering. The flight and maintenance crews then had to work for 40 minutes to shut down the engines.

Because of its role, the crew-escape system has to be especially reliable. As related, one crew member was killed through seat failure, and among minor failures has been deterioration of the cadmium plating in the thruster, which has allowed oil to leak on the output and input cartridges.

The trouble came to light when it was found that a cartridge and energy-transfer line had actually fired on the ground. Fleet inspection showed 59 thrusters to be suffering oil leakage. The cadmium has been replaced by chrome plating.

Another problem was the discovery that letting the hatches over the aft crew stations open beyond the 41° limit could break the remover extension lock. This could cause the hatch to unlock under pressurisation load, and in fact three hatches blew off in flight. Yet another egress system difficulty has been the cost of maintenance. Among other things, the system on each aircraft includes 18 time delays, 26 AND gates and about 560 energy transfer lines, all of which must be frequently inspected, and replaced after quite short intervals, such as four years. It is intended that this complex network will be replaced by a new system based on fibre optics, which might reduce maintenance costs by 80 per cent .

Among other events which had little bearing on the design of the aircraft have been various minor fires, both in flight and on the ground, and a mid-air collision. The collision occurred with a KC-135R tanker, which happened to be behind and above 86-0093. Severe damage resulted to the bomber's fin, rudder and left tailplane, and to the tanker's right forward fuselage.

The latest problem to emerge in the B-1B community has been as a direct result of adopting new roles and modes of operation. Because defensive countermeasures are now more likely to be used in dynamic (as opposed to straight and level) flight, the trajectories of ejected IRCM flares have become more critical. In certain manoeuvres, flares can strike the aircraft's tail, and in one instance a burning flare actually embedded in the fin within feet of the rudder. The long-term solution will be to use a lightweight flare

In landing configuration a 28th BW 'Bone' cruises across the Ellsworth flight line. With many of its maintenance and defensive system headaches behind it, the B-1 is a highly capable power projection vehicle. The SIS2/SEF flight control software updates have had a profound effect on the aircraft's ability to carry nearly full fuel loads during terrain-following flight, in turn vastly increasing the aircraft's effective range in an operational scenario.

B-1B world records

2,000-km circuit with payload
On 4 July 1987 an acceptance flight from Palmdale by 86-0098, B-1B No. 58, included a 2,000-km (1,243-mile) rectangular circuit off the coast of California. Weapons-bay tanks filled with water provided a payload of 30000 kg (66,138 lb). The course was completed at an average speed of 1,077.5 km/h (669.52 mph), setting speed records over this distance with 14 different payloads.

5,000-km circuit with payload
On 17 September 1987, 86-0110, B-1B No. 70, was similarly loaded with a 30000-kg (66,138-lb) payload and then flew a triangular course from Edwards with turning points off the coast opposite Seattle and in southern Colorado. The average speed was 1,054 km/h (655 mph). This set nine records for payloads carried over a circuit of 5000 km (3,107 miles).

Time to height (various weight classes)
On 28 and 29 February and 18 March 1992 aircraft 86-0111 and 86-0121 were used to set time-to-height records in three weight classes:
C.10 (80,000-100,000 kg): 86-0111, 3000 m (9,843 ft) in 1.22 minutes; 86-0111, 6000 m (19,685 ft) in 1.70 minutes; 86-0111, 9000 m (29,528 ft) in 2.18 minutes; 86-0121, 12000 m (39,370 ft) in 5.03 minutes.
C.1P (100,000-150,000 kg): 86-0121, 3000 m in 1.32 minutes; 86-0121, 6000 m in 1.92 minutes; 86-0121, 9000 m in 2.38 minutes; 86-0121, 12000 m in 6.15 minutes.
C.1Q (150,000-200,000 kg): 86-0121, 3000 m in 2.0 minutes; 86-0111, 6000 m in 2.65 minutes; 86-0111, 9000 m in 3.8 minutes; 86-0121, 12000 m in 9.7 minutes.

Circumnavigation
On 11-14 August 1993, two B-1Bs flew around the world with one intermediate landing. On 2-3 June 1995 aircraft 84-0057 and 85-0082 flew a training mission called Coronet Bat which involved flying around the world non-stop, via the Strait of Gibraltar, Indian Ocean and Aleutian Islands. There were six air refuellings, and BDU-50 AIR practice bombs were dropped on the Pacino range in Italy, Torishima range in Okinawa and the Utah Test and Training Range. The distance was 22,865.6 miles (36797.65 km), and the elapsed time 36 hours 13 minutes and 36 seconds, giving an average speed of 631.16 mph (1015.75 km/h). Despite the dogleg route, and need to make three precision bombing runs, this mission set Absolute and Class C.1Q FAI records. This raised the B-1B's total of world records to 38.

Rockwell B-1B Lancer

(perhaps replacing metal parts with plastic) but in the interim the envelope in which chaff and flares can be released has been severely limited.

B-1B today and tomorrow

Probably no aircraft in history has had such a protracted gestation as the B-1B. Undoubtedly no aircraft built in such quantity has been as complicated, and as a direct result few have experienced so many difficulties. Despite this, everyone who flies or maintains the 'Bone' (only press releases call it by the name it was given on 1 March 1990 - Lancer) believes it to be the best bomber in the world.

Certainly, regarded just as a flying machine, the B-1B is outstanding. Russian and Ukrainian bomber pilots envy the 'Bone' drivers their ability to pole this big machine round the sky with a fighter-like stick, while watching a big VSI (vertical situation display). At the same time, it has its limitations. Since 1 July 1994, 10 of the bombers have been active with the 184th BG of the Kansas Air National Guard. Their pilots previously flew F-16s, and the cultural change has been considerable. Few would disagree with the 184th's Lieutenant Colonel Bob Murphy when he says, "I miss the manoeuvrability in a fighter." The B-1B needs 18 miles to make a 180° turn.

In the late 1980s the B-1B had settled in SAC service as a satisfactorily mature aircraft. In 1988 B-1B units competed for the first time in the SAC Bombing Competition. They won the coveted Mathis Trophy for the best radar-bombing scores and the Dougherty Trophy for the best

SRAM launches, and took first and third places in low-level bombing. In 1990 the 28th BW achieved an amazing ORI (Operational Readiness Inspection) score of 0.99, the highest in USAF history, though this was a very special effort and by no means representative.

Throughout the early years of B-1B service the debate continued over stand-off versus penetration. Compared with the B-52 the B-1B is a very superior penetrator, but compared with the B-2 it is extremely vulnerable. A 1988 Congressional study commented: "Stand-off munitions are needed because the B-1B is too valuable for the risky mission of flying over a target..." It continued: "The B-1B is currently ill-prepared for many conventional conflicts where the targets are well defended or multiple sorties are required. As currently configured, the bomber could be used for single sorties against poorly defended targets, but the Air Force has a number of other aircraft well suited to that task."

That was a fairly damning indictment, and despite a great deal of development, on both the aircraft and its payloads, in the third quarter of 1995 little has happened to invalidate this harsh judgement, although the way in which the world has changed has rendered long-range penetration of heavily defended targets much less relevant. While considerable strides have been made to improve the reliability of the B-1B, and as far as the DAS is concerned these efforts will continue into the next millennium, little has so far been achieved – except behind the scenes – to improve its capability to deliver weapons.

Near-elimination of the threat posed by the former Soviet Union has made the use of nuclear weapons by the United States unthinkable. In the summer of 1995 a Russian delegation inspected every active B-1B to ensure that its weapon bays did not have facilities for arming and fusing the B61 or B83 bombs, nor an intermediate-bay bulkhead in the forward position to permit carriage of ALCMs. Current USAF doctrine is that the United States' nuclear bombers are the B-2 and B-52H; of the four combat formations which fly the B-1B today, only one (7th Wing, Dyess) still has a SIOP mission.

This leaves the B-1B with no weapons except a single type of 'iron bomb': the 500-lb Mk 82 AIR (it is intended to be fitted with a launcher for the 2,000-lb Mk 84), requiring 'the risky mission of flying over a target'. Pointedly, the B-1B played no role in the 1991 Gulf War, when its mission was nuclear only, nor in Bosnia.

Most of the post-1991 numerical assessments of B-1B capability against real-world targets are classified, but they are not encouraging. Part of the problem has been the difficulty of making reliable estimates of the defence systems actually in place protecting targets in Russia, Ukraine, Iraq, Bosnia and other potential trouble spots − which are far more varied than in the old days when there was just one giant 'baddie'. Moreover, whereas in nuclear war a loss rate of 50 per cent might be acceptable, today a sustained loss rate of 5 per cent would be considered politically unacceptable. Indeed, even one B-1B shot down would cause problems for the administration in some scenarios.

Today the B-1B crews repeatedly fly gruelling training missions, a significant proportion at night, which involve high-level and low-level bombing against various simulated defences, air refuelling and very long Global Power missions which have even involved non-stop multiple-target flights around the world. Many missions involve distant friendly air forces as either partners or as opposition. In recent years many missions have been flown in strike packages.

When General John Michael Loh became the Commander of Air Combat Command, he said, "The B-1 can fly in packages with fighters and other aircraft designed to suppress air defences. This reduces the B-1's vulnerability to attack and, with the B-1 included, these packages have far greater firepower than if composed of fighters alone." Some strike packages have teamed the B-1B with the F-15C, F-15E, F-16 and EF-111A, each making a particular contribution. In Red Flag exercises strike packages have typically comprised the B-1B, F-15C, F-15E, F-16C and E-3A, and, where forces are to be inserted to capture a site, the C-130.

Continuing upgrades

In the real world, today's B-1B would almost certainly go to war with a 15-ft (4.5-m) tank in the forward bay and 56 Mk 82 AIR bombs in the intermediate and aft bays. Bombing accuracy is highest from the forward bay, but the differences in CEP (circular error probable) between the bays is merely a matter of a few feet. With so expensive a delivery system it is ridiculous not to have the ability to deliver a wide range of weapons, and the picture must change dramatically over the next decade. In this period the following upgrades are predicted.

Apart from striving to reach even higher crew standards, for example reflected in radar bomb scores, the main recent development has been the decision to qualify all backseaters as WSO (Weapon Systems Officers), each able to sit in either the left or the right seat as the OSO or DSO.

The continuing saga of the DAS will run for years to come, and it is too early to predict the outcome. Meanwhile, the Air Force and many contractors continue to try to reduce the RCS (radar cross-section) and the IR signature, improve the defensive chaff and flares, reduce the need for emissions (especially strong ones, however brief, beamed far ahead of the aircraft), study the use of towed or

This underview graphically illustrates the lift-enhancing surfaces on the wing, comprising full-span leading-edge slats and large trailing-edge flaps. In addition to increasing camber, the flaps are of the Fowler type, extending to increase actual wing area.

Nudging into the transonic regime, a B-1B creates its own clouds around the trailing edge of the wing and stabilators. The aircraft is from the 7th Wing, which not only controls the Dyess B-1Bs, but also administers the C-130 tactical transports of the former 463rd Airlift Wing.

Rockwell B-1B Lancer

of B-1Bs in Phase 1 of an ongoing three-part Conventional Mission Upgrade Program (CMUP). One element of the programme due for completion in the near term is integration with a new launcher to carry the Mk 84 2,000-lb bomb. This launcher will fit the 15-ft (4.5-m) bay and will carry either eight or 10 bombs. A recent description of the launcher gives the figure as 10, giving a combined capacity of 30, while an equally recent statement of aircraft capabilities lists the planned overall capacity as 24. Tests are also currently under way to enable the aircraft to carry CBU-87, and CBU-97 and Rockeye II CBUs, and the CBU-89 Gator mine system. The 419th have flown some 600 hours in 150 sorties in support of CMUP, and aim to obtain a 40-millisecond interval for dropping the CBU-87/89 and CBU-97. Bombs collide at faster intervals. Full service clearance is expected by August 1997. At the same time it is intended to obtain limited clearance to use a variety of GBU laser-guided bombs, and limited flight test sorties have already been flown, using ground-based and buddy designators. There are no plans for the B-1B to self designate.

Weapon plans

Several more sophisticated weapons will greatly enhance the B-1B's capability in 1996-2001. These include PGMs (Precision Guided Munitions) of several kinds:

The JDAM (Joint Direct Attack Munition) will be deployed in large numbers. It is a 1,000-lb or 2,000-lb bomb with a guidance kit and a control kit at the tail and nose respectively. The prime contractor will be either Lockheed Martin or McDonnell Douglas, the selection to be made in late 1995 or early 1996. The guidance kit comprises an inertial navigation system which steers the bomb to a target location given by a GPS receiver. The airframe flight-control components include large nose fins. Launched from high altitude, a JDAM will glide up to 12 miles (19 km). It is planned to be issued in very small numbers to B-2 units in 1996-97, each aircraft carrying 16. Once in full production, JDAMs will be supplied to B-1B units around 1998-99, each aircraft carrying up to 24.

The JSOW (Joint Stand-Off Weapon) is not a modified bomb but the AGM-154 winged missile, developed by Texas Instruments. It uses almost the same GPS-located INS guidance as JDAM, but from high altitude can glide up to 40 miles (64 km) carrying a payload in the 1,000-lb (454-kg) class. This could comprise a unitary warhead, but the first payload will comprise a cloud of cluster charges called CEBs (Combined Effects Bomblets), which are highly effective against soft targets. The B-1B will get JSOW around 2001, again probably carrying up to 24.

The WCMD (Wind-Corrected Munitions Dispenser) is an add-on to 40,000 existing payload dispensers which will correct for the difference between estimated and actual wind. The bomber will again drop the weapon on GPS co-ordinates, placing the dispensers at predetermined payload-release points up to 8 miles (13 km) from the drop. On the long drop from high altitude the modest corrections needed to achieve this can be imparted by very small fins. Each dispenser will release 40 sub-munitions, which would normally be the SFW (Sensor-Fused Weapon) or Skeet. Developed by Textron, these heat-seeking copper slugs are designed to home on the relatively thin top armour of tanks. Each B-1B will carry up to 30 WCMDs, compared with 16 for the B-2.

An advanced PGM was the Northrop AGM-137 TSSAM. B-1B units were to have received TSSAM by 2001, but the weapon has now been cancelled in its present form, in favour of the similar JASSM weapon. This is a stand-off precision missile.

While these clever new weapons will be welcome, urgent action is needed to enable the B-1B to do what is likely to be its main job 'for real' throughout the foreseeable future: to maintain a high sortie rate with conventional

even free-flying decoys (as protected many of the first B-52s), and also the use of self-defence missiles fired either ahead or to the rear. Whatever the outcome, it is easy to lose sight of the fact that the B-1B is already as well-protected as any aircraft in the inventory, and in short range, low intensity operations could almost certainly expect to operate with jamming and EW support.

Specific upgrades could be the significantly better targeting capability conferred by fitting a high-resolution FLIR and/or an improved SAR (synthetic aperture radar). Combined with a laser ranger, a FLIR could provide the terrain-sensing information needed for TER FLW in all conditions, without the need for dangerous emissions ahead of the aircraft. It might also enable a forward warning system to counter oncoming missiles to be provided without having to duplicate the emissions of the TWF in the forward hemisphere. Another possibility is to give the right-hand pilot an electronic workstation where the mission could be replanned as it proceeds. This might be needed, for example, to avoid a newly discovered hostile defence site or hit a recently moved mobile target.

One of the highest priorities is obviously to give the B-1B the capability to deliver weapons other than the Mk 82 AIR. The 419th Test Squadron is presently using a pair

Mk 82 AIR bombs from austere sites. Even at a major ACC base the lack of a pre-load facility slows the mission rate up seriously. It takes a C-5 or C-117 to bring in the MHU-196/M trailer, which weighs 40,000 lb (18.15 tonnes), needed for a loaded CWM. When the B-1B returns from a mission the module must be serviced *in situ*. Fifty-six spent impulse cartridges must be removed from each CWM. Then the area is scrubbed to remove carbon, and fresh cartridges put in and the wiring checked. Then 28 bombs must be loaded. Loading the first bomb takes up to 40 minutes, and every subsequent bomb needs not less than five minutes, so loading each CWM takes three hours. If there are three modules, and if there is only one loading crew per aircraft, the gap between missions cannot be less than nine hours. With three crews operating, however, the minimum sortie interval is three hours, and this is probably good enough for most scenarios.

The poor MCR (mission-capable rate) of 55 per cent, the average of all B-1B units, spurred Congress to demand a major Operational Readiness Assessment. This was demanded in the FY94 Defense Authorization Act, and took place at the 28th BW from 1 June to 30 November 1994. The objective was to prove that, in General Loh's words, "The B-1B is a star performer, and when manned and funded at the right level can sustain MCRs in excess of 75 per cent." Secretary of the Air Force Sheila E. Widnall said the challenge was welcomed: "It's really something we should have done a long time ago."

During most of the test the 28th flew training missions from Ellsworth at an accelerated rate. Towards the end it deployed a squadron to Roswell, New Mexico, to simulate flying from an austere location at wartime sortie rates. In fact, thanks to everything being available when needed, the 28th bettered the target. Over the six months of the test the ORA fluctuated between 82.8 and 85.6 per cent, the cumulative average being about 83.8.

It could be argued that the excellent results were meaningless, because they were so unrepresentative. Spare parts, equipment and people were brought in from the 7th BW and the 384th BW, at last bringing the 28th up to 100 per cent in all three respects. This was done at the expense of degrading the other two wings. It did show what was possible, however, given funding and commitment. As General Loh said, "For the first time in the history of the B-1B, we were able adequately to fund and man a unit for its mission." He added, "We showed that if you fund the B-1B to a given level of readiness, it can sustain that readiness. And if you improve the reliability, it can sustain those improved levels of readiness for the long term."

In August 1995 the General Accounting Office, ever seeking flaws in military arguments, claimed that the Air Force's report to Congress on the ORA situation had underestimated the cost of readiness upgrades. The Air Force had said it would need an extra $11 million to achieve a 75 per cent MCR for the entire B-1B force. The GAO said, "The Air Force assumes total success of the planned reliability, maintainability and management improvements," and instead of basing its estimates on a best case it should have used actual ORA data.

The Air Force, like the US administration, cannot afford to say, "There are no powerful enemies any more." One never knows what is around the next corner, and throughout the foreseeable future the B-1B could be by far its biggest and most important deliverer of conventional

The all-grey scheme adds much to the sinister image of the B-1B, but is also symbolic of the aircraft's coming of age and shift to the conventional mission. After Phase II of the CMUP the B-1 will be able to carry up to 24 2,000-lb JDAMs on rotary launchers, while in Phase III JSOW and JASSM will be added to give the B-1 highly accurate weapons. No plans have been made to give an autonomous laser designation capability, although the aircraft is theoretically capable of launching LGBs against targets designated by other systems.

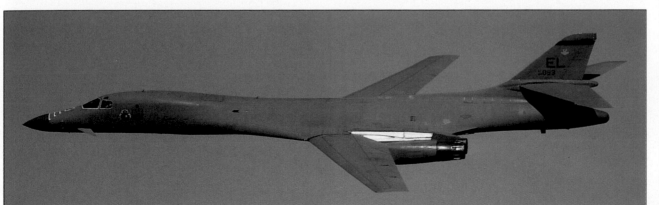

A B-1B of the Ellsworth-based 37th BS 'Tigers' displays the sleek lines of the bomber. By 1996/97 the B-1B will no longer have a SIOP nuclear mission. The 28th BW will be the first to lose this role, followed eventually by the 7th. By 1995 all B-1s were modified so that they could not carry nuclear weapons, although the SIOP mission remains part of the training syllabus. This is undertaken purely in simulators – all flying training being concerned with conventional tasks.

Rockwell B-1B Lancer

weapons. Unfortunately, it needs to have a lot of money spent on it to make the DAS work well enough to allow entirely autonomous operations, to equip the operating units with a wide range of stand-off and precision weapons, and to bring the MCR of the whole force above the 80 per cent level. It is merely a matter of money.

As the Cold War ended and the 1990s emerged as an era of new threats, the USAF devoted considerable effort to devising a 'bomber roadmap' (a term it no longer uses) to explain to Congress – which holds the purse strings – how the manned bomber force is expected to evolve in the final years of the century. Meanwhile, the Clinton administration completed a Bottom-up Review (BUR) to shape the

US military establishment and establish planning assumptions expected to be valid through 2014. None of this planning has ever suggested employing less than the entire force of B-1B Lancers. The 'roadmap' goal of 209 manned bombers (95 B-1B, 94 B-52H and 20 B-2) was USAF policy at the outset of 1995, but has since been challenged by an Institute for Defense Analyses (IDA) study which concluded that a bomber force of 95 B-1B, 66 B-52H, and 20 B-2 was sufficient to meet BUR requirements through 2014. As a result of the study, the USAF will retire 28 existing B-52H bombers in fiscal year 1996 – making the role of the Rockwell B-1B Lancer, the famous 'Bone' more important than ever. **Bill Gunston**

B-1B Individual Aircraft Details

B-1B Lot funding:

Lot I, FY82, one aircraft

82-0001 No. 1	Flight-test only		Leader of the Fleet, later Star of Abilene

Lot II, FY83, seven aircraft

83-0065 No. 2	Maintenance validation	Star of Abilene, Star of Palmdale
83-0066 No. 3		Ole Puss
83-0067 No. 4		Texas Raiders
83-0068 No. 5		Spuds (see 86-0119)
83-0069 No. 6		Silent Penetrator, Rebel
83-0070 No. 7	CWM test aircraft	7 Wishes
83-0071 No. 8		Grand Illusion, Spit Fire

Lot III, FY84, 10 aircraft

84-0049 No. 9	ALCM/SRAM II test	Thunder from the Sky
84-0050 No. 10	Hot/cold climate lab	Surf Rat, Surprise attack
84-0051 No. 11		Lucky Lady, Boss Hawg
84-0052 No. 12		Crashed unnamed
84-0053 No. 13	Ejection-seat tests	Lucky 13
84-0054 No. 14		Silver Bullet, Tasmanian Terror
84-0055 No. 15		Ridge Runner, Sunrise Surprise (see 86-0110)
84-0056 No. 16		Sweet Sixteen
84-0057 No. 17	RCS/EM interference	The Hellion
84-0058 No. 18		Master of Disaster

Lot IV, FY85, 34 aircraft

85-0059 No. 19		Super Glider, Better Duck, Bad Dog
85-0060 No. 20		Night Hawk, unnamed, Rolling Thunder
85-0061 No. 21		Maverick, French Connection, unnamed
85-0062 No. 22		Sky Dancer, Uncaged
85-0063 No. 23		crashed unnamed
85-0064 No. 24		Eliminator, Prairie Thunder
85-0065 No. 25		Trilogy of Terror, Texas Armor
85-0066 No. 26		Special Delivery, Mis[sic] Behavin, Deadwood Express, Missouri Miss, Badlands Bomber
85-0067 No. 27		Wild Thang, later Miss Behavin, Texas Raider
85-0068 No. 28	ACM test	
85-0069 No. 29		Daisy Mae
85-0070 No. 30		Excalibur
85-0071 No. 31		Liberator
85-0072 No. 32	Special mission tests	Polarized
85-0073 No. 33		Wings of Freedom, Cerberus
85-0074 No. 34		Penetrator, Crewdawg
85-0075 No. 35		Banshee, Dakota Demolition, Spirit of '76
85-0076 No. 36		Black Jack, crashed
85-0077 No. 37		Bones, Jap Happy, Hamton, Pride of South Dakota
85-0078 No. 38		Dakota Lightning, Heavy Metal
85-0079 No. 39		Warriors Dream, Classy Lady, Deadwood Dealer
85-0080 No. 40	ECM tests	Lady of the Nite, The Gatekeeper, Screamin' Demon
85-0081 No. 41		Equalizer
85-0082 No. 42		Gunsmoke, Global Power (also 85-0093)
85-0083 No. 43		Dark Star, Overnight Delivery
85-0084 No. 44		Pandora's Box
85-0085 No. 45		America No. 1, Brute Force

85-0086 No. 46		'My Mistress', Soaring with Eagles
85-0087 No. 47		Gremlin, Stars and Stripes
85-0088 No. 48		Phoenix, Loaded Dice
85-0089 No. 49		Midnight Prowler
85-0090 No. 50		Trail Blazer, Tiger Country
85-0091 No. 51	CWL carriage/release	Thor
85-0092 No. 52		Enforcer

Lot V, FY86, 48 aircraft

86-0093 No. 53		Ruthless Raven, Global Power
86-0094 No. 54		Night Hawk
86-0095 No. 55		Mistique, Undecided
86-0096 No. 56		Thunder Child, Wolf Pack
86-0097 No. 57		Iron Eagle
86-0098 No. 58	Used for speed records	Freedom I
86-0099 No. 59	Live Mk 82 tests	Ghost Rider
86-0100 No. 60		Phantom, Night Hawk
86-0101 No. 61		Iron Butterfly, Low Level Devil
86-0102 No. 62		Lady Hawk, Black Hills Sentinel
86-0103 No. 63		Huntress, Lovely Lady, Reluctant Dragon
86-0104 No. 64		American Flyer
86-0105 No. 65		Snake Eyes
86-0106 No. 66		Lone Wolf, crashed
86-0107 No. 67		Vindicator, Valkyries, Bad to the B-One
86-0108 No. 68		Hawk, Alien with an Attitude
86-0109 No. 69		Spectre
86-0110 No. 70	Speed/payload records	Sunrise Surprise
86-0111 No. 71	Time-to-height records	Ace in the Hole
86-0112 No. 72		Vanna, Black Widow
86-0113 No. 73		Charon, Viper, Dakota Reveille
86-0114 No. 74		Wolfhound, Dakota Drifter
86-0115 No. 75		Bump and Run, Top Secret
86-0116 No. 76		Victress
86-0117 No. 77		Millennium Falcon, Pride of North Dakota
86-0118 No. 78		Iron Mistress
86-0119 No. 79		Spud, Christine
86-0120 No. 80		Mad Dawg
86-0121 No. 81	Bottom-bailout tests	Exterminator, Terminator, Zeppelin, Maiden America
86-0122 No. 82		Excalibur
86-0123 No. 83		Molester, Lester, High Noon
86-0124 No. 84		Penetrator, Winged Thunder
86-0125 No. 85		Shack Attack
86-0126 No. 86		The Gun Fighter, Minotaur, Command Decision, Kansas Lancer
86-0127 No. 87		Freedom Bird, Ivan's Nightmare, Nightmare, Kansas Lancer
86-0128 No. 88	Climatic testing	The Hawk, Miss Behavin, Boss, Pony Soldier
86-0129 No. 89		Pegasus
86-0130 No. 90		The Rose, Bad Company
86-0131 No. 91		The 8th's Wonder, Ultimate Warrior
86-0132 No. 92		The Wizard, Oh Hardluck
86-0133 No. 93		Big Bird, The Outlaw, unnamed, Black Hills Bandit
86-0134 No. 94		Green Hornet, Night Mission, Wild Ass Ride
86-0135 No. 95		Make My Day, The Watchdog
86-0136 No. 96		Special Delivery (see 85-0066)
86-0137 No. 97		Wichita Express
86-0138 No. 98		Easyrider Too, Grand Illusion II
86-0139 No. 99		Gallant Warrior
86-0140 No. 100	EMP compatibility testing	Valda J, Peace Warrior

83-0070 – 7 Wishes
7th Wing, Dyess AFB

86-0108 – Alien With An attitude
7th Wing, Dyess AFB

86-0130 – Bad Company
7th Wing, Dyess AFB

86-0107 – Bad To The B-One
7th Wing, 9th BS, Dyess AFB

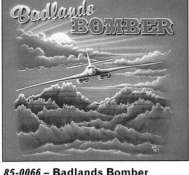

85-0066 – Badlands Bomber
7th Wing, Dyess AFB

85-0075 – Banshee
(now 28th BW, Ellsworth AFB)

86-0133 – Black Hills Bandit
28th BW, Ellsworth AFB

86-0112 – Black Widow
9th BS, 7th Wing, Dyess AFB

85-0077 – Bones *(later Jap Happy)*
(now Pride of South Dakota)

85-0073 – Cerebrus
7th Wing, Dyess AFB

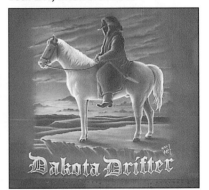

86-0114 – Dakota Drifter
28th BW, Ellsworth AFB

86-0093 – Global Power
37th BS, 28th BW, Ellsworth AFB

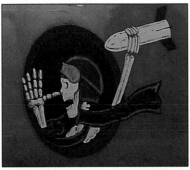

84-0057 – The Hellion
9th BS, 7th Wing, Ellsworth AFB

85-0083 – Overnight Delivery
28th BW, Ellsworth AFB

85-0072 – Polarized
9th BS, 7th Wing, Dyess AFB

86-0128 – Pony Soldier
28th BW, Ellsworth AFB

85-0086 – Soaring With Eagles
28th BW, Ellsworth AFB

83-0068 – Spuds
(now 28th BW, Ellsworth AFB)

84-0055 – Sunrise Surprise
(now 7th Wing, Dyess AFB)

83-0067 – Texas Raiders
(now 7th Wing, Dyess AFB)

83-0065 – The Star of Abilene
(now Star of Palmdale, 7th Wing)

85-0062 – Uncaged
9th Bs, 7th Wing, Dyess AFB

86-0096 – Wolf Pack
28th BW, Ellsworth AFB

United States Air Force

Except for test aircraft, all operational inventory B-1B bombers were initially assigned to Strategic Air Command (SAC), headquartered at Offutt AFB, Nebraska. Strategic Air Command's assigned task was to operate two-thirds of the American nuclear force arrayed against the Soviet Union – the 'strategic triad' comprising US Navy strategic-missile submarines and SAC intercontinental ballistic missiles and manned bombers. SAC thus maintained forces on nuclear alert, including bombers and tankers ready for immediate take-off, and was keeper of the SIOP (Single Integrated Operations Plan) which established targets to be attacked and the means to attack them in the initial phase of an atomic war. Much as the US Air Force itself had been until Vietnam, SAC was led by 'bomber generals' who had pioneered the manned bomber and who had waited three decades to introduce into service the first new bomber since the B-52 of 1955 and the B-58 of 1960.

On 1 September 1991, all SAC B-1B wings were redesignated from 'Bombardment Wing, Heavy' to, simply, 'Wing', the absence of an adjective indicating that they operated both bombers and tankers. (The term 'Heavy' had appeared in parentheses in the names of wings, groups and squadrons prior to 1948, at which time the term was retained but the parentheses deleted). On that date in 1991, all of SAC's B-1B squadrons were redesignated from 'Bombardment Squadron, Heavy' to 'Bomb' squadrons. (They had always been called 'Bomb' squadrons in informal and incorrect shorthand). 1 September 1991 was also the date when the US Air Force reinstated the combat group as a military formation between wing and squadron level; the current term is Operations Group or OG. USAF bombers stood down from nuclear alert on 27 September 1991.

With the easing of Cold War tensions, SAC was disestablished on 1 June 1992 and its bomber force transferred to Air Combat Command (ACC), headquartered at Langley AFB, Virginia. The new Command was officially a merger of two equals, the tactical assets of Tactical Air Command (TAC) and the bombers of SAC (which, on that date, transferred its tankers to Air Mobility Command). In reality, officers who headed the bomber forces saw the change more as a 'hostile takeover' than a partnership of equals. The US Air Force was now being run by 'fighter generals', and an advanced tactical fighter was outpacing bombers as the service's top priority in the post-Desert Storm era. As a result of the emergence of ACC, bombers were to be assigned tailcodes for the first time.

Prior to 1 June 1992 only test B-1Bs had worn a tailcode ('ED'), since tailcodes were never adopted by SAC; thereafter, ACC assigned tailcodes to the bombers. With the reduction in size of the USAF's strategic bomber fleet, two front-line B-1B wings were slated for retirement and their aircraft became available to equip Air National Guard squadrons. Although US nuclear doctrine prohibits members of the Reserve component from taking on a nuclear mission, the emerging emphasis on using the B-1B for conventional warfare made it sensible and cost-effective to put the Lancer in the hands of Guardsmen. Air National Guard (ANG) units report to ACC for operational purposes. In wartime, USAF strategic bombers committed to SIOP would chop to US Strategic Command (Stratcom) at Offutt, while those engaged in conventional bombing would come under unified commanders-in-chief, or CINCs, with regional responsibilities. Test operations were carried out by Air Force Systems Command, which merged with another component to become Air Force Materiel Command on 1 July 1992.

Rockwell manufactured an even 100 B-1B bombers. Four have been lost in crashes and the first B-1B (82-0001), which was essentially a prototype rather than a production machine, was disassembled. Of the 95 surviving Lancers as of 31 March 1995, the force included 82 ACC, 11 ANG, and two AFMC aircraft.

Air Combat Command

Air Combat Command, headquartered at Langley AFB, Virginia, operates US Air Force bombers and CONUS (continental United States)-based, combat-coded fighter and attack aircraft, and organises, trains, equips and maintains combat-ready forces. ACC's Eighth Air Force has responsibility for bomber forces including the 7th and 28th Bomb Wings, while the Twelfth Air Force oversees composite forces including the 366th Wing.

When they entered service, the B-1Bs were extremely anonymous, carrying the SAC badge on the port forward fuselage, below the OSO's window, and the wing badge to starboard, below the DSO's window. Wing insignia were soon adopted and applied to the tailfins of the B-1Bs. The 28th Bomb Wing carried the outline of Mount Rushmore, between parallel blue bands (the upper one joined below a thin orange stripe) and with the word 'Ellsworth' in orange. The 96th Bomb Wing used the Texan state flag with the skull of a Texas Longhorn superimposed. The 319th used an orange (upper) and blue band with a 'sunflake' design forward, consisting of the upper half of a sunburst and the lower half of a snowflake. The 384th used the 'Keeper of the Plains' motif with a Native American holding wheatsheaves and lightning bolts, superimposed on a three-tone blue band. This unit also applied their 'triangle P' World War II insignia on some aircraft for bombing competitions. The reassignment to Air Combat Command saw the introduction of two-letter tailcodes, and squadron fin bands replaced the old wing identities. The SAC badge was replaced by the appropriate squadron badge. Serial number presentation was also changed from the old SAC style which ran the second digit of the year prefix together with the 'last four' below the legend USAF. In Air Combat Command service the aircraft wear the two-digit year prefix below the letters AF, with the last three digits of the serial following in larger letters. Aircraft received the Air Combat Command badge on their fins, between fin band and tailcode, freeing up the space below the OSO window (previously used by the SAC badge) for application of squadron insignia, or, more usually, to repeat the wing badge. Many B-1Bs soon gained names, painted on the undercarriage doors. After a while, B-1Bs in service began to pick up nose art, usually to port only (but on both sides, mirror fashion, on aircraft from the 96th). Between 1988 and early 1991 the 384th used no nose art, instead having aircraft names on both sides of the fuselage painted in red or blue according to flight allocation. Nose art has always had to be approved at wing level, and is often based on wartime bomber nose art. Aircraft at McConnell and Dyess had a large number of nose arts replaced with more politically correct designs during the early 1990s.

7th Wing, Dyess AFB, Texas

On 1 October 1993, the 7th Wing took over 'in place' the facilities, people and equipment of the two Air Force combat wings at Dyess AFB, Texas: the 96th Bomb Wing (B-1B) and the 463rd Airlift Wing (C-130H). The wing's 7th Operations Group also activated on 1 October 1993, the US Air Force having restored the combat group to its order of battle some 25 months earlier. As of 1 October 1995, the 7th was the only B-1B formation with a SIOP, or nuclear, commitment.

The 7th traces its history to an Army observation group established in 1918. It became the 7th Bombardment Group on 1 June 1928 and one of its early commanders, Major Carl A. Spatz, flew the famous January 1929

air-refuelling exercise in the Atlantic-Fokker C-2A (28-120) *The Question Mark* (the future US Air Force chief of staff later changed the spelling of his name to Spaatz). B-17E Flying Fortresses of the 7th were arriving at Pearl Harbor when it was attacked by Japan on 7 December 1941. After flying LB-30 Liberators and B-17Es on Java in 1942, the 7th operated four B-24 squadrons through the end of World War II. Post-war, the 7th Bomb Wing spent 47 years at Carswell AFB, Texas, flying B-29, B-36, and B-52.

With its move to Dyess, the 7th Wing became the only organisation in the US Air Force flying bombers and airlifters. The wing's 7th Operations Group – activated 1 October 1993 –

took over the bomb squadrons (337th BS and 338th CCTS) which earlier had been first to operate the B-1B, and the airlift squadrons (39th and 40th). The latter two replaced the 772nd and 773rd Airlift Squadrons which were inactivated. With the change, the 338th CCTS – which was never designated a bomb squadron – was inactivated.

On 6 June 1994, the 7th Wing's B-1B *The Reluctant Dragon* (86-0103) flew over Normandy for the 50th anniversary of the D-Day landings.

Two 7th Wing B-1Bs flew non-stop around the world in 36 hours 13 minutes on 2-3 June 1995 in a mission

Two years after its maiden flight the first B-1B achieved IOC (and thus stood armed and ready, on alert) at Dyess AFB, on October 1986.

Above: The sinuous and predatory shape of the B-1B is exaggerated in the nose art worn by the 28th BS Sweet Sixteen (84-0056).

called Coronet Bat. The mission was flown by *The Hellion* (84-0057) and *Global Power* (85-0082). The wing's B-1Bs carry the wing badge of a shield bisected by a diagonal stripe, carrying three crosses, on the starboard forward fuselage, below the rear cockpit window. The 7th's legendary (almost) motto, *Mors Ab Alto*, appears below the shield.

Today's 7th Wing inherited its aircraft and aircrew from the 96th Bomb Wing at Dyess AFB, 'the home of the B-1B'. The B-1B replaced the B-52H at Dyess between 1982 and 1984 (the B-52s moved on to Carswell). As SAC's premier B-1 unit the 96th achieved many notable firsts, such as the first live SRAM launch by a SAC crew, in 1987. Since 1993 it has been the responsibility of the 7th Wing to uphold that tradition.

9th Bomb Squadron

The facilities, people and equipment of the 338th went to the newly-arrived 9th Bomb Squadron. The 9th is one of the oldest combat formations in the USAF and had been associated with the 7th since serving as the 9th Night Observation Squadron in France, beginning 6 September 1918. The squadron had been a B-52H operator under the 7th at Carswell but had been inactivated 15 August 1992. Activated concurrently with the change in wing designation on 1 October 1993, aircraft of the 9th are distinguished by a black tail stripe with a white bat superimposed. The squadron badge is applied to port below the rear cockpit window and consists of a simple disc, with searchlight beams forming the Roman Numeral IX.

337th Bomb Squadron

The original post-ACC markings of the 337th BS (maroon/red fin band with yellow griffon) were used from 1 June 1992 until 1 October 1993. On 1 October 1993, 337th BS acquired blue and white checkerboard markings from the 338th CCTS when it became the B-1B training unit. On 1 October 1994, the 337th Bomb Squadron was inactivated and its facilities, people and equipment taken over by the 28th Bomb Squadron, which had been a B-1B operator at McConnell AFB, Kansas. The 337th's squadron badge was carried to port below the WSO's window, consisted of a winged, golden griffon flying past a cloud with four stars visible overhead.

28th Bomb Squadron

A longtime B-1B bomber squadron with the 384th Bomb Wing, the 28th Bomb Squadron's history is described in greater detail in the entry on the 384th Bomb Wing. The 28th BS is now the B-1B RTU (replacement training unit) and uses the fin flash with the blue and white checkerboards previously identified with 338th CCTS and 337th. The squadron badge appears to port below the WSO's window, and consists of an Indian's head.

Aircraft assigned as of 31 March 1995:

83-0065/0071; 84-0050/0051; 84-0053/0059; 85-0062; 85-0065; 85-0067; 85-0071/0074; 85-0082; 86-0100/0101; 86-0103; 86-0105; 86-0107/0110; 86-0112; 86-0117; 86-0119/0120; 86-0122/0124; 86-0126; 86-0130; 86-0132; 86-0135; 86-0137; 86-0140

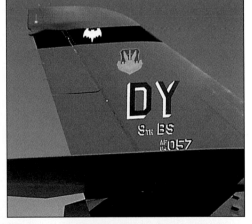

Right: A black fin stripe and high lighted squadron titles leave no doubt as to the ownership of this 9th Bomb Squadron 'Bone'. The stenciled 'Batman' symbol is an unofficial addition but, in many ways, is similar to the bat insignia carried by the Royal Air Force's No. 9 Squadron, which also began life as a specialist nocturnal unit. When the 96th BW became the 7th Wing in 1993, elements of the 338th Combat Crew Training Squadron were reorganised as part of the 9th BS, thereby continuing the lineage of one of the USAF's oldest units.

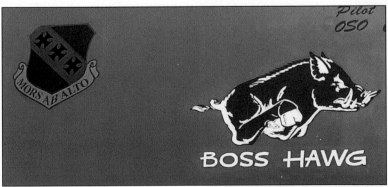

*Above: Alongside **Boss Hawg's** (84-0051) nose art rides the badge of the 7th Wing (formerly the 7th Bombardment Wing). Its motto, Mors ab Alto, translates as Death From on High.*

Right: Blue and white checkers denote a B-1B of the 28th BS. The 28th was originally assigned to McConnell's 384th BW, but is now the B-1B RTU with the 7th Wing.

*Above: The 9th BS's official badge has crossed searchlight beams forming the the Roman numeral for '9' (IX). The subtle grey colours seen here on **Crewdawg** (85-0074) enhance the night-time scene.*

28th Bombardment Wing, Heavy, Ellsworth AFB, South Dakota

The 28th Bombardment Wing, Heavy, was the second B-1B operator. It replaced the B-52H Stratofortress from 1987 with an initial complement of 16 Lancers, later raised to 35. As of 1 October 1995, the 28th did not have a nuclear, or SIOP, commitment.

The 28th traces its history to 1940. The 28th Bombardment Group flew many aircraft types including the B-17 Flying Fortress and LB-30 Liberator in Alaska and the northern Pacific. In post-war years, the 28th operated B-29, RB-36 and B-52. The transition to the B-1B began with the arrival of *Wings of Freedom* (85-0073) on 21 January 1987.

This formation was redesignated the 28th Wing on 1 September 1991 and on that date the 28th Operations Group was activated – the combat group being restored between wing and squadron level by the US Air Force for the first time since 1952. On 1 June 1992 the wing gave up its tankers, transferred to Air Combat Command, and was redesignated 28th Bomb Wing. In July 1994, the 28th began a six-month operational readiness assessment of maintenance, spares, and logistics support for the Rockwell B-1B Lancer bomber. Logistics problems have plagued the

Above: The B-1Bs of the 28th Wing have traditionally carried the four presidents of Mt Rushmore (Washington, Roosevelt, Jefferson and Lincoln) which is a South Dakotan, and national, landmark.

Right: Gremlin (85-0087) wears the badge of the 55-year-old 28th Wing, of Ellsworth AFB.

B-1B force, which currently has a 55 per cent mission-capable rate and which requires a separate 'tail' of parts supplies for each individual airframe by serial number.

For the evaluation, the US Air Force equipped Ellsworth with a full complement of spare parts and crews, which required drawing on assets from two other bomb wings. As part of the

test, one of the 28th Bomb Wing's two squadrons were deployed to Roswell, New Mexico in November 1994 to assess mission-capable rates for B-1Bs operating from a remote location. The assessment has been billed as successful, and as validation of the

role of the B-1B in the US bomber force.

The 28th Bomb Wing's badge is a shield, halved 'jigsaw-style' and surmounted by a Fleur de Lys whose outer feathers are actually whole wings.

37th Bomb Squadron

The first of the wing's flying squadrons was the 37th (activated 1 October 1986). The 37th Bombardment Squadron, Heavy was redesignated as the 37th Bomb Squadron on 1 September 1991, the same day that the wing's 28th Operations Group was activated. Aircraft of the 37th BS wear a black tail stripe with a yellow-gold border containing the word 'Tigers' in a yellow-gold maze. The 37th BS was identified by a Bengal tiger badge.

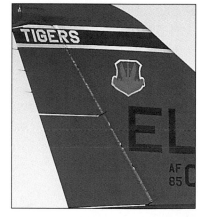

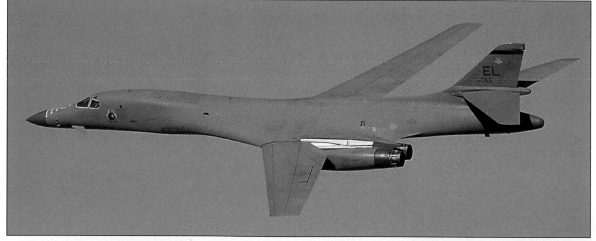

Above and left: The 37th BS was activated at Ellsworth in July 1977 and became a B-1B unit in 1985 – the second for the (then) 28th Bomb Wing. Crews wear a tiger badge and aircraft carry a black and yellow fin stripe with the legend 'Tigers'.

77th Bomb Squadron

The 77th Bomb Squadron had already been at Ellsworth and received its first B-1B in February 1987. The 77th Bombardment Squadron, Heavy, was redesignated as the 77th Bomb Squadron on 1 September 1991. As part of a reorganisation of the B-1B community, the 77th inactivated on 31 March 1995. Ellsworth AFB has since become home, also, to the 34th BS which reports to the 366th Wing

(separate entry). The 77th BS used a blue stripe and some had a likeness of Mount Rushmore superimposed in black outline form.

Aircraft assigned as of 31 March 1995:

85-0061; 85-0066; 85-0075; 85-0077/0079; 85-0083/0087; 85-0089/0090; 85-0092; 86-0093/0094; 86-0096; 86-0098/0099; 86-0102; 86-0104; 86-0111; 86-0113/0114; 86-0128/0129; 86-0133;

Left and right: The blue-striped B-1Bs of the 77th BS carry a simple rendition of the Mt Rushmore carvings. The 77th has been resident at Ellsworth since 1947, flying the B-36 and B-52. The squadron badge depicts a Native American character standing on a flying arrow, with a bomb notched in his bow.

96th Bombardment Wing, Heavy, Dyess AFB, Texas

The 96th Bombardment Wing, Heavy, at Dyess AFB, Texas was the first US Air Force wing to equip with the B-1B Lancer.

The wing dates to July 1942 when the 96th Bomb Group formed in the B-17 Flying Fortress at Salt Lake City, Utah. The wing flew the B-52C, D, E, F and H Stratofortress. Announcement of the wing's new aircraft type was made by President Ronald Reagan on 21 January 1983 and the wing phased out its B-52H Stratofortresses between August 1984 and January 1985.

The wing accepted its first B-1B (of 29) on 29 June 1985. The first production aircraft were resplendent in low-visibility slate grey and dark green camouflage – a colour scheme which changed to 'penetrator grey' in the mid-1990s. Early in the B-1B period, the wing briefly operated Detachment 1 of the 4201st Test and Evaluation

Squadron as part of the bomber's developmental effort. The wing reached IOC (initial operating capability) in the B-1B in July 1986 and the first aircraft stood nuclear alert on 1 October 1986. A B-1B from the 96th (85-0061) made the type's first overseas trip to appear at the Paris Air Salon in June 1987.

On 1 September 1991, the same day on which the wing's 96th Operations Group was activated, the wing was redesignated 96th Wing. On 1 June 1992, when divested of its tankers and transferred to Air Combat Command, it became the 96th Bomb Wing.

On 28 September 1987, a 96th Bombardment Wing, Heavy B-1B

(85-0052) crashed into a range and exploded near La Junta in southeast Colorado during a low-level training flight. The aircraft apparently flew into a flock of birds while at an altitude of approximately 500 ft (155 m). Three of the crew were killed while another three ejected safely. The bomber had been carrying two extra crew members on board.

The 'DY' tailcode was introduced

late and transferred to the 7th Wing on 1 October 1993. The wing's B-1Bs carried a white Longhorn skull silhouette superimposed on a stylised Texas state flag. The official wing badge of a falcon's head, holding a bomb in its beak, appeared below the DSO's window, with the motto *E Sempre L'Ora*. The 96th Bomb Wing stood down on 1 October 1993 when its people, facilities and equipment were turned over 'in place' (together with the assets of the 463rd Airlift Wing) to the 7th Wing.

Wearing a Texas flag on its tail, Spectre, of the 96th Bombardment Wing (Heavy), taxis in at Dyess, in 1990. The following year the unit became the 96th Wing.

4018th Combat Crew Training Squadron

The wing's first flying unit was the 4018th Combat Crew Training Squadron (CCTS), activated 15 March 1985. The initial type training in the B-1B has remained at Dyess but the name of the RTU (replacement training

unit, a term which is technically obsolete but still widely used) has been through several alterations. The 4018th was inactivated on 1 July 1986, before individual squadron insignia were applied to B-1Bs.

338th Combat Crew Training Squadron

The 4018th Combat Crew Training Squadron was replaced by the 338th Strategic Bombardment Training Squadron (SBTS). On 1 January 1987, in another name change, the unit was redesignated 338th CCTS. From 1

June 1992, the 338th CCTS flew with blue and white checkerboards on the fin, a marking which was to change squadrons twice more after the 7th Wing stood up at Dyess (see 7th entry).

Above and left: The blue and white checkerboard once worn by the B-1Bs of the 338th CCTS can now be found on the aircraft of the 7th Wing's 28th BS.

337th Bombardment Squadron, Heavy

The wing's primary flying unit was the 337th Bombardment Squadron, Heavy. This was redesignated 337th Bomb Squadron on 1 September 1991. From 1 June 1992, the 337th BS flew with a maroon or red tail band with yellow griffon.

Left and right: The original tail markings of the 337th BS comprised a maroon fin stripe with a yellow griffon. The unit later swapped marks with the 338th CCTS, adopting its blue and white checkers, but was disbanded in 1994.

319th Bombardment Wing, Heavy, Grand Forks AFB, North Dakota

The 319th Bombardment Wing, Heavy became an operator of the B-1B Lancer in 1988.

The 319th traces its lineage to the 319th Bombardment Group (Medium), activated 19 June 1942 with Martin B-26 Marauders and assigned to the Mediterranean. The unit was inactivated on 18 December 1945. Serving as a fighter-bomber wing after the war, it became the 319th Bombardment Wing, Heavy, at Grand Forks on 1 February 1963, flying the B-52H and KC-135A. (The practice of placing the modifier 'Heavy' in parentheses had been discontinued in 1948.) In 1982 the wing converted to B-52Gs equipped with AGM-86A Air-Launched Cruise Missiles (ALCMs).

Conversion to the B-1B began with the arrival of 86-0122 on 12 January 1988. The wing's initial complement was 17 aircraft. It was redesignated 319th Wing on 1 September 1991, the same day its 319th Operations Group was activated. The wing gave up its tankers and was redesignated 319th Bomb Wing and transferred to ACC on 1 June 1992.

A further series of changes made at Grand Forks was unique to that base and occurred because the base made the transition to tanker operations while, for a time, retaining a modest B-1B force. The Grand Forks wing was redesignated 319th Air Refueling Wing on 1 October 1993 and, together with its 319th Operations Group, was

transferred to Air Mobility Command (AMC) which assumed responsibility for the base at Grand Forks. On that date, Air Combat Command took the unusual step of activating the 319th Bomb Group – separate from AMC's 319th Operations Group – while B-1Bs were on strength before being reassigned elsewhere. This was apparently the first bomb group in the US Air Force since 1952. It was with this unusual designation that the group's B-1Bs participated in the ACC competition Gunsmoke '93. When the 319th BG was disbanded soon after the Gunsmoke event, most of its

B-1Bs went to the 34th BS/366th Wg at Ellsworth AFB. The 319th's badge was a chain-mail clad hand holding aloft a torch, with the motto *Defensores Libertatis* (Defenders of Freedom). The wing's B-1Bs latterly received a 'GF' tailcode, and had a yellow/orange sun motif on tail fin.

***Right and below:** The orange- and blue-striped B-1Bs of the 319th carried an insignia they called the 'sunflake' – a combined sunburst and snowflake on a circular background. B-1s began to replace B-52Gs in 1988.*

46th Bombardment Squadron, Heavy

The 319th operated the 46th Bombardment Squadron, Heavy which transitioned from the B-52 to the B-1B in 1988 (the 319th also operated the tanker-equipped 905th Air Refueling Squadron). The 46th was activated on 1 February 1963 and had operated the B-52H and B-52G. The flying squadron became the 46th Bomb Squadron on 1 September 1991 when the wing's 319th Operations Group stood up. On 1 October 1993, the 46th was assigned to the 319th Bomb Group. The 46th BS and 319th BG were inactivated on 16 July 1994. Squadron markings were not carried.

366th Wing, Mountain Home AFB, Idaho

The 366th Wing is the US Air Force's 'air intervention' wing and traces its heritage to the 366th Fighter-Bomber Wing formed at England AFB, Louisiana in January 1953. The 366th operated F-51, F-86, F-84F, F-100 and F-4 fighters. In Vietnam, the 366th Tactical Fighter Wing ('Gunfighters') flew from Da Nang. After that war, the 366th TFW flew F-111A and EF-111A.

Today, the 366th Wing is one of three composite wings in the USAF but is different from all the others: it is equipped with B-1B (previously B-52G), F-15E, F-15C, F-16C, and KC-135. The composite wing concept was created by USAF chief of staff General Merrill A. (Tony) McPeak after Desert Storm and was put into effect to coincide with the founding of Air Command Command on 1 June 1992. In theory, a composite wing would be able to conduct a war with little or no outside support. In practice, the concept is controversial.

The 366th Wing's badge is worn below the OSO's window and consists of a complex shield containing a Fleur de Lys, crosses and 'flight symbols', with the motto *Audentes Fortuna Juvat*.

The B-1Bs of the 34th BS are the teeth of Mountain Home's 366th Wing 'Gunfighters', though in many respects the Lancers are far less capable than the B-52Gs they replaced.

The badge of the 366th Wing bears the Latin motto** Audentes Fortuna Juvat **(Fortune Favours the Brave).

The 34th Bomb Squadron was the USAF's last operational B-52G unit, but finally exchanged them in 1994.

The mythical thunderbird appears on the badge of the 34th BS and also on the fin stripe of its aircraft.

34th Bomb Squadron

On 4 April 1994, the 34th Bomb Squadron was activated at Ellsworth as part of the 366th Wing based at Mountain Home AFB, Idaho (the 34th had previously operated B-52Gs as part of the 366th Wing but located at Castle AFB, California). The Lancers are stationed at Ellsworth to avoid the unnecessary expense of maintaining the bombers at Mountain Home. The 34th had been activated in June 1992 as the heavy bomber component of the wing and had operated B-52G Stratofortresses prior to converting to the 'Bone' and moving to Ellsworth. Despite being based at Ellsworth the squadron's B-1Bs wear an 'MO' (Mountain Home) tailcode. The unit marking is a black fin stripe with a red thunderbird (a mythological native American creature), trailing horizontal lines, superimposed. The same thunderbird is applied in blue on a white disc below the DSO's window.

Aircraft assigned as of 31 March 1995:
85-0091; 86-0097; 86-0016; 86-0118; 86-0121; 86-0125; 86-0131; 86-0134; 86-0138/0139

384th Bombardment Wing, Heavy, McConnell AFB, Kansas

The 384th Bombardment Wing, Heavy, came into being on 1 July 1987 as a redesignation of the former 384th Air Refueling Wing, Heavy. In the pattern of other Lancer units, it was redesignated 384th Wing on 1 September 1991, the day its 384th Operations Group was activated. It became the 384th Bomb Wing when transferred from SAC to ACC on 1 June 1992. On 1 January 1994, in an unusual change (though not as unusual as the one made at Grand Forks), the wing was redesignated 384th Bomb Group; on that date, the 384th Operations Group was inactivated.

The active-duty USAF gave up B-1B operations at McConnell just as the Air National Guard was beginning to operate the Lancer. The 384th BG was inactivated on 1 October 94 and transferred its aircraft to the co-located Kansas ANG.

The 384th was the fourth and final USAF wing to take the B-1B Lancer on charge, transitioning from the KC-135. Initial authorised strength was 17 B-1Bs. The 100th and final B-1B was delivered to the 384th on 2 May 1988.

In September 1989, three B-1Bs from the 384th (86-0136/0138) deployed to Hickam AFB, Hawaii as part of SAC exercise Giant Warrior '89. Although a B-1B had appeared at an armed forces day show the previous May, it was the first operational deployment to the islands by the type.

On 5 October 1990, a crew from the 28th Bomb Squadron, 384th BMW encountered sudden powerplant failure while pulling up from low altitude during a training mission. The B-1B recovered safely at Pueblo Memorial Airport, Colorado, where the crew discovered only after landing that the number 1 engine was missing. It was later found in a cattle field at Blaine Horne in southeast Colorado. The wing's B-1Bs latterly wore an 'OZ' tailcode (Kansas being the 'Land of Oz') and retained their 'Keepers of the Plains' fin band.

In 1994, the 384th gave up its B-1Bs, most of which went to the 184th Bomb Group, Kansas Air National Guard, farther down the flight line on the same base. The 384th BG was inactivated in October 1994.

The 384th is no more and the mantle of 'Keeper of the Plains' has passed to the 22nd ARW.

The B-1Bs of the 384th bore a Native American motif featuring wheat stalks and lightning bolts.

28th Bombardment Squadron

The wing's flying squadron was the 28th Bombardment Squadron, Heavy, 'Keeper of the Plains', activated on 1 July 1987. It had previously been one of the first B-52H units.

This unit became the 28th Bomb Squadron on 1 September 1991; the 28th BS transferred to the 7th Wing at Dyess AFB, Texas on 1 October 1994. Squadron markings were not worn.

United States Air National Guard

The Air National Guard's official mission is to enforce federal authority, suppress insurrection and defend the nation when mobilised by the President, Congress or both. Guard units augment the US Air Force by participating in operations and exercises worldwide. Far from being 'weekend warriors' as once perceived, Guardsmen are an integral part of US warfighting plans and daily operation. Guardsmen do not, however, participate in the nuclear, or SIOP, commitment and Guard Lancers will perform conventional missions only.

When they transferred to the Guard, B-1Bs had their ACC fin-shields replaced by the ANG insignia, and also lost the wing badges previously applied below the DSO/OSO windows. The arrival of the B-1B in ANG service is a major milestone in the Guard's history and an important element of the new USAF 'bomber roadmap'.

116th Fighter Wing, Georgia ANG, Dobbins AFB, Georgia

The USAF is belatedly proceeding with long-stalled plans to move its F-15A MSIP Eagle-equipped 116th Fighter Wing from Dobbins AFB, Georgia (in Marietta, near Atlanta) to Robins AFB, Georgia and to convert the wing to the B-1B. The B-1Bs are expected to retain the current 'GA' tailcode.

128th Fighter Squadron

The wing operates the 128th Fighter Squadron, which began as an observation squadron in 1940 and has operated numerous aircraft, including most post-war jet fighters. As of October 1995, the squadron had completed transferring its F-15A MSIP Eagles to the 125th Fighter Squadron, Florida Air National Guard at Jacksonville, where they replaced F-16A Block 15 ADF Fighting Falcon aircraft. Funds for conversion to Lancer bombers were expected to be included in Fiscal Year 1996 appropriations (signed on 4 October 1995) and the move of Lancers to Robins was slated to begin in February 1996.

184th Bomb Wing, Kansas ANG, McConnell AFB, Kansas

On 1 July 1994 the 184th Fighter Group ('Jayhawks') which had long been an Air National Guard (ANG) F-16 Fighting Falcon training and operating unit was redesignated the 184th Bomb Group to reflect the group's conversion to the B-1B Lancer. The group was located at McConnell AFB in Wichita, Kansas and became the first ANG unit to operate the bomber. The group received most of the aircraft – and used some of the facilities – of the former 28th Bomb Squadron/384th Bomb Wing which had been elsewhere at the same airfield.

Unlike the active-duty Air Force which reinstated the practice in 1991, the Air National Guard has long used the combat group as its basic military formation. However, on 1 October 1995, the 184th BG became the 184th Bomb Wing. At the same time, the 184th Operations Group was established to oversee the 127th BS.

Above: The ownership of this 184th Bomb Wing 'Bone' is left in little doubt.

Left and below: ACC became the 127th Fighter Squadron's gaining (wartime) command in October 1991, when the unit was still an F-16 squadron. This made the subsequent transition to the B-1B much smoother.

127th Bomb Squadron

The ANG previously had operated two squadrons at McConnell; one was inactivated and, on 1 July 1994, the 127th Fighter Squadron (also dubbed 'Jayhawks') was redesignated the 127th Bomb Squadron. The 127th began as an observation squadron on 30 July 1940. In the post-war Air Guard, the squadron flew F-51Ds, F-84Cs, F-80Cs, F-86Ls, F-100s, F-105s, and F-4s prior to F-16 operations. The squadron's aircraft carry no tailcode but do have a toned-down stripe across the top with the word 'Kansas' superimposed.

Aircraft assigned as of 31 March 1995:

85-0060; 85-0064; 85-0069/0070; 85-0080/0081; 85-0088; 86-0095; 86-0115; 86-0127; 86-0136.

Air Force Materiel Command (AFMC)

412th Test Wing, Edwards AFB, California

412th Test Wing ('ED' tailcode) is the current designation for the organisation known until 1 October 1992 as the 6510th TW, at Edwards. The number was chosen for a historical reason: the 412th Fighter Group operated the first American jet fighter, the P-59 Airacomet, at Muroc Army Airfield (now Edwards) during World War II. The 412th and its predecessor the 6510th Test Wing (which also used 'ED' tailcode) tested new aircraft and systems as part of the Air Force Flight Test Center (AFFTC) and supported the Air Force test pilots' school. (Edwards was also home to the SAC-owned 4201st Test Squadron which provided personnel

for B-1B tests but operated no aircraft.) The 6510th operated the B-1B Combined Test Force (CTF) which began evaluating the Lancer in 1988, starting with the first aircraft (82-0001). The CTF was absorbed by the 6510th TW's 6510th Test Squadron in about 1990. The 412th TW has never been part of Strategic Air Command, which 'owned' all other B-1Bs in service until being disbanded on 1 June 1992. In keeping with USAF practice revived on 1 September 1991, this wing has an operations group, the 412th Logistics Group. Some aircraft may have briefly worn the AFFTC (Air Force Flight Test Center) fin cap, white with blue diamonds superimposed.

419th Flight Test Squadron (FLTS)

The 6510th wing's 6512th Test Squadron (one of nine flying squadrons testing various aircraft types) operated two B-1Bs. On 1 July 1992, AFSC was merged with Air Force Logistics Command to create Air Force Materiel Command (AFMC). The 6510th TW retained its designation under the latter command until 1 October 1992 when it was renamed the 412th TW. At this time, the newly redesignated 412th wing's 419th Test Squadron (TESTS, not TS as often abbreviated)

acquired from the wing's 410th Test Squadron the two B-1B Lancers employed for avionics tests and other test flying. The 410th Test Squadron began as the 6510th TESTS, and was redesignated 410th Test Squadron on 2 October 1992; on 1 March 1994 it was redesignated the 410th Flight Test Squadron (FLTS). The Edwards B-1B operator was always one of nine flying squadrons in the wing operating various types of aircraft as part of the USAF's test programme. On 1 October

1993, B-1Bs were moved from the 410th TESTS to the 419th TESTS, which also operates B-52Hs. The latter was redesignated 419th FLTS on 1 March 1994.

Above: The No. 1 B-1B (82-0001) made its three-hour 20-minute maiden flight from Palmdale to Edwards AFB. A B-1 test unit has been based at Edwards ever since.

The first USAF B-1B arrived at Edwards in October 1984 and did not leave until June 1985, when it was handed over to SAC. Here a B-1B of the 410th TS/412th TW closes on one of the same wing's NKC-135As during the 1993 Edwards AFB open day.

Below: Today, B-1Bs fly alongside B-52Hs with the 419th Flight Test Squadron, as part of AFMC's 412th Test Wing. The B-1B test force is currently involved in a heavy schedule of weapons integration and qualification flying.

Moscow Air Show

Although the non-appearance of the new Mikoyan 1.42 prototype was a disapppointment (if not a surprise), the annual Mosaeroshow at the LII Gromov Flight Research Institute's Zhukhovskii airfield gave visitors an unparalleled opportunity to see at close quarters the struggling Russian aviation industry's latest and most interesting projects.

Below: The Il-76MF is a stretched military transport version of the Il-76, powered by four Aviadvigatel PS-90AN turbofans. The aircraft has plugs fore and aft of the wing, lengthening the cargo hold by 6.6 m (21 ft 8 in). The prototype made its maiden flight on 1 August, yet was able to give a spirited display at Zhukhovskii later the same month. The civilian stretched, re-engined variant is designated Il-76TF.

Left: Yakovlev's only remaining military programme is the Yak-130D, developed in partnership with Aermacchi to meet a Russian air force requirement for an L-29/L-39 replacement. The production aircraft will reportedly be smaller than the prototype seen here.

Below: The Tu-22M (seen here in Tu-22M-3 'Backfire-C' form) continues to form the backbone of Russia's strategic strike force, and has been adapted to perform a number of conventional and support roles. The Tu-22M-3 is expected to serve into the new millennium.

Below: Framed by the distinctive nose of the Su-32FN is a prototype Su-33. Despite its designation, the Su-33 is very much a navalised version of the basic, first-generation 'Flanker-B' and does not have the advanced avionics and FCS of the Su-35 family. Recent reports indicate that the MiG-29K remains a threat.

Above: The ninth Su-35, wearing a desert pattern splinter camouflage originally applied for a Dubai air show appearance, makes a high Alpha flypast. The Sukhoi OKB had promised to show the 11th prototype, which is fitted with multi-axis thrust vectoring nozzles but, as at Farnborough in 1994, the aircraft did not appear.

Below: Once something of a mystery ship, the Su-27IB performed a spirited flying display, while the Su-34 (and Su-32FN) for which it acted as aerodynamic prototype remained on the ground as static exhibits. The big 'Flanker' is intended primarily as an Su-24 replacement.

Above: A MiG-29UB taxis out, past lines of miscellaneous test aircraft, including an early, ventral-finned MiG-29 and even an Su-15, one of at least three 'Flagons' still present at Zhukhovskii, and reportedly still flown. Such clusters of derelict-looking aircraft are common on the massive airfield and, during the show, many aircraft on such parking areas became active and took part in the display, to the surprise of some Western onlookers.

Above: The Mikoyan Design Bureau participated actively in the flying display, and even some of their older designs gave flying displays. Here a MiG-23UM pulls up into a climb, vortices streaming away from the inboard leading edge. The red, yellow and black device on the nose is similar to a design applied to Bulgarian MiG-23BNs and is intended to represent an eye to scare off birds.

Above: Budgetary constraints notwithstanding, the demonstration regiment based at Kubinka operates three fast-jet flying display teams, all of which appeared at Zhukhovskii. The 'Swifts', seen here, fly a mix of MiG-29s and two-seat MiG-29UBs, while the other teams fly the Su-27 (the 'Russian Knights') and the Su-25 (the 'Hussars'). The Swifts display involves a great deal of precise formation flying, and the expending of many IR decoy flares.

Above: The 1995 Mosaeroshow marked the first public appearance by the MiG-31M. This aircraft carries the finned wingtip ESM pods often associated with the updated 'Foxhound' and has underwing R-77 (AA-12 'Adder') missiles, but not the long-range R-37 missiles usually carried semi-conformally under the belly.

Left: MiG-29UB leads MiG-31, MiG-25PU, MiG-23UB and MiG-21UM in a formation demonstrating Mikoyan's fighter-building pedigree. The 1.42, claimed to be more advanced than the F-22, did not appear. Still not ready to fly, a static appearance by 1.42 was cancelled on security grounds, although there were persistant rumours of a two-hour glimpse, which did not materialise.

Right: This MiG-21UM is one of the dozen or so 'Fishbeds' still present at Zhukhovskii. This aircraft gave a spectacular flying display, and Mikoyan showed their MiG-21-93 upgrade prototype in the static park. The MiG-21's plentiful thrust and big wing make it a lively performer, and updating the aircraft with modern systems can represent a cost-effective solution to a nation's air defence requirements.

Left: Behind an array of largely unsuitable weaponry lurks the first prototype Mikoyan MiG-ATF, competitor for the same L-29/L-39 replacement requirement as the Yakovlev Yak-130D. The MiG-ATF uses French avionics, while the ATR will have Russian. The ATB will be a light attack version, while carrier-suitable and single-seat derivatives have also been planned. All are to be powered by the French SNECMA Larzac engine, or Russian-built derivatives of the engine.

Below: The MiG-29K is reportedly back under consideration for service aboard the Kuznetsov, following dissatisfaction with the Su-33 and a personal intervention by Defence Minister Pavel Grachev. With its multi-role capability and advanced Zhuk radar, the MiG-29K is significantly more capable than the Su-33, and, being smaller, more can be fitted onto a given carrier deck. The MiG-29K is a minimum-change navalised derivative of the advanced MiG-29M, and has the same weapons system and avionics.

Above: One of the two prototype Ka-31s (hitherto known as the Ka-29RLD) made its public debut at Mosaeroshow '95. Equipped with a massive retractable antenna array below the fuselage, the aircraft is intended for the AEW and radar picket roles, and has a claimed detection range of up to 150 km (93 miles) against a fighter-sized target.

Left: The first example of the Technoavia SM-92P Finist was sold to a customer in the UK (reportedly an RAF pilot) in January 1995. This aircraft is a Technoavia demonstrator, but its military-style colour scheme reflects interest shown in the aircraft by a number of paramilitary and police forces.

Right: Russian air shows are often a bizarre mixture, with pleasure flights, balloon rides, glider displays and parachute jumps appearing alongside the latest high-tech hardware. Here DOSAAF members jump from an An-2.

Below: The Mil Mi-28N is a dedicated night/all-weather version of the basic Mi-28, with a new undernose sensor package including FLIR, LLLTV and with a mast-mounted millimetre wave radar. It is understood that the prototype was converted from one of the four Mi-28s, and has late-standard tail rotor and engine exhaust suppressors.

Left: Mil and its associated factories displayed a bewildering array of helicopter variants. Here an Mi-26T leads the Mi-8TG, modified to run on Liquid Petroleum Gasoline (LPG) and kerosene for take-off and landing. The LPG is stored in the large external tanks. Any Mi-8 can be modified to run on LPG (which reduces emissions in flight) at normal maintenance centres.

Below: Three Kamov Ka-50 'Hokums' gave an unusual co-ordinated display. Two of the aircraft were pre-production machines (the 11th and 12th Ka-50s built), and appeared in full army colours, while the other was the ninth prototype. The static display contained a mock-up of the intended two-seat night/all-weather attack version.

Below: The Mi-24PS is a dedicated police version of the 'Hind' with a nose-mounted FLIR, searchlights in place of the old missile guidance radome, and with a cluster of what look like loudspeakers under the starboard side of the nose. Frames around the doors were intended to allow rapid abseiling from the cabin. The example shown at Zhukhovskii wore full militia colours.

F-16 Operators: Part 2

United States Navy

In January 1985 the US Navy announced its plans to purchase the F-16 as an adversary aircraft. The F-16N was a modified version of the F-16C Block 30, featuring an F110-GE-100 engine. Major differences were the deletion of the 20-mm cannon, wing strengthening to cater for prolonged high-*g* manoeuvring, and replacement of the APG-68 radar with the earlier APG-66. Radar reflectors were added to enhance cross-section. The first F-16N flew on 24 March 1987, and deliveries began to the Navy soon after. An initial batch of 14 aircraft comprised eight F-16Ns (BuNo. 163268/163277 and four two-seat TF-16Ns (BuNo. 163278/163281), followed by a second batch of 12 F-16Ns (BuNo. 163566/163577). Following completion of deliveries, five F-16Ns were assigned to each of the adversary squadrons, and seven to the NFWS. A single TF-16N was assigned to each unit.

In Navy service the F-16N suffered from structural problems, and the fleet was grounded in 1991 while these were attended to. As the decade progressed, the F/A-18 Hornet and F-14 Tomcat began to assume an ever greater proportion of the adversary mission. In 1995, following the disestablishment of VF-43, the Navy announced that the F-16N fleet would be retired. Seen as a luxury, the small force did not prove economical to support. At the time of writing the F-16Ns were expected to be transferred to Bahrain, the deal including the return to the US of Northrop F-5Es.

Two West Coast and two East Coast units received the F-16N. This aircraft is from VF-45, wearing their original markings with red star and 'AD' codes.

VF-43 'Challengers'
NAS Oceana, Virginia

On relinquishing the IAI F-21A Kfir which it had operated for three years, VF-43 began flying the F-16N in June 1988, but the squadron's first aircraft were borrowed from VF-45 and retained that unit's markings. In mid-1989 the squadron began receiving its own complement of aircraft, which comprised five F-16Ns and a single TF-16N. VF-43 used the Falcons alongside a mixed bag of A-4s and F-5s in the adversary role, the squadron also employing the T-2 Buckeye for spin training. The squadron supported work-ups for the Atlantic Fleet Tomcat community co-located at Oceana. In 1994, as part of a round of unit disbandments, VF-43 was deactivated.

Squadron markings consisted of a pentagon upon which was superimposed a mailed fist crushing a MiG fighter. The squadron number was presented on the ventral fins, and the two-digit Soviet-style codes were in blue.

With VF-43 the F-16N served alongside the A-4 Skyhawk (and F-5E) to provide a complete adversary service to Atlantic Fleet fighters.

VF-45 'Blackbirds'
NAS Key West, Florida

Since 1976 VF-45 had operated A-4 Skyhawks in the dissimilar air combat role, supporting fleet exercises in the area. In October 1987 it became the first of the Atlantic Fleet adversary units to receive the F-16, its initial complement comprising 10 F-16Ns and two TF-16Ns. Subsequently half of this number was loaned, and then permanently assigned, to VF-43 at Oceana.

Markings initially consisted of a red star on the fin and red two-digit codes on the

nose. The 'AD' tailcode (shared by VF-43) was also worn. The squadron badge consisted of a blackbird with boxing gloves, underneath which was the legend '4 and 20' in reference to the nursery rhyme. This badge was subsequently worn on the fins of the aircraft

VF-45 flew the F-16N until the retirement of the type from Navy service in 1995.

In the early 1990s VF-45 aircraft featured a 'blackbird' badge instead of the original red star. At the same time, the two-digit codes changed to green from red.

VF-126 'Bandits'
NAS Miramar, California

In April 1987 VF-126 became the first US Navy squadron to receive the F-16, acquiring six for its fleet adversary training commitment. This was performed in support of the co-located West Coast Tomcat community. Markings consisted of a small red star on the fin, two-digit red codes under the cockpit (rather than on the nose) and a white modex presented at the top of the fin, incorporating the unit's 'NJ' tailcode. The six aircraft were used until complete retirement of the F-16N from Navy service in 1995.

Although it shared a base with the NFWS, VF-126's task was to provide adversaries for Pacific Fleet fighters. The unit often deployed to NAS Fallon, the main West Coast site for pre-cruise work-up and home to the adversary F-5Es and F/A-18s of VFA-127.

Navy Fighter Weapons School ('Top Gun')
NAS Miramar, California

F-16Ns began arriving at the NFWS in June 1987, dramatically improving the unit's capabilities to replicate advanced Soviet aircraft and to teach advanced air combat techniques to already proficient squadron air

crews. A total of eight F-16s were assigned to the school, these featuring a variety of schemes through their careers. One aircraft was given a desert sand scheme, and another had a striking green/grey scheme.

The latter aircraft was marked with 'Marines' titles to signify that service's participation in the NFWS programme. The unit's marking, consisting of a MiG caught squarely in a gunsight pipper, was worn on

the fin.
In common with other F-16N users, the NFWS finally gave up its aircraft in 1995, having fully transitioned to the F/A-18 and F-14 to fulfil its adversary needs.

The NFWS used the F-16N to replicate threats from aircraft such as the MiG-29 and Su-27.

A variety of schemes has been worn by NFWS aircraft, although most retained the original three-tone camouflage.

National Aeronautics and Space Administration

Langley Research Center
Langley Field, Virginia

Around 60 per cent of NASA Langley's work is devoted to future aircraft design, and to support its experiments the Center operates a single F-16A (N516NA). This is used for a variety of high-speed trials, and is supported by a grounded F-16B. The F-16A retains standard two-tone grey USAF camouflage, bearing the NASA logo and individual aircraft number on the fin, with the civil registration applied on the side of

the rear fuselage.
Much earlier the second FSD F-16A was used by Langley for a pylon decoupler test. Between April and November 1994 Langley also operated the single-seat F-16XL-1, normally based at Edwards. Used for experiments into take-off performance and noise as part of a future airliner study, the XL received a smart black and white scheme for these trials.

Above: For a period in 1994 Langley operated the F-16XL-1, in this smart scheme, for trials into noise footprints.

Below: This F-16A currently serves at Langley as a general-purpose trials platform. Another aircraft is on strength as a spares source.

Dryden Flight Research Center
Edwards AFB, California

Named after Dr Hugh L. Dryden, the Edwards facility is NASA's principal flight research site, investigating high-performance aircraft. Dryden was the principal facility flying the AFTI/F-16 (NF-16A), this programme being undertaken jointly with the USAF, US Navy and US Army. A series of test phases with this aircraft in various configurations began in July 1982, and although NASA conducted the tests, the AFTI aircraft never received a NASA number.

An ongoing programme which is undertaken purely by NASA is the use of the two F-16XL prototypes to test various supersonic laminar flow wing sections, and other technologies intended for use in a future supersonic airliner. NASA had initially co-operated with General Dynamics in the original design of the F-16XL, and in January 1989 signed a leasing deal with the company to use the two redundant prototypes. Having been stored since 1985 at Fort Worth, the single-seat aircraft

returned to Edwards in April, assigned NASA number 849. The two-seater has also joined the SLFC programme, originally assigned number 846, but subsequently renumbered as 848.

Above: The two F-16XLs are assigned to NASA Dryden for testing wing sections incorporating advanced supersonic low drag laminar flow sections.

General Dynamics/Lockheed

Lockheed Martin Tactical Aircraft Systems
Fort Worth, Texas

What is now the LMTAS was originally known as the General Dynamics Tactical Military Aircraft Division. Following Lockheed's December 1992 purchase of the plant, it was renamed Lockheed Fort Worth Company on 1 March 1993. The name changed to its present title in 1995 after Lockheed's merger with Martin Marietta.

Throughout the Fort Worth association with the F-16, the manufacturer has operated several aircraft for its own purposes. On occasion these are bailed back from the Air Force for short trials

programmes (as recently happened with the F-16ES demonstrator), while some have been borrowed from a variety of sources for international air shows.

One aircraft from the original FSD batch, 75-0572, has been used over the years for a variety of manufacturer's trials, including the testbed for the J79 engine. The aircraft, as the F-16B-2, was fitted with advanced air-to-ground equipment and Falcon Eye FLIR as a technology demonstrator for the close air support role, and has supported many sales drives, including that to the US Navy.

75-0572 has been used for many years by GD/Lockheed as its main testbed. The camouflage was applied for the F-16B-2 CAS trials.

Bahrain   Bahrain Amiri Air Force

This emerging Middle Eastern country received 12 GE F110-powered Lockheed/Martin F-16C/D Fighting Falcon Block 40D/40E aircraft in March 1990. They were intended to supplement Bahrain's single squadron of Northrop F-5 Tiger IIs purchased five years earlier. Receiving the serials 101, 103, 105, 107, 109, 111, 113, 115 (FMS 90-0028/0035) for the F-16Cs and 150/152/154/156 (FMS 90-0036/0039) for the F-16Ds, the aircraft ordered in 1987 were delivered under the Peace Crown programme and saw action as part of the coalition forces during Operation Desert Storm.

As a result of the Gulf War, Bahrain is now eligible for low-cost equipment following the United States' 1994 Defense Authorization Act. An offer has recently been made to exchange 18 surplus US Navy F-16N Fighting Falcons for the surviving Northrop F-5E/Fs, which would bring a measure of standardisation to the defence force. Three Sharpshooter targeting pods for the F-16s ordered in late 1993 are expected to be delivered in 1996.

This aircraft was the first of four F-16Ds for Bahrain. The single squadron is based at Sheikh Isa AB on the east coast of the island. More aircraft are sought to replace the Northrop F-5s.

Belgium   Belgian Air Force (Force Aérienne Belge/Belgische Luchtmacht)

Belgium was the first of the four NATO start-up partners to receive the F-16 when twin-seat F-16B, FB-01, was delivered on 29 January 1979. The aircraft were produced by SABCA/SONACA at Gosselies as a replacement for the ageing Lockheed F-104G Starfighter. The country's original order was for 116 examples comprising 96 single-seat F-16As and 20 twin-seat F-16Bs, serialled FA-01/96 and FB-01/20 (FMS 78-0116/0161; 80-3538/3587, 78-0162/0173; 80-3588/3595) respectively. IOC (initial operating capability) was reached in January 1981, by which time 18 single-seat and five twin-seat aircraft had been delivered.

The first 25 F-16As and 10 F-16Bs were built to Block 1/5 standard, although later upgraded to Block 10 standard. The following 20 As and two Bs were delivered factory fresh. The remainder were built as big-tailed Block 15 aircraft, with deliveries of the original order being completed in the latter part of 1985.

In February 1983 plans were announced for the purchase of an additional 44 aircraft (40 F-16As and four F-16Bs) to re-equip a third wing and replace the Dassault Mirage V. Serialled FA-97/136 and FB-21/24 (FMS 86-0073/0077; 87-0046/0056; 88-0038/0047; 89-0001/0011; 89-0025/0027; 87-0001; 88-0048/0049; 89-0012). Belgian aircraft differ slightly from other NATO machines in having been retrofitted with ESD Carapace ECM, resulting in the deletion of the small blade antennas under the nose of the Block 15s, and the addition of bulged fairings on the intake sides. Brake parachutes were fitted to the final batch and have been have been retrofitted to the remainder of the fleet. The air force also tested the aircraft with the MATRA Magic 2 missile as an alternative to Sidewinder.

June 1993 saw the Belgium government commit itself to the F-16 mid-life update programme. This covers some 48 airframes and involves a major avionics upgrade including the installation of GPS, MLS, an improved radar and advanced IFF. The air force is undergoing a restructuring that will reduce the flying combat units of the TAFC (Tactical Air Force Command) from three to two wings, with a total of six squadrons of 12 aircraft each.

To achieve this level of operational capacity it was intended to withdraw a number of early Block 10 F-16s and place them for disposal. With attrition having accounted for 16 of this variant, approximately 45 aircraft (all of the F-16As and a few F-16Bs) were ferried to the former USAFE logistics airfield at Weelde where they have been placed in long-term store. Belgium had been hopeful of finding a buyer for some of these aircraft, but with a glut of early model F-16s now available it has found itself in the position whereby it would not be cost effective to sell the aircraft. It is likely that these F-16s will be held as a reserve or broken down to provide spares for the remaining aircraft in use.

1 Smaldeel/Escadrille

1 Smaldeel became the last Belgian squadron to transition to the F-16 Fighting Falcon. Located at Florennes air base within the structure of 2 Wing, the squadron received its first aircraft in mid-1989. At that time the air force was still adopting a relatively high-visibility approach to squadron markings which resulted in No. 1 Squadron adopting a black-and-yellow fin strip with a black-and-white diamond in the central position. Further down the fin was a thistle motif taken from the official squadron badge. This comprises a green thistle surrounded by a belt containing the motto 'Nemo Me Impune Lacessit' (No man provokes me with impunity).

During 1992 a special scheme was created for aircraft FA-111, inspired by the squadron's black and yellow colours and designed to celebrate the unit's 75th anniversary. No. 1 was to also receive Belgium's final F-16A, FA-136, which arrived sporting a triangular badge inscribed 'The little last one'.

1 Sm/Esc celebrated its 75th anniversary in 1992, and produced this smart scheme accordingly. Prior to gaining F-16s in 1989, the unit had flown Spitfire XIVs, F-84E/Gs, F-84Fs and Mirage 5s.

Above and right: The tails of 1 Sm/Esc aircraft carry the thistle badge from the squadron's official emblem. The fin-band design is shared with 2 Sm/Esc.

2 Wing at Florennes was slated to receive all of the second order of Block 15 F-16s, with aircraft being assigned to the two squadrons in alternate order. With the closure of 1 Wing at Beauvechain, however, some reallocation of airframes is taking place to ensure there is a more even distribution of higher-houred aircraft between the two surviving wings.

Since completing conversion to the F-16 the unit has only lost one aeroplane, when a member of the ground crew 'borrowed' F-16A FA-105 on 5 September 1989 while on detachment to the Norwegian air base at Ørland. The jet crashed shortly after take-off during this unauthorised flight.

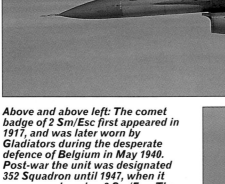

2 Smaldeel/Escadrille

The first of the squadrons at Florennes to receive the F-16 Fighting Falcon, No. 2's deliveries began in early 1988. Setting the trend for the wing, the squadron adopted a blue fin band outlined in white with a black-and-white diamond superimposed in the centre. The squadron also chose to include its red comet emblem lower down the fin, which symbolises the squadron motto 'Ut Fulgar Sulca Aethera' (Cleave the air like lightning) and which was also worn by its former Mirage 5BA mounts when the unit was assigned to 3 Wing at Liege/Bierset. In 1992, to mark the squadron's 75th anniversary, FA-120 received a commemorative blue colour scheme with the unit's red comet superimposed upon it.

Above and above left: The comet badge of 2 Sm/Esc first appeared in 1917, and was later worn by Gladiators during the desperate defence of Belgium in May 1940. Post-war the unit was designated 352 Squadron until 1947, when it was renumbered as 2 Sm/Esc. The unit flew Spitfires, F-84Es, RF-84Fs and Mirage 5BAs prior to 1988, when the Falcon appeared.

Right: 2 Sm/Esc applied one of the smartest schemes ever to adorn an F-16 on the occasion of its 75th anniversary in 1992.

23 Smaldeel/Escadrille

23 Squadron operates from Kleine Brogel air base as part of 10 Wing. The squadron transitioned to the F-16 Fighting Falcon alongside its sister squadron during 1982, when it retired the venerable Lockheed F-104G Starfighter. The unit initially received

23 Sm/Esc painted this F-16 in a special scheme during 1991, highlighting the unit's devil badge and red/white fin-stripe.

early Block 1 aircraft before trading these in for the larger-tailed Block 15s, these once again being allocated alternately.

Sporting a red-and-white saw-tooth fin band with the unit's red devil motif as a centrepiece, the aircraft also wear 10 Wing's red lion and golden crown upon a blue shield. Although individually assigned, the aircraft generally function as a pool for the wing's squadrons with whoever is on the early 'push' providing the bulk of the aircraft for the day's flying.

The squadron celebrated its 40th

anniversary in 1991 and painted F-16A FA-91 in an attractive red-and-white colour scheme with the unit's red devil superimposed on the red tail.

The squadron was one of the first in NATO to have female aircrew, this being highlighted when FA-113, which had been transferred from No. 1 Smaldeel, overturned onto its back when attempting to take a taxiway exit too quickly at Hradec Kralove while attending the Czech International Air Fest in May 1995. The accident occurred when the aircraft (as

number two of a pair) landed in formation with the leader, only to begin aquaplaning due to heavy rain. The leader ordered go-around and applied reheat, which swamped his No. 2, who was then unable to stop on the remaining runway length. The pilot, FAB's sole female fighter pilot, ejected as the aircraft began to overturn.

In addition to the fin-stripe, which contains the unit badge of a devil holding two bombs, 23 Sm/Esc aircraft carry the 10 Wing badge.

31 Smaldeel/Escadrille

Belgium's No. 31 'Tiger' Squadron has been a part of 10 Wing since 20 December 1951, when along with its current sister unit, 23 Smaldeel (and in company with 27 Smaldeel which disbanded in June 1962), it moved from Bevekom to Chievres with Supermarine Spitfire Mk XIVs. Today No. 31 is located at Kleine Brogel air base where it operates Block 15 F-16 Fighting Falcons, having transitioned from the venerable Lockheed F-104G Starfighter in 1982, a type it operated for 18 years.

Although lapsing into realms of garish improvisation when attending the annual

NATO Tiger Meets, the squadron generally has a very sober approach to unit markings and chooses to portray a small tiger motif alongside its 10 Wing red lion on a blue shield. During 1991, however, when celebrating its 40th anniversary, the squadron produced perhaps one its most tasteful schemes to date.

Below: 31 Sm/Esc produced this remarkable special scheme during 1991 to commemorate both the unit's 40th anniversary and its status as a NATO 'Tiger' squadron.

Above: Standard squadron aircraft wear relatively muted markings consisting of a tiger's head (for the squadron) and the 10 Wing badge. The unit transitioned from F-104Gs in 1982.

F-16 Operators: Part 2

349 Smaldeel/Escadrille

Identifiable by its motif of a spiked ball on a chain (known locally as the Godendag), 349 Squadron is one of two Belgian squadrons specifically charged with air defence. The unit currently resides at Beauvechain air base as part of 1 Wing, but is scheduled to relocate to Florennes in March 1996 to become the third squadron assigned to 2 Wing.

Initially operating the early Block 1/10 F-16s, the squadron became the first European unit to reach IOC, in January 1981. Markings include a blue fin strip outlined in white, with the Godendag as the centrepiece. This squadron has now received Block 15 aircraft and adopted low-visibility markings which, although primarily the same as carried previously, are now portrayed in grey on a lighter grey background. To make unit identification easier, within the grey stripe is inscribed '349 SQN'. On the rudder the aircraft carry the 1 Wing golden falcon superimposed on a light blue circle.

During 1987 the squadron celebrated its 45th anniversary, which prompted the application of a special colour scheme to F-16A FA-49.

Above: The current markings of 349 Sm/Esc consist of a toned-down grey fin-stripe, with a small 1 Wing badge below. The fin-stripe contains a representation of the Godendag.

Left: 349 Sqn's original markings consisted of a blue fin-stripe with the Godendag. The unit had its origins in the wartime RAF, forming in 1942 and subsequently flying Spitfires during the liberation of Europe. It subsequently operated the Meteor F.Mk 4, Meteor F.Mk 8 Hunter, Avro Canada CF-100 and F-104G before gaining the F-16 in early 1981 to be the first European service operator of the type.

350 Smaldeel/Escadrille

As a sister unit to 349 Squadron at Beauvechain air base, 350 Squadron was the second Belgian air force F-16 unit to reach IOC. Again initially operating with Block 1/10 aircraft, which it began receiving in 1979, the squadron has now transitioned on to the larger-tailed Block 15 model. Unit markings were originally comprised of a red fin strip with the head of Ambiorix as the centre emblem. Today the unit has adopted a low-visibility stance akin to 349 Squadron, and also portrays the wing insignia on the rudder. During 1987, 350 Squadron celebrated its 45th anniversary and produced a very attractive commemorative scheme.

350 Squadron will re-locate to Klejne Brogel air base by March 1996 as part of the Belgian air force's restructuring programme, while the bulk of its earlier Block 10 mounts are now in long-term storage at Weelde air base.

During F-16 Fighting Falcon operations, 1 Wing has lost 16 aircraft in accidents, all early Block 10 aircraft, including two twin-seat F-16Bs.

350's badge depicts Ambiorix, a Gaul warrior. The unit's motto translates as 'Belgians, bravest of the Gauls'.

Operational Conversion Squadron

The OCS formed at Beauvechain air base to oversee conversion of new pilots to the F-16, and is equipped mainly with two-seat F-16Bs with a handful of F-16As. The unit adopted a blue fin band outlined in red with the wing's golden falcon as the centrepiece, but today it too has adopted low-visibility markings. The OCS is scheduled to relocate to Kleine Brogel and its role will be absorbed by 10 Wing.

Currently the OCS aircraft (mostly F-16Bs) wear the golden eagle wing badge of 1 Wing at Beauvechain. When the unit moves to Kleine Brogel they will adopt the 10 Wing badge.

Denmark

Royal Danish Air Force (Kongelige Danske Flyvevaaben)

Denmark was a member of the quartet that brought the F-16 Fighting Falcon to Europe, gaining its aircraft from the SABCA production facility at Gosselies. The initial order was for 46 single-seat Block 1/5/10 F-16As serialled E-174/203 (FMS 78-0174/0203) and E-596/611 (FMS 80-3596/3611), and 12 two-seat F-16Bs serialled ET-204/211 (FMS 78-0204/0211) and ET-612/615 (FMS 80-3612/0615) to equip four squadrons. The first aircraft, ET-204, was received from Gosselies on 18 January 1980 and was handed over to Esk 727 10 days later. The first single-seater, E-174, was delivered on 18 February 1980 and passed into the hands of Esk 727 two days later. Subsequent airframes were delivered from the Belgian production line at a rate of approximately 1.5 a month during the first year, giving the air force a total of 17 F-16s at the beginning of 1981.

Deliveries were completed by the end of 1984, by which time a further batch of eight F-16As with serials E-004/008 (FMS 87-0004/0008) and E-016/018 (FMS 88-0016/0018), and four F-16Bs (ET-197/199; FMS 86-0197/0199 and ET-022; FMS 87-0022) had been ordered. These later airframes were of the larger-tailed Block 15 variety and came from the Fokker production line in the Netherlands rather than SABCA.

The earlier Block 1/5 F-16s were gradually upgraded to Block 10 standard by the RDAF at Aalborg under a programme known as Pacer Loft 1. Another batch of 12 aircraft was planned in 1989 as part of a three-year modernisation programme. However, these fell foul of defence spending cuts that also saw the demise of the two Saab Draken squadrons. Three F-16As intended for partial replacement of the seven examples lost in accidents were purchased from the United States. These three jets (82-1024, 83-1075 and 83-1107) were former aircraft of the 170th Fighter Squadron, Illinois Air National Guard. Deliveries to the RDAF occurred during July 1994. The aircraft have since undergone modification to bring them up to a compatible standard with the remaining aircraft in the Danish inventory and are expected to enter service during 1996 as E-024, E-075 and E-107, respectively.

Four of the seven RDAF F-16 losses have occurred as a result of mid-air collisions. This apart, the RDAF safety record in respect of the F-16 is second to none in Europe, with no major incidents or losses having occurred since 1987.

Denmark is putting 61 aircraft through MLU to add wide-angle HUD and other improvements.

Eskadrille 723

Esk 723 began transitioning from the Lockheed F-104G Starfighter to F-16 Fighting Falcon on 1 January 1983. Conversion was undertaken at Skrydstrup air base under the watchful eye of Esk 730 before the squadron returned to its home base of Aalborg.

Tasked with the fighter attack mission, the squadron became operational on 31 March 1984. The aircraft carry a minimum of identification and sport a small squadron emblem of a winged blue/silver shield with an eagle superimposed and the legend 'Valet Vigilat'. This is located on the port side of the engine air scoop.

Danish aircraft carry little in the way of unit identification, this usually being restricted to an intake badge.

Above: Eskadrille 723's badge consists of an eagle, beneath which is the unit's motto.

Eskadrille 726

Esk 726 was the fourth and last RDAF squadron to equip with the F-16 Fighting Falcon. Based at Aalborg alongside Esk 723, this squadron was also a former F-104G Starfighter. Esk 726's last flight with this venerable aircraft occurred on 29 December 1983.

After achieving operational readiness, the squadron was given the additional task of pilot training for the RDAF, a role it shared for a time with Esk 727. However, upon the

Left: Eskadrille 726's badge consists of a three-clawed motif. The unit also wears a badge on the fin.

demise of the Saab Drakens of Esk 725 and Esk 729, the unit was assigned the task of tactical reconnaissance. To fulfil this role it received not only the Red Baron reconnaissance pod with Vinten cameras, but was allocated the 12 new Block 15 aircraft shortly after the start of their deliveries in December 1987. In 1996 the

Left: To fulfil the reconnaissance role, Esk 726 uses the Red Baron pod previously carried by Drakens. A new low-drag pod is under development.

Esk 726 was assigned all of the 12 Block 15 OCU aircraft purchased in a follow-on batch.

Danish F-16 force is expected to begin operations with a lower-drag Per Udsen reconnaissance pod.

Once again unit insignia are rather nondescript, but in line with other Danish squadrons the aircraft sport a winged red shield with three falcon claws superimposed upon it, with the motto 'In Corpore'. Again, this is located on the aircraft's port side just aft of the engine intake.

Eskadrille 727

The first squadron to receive the F-16 Fighting Falcon in the RDAF, Esk 727 formed its first contingent of pilots on 1 July 1980 even though the unit had been receiving aircraft at its Skrydstrup base for the previous six months. Esk 727 was declared operational on 1 April 1981. The squadron undertook an operational work-up to fulfil its fighter attack mission while simultaneously participating in the MOTE (Multinational Operational Test & Evaluation) programme alongside the United States, Norway, the Netherlands and Belgium. Another of the unit's responsibilities was to provide the initial cadre of pilots for its sister squadron Esk 730.

Aircraft assigned to the squadron can be identified by the small, blue, winged shield located on the port side intake, with a silver Thor's hammer superimposed upon it.

Thor's hammer is the badge of Esk 727. The aircraft shown right also carries a zap from No. 5 Sqn, RAF.

Eskadrille 730

Esk 730 was Denmark's second squadron to receive the F-16 Fighting Falcon. The retired North American F-100 Super Sabres were returned to US charge as per the FMS agreement, for onward transfer to Turkey. Transition to the F-16 began on 1 January 1981 and was completed on 11 August 1982, at which time the unit was declared operational. It was then charged with its fighter attack mission and also that of pilot conversion for the RDAF.

Esk 730 uses a bull as its badge, and this featured strongly in a rare special scheme applied to this aircraft for the unit's 40th anniversary in 1994. The bull motif is also painted on the dummy Sidewinders.

Egypt   Egyptian air force (Al Quwwat al Jawwiya Ilmisriya)

Despite the 1979 rapprochement with Israel that helped to defuse Middle East tensions, Egypt has maintained its formidable armed forces and remains a decisive force in that area. In June 1980, Egypt signed a letter of agreement for its initial purchase of 40 General Dynamics F-16A/B Fighting Falcons. Comprising 34 Block 15 F-16As and eight F-16Bs serialled 9301/9334 (FMS 80-0639/0643; 81-0643/0661; 82-1056/1065) and 9201-9208 (FMS 80-0644/0648; 81-0662; 81-0883; 82-1043) respectively, they were delivered under the Peace Vector 1 programme. The first aircraft were handed over in a ceremony at Fort Worth during January 1982, with deliveries to Egypt commencing the following March.

It is interesting to note that one aircraft from this initial order, F-16B Block 15P 81-0883 (later 9207), was produced on the Fokker production in the Netherlands. Having originally been laid down for the KLu with construction number '6E-24', this was changed to '9F-7' to accommodate the transfer to Egypt.

The initial order was followed by the purchase of 40 Block 32 F-16C/Ds, the first of which was delivered to Egypt on 11 October 1986. In October 1987 a further agreement was signed under the Peace Vector III programme for another 47 F-16C/Ds, although on this occasion the aircraft were to be to Block 40 specification and to have BVR capability through the use of the AIM-7 Sparrow missile. A third batch of 46 F-16C/Ds was ordered in June 1990 under Peace Vector IIIA, these to come from the Tusas Aircraft Industries production line at Murted in Turkey. This latest order, which is still in production, will give Egypt a total force of 175 F-16s of all derivatives.

Those Block 32 and Block 40 F-16C aircraft produced at Fort Worth were serialled 9501/9534 and 9901/9935 (FMS 84-1332/1339; 85-1518/1543; 89-0278/0279; 90-0899/0930) and the F-16Ds 9401/9406 and 9801/9812 (FMS 84-1340/1345; 90-0931/0937; 90-0954/0958) respectively, while those emanating from Turkey were 9951/9984 (FMS 93-

0485/0530) and 9851/9862 (FMS 93-0513/0524).The early batch of Block 32 aircraft equipped the 242nd Regiment at Beni Suef during 1986. One jet, 9501, remained in the United States to undergo development work with the General Dynamics test facility at Edwards AFB until 1992.

Illustrating Egypt's two batches of F-16C/Ds are a Block 32 single-seater (below) and a Block 40 two-seater (above). The F-16C wears a pre-delivery test registration derived from its FMS serial (84-1333), while the D should be painted 9802.

Greece Hellenic Air Force (Elliniki Aeroporia)

Greece announced its decision to purchase the F-16 in November 1984, with a view to partially replacing its ageing but large fleet of Northrop F-5A Freedom Fighters. The order for the aircraft, 36 Block 40 F-16Cs and six F-16Ds, was signed in January 1987 and made Greece the 14th nation to operate the Fighting Falcon.

The first F-16D, 88-0144, was handed over in a ceremony at Fort Worth on 18 November 1988, with F-16C 88-0110 following a few weeks later. Crew training was initially undertaken in the United States. The first aircraft for 111 Pterix (Wing) arrived at the Nea Ankhialos base in January 1989, and the final delivery of the Block 40 aircraft took place in October 1989.

The aircraft delivered under the Peace Xenia programme are serialled 110-143 for the F-16Cs and 144-149 for the F-16Ds, which are the last three digits of their FMS serials. Service allocation to the wing's two squadrons, 330 Mira and 346 Mira, has been on an alternate basis with the former receiving the odd-numbered aircraft and the latter the even-numbered. Squadron markings have not been worn in the past, although attitudes towards such events are gradually changing, as has been seen on the Hellenic Mirage 2000s.

Attrition has been light in the seven years of operation, with only one known loss occurring. An unidentified aircraft collided with a Dassault Mirage 2000 from 114 Pterix at Tanagra near Pelagos on 26 November 1992, resulting in the loss of both aircraft.

An additional 40 F-16s (32 Cs and eight Ds) have subsequently been ordered for delivery during 1997/08. These are Block 50 aircraft and will replace the last remaining Northrop F-5s currently serving with 341, 343 and 349 Mira. In the meantime, the air force is awaiting the delivery of 24 Martin Marietta LANTIRN navigation and 16 LANTIRN targeting pods.

Greece's Block 30 aircraft differ from standard aircraft by being fitted with brake parachutes and nose-mounted ID light.

Above: One of two patches worn by 330 'Keraunos' Mira pilots. The other depicts a falcon and a lightning bolt.

Above: Armed with practice 'blue bombs' on TERs, this F-16 is operated by 346 'Jason' Mira at Nea Ankhialos as part of 111 Pterix. In addition to its front-line duties, 346 Mira is also the type OCU.

Indonesia Indonesian Air Force (Tentara Nasional Indonesia – Angkatan Udara)

Introduction of the F-16 into the Indonesian air force occurred in October 1989 following the signing of a letter of agreement in August 1986 for the supply of eight Block 15 F-16As and four F-16Bs.

The choice of the F-16 to replace the country's ageing fleet of Soviet MiG-21 'Fishbed' fighters and other types indigenous to the Eastern Bloc was undertaken not only to provide a credible defence posture in the region but also partly for prestige and morale purposes. The aircraft, serialled S.1601/1604 (FMS 87-0721/0724) for the F-16Bs and S.1605/1612

(FMS 87-0713/0720) for the F-16As, began arriving at Madiun-Ishwahyudi air base in December 1989 under the Peace Bima-Sena programme, with deliveries being completed during 1990. The F-16s currently operate alongside the BAe Hawk Mk 53s and the Northrop F-5E/Fs of No. 14 Squadron from Madiun air base.

Indonesia hopes to be in a position to purchase additional F-16s during 1996 to bring its squadron up to a strength of 16 aircraft. The country's next five-year plan, which begins in 1996, anticipates the funding of an additional squadron of F-16s.

TNI-AU F-16s wear an unmistakable camouflage scheme, and are further distinguished by having brake chutes. The order of 12 included four two-seaters (below). More purchases are scheduled if funding permits.

Israel   Israeli Defence Force/Air Force (IDF/AF) (Heyl Ha'Avir)

Following the Camp David Peace Treaty between Israel and Egypt, both countries were rewarded by the United States with substantial deliveries of the General Dynamics F-16 Fighting Falcon. Up until that time the offer of such sophisticated hardware had been made to only the United States' closest allies, such as NATO, South Korea and Iran. The latter country, through its revolution, ruled itself out of the equation. Israel became the F-16's first Middle East customer and received many of the airframes already under construction for the Imperial Iranian air force (IIAF). Israel's initial approach to the United States in respect of the F-16 had been met with a polite refusal; at that time, it had hoped to purchase some 250 examples with 200 being built under licence within Israel. In spite of this initial stumbling block, subsequent events saw Israel become one of the largest users of the type.

Although no formal treaty existed between the United States and Israel, the sale of F-16s was granted under the Carter administration when arms transfer restrictions prevented such sales to other so-called 'friendly' countries. Israel therefore was at the very forefront of the F-16 community when it announced plans in August 1978 to procure 75 F-16A/B Blocks 5 and 10 models for the IDF/AF.

Deliveries of the initial four aircraft began in July 1980 following an 11-hour, 6,000-mile (10160-km) flight from Pease AFB, New Hampshire. Further aircraft were delivered under the Peace Marble programme, enabling IOC to be reached within weeks of the aircraft arriving in Israel. The first 18 single-seat and eight two-seat aircraft were Block 5 aircraft which incorporated a number of internal changes unique to Israel, including the installation of chaff/flare dispensers.

Before deliveries of this first F-16 order to Israel were complete the type saw its baptism of fire when, over the Beka'a Valley during 1982, F-16s notched up an impressive tally of 44 aerial victories over Syrian MiGs. This action followed the raid on the Iraqi nuclear reactor at Osirak on 7 June 1981, an operation that had originally been assigned to the IDF/AF McDonnell Douglas F-4E Phantom IIs but which shortly before its implementation was reassigned to the newly arrived F-16s.

As a result of these so-called acts of 'military recklessness', Ronald Reagan delayed delivery of the final 22 aircraft from the original order although, ultimately, the aircraft did find their way into IDF/AF service. The order comprised 26 Block 5 and 49 Block 10 airframes. Many of the airframes were upgraded, featuring not only structural changes that included the larger Block 15 tailplanes to give increased pitch authority, but also wiring improvements facilitated in the later Multi-Stage Improvement Program (MSIP).

The F-16C/D version of the Fighting Falcon followed the earlier F-16A/Bs into service with the IDF/AF. The C is known

locally as Barak (Lightning) and the D as Brakeet (Thunderbolt). Deliveries began in October 1987, with Israel once again becoming one of the first customers for this upgraded version. Fifty-one Block 30 F-16Cs and 24 F-16Ds were delivered under Peace Marble II, with many if not all of the latter being delivered with or being retrofitted with a prominent dorsal spine. This modification is believed to house new avionics, possibly including the Elisra SPS 300 ECM jamming system often associated with the defence suppression role. These aircraft are operated in an operational mode rather than as continuation trainers.

Most of these aircraft, both C and D models, have now been upgraded to the more capable Block 40 standard with the provision for LANTIRN and HARM, and featuring GPS, APG-68 radar, automatic terrain following and the common engine bay. Following the cancellation of the indigenous Lavi fighter programme in August 1987, Israel, in May 1988, placed a follow-on order for a further 60 production Block 40 F-16C/Ds. The order was divided evenly between Cs and Ds. Subsequently, a repeat order for an equivalent amount of aircraft has been placed for delivery between 1997 and 1999. These will effectively see the replacement of the remaining Douglas A-4N Skyhawk fighter-bombers, the McDonnell F-4E Phantom IIs and probably the Kurnass 2000. Israeli F-16s have been subject to a variety of modifications, many of which substitute indigenous equipment for that of US origin. Details are given in the variant entry.

As compensation for Israel's non-intervention during the Gulf War, the IDF/AF was allocated 37 surplus USAF F-16As and 13 F-16Bs. The aircraft had been made

Above: This aircraft was from the first batch of Block 5 aircraft delivered to Israel from July 1980.

Below: Seen on test in the US, '506' is one of the Block 40 aircraft delivered from July 1991.

available through the ending of the Cold War. These aircraft – either drawn from storage at AMARC or delivered direct from converting ANG units – will be upgraded in Israel to IDF/AF standards by IAI. They are intended to replace the last of the Kfir fighter-bombers which have now been placed in storage at Ovda to await resale to potential customers.

Serialling of Israeli F-16s is designed to create the illusion that there are significantly more aircraft in service than there really are. The F-16A/Bs of the first order were numbered 100 to 138, with a number of gaps, for the Block 5 aircraft (FMS 78-0308/0325) and 001/017 for the eight two-seat F-16Bs (FMS 78-0355/0362). The Block 10s were 219 to 299 (FMS 78-0326/0354, 80-0649/0668).

Block 30 aircraft (FMS F-16C 86-1598/1612, 87-1661/1693, 88-1709/1711, F-16D 87-1694/1708, 88-1712/1720) received numbers in the ranges 301 to 399 and 020 to 083 respectively, not only having the accepted gaps but also not following in sequential order with the allocation of FMS serials. The 60 Block 40 aircraft so far delivered were serialled 502 through to 558 for the single-seat C model (FMS 90-0850/0874, 91-0486/0489) and 601 to 687 for the Ds (FMS 90-0875/0898, 91-0490/495). The surplus USAF aircraft (78-0012, 0014, 0018, 79-0288, 0289, 0291/293, 0295, 0297, 0299, 0302, 0304, 0305, 0319/0321, 0325, 0328, 0333, 0339, 0356, 0358, 0369, 80-0491, 0501/0503, 0514, 0516, 0517, 0532, 0534 and 78-0086, 0095, 0106, 0108, 0109, 0111, 0114, 0115, 79-0410, 0423/0425, 80-0624, 0632) have been appearing in the 700-series serial range.

Such is the method of IDF/AF serialling that the last two digits of the individual aircraft number remain with the jet for its entire life, while the initial digit is assigned to that aircraft's modification state. No information has been forthcoming from Israel regarding serial changes, other than a couple of publicity photographs depicting F-16Bs with serials in the 100 series which slot in around those allocated to the Block 5 F-16As. If the method adopted with both the Phantom and Kfir when they were modified continues, then, in due course, some aircraft may well be reserialled if they receive any significant designation change.

Israel's understandable concern with security makes it difficult to ascertain squadron details. The following entries have been compiled from unofficial sources.

As suggested by the stylised 'X' on the fin, this F-16C Block 30 is flown by the IDF/AF flight test centre. It is believed to be the first of the batch, which arrived in Israel in late 1986.

This F-16D Block 30 Brakeet wears the fin-badge and well-known rudder stripes of 101 Sqn, the 'First Fighter' unit. This operates a mix of Cs and Ds, their two-seaters featuring the enlarged spine with mission avionics.

aircraft that have so far been noted in service with 144 Squadron have received Israeli serials in the 700 range. Unusually, they have not been repainted in the standard Israeli camouflage scheme and, apart from the fin receiving a coat of grey paint, the aircraft are being operated in a standard USAF scheme. The unit's large stylised yellow bird marking has been applied in red and detailed in yellow.

190 Squadron

This squadron formed at Ramon air base alongside No. 140 Squadron when it too began to receive F-16A/B model made available by the upgrading of the Ramat David-based 110 and 117 Squadrons. These aircraft are operated with markings comprising a red disc with an eagle's head and a superimposed F-16.

In a period of much change, rumours exist that 190's number plate will be transferred to a squadron due to form on AH-64A Apaches. This would allow 190's F-16A/Bs to be used either to support the other two Ramon-based squadrons or to enable the transition of one of the surviving Douglas A-4N Skyhawk squadrons prior to the receipt of the expected further delivery of late model F-16C/Ds.

253 Squadron

This squadron is the third of those based at Ramon air base to operate the Fighting Falcon, and was the first at that base to transition to the type. The unit was the third to convert to the F-16A/B, after Nos 110 and 117 Squadrons. Squadron markings comprise a yellow falcon on a blue disc.

Variously reported as wearing 190 or 253 Sqn badges, this is an F-16A Block 10.

101 Squadron

Located at Hatzor air base just to the south of Tel Aviv along highway 40 with Canaf (Air Wing) 4, this unit is known simply in Israel as the 'First Fighter Squadron'. The unit transitioned from the indigenous Kfir C7 to the Block 30 F-16C/D during 1987. The unit subsequently exchanged these Block 30 examples for the new Block 40 aircraft delivered during the early 1990s under Peace Marble III.

These latest aircraft operate in the standard Israeli desert camouflage scheme, with a red/white diagonally striped rudder. The upper part of the fin sports a badge comprised of a winged skull wearing a flying helmet superimposed on a black disc. The squadron appears to be operating a fairly even mix of F-16C and D airframes.

105 Squadron

A sister squadron in Canaf 4 at Hatzor is No. 105 Squadron, which received its F-16C/D aircraft during 1991 from the last deliveries under Peace Marble III. Receipt of both the Barak and Brakeet enabled the squadron to dispose of its ageing McDonnell F-4E Phantom IIs, which in turn were passed on to the remaining users of the type at Hatzerim.

Configured in a similar manner to 101 Squadron, No. 105 has chosen to adopt more lavish markings, with the entire tail section covered with a large scorpion applied in the lightest shade of the basic camouflage pattern. Above this is a small badge comprising a red scorpion on a red, white and blue disc. The extended fairing containing the ECM and braking parachute has also received a red/white chevron.

109 Squadron

No. 109 'Valley' Squadron is located at Ramat David air base in the northern half of Israel (Canaf 1). The unit was the last of the squadrons at the base to convert to the F-16. In 1991 it disposed of its Kfir C7s for what is believed to be the upgraded Block 30 F-16C/Ds previously operated by No. 101 Squadron. Upon receipt of these aircraft their entire fins were covered with the silhouette of a bird of prey with outstretched wings, applied in the palest of the three camouflage colours. The fin also sports a small red disc containing a black bird of prey perched on a white crescent moon.

110 Squadron

Another Ramat David-based squadron, No. 110 is equipped with the Block 30 F-16C/D. The unit was the second in Israel to receive the Fighting Falcon when it received the F-16A/B in 1981. Its latest aircraft were received in 1987. They are decorated with a large hawk's head covering the tail fin and a smaller squadron badge consisting of a stylised bird carrying a dart-like bomb. The

aircraft also feature a small lightning flash superimposed on a green-and-black rectangle on the tail ECM/parachute fairing.

117 Squadron

The third F-16 squadron to be based at Ramat David is 117 Squadron, which was the first in Israel to transition to the Fighting Falcon in 1980. Up until that time the squadron had been operating the highly successful but very old Nesher. The unit was then charged with service introduction on the F-16A/B and is known as the 'First Jet' squadron.

No. 117 transitioned to the more capable F-16C/D during 1987 and took on charge the Block 30 aircraft being delivered under Peace Marble II. The aircraft today sport a jagged silver-grey lightning flash down the sides of the fin, with an aircraft silhouette and crescent moon in white on a red disc.

140 Squadron

Based at Ramon air base in the heart of the Negev Desert, No. 140 Squadron acts as the operational conversion unit for the Israeli IDF/AF F-16 community. The unit is equipped with a selection of early Block 05/10 F-16A/Bs which it received in 1987 from the converting 110 and 117 Squadrons at Ramat David.

These aircraft are not as garishly marked as those assigned to both Hatzor and Ramat David, which might reflect a base policy rather than an individual unit preference. The jets do carry a small fin badge with a

yellow bird of prey superimposed on a green disc.

144 Squadron

The latest squadron to transition to the F-16 is Hatzor's third squadron and the final Israeli unit to operate the indigenous Kfir C7. The unit began to transition to the F-16A/B during 1994, receiving those aircraft transferred from surplus USAF stocks. (It is thought that a number of the surplus USAF machines will be used as a spares source. There are sufficient airframes to form a 10th squadron, but to date no evidence exists that this has taken place.) 144's former aircraft were placed into storage at Ovda with other examples that had been retired in previous years.

The F-16s received attention and upgrading by IAI, although this appears to have been undertaken at Hatzor. Those

Below: The giant scorpion badge identifies 105 Sqn, this aircraft being an F-16C Block 40.

Netherlands

Royal Netherlands Air Force (Koninklijke Luchtmacht)

The Netherlands, along with Belgium, Denmark and Norway, was one of the start-up partners for the multinational F-16 programme. Its initial purchase was for 102 aircraft, eventually increasing to 213 following an announcement made in March 1980 and approved by the Dutch Parliament in December 1983.

The aircraft are tasked as part of the NATO 2nd Allied Tactical Air Force (2 ATAF) in the role of close air support (CAS) with a secondary requirement of air superiority over the battlefield and within the region allotted to the Netherlands within NATO. The KLu began receiving its F-16s on 7 June 1979, when the first example off the Fokker-VFW production line was delivered

to Leeuwarden having undertaken its maiden flight the previous month. Production by Fokker-VFW followed that by SABCA and produced all of the aircraft to fulfil the Dutch order, as well as the majority of those procured by Norway. One F-16B originally laid down for the Netherlands was diverted to Egypt. The final Dutch delivery took place in March 1992.

The Koninklijke Luchtmacht was structured around nine front-line squadrons and an operational conversion unit. Following a defence white paper in 1991 and a subsequent review in 1993, prompted by the changes in the former Soviet Union, the air force was reorganised and restructured. From this, the F-16

community was reduced to six front-line squadrons assigned to three front-line bases as opposed to the nine previously stationed at five different locations. The KLu also maintained a training detachment as part of the 162nd Tactical Fighter Training Group, Arizona Air National Guard at Tucson International Airport. This arrangement ran from December 1989 to April 1994, during which time both Dutch instructors and aircraft were operated from this US facility.

With a force reduction in hand, the KLu intends to dispose of 20 aircraft during 1996 with a further 16 being sold after 2000. In the meantime, the remaining aircraft will undergo a mid-life update programme which will lengthen the operational use of

the aircraft until about 2010, when a replacement will be sought. To date, 27 aircraft have been lost in accidents while a number of the earlier aircraft are now being retired and used for ground instructional duties.

Three of the active KLu 'swing-role' F-16 squadrons are dedicated to the NATO Rapid Reaction Force. Drawn from Nos 306, 315 and 322 Squadrons, one unit is assigned on rotation to the UN Deny Flight peacekeeping force in Bosnia and operates in respect of the UN mandate from Villafranca-Verona air base in northern Italy.

The 213 F-16s delivered to Holland comprised 12 Block 1 single-seaters: J-212/223 (FMS 78-0212/0223), 14 from Block 5: J-224/237 (FMS 78-0224/0237), 20 from Block 10: J-238/257 (FMS 78-0238/0257), and 131 from Block 15: J-258 (FMS 78-0258), J-616/648 (FMS 80-3616/3648), J-864/881 (FMS 81-0864/0881), J-192/207 (FMS 83-1192/1207), J-358/367 (FMS 84-1358/1367), J-135/146 (FMS 85-0135/0146), J-054/063 (FMS 86-0054/0063), J-508/516 (FMS 87-0508/0516), J-710 (FMS 87-0710), J-001/021 (FMS 88-0001/0012, 89-0013/0021). All of the Block 1 and 5 aircraft were brought to Block 10 standard between 1982 and 1984, while the Block 15 aircraft have been subject to an Operational Capabilities Upgrade (OCU) since late 1987.

Some 36 twin-seat F-16Bs were procured, six Block 1 aircraft: J-259/264 (FMS 78-0259/0264), two Block 5: J-265/266 (FMS 78-0265/0266), five Block 10: J-267/271 (FMS 78-0267/0271), the remaining 23 all being larger-tailed Block 15 aircraft: J-649/657 (FMS 80-3649/3657), J-882 (FMS 81-0882), J-884/885 (FMS 81-0884/0885), J-208/211 (FMS 83-1208/1211), J-368/369 (FMS 84-1368/1369), and J-064/068 (FMS 86-0064/0065, 87-0066/0068).

In 1989 the KLu staged this formation in recognition of 10 years of F-16 operations. Notable is the 313 Sqn aircraft (J-364) wearing the unit's previous badge.

306 Squadron

The unit was the second of those operated from Volkel air base to receive the F-16. Charged with a mixed task of tactical reconnaissance and close air support, the unit is assigned to both 2 ATAF and the NATO Rapid Reaction Force. It therefore shares peacekeeping duties with Nos 315 and 322 Squadrons and currently rotates both aircraft and crews onto Deny Flight operations. For its reconnaissance task the unit has retained the Orpheus pod previously used on the F-104G Starfighter, which is carried on the centre-line station. Aircraft configured with the pod are known as F-16A(R)s.

Although for logistic reasons the squadron operates from Volkel, its war-time assigned base is that of De Peel. This base is currently in a reserve state but is activated on a number of occasions each year when the squadron relocates. Under the 1993 defence review, De Peel is scheduled to be closed. No. 306 Squadron will remain at Volkel, but there are sufficient hardened shelters available at other KLu bases to house the unit should it become necessary, with Eindhoven being identified as the first choice.

306's aircraft are operated in the standard two-tone grey camouflage scheme

Above and left: 306 Sqn has always been the KLu's reconnaissance unit, and now operates Block 15 F-16s with the Orpheus camera pod. The squadron applies different bands on either side of the fin.

and display markings comprised of a golden head of an eagle and five white stars in a vertically divided black-and-blue circle. Most aircraft also wear a blue/yellow/black band or black/white 'Limburg' band on one side and the red/white Volkel band on the other.

311 Squadron

The squadron began receiving the first Block 15 aircraft in May 1982 to fulfil its fighter attack mission. Declaring itself operational on 1 October 1983, No. 311 forms part of the Volkel wing assigned to NATO's 2 ATAF.

The squadron initially received the FY 1980 batch of Block 15 F-16s but, with the current state of modification and with aircraft being detached for Deny Flight duties, 311 currently operates a mix of Block 10 and 15 examples. It appears that very few aircraft are wearing the squadron emblem of a black-and-white eagle with golden claws and a beak in a blue circle. The vertical fin sports a red/white checkered band that is known locally as 'Brabants Bont' and derived from the local region's flag.

Below: 311 Sqn introduced revised marks but still featuring the eagle. The squadron was formed in 1951 to operate F-84Es, subsequently flying the F-84G, F-84F and F-104G. In 1960 it adopted a nuclear strike role.

Left: Wearing the unit's traditional eagle markings, this F-16A Block 15 poses with a 32nd TFS F-15C. The F-15s were based on Dutch soil.

312 Squadron

No. 312 is the third of the Volkel squadrons to convert to the F-16 and the last Dutch user of the venerable F-104G Starfighter. Assigned to NATO's 2 ATAF in the fighter attack role, the unit was initially equipped with the final batch of Block 15 airframes from the original order. Due to increased KLu commitments as part of both the Rapid Reaction Force and UN peacekeeping duties, the squadron – like its sister unit – operates a mixture of Block 10 and 15 aircraft.

Squadron markings, when applied, are two golden crossed swords and a bolt of red lightning in a black circle. The fin features the red/white checkered 'Brabants Bont'.

The crossed swords badge of 312 Sqn was applied in 1991 to this aircraft (above) for the unit's 40th. Regular squadron aircraft wear the badge much smaller on the fin (right).

313 Squadron

No. 313 received its first F-16, J-359, at Twenthe on 1 June 1989 but did not become operational on the type until 1 April 1990. The unit was tasked originally in the fighter-attack role as part of NATO's 2 ATAF but, following the inactivation of No. 316 Squadron on 1 April 1994, 313 was assigned the role of training and was declared non-operational from that time.

The first few aircraft assigned to the unit received a toned-down version of the marking that had been previously carried on the Canadair NF-5s. This comprised a golden eagle alighting on a white runway in a blue circle. On the F-16 these markings were depicted in differing shades of grey. Shortly after converting to the Block 15 F-16, a new tiger head marking was adopted which was approved shortly before the unit was declared operational in 1990. This marking is a full-colour tiger's head on a blue disc. The aircraft also wear across the fin a red band with the local 'Twenthe Ros' horse symbol in white superimposed upon it.

Below: 313 Sqn adopted the tiger as its badge to qualify for NATO 'Tiger' club status. These 'specials' were produced for a Tiger Meet.

Above: The squadron badge is now a tiger's head, although this pair displays it facing both fore and aft.

Below: The 'Twenthe Ros' fin-band consists of a series of prancing horse figures on a red stripe.

F-16 Operators: Part 2

314 Squadron

314 Squadron was one of the final Dutch squadrons to form on the F-16 and received its first aircraft in April 1990. Equipped with Block 15 aircraft in the fighter attack role as part of NATO's 2 ATAF, the unit relocated from Eindhoven to Gilze Rijen in the transition period. Under the 10-year defence plan the squadron was destined to move again, this time to Leeuwarden in 1996. Following the 1993 review it was decided to inactivate the squadron on 1 January 1996, although in the end this date was brought forward to 6 July 1995, when all flying ceased.

During its short career with the F-16, the squadron adopted similar markings to those previously carried on the Canadair NF-5, comprising a golden centaur holding a bow and arrow in a red circle. On the F-16, however, this marking was portrayed toned down in several shades of grey, although the fin carried a white band enclosing black fox heads with red tongues.

Right: 314 Sqn's aircraft wore a toned-down centaur badge on the fin. The squadron was disbanded in 1995 as the KLu F-16 force contracted to six front-line squadrons.

Right: In 1992 314 celebrated its 40th anniversary with this special scheme. The unit was previously an NF-5 operator. In 1971 the unit was temporarily known as '630 Sqn' as it was in the process of forming 316 Sqn (314+316=630). The NF-5 served from 1970 to 1990.

315 Squadron

315 Squadron was the first of the former Canadair NF-5 users to transition to the F-16A/B. Equipped with Block 15 aircraft, the unit is charged with the role of fighter attack as part of NATO's 2 ATAF and is also assigned to the Rapid Reaction Force. As such, it shares periods of detachment to Villafranca-Verona air base in Italy as part of Deny Flight operations supporting the UN mandate and peacekeeping force in Bosnia.

Home-based at Twenthe, 315's aircraft carry a marking comprised of either a grey lion's head on a grey disc or a yellow lion's head on a blue disc. At the tip of the fin is a red band with white 'Twenthe Ros' horses superimposed upon it.

Seen at Verona in 1993, this 315 Sqn F-16A Block 15 carries four Sidewinders for its participation in Deny Flight.

The lion's head tail badge was initially worn in toned-down greys (below), but is now presented in full colour.

316 Squadron

The final unit to transition to the F-16 in Holland was 316 Squadron. When it reformed at Gilze Rijen in June 1991 the unit was assigned the task of F-16 conversion, a role it took over from No. 323 Squadron. For this task it received four Block 15 F-16As and eight F-16Bs. The unit relocated to Eindhoven on 30 September 1991 and was scheduled under the 10-year defence plan to move to Twenthe in 1996. However, following the 1993 review it was decided to inactivate the unit and it disbanded on 1 April 1994, passing its conversion task to No. 313 Squadron.

1993 saw the 40th anniversary of 316 Sqn, with this aircraft receiving a special scheme including the hawk badge.

During its short period of operation the aircraft operated with a badge comprising a yellow disc containing a white hawk. The fin tip sported a white band containing a number of black fox heads with red tongues.

316 Sqn undertook the OCU role during its brief existence. Only four single-seat aircraft were assigned to the unit, the majority being F-16Bs.

322 Squadron

322 Squadron was the first Royal Netherlands air force squadron to become operational on the F-16, achieving that level in May 1981. Equipped with early Blocks 1, 5 and 10 aircraft, the unit was assigned the fighter attack role although it maintained a bias towards its former air defence tasking. From 1982 to 1984 its early airframes were upgraded to Block 10 standard. Today 322 operates predominantly Block 15 airframes, with the earlier aircraft having been reassigned. With the upgrade to the larger-tailed Block 15s came assignment to

Above: Another KLu anniversary special, this time for 322 Sqn's 50th. The unit was established within the RAF in 1943 flying Spitfire Mk Vs and subsequently Mk XIVs.

NATO's Rapid Reaction Force and deployment to Italy as part of Deny Flight.

Unlike F-104 Starfighter days, when the Leeuwarden wing carried dual markings, No. 322 Squadron aircraft sport the grey parrot emblem. They also wear a blue/white fin tip band containing the red motifs of the Frisian flag.

Above: 322's 'Polly Grey' parrot badge is one of the best-known in the Klu. The squadron's motto is 'Niet Praten, Maar Doen', translating as 'No words, only action'. The fin-band is for the Frisian district.

323 Squadron

323 Squadron began conversion to the F-16A/B alongside its sister squadron at Leeuwarden and became operational early in April 1982. Initially equipped with early Blocks 1, 5 and 10 airframes, the squadron was charged with the dual roles of fighter attack and operational conversion. It was tasked with the latter role following the inactivation of the CAV in March 1986, and to achieve this had received the bulk of the early build F-16Bs.

The conversion role was withdrawn partially in 1989 when KLu training was transferred to the United States along with eight F-16As and four F-16Bs. The remaining part of this package was finally removed in September 1991 when the conversion role was tasked to the newly formed No. 316 Squadron at Eindhoven, although 323 picked up the additional tasking of Fighter Weapon Instructor Training. 323 Squadron has continued to operate a mix of aircraft from all four blocks.

The assigned aircraft operate with the emblem of a yellow and red Diana the Huntress on a black disc. The fin tip is painted with a blue/white band containing red motifs of the Frisian flag.

323 Sqn was formed in 1948 and was the KLu's first jet squadron, flying Meteor F.Mk 4s. The Diana the Hunter badge has been retained throughout its history.

Training and Conversion All-Weather (TCA)

Conversion of F-16 pilots within the Royal Netherlands air force was initially carried out by this unit at Leeuwarden, but in March 1986 the role was transferred to No. 323 Squadron. During the period of operation the assigned aircraft sported a blue circle on the fin containing a cartoon whale with a black radome for a nose. The unit was initially known as the Training en Conversie Afdeling, and previously flew the TF-104G. The title was subsequently anglicised.

Test Groep

The Test Groep is located at Volkel and undertakes trials and tests, borrowing aircraft from the operational units. It does have one F-16B assigned, J-653. This aircraft wears a modified national insignia as its unit badge with the winking owl crest superimposed.

Until 1986 the TCA/CAV carried out type conversion. Aircraft wore a cartoon figure with F-16 nose.

Norway   Norwegian Air Force (Kongelige Norske Luftforsvaret)

Although Norway has one of the largest coastlines anywhere in Europe to defend, it relies heavily on natural defences. Nonetheless, to police Norwegian waters and provide a credible aerial defence, Norway was quick to join the four-nation consortium for the introduction of the General Dynamics F-16A/B Fighting Falcon.

Norway identified a requirement for 72 F-16s to meet its needs, divided between 60 single-seat F-16As and 12 twin-seat F-16Bs. These were to be built by Fokker-VFW at Schipole, with the maiden flight of the country's first aircraft taking place on 12 December 1979. The aircraft were designed to replace both the Lockheed F-104G

Starfighter and the Northrop F-5A Freedom Fighter.

The F-16s were delivered between 15 January 1980 and 4 June 1984. They equipped four front-line squadrons, one of which would also have the role of operational conversion unit. Norway's aircraft differed from those supplied to NATO, as Norway had requested an extended tailcone for housing a braking parachute made necessary by the winter operating conditions, something that was not considered a problem for those countries in the central European region, although both Belgium and the Netherlands subsequently retrofitted chutes.

All the squadrons are charged with a primary role of air defence, with a secondary commitment of coastal defence for which the Penguin Mk 3 missile is the main armament. The aircraft were all from early production, split fairly evenly between the small-tailed Block 1/5/10 and big-tail Block 15s. The RNoAF is planning a mid-life update (MLU) programme for its aircraft which will enable them to continue in service until 2020.

With attrition standing at six aircraft in 1987 (nearly one-tenth of those procured), Norway had been hoping to buy six replacements comprising four F-16As and two F-16Bs. In the end, this was reduced to

two more Block 15 two-seat F-16Bs which came from the Fort Worth production facility rather than Fokker at Schipole. By the time these were delivered attrition had claimed 12 aircraft, and a further two have been lost since, which brings the total to 14, or one-fifth of those received.

The 74 aircraft received were F-16A Block 1 78-0272/0274, Block 5 78-0275/0284, Block 10 78-0275/0299, Block 15 78-0300, 80-3658/0688, and F-16B Block 1 78-0301/0302, Block 5 78-0303/0304, Block 10 78-0305/0307, Block 15 80-3689/3693, 87-0711/0712. In all cases, Norway uses the last three digits of the FMS serial for identification.

331 Skvadron

331 Skv retired it ageing Lockheed- and Canadair-built F-104G/TF-104G Starfighters in June 1981, the survivors being transferred to Turkey the following month. The unit had already by that time begun to transition to the F-16 in parallel with 332 Skv at Rygge, returning to its Bodø base on completion of the conversion course. At that time the unit had received early Block 1/5/10 airframes but converted to the larger-tailed Block 15 in early 1984, and in doing so received the final aircraft of the

Below: In addition to the fin-stripe, 331's aircraft also carry the squadron badge. This machine has been 'zapped' by 416 Sqn, CF.

Norwegian order.

The squadron has had its fair share of incidents and has lost five F-16s in the 12 years of front-line operation. One of these crashed as a result of a mid-air collision over the Nellis Range during the 1986 Red Flag; the second machine recovered but had to

be sent to Ogden ALC for substantial repairs.

Aircraft assigned to the unit are identified by the red/white/blue fin flash and the blue lightning flash under the cockpit, both markings being legacies of the Sabre and Starfighter days.

A quartet of 331 Skvadron aircraft displays the single-tone grey scheme worn by Norwegian F-16s. The unit applies a blue lightning flash below the cockpit as well as the fin-flash.

332 Skvadron

332 Skv had been inactive for five years following its disbandment as a Northrop F-5A user. It was recommissioned at Rygge to become the first Norwegian F-16 squadron and to serve as the type's operational conversion unit (OCU).

The unit received alternate airframes from the Block 1/5/10 production run, sharing the deliveries with 331 Skv, with which 332 worked up. When 331 Skv then transitioned to the larger-tailed Block 15 examples, its former aircraft were returned to Rygge where they were redistributed to the emergent 338 Skv. This re-shuffle saw 332 Skv receive principally the Block 1/5 F-16A airframes which had been upgraded to Block 10 standard, leaving 338 Skv to pick up the remaining Block 10s. The unit also employed a high proportion of the twin-seat F-16B aircraft in its conversion role. Unit attrition has seen four aircraft, three F-16B and one F-16A, lost in accidents.

332's aircraft operate in an all-over single grey colour scheme with national insignia displayed just aft of the cockpit. The fin flash is black and yellow.

Apart from the fin-flash 332 Skv aircraft wear no unit identifications, not even the axe insignia worn by the previous F-5s. The unit was established in the RAF in January 1942, and flew Spitfires on fighter sweeps and convoy patrols in the European theatre.

334 Skvadron

In late 1982 334 Skv moved from Rygge to Bodø to convert to the F-16A/B, becoming the first Norwegian unit to receive Block 15 airframes. No. 334 converted from its Canadair CF-104 Starfighters, the latter then moving into storage at Sola air base. The unit had also previously operated the F-5A Freedom Fighter. Charged primarily with air defence, No. 334 is also operational in the anti-shipping role using locally-built Kongsberg Penguin anti-ship missile.

Conversion was completed in 1984 and in 11 years of operation the unit has only suffered one total loss, when the first Block 15 aircraft, 78-0300, was lost in a crash at Morsvikfjord, Nordland on 5 July 1988. Although the pilot was killed in this incident, the unit has the best safety record of all the Norwegian squadrons.

Aircraft assigned to 334 Skv can be identified by the red/white fin flash.

334 Skvadron formed in late May 1945 as a Mosquito unit within the RAF. Today it uses F-16s in both the air defence and anti-shipping roles.

338 Skvadron

338 Skv was the last Norwegian squadron to receive the F-16A/B, completing the planned four-squadron fleet. It received its Block 10 aircraft at Ørland following the transition of 331 Skv to the Block 15 in 1984. Initially, there were insufficient aircraft and pilots for the unit to be declared fully operational, a result of both the upgrade programme being applied to the earlier Block 1/5 airframes and a general pilot shortage created through airline recruiting.

When 338 Skv did reach its full establishment it received the bulk of the Block 10 airframes. Four aircraft have been lost between 1987 and 1990, including a mid-air collision, and the squadron has since been supplemented with Block 15 aircraft transferred from the Bodø wing.

Identification of those aircraft assigned to 338 Skv is by the black fin flash containing a yellow lightning bolt; above this can be found a black bow and arrow.

338 Skv wears both its lightning bolt fin-flash and a bow symbol. Norwegian pilots wear Dayglo flight suits for greater conspicuity in the event of ejecting over snow.

Pakistan   Pakistan Air Force

Pakistan has maintained a well-armed military because of its ongoing differences with India and other regional issues, such as Islamabad's support for the Mujahideen rebels that were fighting the Soviet-supported Afghan government. Pakistan's air force has had close ties with a number of countries within its history, including Great Britain, then the United States and finally China, with whom links continue.

Introduction of the General Dynamics F-16A/B Fighting Falcon came about following a letter of agreement that was signed in December 1981. This initial order came in the shape of 32 single-seat F-16As and eight twin-seat F-16Bs. These were allocated US serial numbers 81-0899/0930

Pakistani F-16s do not wear unit identification, but it is known that this aircraft serves with No. 11 Sqn.

and 81-0931/0938, respectively, under the terms of Foreign Military Sales (FMS). Before the contract became too far advanced the order was modified to 28 F-16As and 12 F-16Bs, reflecting Pakistan's possible future need to conduct all of its own in-house training. The combat effectiveness of the force was altered very little since both versions are combat-capable, a point which was emphasised by subsequent events.

Changes within the FMS serialling

department saw aircraft 81-0927/0930 cancelled and 'new' F-16Bs 81-1504/1507 being added. This apart, the FMS serials are not reflected in the PAF serialling system.

All the aircraft were built to Block 15 standard, with the first being accepted at Fort Worth in October 1982. The initial delivery of two F-16As and four F-16Bs was carried out in January 1983 when the jets were flown to McDill AFB, Florida before

Two of the embargoed second batch are seen at Davis-Monthan, where they have been in storage pending a decision as to their future.

being inflight refuelled across the Atlantic Ocean to the Azores and then to Dhahran, Saudi Arabia. The first two legs were flown by American delivery pilots although four PAF pilots occupied the rear seats in the F-16Bs. The flight from Dhahran was completed utilising only PAF personnel, all of whom had undertaken training and conversion under the auspices of the 421st Tactical Fighter Squadron at Hill AFB, Utah.

This first batch of F-16s equipped three front-line squadrons, one of which also served as an operational conversion unit. Deliveries were completed in 1985 and in the following few years the aircraft proved themselves in combat, claiming a number

defending Pakistan airspace, standing an alert commitment which it rotates with the other two F-16 squadrons.

The aircraft display no unit insignia and only toned-down national markings. It was originally assigned aircraft 84-704 through to 84-716, although by now it is probable that aircraft have been interchanged.

The squadron took the honour of claiming the first success against violating Afghan air force aircraft when, on 17 May 1986, Squadron Leader Qadri intercepted a flight of Su-22 fighter-bombers. Two Sukhois were despatched, the first with an AIM-9 Sidewinder AAM causing it to crash 9 miles (23 km) inside Pakistan territory, and the second with the use of cannon.

11 'Arrows' Squadron

Pakistan's first F-16 squadron formed in 1982 at Sargodha air base as part of 38 (Tactical) Wing. The squadron has a dual role operating as both a front-line fighter unit and the operational conversion unit. The intake of pilots into the F-16 community is such that the OCU only operates for around five months of each year. The remaining period sees the unit become another line squadron.

No. 11 is equipped with just three F-16As, 701 to 703, and most of the two-seat F-16Bs. Being co-located with No. 9 'Griffins' Squadron, it is able to borrow aircraft as and when required. The aircraft of No. 11 display no individual unit insignia.

14 'Shaheens' Squadron

The third and last PAF squadron to re-equip with the F-16A/B was No. 14 'Shaheens'. Reforming at Kamra air base in September 1986, it received the last 12 aircraft from the original PAF order, 717 to 728. The unit is stationed the farthest north among the F-16 community and has experienced more than its fair share of live intercepts. One of these was conducted on 4 August 1988 when Squadron Leader Bokhari in aircraft 85-725 shot down a Soviet Su-25 'Frogfoot' which had strayed 7 miles (11 km) inside Pakistan air space.

Further victories were claimed on 12 September 1988 when two MiG-23s were shot down by Flight Lieutenant Khalid Mahmood while flying aircraft 85-728. He then destroyed an Su-22 on 3 November 1988 with an AIM-9L fired from 84-717. An An-26 'Curl' was destroyed by the squadron commander on 21 November 1988, which was the first time authority had been given to a PAF pilot to shoot down a non-fighter aircraft.

Under test from Fort Worth, this is one of the second batch aircraft seen prior to the embargo.

of kills against trespassing Afghan fighters.

In September 1989, when relations with the United States were at an all-time high, plans were announced for Pakistan to acquire 71 additional F-16A/Bs and three Lockheed P-3 Orions. A down payment of $658 million out a total cost of $1.75 billion was paid by the Pakistan government and production commenced. However, sanctions were imposed by Congress in 1990 under legislation banning deliveries of military equipment unless the President could certify that Pakistan does not possess nuclear weapons.

This meant the 28 aircraft completed before the stop work order was issued were embargoed and placed into storage within the AMARC complex at Davis-Monthan AFB, Arizona. The continuing wrangle over these aircraft is likely to drag on for some time but there seems little likelihood that they will ever be delivered to Pakistan. As a result, the Pakistan government has requested the return of the original down payment.

The US offered to assist in the sale of the embargoed aircraft to another friendly country. Senator Larry Pressler, the US politician responsible for the legislation which has blocked the delivery of the aircraft, has proposed that 11 of the aircraft be sold to the Philippines and 17 to Taiwan, and that the proceeds from the sales be

used to reimburse Pakistan. The Clinton administration has given the proposal a cautious welcome, but to date little interest has been shown by the countries concerned and the aircraft continue to languish in desert storage. In late 1995 moves were afoot to release the embargoed Orions, and to refund Pakistan with the F-16 acquisition funds.

Attrition in Pakistan on the original batch of aircraft has been low, with only four machines – three F-16As and a single F-16B – thought to have been lost. The Pakistan serials for the first batch of aircraft are F-16A 82-701/702, 83-703, 84-704/719, 85-720/728 (FMS 81-0899/0926) and F-16B 82-601/604, 83-605, 84-606/608 and 85-609/612 (FMS 81-0931/0938, 81-1504/1507). The second batch, although not complete, has been completed in full PAF markings which are F-16As 91-729, 92-730/738, 93-739 to at least 741 (FMS 90-0942/0947, 92-0404/0410) and F-16Bs 91-613, 92-614/619, 93-620/621 (FMS 90-0948/0952, 92-0452/0455).

9 'Griffins' Squadron

Based at Sargodha and forming part of No. 38 (Tactical) Wing, No. 9 'Griffins' Squadron was the second unit to convert to F-16A/B. The squadron plays a major role in

Left: An F-16B touches down at Sargodha. The Pakistani aircraft have a unique camouflage with a central band of dark grey and small patches on the tailplanes.

Below: Pakistan is one of the nations to have used its F-16s in action, having claimed several Soviet and Afghan aircraft along its western borders.

Portugal   Portuguese Air Force (Força Aérea Portuguesa)

During June 1990, the US Congress was notified that Portugal intended to purchase 20 F-16A/B Fighting Falcons from surplus aircraft within the US inventory. These were to be used to replace the LTV A-7P Corsair IIs currently being used as a stop-gap in the interceptor role with Esquadra 304 at BA5/Monte Real.

These aircraft were originally scheduled to be delivered during 1992. After a period

of work-up, they would allow the A-7Ps to be released from their commitments and relocate to BA4/Lajes. Portugal ultimately selected new-build Block 15 OCU F-16A/Bs and delivery of the first four aircraft, F-16As 15102, 15103 and F-16Bs 15119 and 15120, took place on 8 July 1994. They were flown direct from Fort Worth to Monte Real where they were assigned to Esquadra 201. The official handover of F-16A 15101 and

F-16B 15118 in the USA had been carried out on 18 February, making Portugal the eighth NATO air force to operate the Fighting Falcon. These two machines were retained for development work although they have now been delivered.

Allocated serials are 15101/15117 (FMS 93-0465/0481) for the F-16As and 15118/15120 (FMS 93-0482/0484) for the F-16Bs.

Portugal's aircraft have a primary air defence commitment, and are consequently fitted with the HF radio and ID light associated with the USAF's ADF version. However, the AIFF equipment fitted to similar ADF aircraft has not been issued to Portugal, although the aircraft are Sparrow-capable.

Portugal bought three two-seaters in its batch of 20 aircraft, these being to Block 15 OCU standard but lacking the bulge on the lower fin.

Singapore   Republic of Singapore Air Force

Singapore, although no more than a city state on a small island, occupies a strategic corner of Southeast Asia astride the critical Strait of Malacca, where much oil produced in the Middle East transits en route to Asia. Singapore was originally to be the launch customer for the degraded General Electric J79-powered F-16 that was being offered to a number of smaller 'friendly' countries. The RSAF ordered eight examples in January 1985, with an option on 12 more. In mid-1985, when it became clear that the standard F100-powered version would be available, the order was amended to reflect this upgrade.

Four Block 15 OCU F-16A and four F-16B aircraft were delivered under the Peace Carvin programme to replace Singapore's ageing Hawker Hunters. The first aircraft, F-16B FMS serial 87-0401, was handed over at Fort Worth on 10 February 1988, becoming the 2,000th F-16 delivered. However, these jets spent two years at Luke AFB, Arizona before finally transferring to Singapore to be commissioned at Tengah air base in February 1990 with No. 140 Squadron.

During their period with the then-58th TFTW at Luke AFB, the aircraft were operated in a standard USAF scheme with 'LF' tailcodes and a red fin band. This band contained the Singapore national insignia as its centrepiece, reflecting the aircraft's ownership. During August 1989 the aircraft were observed at Luke AFB operating in full RSiAF markings, including the assigned serials 881 to 888, but three months later when the unit participated in Red Flag 1/90

they had reverted to full USAF marks of 87-0397/0404.

Requiring a further 18 aircraft to bolster its combat fleet, Singapore carried out a detailed evaluation of both later generation F-16s and the F/A-18, the outcome of which fell in favour of the Block 50D/52D F-16C/D. As yet no decision has been announced as

to which engine will be adopted, but eight single-seat and 10 two-seat versions were ordered on 9 July 1994 for delivery commencing in March 1998 and ending in December 1999. Once again, nine of the aircraft will be retained at Luke AFB for crew training, a role currently being undertaken at the same location by the

The sharp end of Singapore's defences are the F-16A/Bs of No. 140 Sqn. In service they wear a red fin-stripe.

425th Fighter Squadron of the 56th Fighter Wing using leased F-16A/Bs.

South Korea   Republic of Korea Air Force (RoKAF)

With the country's capital, Seoul, only minutes' flying time from the border with intransigent North Korea, the air force plays a major role in the defence of the Republic of Korea.

There are upwards of 600 tactical jet aircraft in North Korea. This fact prompted the RoKAF in 1981 to upgrade and enhance its own force of air defence fighters with a modest order of Block 32 General Dynamics F-16C/D fighters. Budgetary constraints restricted this order to 36 aircraft, which began to be delivered during March 1986 under the Peace Bridge programme. In the

This aircraft is the first of the Block 52 batch for Korea, displaying the unique camouflage of this user. The later aircraft of the batch are being built by Samsung Aerospace.

process, the Republic of Korea became the first foreign operator of the new enhanced version of the Fighting Falcon.

A speech by President Chun Doo Kwan on 27 June 1986 saw this programme christened Victory Falcon. Two years later,

in June 1988, a top-up order was placed for another four F-16Ds.

In a more ambitious Korean Fighter

Programme (KFP), formerly known as the F-X programme, the F-16 lost out to the competing F/A-18 Hornet. This ultimately led to an announcement by the Korean government on 20 December 1989 of plans to order 120 of the latter. The decision was apparently based on a lucrative offset offer but subsequently became bogged down in

funding technicalities. The government opted for a total reversal and pursued procurement of additional F-16 fighters instead.

In the new deal, the RoKAF will receive 120 Block 52 Pratt & Whitney F100-229-powered F-16C/Ds. Twelve of these are to be built at Fort Worth in the United States,

The first RoKAF batch were Block 32s, and were assigned to the 11th Fighter Wing where they replaced F-4Ds. Korean F-16s train regularly with their USAF counterparts.

36 are to be provided as knock-down kits and assembled in South Korea by Samsung Aerospace, and the remaining 72 are to be built under licence.

The initial order for aircraft saw the jets delivered in a two-tone light grey colour scheme with toned-down national markings. Serialled 85-1574/1583, 86-1586/1597 and 87-1653/1660 for the single-seat F-16Cs and 84-1370/1373, 85-

1584/1585 and 90-0938/0941 for the F-16Ds, they were assigned to the 11th Tactical Fighter Wing at Taegu air base.

Integration with the United States Air Force in Korea has produced a very successful cross-training programme and led to one of the wing's squadrons, the 162nd TFS, participating in the large bilateral military exercise, Team Spirit, during 1986. Such participation has continued.

The first 48 Block 52 aircraft built wholly or in kit form are serialled 92-4000/4027 for the single-seaters and 92-4028/4047 for the two-seaters. Serials for those to be produced under licence have yet to be made public. Initial deliveries of these aircraft commenced on 2 December 1994.

Taiwan   Republic of China Air Force

After the vacillation of US policy towards China, both Nationalist and Communist, the recent decision by the US government to relax its informal embargo against the sale

of fighter aircraft to Taiwan has resulted in a substantial order for 150 F-16s. It is believed these aircraft will be F-16A/B Block 20 variants. Pending delivery, the US Air

Force has leased a number of Northrop T-38A Talon aircraft to the Chinese air force to provide extra training for F-16 pilots.

The decision to purchase the F-16 along

with 60 Mirage 2000-5 aircraft will probably result in the abandonment of further upgrades to the Ching-Kuo indigenous fighter. Orders for that aircraft were slashed in 1992 from the planned 250 aircraft to only 130.

Thailand   Royal Thai Air Force

Thailand has occupied its strategic location in Southeast Asia without ever being occupied by an invader. In 1985, Thai leaders turned to the F-16 Fighting Falcon as a counter to the Vietnamese MiG-23s. In April 1985 the US Congress was told of Thailand's intent to purchase 12 F-16s. At that time the F-16/79 was considered the likely version but, ultimately, it was standard Block 15 F-16A/Bs that were delivered. In July 1987 plans were announced for Thailand to receive an additional six F-16s and a letter of agreement was signed in December 1987.

Thailand took delivery of its first aircraft at a ceremony at Fort Worth in May 1988. Eighteen more F-16s were ordered in January 1992, with the first being handed over at Fort Worth on 11 September 1995. These are to equip a second unit (403 Sqn). The air force is also looking for funding to equip a third front-line squadron but it is doubtful whether it will receive approval for more fighters before the start of the 1996 fiscal year. It is thought that the government wants the air force to fully absorb its second F-16 squadron before further funding is made available. Both the F-16C/D Block 50/52 and the F/A-18 are under scrutiny, with Russia offering the Su-27/35.

Thai aircraft are operated in a lighter scheme than used by the USAF, although with similar disruptive camouflage pattern. Identification of individual aircraft is by four

methods: the construction number, the serial of its former identity (which in the case of the F-16 is an incorrectly presented FMS number), the squadron code and the Thai serial.

Two serials are generally carried, the original FMS one on the tail and a Thai air force serial which is in Thai script. For example, in the Thai serial BK.19-13/37, BK.19 is the Thai aircraft designation for F-16. The next two digits represent the order of delivery, i.e. the 13th example, followed by the last two digits of the

Buddhist year of delivery 2537. Serial BK.19-13/37 is carried on aircraft 91062 (really 91-0062), which also carries a squadron code. This particular F-16 is assigned to 103 Squadron at Korat air base, so it wears the number 10313, which indicates it is the 13th example assigned to No. 103 Squadron.

The Thai air force Block 15 OCU F-16As have FMS serials 86-0378, 87-0702/0708, 90-7020/7031, 91-0062/0067 with the F-16Bs being 86-0379/0381, 87-0709 and 90-7032/7037.

The first batch of F-16s were assigned to 103 Squadron (above), wearing a lightning bolt fin badge. The second batch aircraft emerged from the Fort Worth factory with the cobra badge of 403 Sqn, previously an F-5 operator (left). Deliveries of these aircraft began in September 1995.

Turkey   Turk Hava Kuvvetleri (Turkish Air Force)

The introduction of the F-16C/D Fighting Falcon into the inventory of the Turk Hava Kuvvetleri during 1987 heralded the beginning of what amounts to a programme to lose the stigma of being NATO's poor relation. The choice of F-16 by the Turkish air force was based on sound evaluation of the type's potential coupled with an agreement to allow licence production of the type by the Turkish Aerospace Industry (TUSAS) from its Murted facility. It was in September 1983 that Turkey announced plans to buy 160 F-16s (132 F-16C and 28 F-16D). This evolved into the current order for 240 aircraft, which may possibly rise to 320. The F-16s are designed to replace the Lockheed F-104G/S and Northrop F-5A/B now in service with five tactical air forces – and eventually the McDonnell F-4E Phantom II with three others – allowing Turkey to standardise on a single front-line type.

Two aircraft in knock-down form were delivered to TUSAS in March 1985, and the first flight of a TUSAS-constructed aircraft took place on 20 October 1987. The company will be responsible for supplying

all but the eight aircraft which were manufactured in Fort Worth.

Turkey officially received its first F-16D in a ceremony at Fort Worth during July 1987. Delivery of the first service aircraft under Peace Onyx 1 occurred in October 1987 when 141 Filo, as part of 4 AJU, began receiving the first of 44 Block 30 F-16s. The remaining aircraft on order under Peace

Onyx II are of the more capable Block 40/50 configuration which are compatible with the LANTIRN night-attack system.

The aircraft are operated without individual squadron insignia and have adopted a standard USAF camouflage scheme, as well as utilising the FMS serial range for aircraft identification.

Aircraft so far ordered are F-16C Block

30s 86-0066/0072, 87-0009/0021, 88-0019/0032 with Block 40s 88-0033/0037, 89-0022/0041, 90-0001/0021, 91-0001/0021, 92-0001/0021, 93-0001/0014; F-16D Block 30s 86-0191/0196, 87-0002/0003, 88-0013 with Block 40s 88-0014/0015, 89-0042/0045, 90-0022/0024, 91-0022/0024, 92-0022/0024.

Armed with four AIM-9 Sidewinders, this THK F-16C Block 40 is seen during a Deny Flight mission over Bosnia.

4 Ana Jet Us

The first Filo (squadron) to receive the F-16C/D was 141 'Kurt' Filo located at Akinci air base, which was formerly known as Murted. The squadron is part of 4 Ana Jet Us, one of the four wings assigned to 1 Turk Hava Kuvvetleri Komutanligi. The unit began converting to the Block 30 F-16 during 1988 and was followed into the world of Fighting Falcon operation by its sister unit 142 'Ceylan' Filo a short time afterwards. Both squadrons were equipped with aircraft from the initial order of 34 Block 30 F-16Cs and nine F-16Ds.

Also located at Akinci air base is the 'Oncel' Filo, which is effectively the F-16 operational conversion unit and which shares aircraft with the two resident front-line units. These Block 30 aircraft have been upgraded with an improved ECM system to enhance the variant's survivability in a high-threat environment.

6 Ana Jet Us

F-16s were delivered to 6 AJU at Bandirma air base between May 1991 and May 1993 to equip both 161 'Kartal' Filo and 162 'Zipkin' Filo. In both cases the Fighting Falcon replaced the venerable Lockheed F-104G Starfighter within the wing structure. 161 Filo was the first Turkish squadron to receive the upgraded Block 40 aircraft. In February 1994 the LANTIRN pod was also introduced, giving the Turk Hava Kuvvetleri a truly multi-role capability.

8 Ana Jet Us

Situated the farthest east of Turkey's F-16 operators, 8 AJU at Diyarbakir is part of the 2 Turk Hava Kuvvetleri Komutanligi and has been the fourth and last wing so far to receive the Block 40 F-16C/D. Its two subordinate squadrons are 181 'Pars' Filo and 182 'Atmaca' Filo.

When current orders are fulfilled, the THK will have purchased 240 F-16s. This is one of the first batch of Block 30 aircraft serving with 4 Ana Jet Us at Murted.

Introduction of the F-16 to Diyarbakir began during the early part of 1994 and conversion was completed during 1995. This effectively saw the final retirement of the F-104G Starfighter. The unit also had operated former Canadian Forces CF-104s. Aircraft received by the wing were the last procured under the Peace Onyx 1 programme and further deliveries are expected to be Block 50 aircraft, the initial batch of which has recently received the necessary funding.

9 Ana Jet Us

192 'Kaplan' Filo was the first unit within the structure of 9 AJU at Balikesir to receive the F-16. These Block 40 aircraft began to

192 Filo is a NATO 'Tiger' unit, and this aircraft wore a small badge on the fin for the 1994 Tiger Meet at Cambrai.

be delivered during June 1993, which allowed both 192 and later its sister unit 191 'Kobra' Filo to transition from the F-104 Starfighter.

Both units, along with those from the other wings, undertake UN peacekeeping duties as part of Operation Deny Flight in Bosnia. They rotate aircraft and crews through Ghedi-Brecia air base in Italy from where the detachment operates. In conjunction with all other Turkish fighter units, 9 AJU undertakes alert facilities from Incirlik on Turkey's southern border with Iraq, although the Turkish aircraft operate independently of forces deployed there under a UN mandate.

Venezuela   Venezuela Air Force (Fuerza Aérea Venezolana)

In May 1982, Venezuela signed an agreement for the purchase of 24 Block 15 F-16A/Bs to replace the ageing fleet of Mirage IIIEV and Mirage 5V fighters in the air defence and ground attack roles. This allows the surviving Mirage airframes to be returned to Dassault for upgrading to Mirage 50V standard.

The sale almost foundered, as it had with a number of other countries, when the US government offered the F-16/79 which Venezuela felt would not meet its requirements for long-term maintainability and range. The Pratt & Whitney F100 engine ultimately was selected and the first aircraft was handed over at a ceremony at Fort Worth in September 1983. Deliveries under the Peace Delta programme commenced with six aircraft on 16 November 1983, with IOC being reached on 10 December the same year. The aircraft themselves are operated in a very non-standard F-16 colour scheme of two-tone brown and green. Although no unit insignia are worn, the combat command red chevron logo is carried on the tail.

The Fighting Falcons went to equip Escuadron 161 'Caribes' and 162 'Gavilanes' as part of Grupo Aéreo De Caza No. 16 at El Libertador air base on the outskirts of the city of Maracay. Crews have undertaken a number of exchange visits with the United States and were considered proficient enough to be invited to participate in a Red Flag exercise at Nellis AFB, Nevada in June 1992. The aircraft were involved in the limited *coup* attempt in November 1992, in which they sided with the government forces and were responsible for at least one aerial kill.

Attrition has been light in the 10 years of operation, with only one known loss. Consideration is currently being given to the purchase of an additional batch of F-16s to replace the recently upgraded Canadair VF-5

Freedom Fighters. All the surviving F-16s from the original order have received the Operational Capability Upgrade, and in late 1995 were having the Honeywell H-423 INS fitted, with GG1342 ring laser gyro.

The Venezuelan serialling system has always been a mystery and seems to defy any logic, but identities are known and are as follows: F-16As 0051 (82-1051), 0094 (84-1349), 0220 (84-1357), 0678 (83-1187), 1041 (82-1050), 3260 (83-1188), 3648 (84-1356), 4226 (84-1351), 4827 (84-1354), 5422 (84-1352), 6023 (84-1350), 6426 (84-1353), 6611 (82-1052), 7268 (84-1346), 8900 (84-1353), 8924 (84-1348), 9068 (84-1347), 9864 (84-1355), and F-16Bs 1715 (82-1053), 2179 (82-1054), 2337 (83-1189), 7635 (83-1190), 9581 (82-1055), 9583 (83-1191).

Venezuela is the only F-16 operator to employ a standard tactical camouflage. The aircraft serve with Grupo 16 at Maracay.

Hrvatske Zrance Snage
Croatia's embargoed air force

Despite a UN arms embargo, Croatia has managed to build up an air arm of impressive size, allegedly with German assistance or collusion. As the tide of the war in the Balkans has changed, the Croatians have gone from being on the defensive to conducting offensive actions against Serb areas, and have used their new found air power to devastating effect. *World Air Power Journal's* **Austrian correspondent was given unprecedented access to the air force by its commander, General Imra Agotic.**

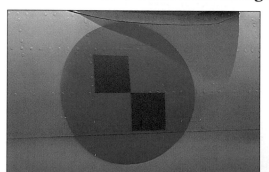

Above: One of an unknown number of MiG-21bis fighters allegedly sourced from the former East German air force, or built from spares according to the Croats.

Left: The post Cold War period has seen an explosion of new nations and new national insignia. This simple blue and red roundel is used by Croatia.

Below: A pair of MiG-21s are readied for flight. Croatia began its air force using lightplanes and a trio of MiG-21s which defected from the old Federal Yugoslav air force. No serials or codes are visible on any of the newly acquired aircraft.

Despite the UN arms embargo imposed on all of the newly independent states of the former Yugoslavia, they all have established their own armed forces, usually with some form of air arm. Croatia in particular has been able to build up an increasingly large and capable air force since 1992. This, the HZS (Hrvatske Zrance Snage), has now been blooded, mounting many combat sorties during operations in western Slavonia in May 1995 and against the Krajina Serbs during August 1995. *World Air Power Journal's* Austrian correspondent recently visited Croatia at the invitation of General Imra Agotic, the HZS Commander.

When Croatia split away from Yugoslavia in 1991, the new republic immediately began to form its own armed forces. The Hrvatske Zrance Snage was formed during the third quarter of 1991, even before the new nation had been officially recognised by the international community. General Agotic recalled that "at first, there were only difficulties and problems. In most of the branches of the force, there was

almost nothing left (by the retreating Serbs). We had a dramatic lack of equipment, but not of pilots. Sports and agricultural aircraft formed flying brigades under the command of local frontal sectors. Some damaged helicopters were also taken from the JNA and RSK forces. But often our planes could not reach trouble spots because all the jets were in Serb hands, and our pilots had the same experiences as the Fieseler Storch crews in World War II.

Confrontation with Yugoslavia

"When it became clear that there could be no peaceful solution in the face of Greater Serbian designs on parts of our nation, I was selected by president Tudjman to head our team in the difficult talks with the JNA (Jugoslav National Army) commanders in Zagreb. After the loss of Slovenia and the capture of eastern Slavonia, tension increased around the large JNA camps and barracks in and around Zagreb. Negotiations started on 8 October 1991 and lasted until the 2 January 1992, the day the first Vance peace plan became valid. We were able to reach an agreement on the withdrawal of the JNA armoured columns, and seized a nucleus of equipment for

Above: Judged too 'dirty' to be kept in service by the Luftwaffe, with its depleted uranium core, the R-60 AA-8 'Aphid' nevertheless remains a highly effective short range AAM, and represents the primary weapon of the Croat MiG-21s.

Right: Although equipped with Soviet-bloc aircraft, and trained in Communist Yugoslavia, Croatia's fighter pilots wear Western equipment and consider themselves part of a Western-type air arm.

Below: A Croat pilot straps into his MiG. The Croat MiG-21s carry the national shield on their fins, and a squadron emblem (a Knight's head) on their noses.

Above: It is believed that Croatia can arm any (or all) of its Mil Mi-24 'Hind-Es' although it chooses not to do so. This aircraft is seen in the armed configuration with gun turret, underwing rocket pods and wingtip missile launch rails. The old East German air force never used the 'Hind-E' so these aircraft may be ex-Ukrainian.

Left: All Croatian aircraft wear the national crest, a red and white checkerboard design, surmounted by an ornamented crown representing Croatia's provinces. This also forms the centrepiece of the national flag.

our future forces and – maybe the most important – we gained a break before the oncoming clashes. But we were unable to prevent the JRV (Federal Yugoslav Air Force) from taking away or destroying almost all their infrastructure on Croatian soil. I was nominated as Chief of Staff of the air force and air defence by our first Defence Minister, Martin Spegelj."

Agotic's appointment as Commander of the HZS was instrumental in transforming it from an ill-equipped liaison and light support force into a modern air defence force. He was a radar specialist and had been responsible for radar-surveillance and radar-guidance units during his JRV service. Exercise Posejdon '94, the first major Croatian exercise, was held in November 1994 and helped to demonstrate that the HZS was already able to support its own ground

troops and to simultaneously protect the airspace of the non-occupied territory of Croatia. The radar network covered all of the area within its internationally recognised borders and especially the airspace closest to Serbia, around Banja Luka and the southern area around Udbina and Knin.

The recent operational sorties during the recapturing of western Slavonia in May 1995 and the invasion of Krajina in August 1995 underlined the air force's readiness. Croatia's invasion of Krajina (Operation 'Storm') was accompanied by the mass movement of the local Krajina Serbs, although there has been controversy as to whether they left voluntarily (or on Serb instructions) or as a result of Croat 'ethnic cleansing'. The operation has restored one portion of what Croats see as their rightful borders, but has also removed some potentially dangerous Serbian forces from the Croatian periphery.

Provocation from Udbina

In this context, the capture of Udbina airfield was particularly important, its significance being explained by General Agotic shortly before the invasion: "Two Galebs from Udbina recently flew a sortie against positions within the UNCRO demarcation corridor, despite the 1991 decision not to use air power and artillery within the 20-km zone. Two Kenyan UN observers were wounded. Although plotted by NATO, there was the decision in Sarajevo not to intercept them under Deny Flight rules. We agreed very much with NATO's bombing of Udbina last fall, but this incident shows that Udbina is again very active. The RSK or Krajina Serbs are operating around four MiG-21s, eight to 10 SOKO Oraos and eight Jastreb/Galebs.

"Udbina is even today within our artillery range and is not our biggest problem. The main

threat to Croatia is posed by the air base at Banja Luka in Serb-controlled northern Bosnia. There are two squadrons with a mix of Orao, Jastreb and Super Galeb fighter-bombers. They are accompanied by sophisticated radar and SAM systems and you have people using all this without any scruples, as you can see by what happened when Scott O'Grady met their SA-6! They are very active there and the four aircraft downed by Aviano F-16s last year were from Banja Luka. They would not be half as professional without the specialists and technical support from the Serbian motherland. Sometimes their capability is upgraded by provocative sorties by 'rest-Serbian' MiG-21s and – more rarely – by MiG-29s. Belgrade's MiG-29s pose little direct threat for us. They fly very little, and do not have enough pilots. Don't forget, Croatians and Slovenes provided 80 per cent of the JRV pilots!"

Birth of the HZS

After the Croatian declaration of independence, Croat pilots in the JRV (the air force of the former Yugoslavia) regiments were observed closely. As the danger of arrest rose, three pilots flew their aircraft to Croatian airfields, which were hastily prepared for jet flying. In 1991/92 the HZS had only three operational MiG-21s, serialled 101 to 103. 102 was named Osvetnik Vukovara, while 103 carried the name Osvetnik Dubrovnika. The first defector was Ing. Peresin, who flew from Bihac to Austria in October 1991 where his old MiG-21R, flown in without the camera pod, was kept by the Austrians. He saved himself, although his aircraft was interned and eventually became a target on an Austrian firing range.

It was Agotic's job to create a viable military aviation arm out of these and other resources. His main priority was to establish an air defence system, as he explained: "What harmed us most in the early days was that we lacked some kind of radar surveillance. It was my primary aim to convince the politicians to put the main efforts within the military build-up into creating a 'roof' over Croatia. Rudi Peresin and other pilots like Danijel Borovic, who landed at Split, began flying missions on the few MiGs at that time, much to the surprise of our opponents. All except one of these aircraft were lost, mainly to Serbian ground fire." The first to be lost was 101, downed during a reconnaissance mission near Zupanja in June 1992. Another was downed near the Save bridges in 1992 and 1993. Two replacements were acquired by late 1993, but one of these was also destroyed.

"On the other hand, our troops and air defence units have shot down more than 100 enemy aircraft during the fighting for the so-called UNPAs (United Nations Protected Areas). In May 1992 some MiG-21s and a sole MiG-29 were destroyed around Slavonski Brod. When it became clear that the UN weapons embargo would last for the unforeseeable future, we tried to increase our aircraft strength. This was very complicated and expensive, but also very necessary. It was an important morale booster for our people to see that Croatia was not defenceless against its sometimes mad enemies."

Surviving the embargo

Despite the UN arms embargo, the Croatians have been very successful in augmenting their air force, even though the UN actually operates centres for UNCRO and UNPROFOR at Zagreb and Split, so that the increase has occurred right before the eyes of all the observers. The build-up has been generously funded, with $1.86 billion (30 per cent of the total gross national product) spent on defence.

The daily routine in all the units gives the visitor an impression of well organised professionalism within an air force at war. All the uniforms, the flying kit, the g-suits and even the GenTex-helmets are of Western origin and are NATO standard. All the ground crew wear US-style camouflage uniforms and expensive Gore-Tex boots. As one of them pointed out, they all feel that they are a Western-thinking air force with Eastern-origin aircraft.

Today it is estimated that between 15 and 25 MiG-21s serve with the HZS, including two-seat 'Mongols'. Six were seen at Zagreb/ Pleso recently, with another five at the ZMAJ hangars at Velica Gorica. At the Posejdon '94 exercises and during the most recent 30 May parade, 10 aircraft were displayed. Although

only 10 have been seen simultaneously, it is believed that the air force would not show all of its fighters to the public at once. The exact number of MiG-21bis and MiG-21U airframes on charge, and their ountry of origin, remain among the young state's best-protected secrets. To preserve secrecy, the MiG-21s do not wear visible serial numbers or codes. The official line is that the aircraft were built from spares at the ZMAJ (Dragon) facility at Velica Gorica near Pleso, but this would seem to be impossible.

Some sources have suggested that the MiG-21s are from former East German stock. Several factors point to the aircraft being of NVA-LSK origin (Nationalen Volksarmee-Luftstreitkrafte und Luftverteidigung/[East German] National Army Air Force and Air Defence). Ever since the co-operation between the Croatians and the Germans during World War II, there have been close links between those two nations and between Croatia and Austria. These were refreshed when Austria's Foreign Minister Alois Mock was the first to suggest international recognition of the new Croatia in 1991. Today, a number of squares in Croatian towns are named after him.

In the cockpits of the MiG-21s, the basic electrical support and communications equipment carries manufacturers' plates from Siemens, Korting and Nordmende, and the new aircraft wear a camouflage scheme similar to that applied to East German MiG-21s. Former East German personnel have been reportedly spotted

Right: This badge decorates several of the Croatian Mi-24s. It depicts a heavily armed insect, with rocket pods and a Swatter in the tail. The aircraft on which this badge was photographed was stripped of armament.

Below: When initially delivered the Croatian 'Hinds' wore prominent red cross markings, and the fiction was maintained that these were high-speed, armoured but unarmed casevac and air ambulance aircraft. Some aircraft do fly without armament fitted, but are believed to be capable of being armed within hours.

by the United Nations instructing HZS air and ground crews.

Some circumstantial evidence points to the MiG-21s being part of a major arms supply programme by Germany. Many Croatian personnel at the airfields speak German quite well (apparently after recent language courses) and many cars seen at Pleso airfield bear German licence plates. Former East German maintenance personel, notably from the old JG 8 have identified the aircraft as being their former charges pointing to the inclusion of MiG-29-type IFF equipment which was apparently unique to the East German MiG-21 bis. This is externally indicated by the absence of a standard undernose panel, and by extra switches on the starboard side of the cockpit.

Hrvatske Zrance Snage: Croatia's embargoed air force

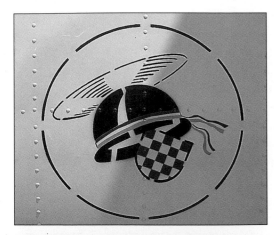

Left: The total number of Mi-17s on charge with the Croatians is unknown, but the type represents an extremely effective assault and support helicopter type. The aircraft wear a variety of camouflage schemes and a number of unit insignia have been observed. The badge illustrated above is clearly of a tiger.

Above and below: A late-standard Mi-17 (or Mi-8MTV) 'Hip-H' and the simple squadron badge it wears on the cabin entrance door. Some of the Croat 'Hips' were obtained from Aeroflot, while others probably came from the Ukrainian armed forces. The Croatian 'Hips' have undernose weather radar and may be capable of being armed, but this cannot be confirmed.

The Mil Mi-24's camouflage shows obvious signs of having been repainted to hide the helicopter's previous markings. A large, almost rectangular pattern coincides with the spaces where former East German 'Hinds' carried their tactical numbers, with similar spots of new paint over the location of the old national insignia. The Germans never used the Mi-24V 'Hind-D' however, and this makes it likely that the helicopters are ex-Ukrainian. In front of the big overhaul-facility of the ZMAJ complex at Velica Gorica are parked a number of Do 28 light transports, a type recently phased out by the Luftwaffe. And on one An-2 'Colt', configured as a mini-AWACS, one can easily read an overpainted ex-DDR registration.

Other possible sources for the MiG-21s are some of the impoverished states of the former Soviet Union such as Ukraine, Belarus or Moldova. Such states have a surfeit of combat aircraft (especially older types like the MiG-21) and are hungry for foreign currency. Ukrainian Il-76MDs and -TDs have regularly been seen at Zagreb/Pleso, but without any UN markings. The camouflage schemes on the MiG-21bis are similar to some old Soviet schemes, as well as to the East German camouflage. Although the former CIS countries are traditionally more related to the Serbs, economic factors could overturn these links very quickly.

The exact disposition of the MiGs is also a closely guarded secret, and only those aircraft operating from certain airfields have been seen publicly. The HZS MiG-21bis fighters at Zagreb/Pleso, for example, share the same runway as the UN aircraft.

The high command of the HZS is located in the centre of Zagreb in a small mansion which, interestingly, housed the staff of the Luftwaffe's Fliegerführer Balkans during World War II, and later housed a corps HQ of the old JRV air force. General Imra Agotic's staff is responsible for the flying elements and for the ground-based air defence troops. The latter are divided into AAA and SAM elements, but come under the direct operational control of frontal sector commanders. There is no high-altitude SAM network at the moment.

Bases and operations

Flying units are located at five known airfields (below), and there are military airfields at Cerklji, Portoroz, Rijeka, Split and Varazdin. There are permanent squadrons (Eskadrilas) nominally based at each, though these often have detachments elsewhere. The HZS officially states that squadron numbers or names are not used, but it seems more likely that these exist but are secret. The MiG-21s, for example, wear a unit insignia consisting of a crest with a knight's helmet and a red and white checkered shield bearing the number '1', and this has been reported as being the badge of the 1st Fighter Squadron.

Whatever its designation, the fighter squadron (Eskadrila Lovacka) is based at the eastern end of the Zagreb/Pleso airport, using the same runway as the civil and UN traffic. The aircraft are in excellent condition and do not convey a Third World image, despite their age. Training missions are flown every day, normally lasting about 30 to 40 minutes. As serious pilot training on jets had not started before 1992, all the

current operational MiG-21 pilots were ex-JRV officers. About 80 per cent of the pilots in the JRV were of Croatian and Slovene nationality, and many returned to their homes after the dissolution of Yugoslavia, so there is no lack of flyers. The first newly trained pilots should become operational in mid-1996. The typical pilot is flying between 150 and 180 flying hours annually, twice the Eastern European average. Armed combat missions have also been flown from Zagreb, including the missions mounted against the Serbian positions around the Save bridge during the recapture of western Slavonia. On one of these sorties Ing. Rudolf Peresin (who had flown his MiG-21R to Austria in 1991) was reportedly shot down and captured by the Serbs on 2 May 1994. Dogfights against RSK (Republic of Serb Krajina) or Serbian air force jets have not taken place.

Zagreb/Pleso is also the main base for the transport squadron (Eskadrila Transportnih Aviona), which is equipped with An-2s. Some of the An-2s were inherited from the JRV and others may have been on the Yugoslav civil register, while more may have come from Germany. The outdated 'Colt' has proved very versatile in Croatian service. At the beginning of the conflict, the type was used as an attack aircraft with hastily built bomb sights and a variety of different bombs, some made out of propane gas cylinders. These were often simply thrown out of the open door. During the siege of Vukovar in 1991, Croatian An-2s achieved remarkable results against key Serb positions and command-posts. Even pilots of Serbian origin flew with the Croatians. When one of them was shot down and killed, the highest Croatian medal was sent to his mother in Serbia.

Above: Croatia's helicopters are widely dispersed around a large number of airfields, and is difficult to state with certainty where any particular unit might be based. The helicopter force was used during summer 1995 in the attacks against the Krajina and in the Slavonia campaign.

Augmenting the transport An-2s are a handful of early warning/surveillance-modified An-2s. These can be recognised by the presence of additional antennas under the belly and on the spine. At least one of these wears a badge with 'Split' aft of the cockpit windows on the right side. It is not known if the installation and integration of the mission equipment was undertaken before or after the aircraft came to Croatia. These versions, like the normal transports, can be seen all around the country.

Transport fleet

The An-2 is not regarded as being the ideal transport aircraft type by the Croatians, as General Agotic explained: "Unfortunately, the JRV An-26s once based at Zagreb were flown to Serbia before their withdrawal. We desperately need some larger transports. I hope that in the very near future we will solve this problem, since transport aircraft and trainers are not covered by the UN embargo. We are working on the concept of mobile brigades, and transport aircraft are the key element for this concept."

There may be an element of disinformation here, since some sources suggest that the Croatians actually have three An-26s. The Croats' unwillingness to admit to operating these aircraft may reflect sensitivity as to their source (perhaps from Germany), or that the aircraft do not exist. Other aircraft types said to be in Croat service but not officially admitted include a single Do 28, 12 Gazelle helicopters, two Oraos and six Super Galebs (after the MiG-21s arrived these ground attack aircraft may have been grounded due to lack of spares or by the disproportionate cost of operating a type in such small numbers). The air arm also operates a Gulfstream and a pair of Challengers in the VIP role.

A smaller group of MiG-21bis fighters is operating from Pula, on the western cost of the Istrian peninsula. Here, as at Zagreb/Pleso, a pair of armed aircraft maintains a five-minute alert status. It is likely that a similar alert is undertaken at Split, or perhaps at another base

in the south of Croatia. The normal armament consists of two Vympel R-60 (AA-8 'Aphid') IR-homing air-to-air missiles. An agreement negotiated with the JNA in 1991 resulted in the establishment of a 20-km (12-mile) exclusion zone for heavy weapons and fighter aircraft around the whole demarcation line. Therefore, there are no jets are based at the airfields of Zadar and Dubrovnik, although these are fully capable of supporting MiG-21 operations.

The MiG-21 and the future

Although senior Croatian officers acknowledge that they would like to obtain a more modern, Western fighter type, there has been general satisfaction with the MiG-21. General Agotic stated that "We are satisfied with the MiG-21bis for the moment because we can use them for close air support and air defence missions since all of those involved with the type know it very well from the past. Relating to the embargo, I would make only one statement. I think that our crews could provide some peaceful solutions even today. As the UN knows very well, we could retain control of these UNPAs without its assistance. So we all hope that the refreshed mandate of UNCRO will increase its efforts to gain some results. We will see in a few months what has happened. At the moment, the embargo is real for us and does not allow any thought of new aircraft. Without the embargo there is a need for a true multi-role fighter in the F-16 class. I feel that we need two squadrons of a modern multi-role type, capable of mounting offensive combat air patrols. This aircraft would be of Western origin. As long as I am in command, the procurement of a Soviet type would only be a possibility if no other options were open. Although there are a few here who know Russian systems, any Russian aircraft that would meet our requirement would be as new as something of Western origin. A small number of medium or heavy transports and a SAM system for higher airspaces are other urgent priorities. We are looking into the future with definable concepts."

The second most important airfield in Croatia is Zemunik, near Zadar, near the middle of the country's coastline. It has remained the major

training base since JRV times, despite the proximity of RSK-held territory (20-25 km/12-15 miles away). The fixed-wing training squadron (Eskadrila Trenaznih Zrakoplovo) is the main user of the excellent airfield, and takes advantage of the high number of clear days in this former tourist area. At the moment, there are only light aircraft like the UTVA-75, the Cessna 172 and 188 available. The huge performance gap between these and the MiG-21UM should ideally be filled by a modern turboprop trainer in the PC-9/Tucano class, although the capture of Udbina in Operation 'Storm' did provide an interim solution. Ten aircraft (a mix of Soko J-1 Jastrebs, G-2 Galebs and G-4 Super Galebs were captured intact, along with spares and some 100 BL755 CBUs. The G-2 and G-4 are both tandem seat trainers with a significant secondary ground attack pilot, and should ease the transition to the MiG-21, as well as augmenting the MiGs in the fighter bomber role, for which they are not ideally suited. A Croatian Army press release issued immediately after the Krajina operation stated that the captured aircraft would be placed in service as soon as technical documentation was completed, and anticipated that this would take between two and three months. In the early days, the light aircraft were used operationally for spotting and reconnaissance, while Microlights were used for Special Forces insertion. As Zagreb has a 400-year university tradition, Zemunik has never had a problem in gaining enough young flying students. The whole training syllabus is extremely academic, so there are no NCO pilots. Flying training – apart from the initial screening – begins in the second year of the course. A real helicopter training programme is not underway at the moment, but helicopters are maintained for basic training. Two Hughes 500s, a Bell 205 and an unknown number of Bell 206 Jet Rangers are flying with the police forces, but these are operated very intensively and are not available to the HZS.

The transport helicopter squadron (Eskadrila Transportnih Helikoptera) is based at Lucko, southwest of Zagreb. From here, a mix of older Mil Mi-8s, Mil Mi-8Ss and some new Mil Mi-17s (called Mil Mi-8MTVs by their crews) operate throughout the country. At least one

At least two of Croatia's Mi-17 fleet are all-white VIP aircraft, for the use of President Tudjman and government ministers. These aircraft are notable for being Mi-17s, but with many of the features of the Mi-8S Salon, such as large windows and cabin soundproofing. Such dedicated transport Mi-17s are quite uncommon.

Mi-17 is almost brand new and fitted with Garmin GPS and an FMS display in the right cockpit console. There is also an overall-white Mi-17, equipped with vibration dampers on the rotor and with an air-conditioning set. This helicopter is held ready for use by President Tudjman. Some 24 of the 'Hips' are ex-Aeroflot and were acquired on the black market in 1993. Several may in fact be ex-CIS air force military versions acquired by Aeroflot for spares, or by the broker specifically for resale.

The last and smallest military airfield is Divulje, 15 km (9 miles) north of Split. There are no known squadrons based here, but the Lucko-squadron maintains a detachment of Mi-17s for basic SAR duties along the coastline and for ambulance flying.

The ZMAJ maintenance and overhaul facility at Velica Gorica near Zagreb/Pleso is responsible for all field modifications and for regular maintenance work on all Croatian aircraft and helicopters. Compared with similar installations in Eastern Europe, ZMAJ is different. Workers, the various hangars and their freshly-asphalted aprons all look very much cleaner, like those in Western European countries. A number of different aircraft are parked outside, including Do 28s, MiG-21UMs and assorted light aircraft, as well as Mil-8S and Mil-17 helicopters.

'Hind' force

Although nominally based at Pleso, the Mil-24V assault helicopters of the combat helicopter squadron (Eskadrila Borbenih Helikoptera) are usually to be seen at Velica Gorica. Around 12 examples of the 'Hind' are now flying in Croatia, but as much secrecy surrounds these aircraft as the MiG-21s and they are bereft of serial numbers or code letters. The official position is that only a few examples are armed and the majority have their weapons removed and are used only for training and for medevac duties outside the high-risk positions,

Above: The antenna fit on one of the Croatian 'electronic' Antonov An-2 'Colts'. These aircraft may have been modified by a UK-based company, and their exact role and capabilities remain unknown.

Below: This An-2 shows clear signs of having benefited from cannibalisation, with a camouflaged rudder from another aircraft. In the early days, An-2s operated as makeshift bombers, rolling home made bombs out of their cabin doors. At least some of the air arm's Antonov An-2s are believed to have come from former East German stocks. The colour scheme on this aeroplane is reminiscent of the colours seen on some Interflug aircraft.

because some older, slower HZS Mi-8s were shot down on such missions in the past.

General Agotic stated for the record that "I have reported six armed aircraft to the OSCE. All other airframes are only used for training and are constantly unarmed. At the moment I can not reveal any more details on numbers, origins and units. One-third of our territory is occupied and we don't want to let our enemies know exactly where types are based and how many aircraft of which type there are. Also, we are not driven to do anything which might cut vital links to friendly nations. Regarding the combat support helicopters, I only can repeat that they were purchased only to evacuate wounded soldiers and civilians out of so-called 'hot spots'. Several Mil-8s were destroyed on such occasions. Their armament will only be used to defend themselves and the victims on the ground before going in."

Of four aircraft seen recently, two were unarmed, without any missile rails and cannons. The other pair was configured for the AT-6 'Spiral' and had the 'Natasha device' radar-homing and warning system mounted on the fuselage sides between the cockpits. One of the unarmed aircraft carried a Garmin GPS blade antenna in front of the rear cockpit. Large red cross markings, seen when the Mi-24s were introduced, have since been removed.

The HZS has become an important safeguard for Croatia and is able to project power over the borders of the young nation. The nature of the present conflict sometimes makes it inevitable, however, that the force should be used against both the Serbs and, also, sometimes against the UN. The UN embargo is seen as being half-hearted, uneven and unfair (it takes no account of the vast stockpile of weapons Serbia inherited from the old Yugoslavia) and the renewed mandate of the UNCRO is unpopular. The embargo, as someone pointed out, makes the necessary material only more expensive. Croatian officers have no doubt that Croatia and the HZS are strong enough to retake the Serb-occupied territories without any international participation, and they resent not being allowed to do so. They are under no illusions about the cost such operations would entail, but they are sure they could stand the losses.

Georg Mader

Força Aérea Portuguesa
Portuguese Air Force

Unkindly regarded by some as being a 'semi-detached' member of NATO, Portugal's withdrawal from its overseas empire has allowed it to concentrate more fully on its in-theatre assets and European commitments – including peace keeping in the Balkans. An ongoing modernisation and expansion programme has been undramatic, but has left the air force in a much strengthened position, with a useful mix of relatively up-to-date aircraft, weapons and systems, able to fulfil a wider variety of roles. Within 15 years the nation's air defence has gone from the Korean War-vintage F-86 to the F-16. In modernising its air force, Portugal has taken advantage of the post-Cold War cascade of surplus equipment from wealthier states, and has continued to exploit its longstanding links with Germany, whose air force undertook advanced tactical training in Portugal for many years.

The history of military aviation in Portugal dates back to May 1911, when a balloon company was formed within the army's Telegraphic Service. One year later, the Escola Militar de Aeronáutica (Military Aviation School) was activated and, in 1917, the Aeronáutica Militar and Aviaçao Naval came into being. Portuguese pilots and observers were attached to British and French squadrons during World War I. On 16 September 1924, the so-called Aeronáutica Militar was upgraded to the status of an arm of the Portuguese army.

Although Portugal declared its neutrality during World War II, it nonetheless permitted the RAF to base maritime reconnaissance aircraft at Lajes, Azores, thanks to a mutual defence treaty signed in 1373 with the United Kingdom.

The 1950s was a decade of activity for Portugal's military aviation. On 27 May 1952, the Aeronáutica Militar and the Aviaçao Naval joined in a fully independent air force, the Força Aérea Portuguesa (FAP). In 1956, the Paratroop Rifle Command was transferred from the Army to the FAP, and was to play an important part in the African wars. During the same year, the air force was organised into three air regions that covered all national territory as well as the African and Asian colonies.

Portugal was a founding member of NATO, joining in 1949 when Cold War clouds began to gather over Europe. Despite this, Portugal assigned few operational units to the command. Instead it concentrated on providing services to the strategically important Azores Islands and its air base at Lajes. Also, throughout the 1960s and 1970s, it was distracted by prolonged fighting in Africa. When Spain joined NATO in 1982, there was some hope of establishing a unified Iberian Command, but this failed to materialise. The air defence and surveillance radar system has now been upgraded to the point where useful co-operation with its neighbours can be initiated.

Colonial rebellion in Africa

Portugal's colonial history dates back as far as 1337, when explorers reached the Canary Islands. Over the many years that followed, Portuguese ships explored the known (and unknown) world. More sizeable possessions were taken throughout Africa (Angola, Guinea, Mozambique), South America (Brazil) and the Far East (East Timor, Macau and Goa).

By the early 1960s, Portugal's surviving (and substantial) colonial possessions in Africa and the Far East began to reject Portuguese authority and gave birth to several armed independence movements. As a result, between 1961 and 1974 the small Portuguese air force undertook every kind of conceivable mission and amassed substantial combat experience during the African colonial wars. These events shaped its structure and its operating concepts. Indeed, throughout its life the FAP has undergone many changes, and faced challenges out of all proportion to its size.

War in Portuguese Guinea

The first scene of armed rebellion was Portuguese Guinea, in 1963. Portuguese Guinea (a colony since 1446 and now modern-day Guinea-Bissau) is a small country situated on Africa's Atlantic west coast, between Senegal to the north and Guinea (formerly French Guinea) to the south. Fighting broke out in August 1959 with the PAIGC (Partido Africano de Independencia da Guiné e Capo Verde). Its supporters were trained in Algeria, Cuba, China and the Soviet Union and found a safe haven in both of Portuguese Guinea's neighbouring nations. Its headquarters were in Conakry, capital of Guinea. At first only a handful of FAP T-6s were available to deal with the emergency, until supplemented by Republic F-84Gs in 1963.

Portuguese tactics, in response to the actions of the increasingly well-armed and very mobile guerrilla groups, centred around heavily-defended fire-bases scattered across the country. As rebel activity increased, so did the FAP presence. The main operational base was BA 12, at Bissalau, near the capital of Bissau. In 1967, the newly established Esq. 121 'Tigres' stood up with eight ex-Luftwaffe G91R4s at BA 12, along with additional T-6s and Do 27 liaison aircraft. The G91s flew in support of Portuguese troops and against the PAIGC's supply trails near the Senegalese and French Guinean borders. All active aircraft were forward deployed during operations and rearmed and refuelled as close to their operational areas as possible. During its African combat career, the 'Gina' proved to be a reliable and sturdy fighter-bomber and reconnaissance platform, operating mostly in adverse conditions. Five of the type were lost to enemy action, at least two of them shot down by SA-7 missiles. In at least one

instance Esq. 121 engaged MiG-17s from Guinea-Bissau, with inconclusive results.

In May 1968 General Antonio de Spinola was appointed Governor. He initiated massive spending on a 'hearts and minds' campaign, building local schools and hospitals. He also ordered 12 Alouette III helicopters, which were essential for operations in a country that was comprised largely of marsh and soft terrain. The Alouette IIIs were part of Esq. 121, as was a flight of Nord Noratlas transports, permanently based at BA 12. The Nords undertook all local supply flights, but transport missions to and from Portugal were provided by DC-6s of the air force's Transportes Aéreos Militares (TAM).

By 1970 the campaign in Portuguese Guinea had taken on a much tougher approach and the FAP was using napalm and defoliants against PAIGC targets. Attempts to persuade President Touré of Guinea (which had become an independent Marxist state in 1958) to cease supporting PAIGC failed. As a result, Portugal masterminded a 1972 'invasion' of Conakry. The seaborne assault failed to rouse hoped-for public support, but did succeed in freeing a number of Portuguese prisioners of war.

PAIGC received limited air support from a number of diverse sources. Conakry-based Nigerian MiG-17s were used for reconnaissance flights, while Soviet-supplied Mi-4s carried out supply flights in the east of the country. Several FAP aircraft, including at least three G91s, were lost to SA-7s and AAA fire, and over seven years of fighting PAIGC claimed to have shot down 21 aircraft.

MFA *coup*

PAIGC declared an independent republic in September 1973, and carried out elections in the portions of the country under its control. Events in Portugal at this time began to have an effect on the military operations in Africa. Public unease at the cost of such operations, coupled with professional dissatisfaction at the way they were being conducted, gave rise to the clandestine Armed Forces Movement (MFA). On 25 April 1974, the military seized power in a nearly bloodless coup, establishing a provisional military government which installed Spinola as President. As a result, independence was granted to Guinea-Bissau on 10 September 1974. The FAP

BA 5, at Monte Real, is home to the FAP's front-line fighter force of 17 F-16A Block 15 OCU aircraft. The F-16s are armed with AIM-9 Sidewinder and AIM-7 Sparrow AAMs.

Three of the FAP's Fighting Falcons are two-seat F-16Bs. An F-16B undertook the FAP's first overseas deployment of the type, visiting Soesterburg, in April 1995.

Above: The fighter mission is no longer a primary one for the A-7Ps of Esq. 302 and 304. Instead, their attack capability has been improved through the acquisition of the AGM-65.

Above: Until the arrival of the F-16, air defence A-7s made frequent deployments to the Azores and practised their ACM skills regularly.

Below: Esq. 302 and 304 share their Corsairs and squadron badges rarely appear on any aircraft. This is true across the FAP.

Above: Portugal's six TA-7Ps began to arrive in May 1985, as part of the air force's second batch of A-7s. Prior to that, only a single leased TA-7C was in use.

undertook the withdrawal of most military and civilian personnel by 15 October. Some Do 27s and Alouette IIIs were left behind to form the nucleus of the Guinea-Bissau air force.

While the situation in Portuguese Guinea was worsening, trouble flared up further south in Angola. Angola had been a colony since 1655, and an overseas province of Portugal since 1955. The Marxist Movimento Popular de Libertação de Angola (MPLA) was founded in 1956 and its actions forced the stationing of FAP C-47s and PV-2 Harpoons at Luanda to support the army. A second opposition group, the União das Populações de Angola (UPA), was established in 1958.

The first serious MPLA attack came on the prison at São João, and was followed by assaults on police stations and other prisons. Several major towns soon came under siege and the small Portuguese army element in Mozambique was stretched to breaking point. A number of civilian aircraft, such as Piper Cubs, were pressed into service as light transports to resupply outlying settlements, while DC-3s and Beech 18s were used as makeshift bombers. These and the other FAP aircraft were joined in June 1961 by F-84Gs from Esq. 21. The Thunderjets formed a new unit at Luanda, Esq. 93, alongside the Harpoons which were now operated by Esq. 91. Napalm and fragmentation bombs became the FAP weapons of choice and a substantial paratroop-dropping effort was sustained, first by the C-47s and later by Noratlases, to relieve several towns under siege. On 1 June 1962 the air base at Luanda formally became BA 9, and other small air bases were established at Negage and Henriques de Carvalho.

Bizarrely, as the war progressed the UPA was transformed into the Frente Naçional de Libertaçã de Angola (FNLA), with US support from the Kennedy administration. The US saw that a new indigenous government would eventually emerge from the fighting in Angola and wanted to counter the Marxist-inspired MPLA with a more pro-Western group. Fighting continued, mostly in the north of the country, and the Noratlas detachment made regular parachute drops with the 21st Battalion of the Regimento de Caçadores Paraquedistas to garrison towns.

Invaders from the USA

Although Portugal was the subject of a US arms embargo due to its African conflicts, seven B-26s were sold to the FAP in 1965. These helped to compensate for the F-84G losses, which stood at five (mostly through accident rather than action) and growing Soviet support for the MPLA. The B-26s were obtained through a Tucson-based private firm, Aero Associates, which became embroiled in allegations of arms smuggling, but the B-26s all reached Angola to supplement the PV-2 Harpoon bombers. Yet another guerrilla group materialised in 1966, when a breakaway MPLA group established itself as the União Naçional de Independência Total de Angola (UNITA), under the leadership of Jonas Savimbi. FAP aircraft maintained constant attacks against the MPLA, which was advancing inexorably westward towards the capital. Several major offensives were launched during the early 1970s, backed up with aid from other white African nations, but the largely conscript army became increasingly reluctant to carry on fighting.

The arrival of G91R4s in 1972 (some coming from FAP units stationed in neighbouring

Mozambique) boosted the FAP's combat power. Helicopters also became an increasingly important part of operations. The Alouettes were used to move troops rapidly to trouble spots and by 1969 they had been joined in country by the first Pumas. F-84Gs, B-26s, T-6Gs and even armed Do 27s kept up a constant cycle of air attacks on rebel positions.

However, the strain of fighting across Africa was proving too much for Portugal. The MFA coup heralded the end of Portugal's involvement in Angola, which was offered independence in 1 July 1974. A massive exodus of Portuguese nationals followed, as over 300,000 people abandoned their homes by 11 November 1975, Independence Day. On one of the final days of the evacuation in 1975, a TAP Boeing 707 departed Luanda with no fewer than 342 people on board and a further 19,000 lb (8618 kg) of cargo. Military equipment left behind was soon put to use in the civil war that followed the Portuguese withdrawal – a war that continued unabaited until 1988, and rumbles on periodically to this day.

Mozambique

The third chapter of Portugal's African wars belongs to Mozambique. Following the other colonies' struggle for independence, Mozambique saw the rise of Eduardo Mondlan's Frente de Libertaçãco de Moçambique (FRELIMO) movement in 1962. Again, only small numbers of FAP C-47s and T-6s were on hand when serious trouble broke out in 1964. In a short space of time, 16,000 troops had arrived in the country and additional T-6s, PV-2s (eight), Do 27s (12) and some Alouette IIIs were despatched to support them. FRELIMO operated from bases in Tanzania and later Zambia, and directed frequent rocket attacks at the strategic Cabora Bassa dam, which was protected by thousands of Portuguese troops.

The FAP commitment to Mozambique became larger than that in either Guinea or Angola, though combat operations did not begin in earnest until 1968. A network of new air bases was set up as a result. BA 10 was established at Beira, and it was home to the T-6Gs, PV-2s and Auster D.5s of Esq. 101, along with Noratlas transports. Aérodromo-Base (AB) 7, at Tete, housed more T-6Gs, Do 27s, Auster D.5s and Alouette IIIs, alongside G91R4s of Esq. 702 'Os Escorpioes'. Additional G91s were based at Nacala (AB 5), with Esq. 502 'Os Jaguares'. AB 6, at Nova Freixo, was occupied by yet more T-6s, Austers and Alouettes. The C-47 transports of Esq. 801 were based at AB 8, Lourenço Marques.

FAP vs FRELIMO

Now under the command of Samora Machel (later to become President), FRELIMO began vigorous operations against the Portuguese from 1970. South African-registered crop-sprayers were used to spray herbicides over FRELIMO's border strongholds, in an attempt to deny them food. These aircraft departed the country prematurely, after AAA fire shot down escorting T-6s and one of the crop-sprayers.

Once again Portugal found itself fighting a losing battle with a conscript army. After the April 1974 revolution in Portugal, Esquadras 502 and 702 merged and relocated to BA 9 in Luanda, Angola, supplanting the old F-84G Thunderjets which equipped Esquadra 93. The G91s returned to Portugal in 1974 in anticipation of an indepen-

dence offer. Mozambique gained independence on 25 June 1975 and took possession of several T-6s and Noratlases for its own use.

The FAP's African campaigns were a drain on its resources, but also spurred a re-equipment through necessity. In 1959 BA 5 received the first of a total of 50 F-86F Sabres intended to equip Esquadra 51 'Falcoes'. In 1970 another 50 Sabres were acquired, this time ex-Luftwaffe Canadair-built Mk 6s of which only 15 were put in service, the remainder being used as spares, as were half a dozen Norwegian F-86Fs acquired in 1968-69. The Sabres continued to serve as Portugal's only dedicated interceptors until 1980. The link they established with Germany led directly to the acquisition of the G91 and continues to this day.

Seven years after the initial Sabre acquisition the first Fiat G91 fighter-bombers arrived, intended then for use primarily in the African wars. In total, 40 former Luftwaffe G91R4s were delivered between 1965 and 1966. Between 1976 and 1981 Germany supplied an additional 34 G91R3s and 11 two-seat G91T3s, which were joined by 36 G91R3s and 15 G91T1s largely used as a spares source. These aircraft were part payment for the Luftwaffe's use of Beja as a weapons training base.

The G91 in service

After the inactivation of the African squadrons, Esquadra 62 'Jaguares' stood up with G91s in August 1974 at Montijo, but four years later was renumbered as Esquadra 301. From August 1980, eight-aircraft detachments were provided by the 'Jaguares' at BA 4 Lajes. The number of G91s grew and on 31 January 1981 Esquadra 301 'Tigres' was activated, operating the aircraft until January 1989 when it was disbanded. The active G91 fleet was extensively refitted by OGMA, which added new navaids and ejection seats, passive ECM and Sidewinder capability. By 1987 Esq. 301 was flying 33 G91R3s, while 23 G91R4s were allocated to Esq. 303. Aircraft based at Montijo were tasked with a secondary air defence role until 1989, when they were replaced by equally unsuitable Sidewinder-armed A-7 Corsair IIs. In June 1993 the Fiat G91R3s and T3s equipping Esquadra 301 'Jaguares' were phased out, and the following month the squadron relocated to Beja and re-equipped with Alpha Jets. The G91 had become too expensive to support, particularly as the Italian air force had retired its last single-seat G91Rs in April 1992. The availability of a substantial number of ex-German Alpha Jets at bargain prices was also a persuasive factor. Esq. 301 retired the last of its G91s, including an extravagantly tiger-striped aircraft and an immaculately polished silver example, in a ceremony held on 17 June 1993.

On 28 January 1977 the first of six T-38A Talon supersonic advanced trainers arrived on loan from the USAF for Esquadra 103, then exclusively equipped with T-33As. The Talons were joined by another six in 1980, the same year that the seasoned Sabres were phased out of service. In 1987 the unit, with its T-Birds and Talons, relocated to BA 11 Beja. On 14 October 1991 the last six truly veteran T-33s were finally withdrawn from Esquadra 103, which had been activated in 1953 with the same aircraft. To support the air-defence configured A-7s, eight of the T-38s were wired for Sidewinder carriage and declared as 'fighters' armed with AIM-9Ps. The T-38s

The delivery of ex-Luftwaffe Alpha Jets, to Beja-based Esq. 103 and 301, has resulted in a substantial improvement in the FAP's training capability. The Alpha Jets also have a useful light attack capability.

At least two colour schemes are worn by the FAP's Alpha Jets – both are a throwback to their Luftwaffe days. The Luftwaffe has been a regular supplier of (second-hand equipment) to Portugal since the 1950s.

Portugal's P-3P Orions arrived in this grey/white colour scheme, once common to Orions around the world. They have since adopted a very distinctive two-tone grey scheme. They are flown by Esq. 601, from BA 6, Montijo, and (finally) replaced P-2 Neptunes that had been withdrawn in 1977.

Esq. 601's six P-3Ps (which are all updated, former RAAF P-3Bs) have been heavily involved in Operation Deny Flight. A detachment at Sigonella has maintained surveillance of the Adriatic along with patrol aircraft from other NATO nations.

Esq. 501, based at BA 6, Montijo, operates a pair of stretched C-130H-30s alongside its standard Hercules. Both aircraft were delivered as C-130Hs, and modified by OGMA, at Alverca.

Between 1977 and 1978, six C-130Hs were delivered to the FAP, and all are operated by Esq. 501. They replaced Douglas DC-6s and Nord Noratlases, which were worn out by Portugal's African campaigns.

Basic transport and VIP CASA C.212s are flown by Esq. 502, from Sintra, north of Lisbon. The squadron also has a single C.212 navigation trainer

Sintra is also home to a plethora of modified C.212s, flown by Esq. 401. This is one of its ECM trainers fitted with a fin-tip antenna and under fuselage infra-red/ultra-violet sensor for geophysical survey missions.

were eventually retired as fighters when the second batch of A-7s arrived from the United States, and retired completely when the Força Aérea Portuguesa took delivery of former Luftwaffe Alpha Jets in 1991.

To replace its T-33s, Portugal signed a letter of intent with the Skyfox Corporation, which was offering its radical T-33-derived Skyfox Trainer. The Skyfox replaced the T-33's original J33 turbojet with two pod-mounted TFE731 turbofans, redesigned the tail, wings and forward fuselage and added all new avionics and a new ejection seat. The resultant aircraft bore only the vaguest resemblance to a T-33. A prototype was flown in 1983, and the project was later taken over by Boeing. The FAP proposed that OGMA would undertake its Skyfox conversions, but insufficient orders were obtained from other sources to motivate Boeing to continue with the project. Portugal was next touted as the launch customer for the equally unsuccessful side-by-side seating Promavia Jet Squalus trainer, in 1989, but plans to assemble this aircraft in Portugal fell through too.

The FAP today

Today, the Força Aérea Portuguesa, with a total strength of some 240 aircraft/helicopters and 10,000 men and women (of whom 2,000 are civil servants), is immersed in a limited modernisation and upgrade process. In common with other NATO members in the post-Cold War era, FAP units train intensively for 'out of area' operations such as those exemplified by Operations Deny Flight and Sharp Guard. One of the most recent relevant changes was the transfer of the 2,000-man Parachute Brigade to army control.

In 1994 a new serialling system was introduced that replaced the existing four-digit aircraft serials with five-digit codes. All non-operational aircraft serials are now prefixed with a '0', and operational aircraft with a '1'. The second number denotes the aircraft's role and is allocated as follows: 0 – gliders; 1 – single-engined trainer; 2 – multi-engined trainer; 3 – liaison and observation; 4 – maritime patrol; 5 – fighter/ground attack; 6 – transport; 7 – VIP/special missions; 8 – not yet in use; 9 – helicopters.

Command structure

The Força Aérea Portuguesa is structured into three main commands: **COFA** - Comando Operacional de la FA (air force operational command); **CLAFA** - Comando Logístico y Administrativo de la FA (air force logistic and administrative command); and **CPESFA** - Comando de Personal de la FA (air force personnel command). In addition, several of its squadrons are assigned to the NATO commands CINCSOUTH, SACLANT and SACEUR. The nucleus of the air force is distributed among the complex of Base Aéreas – BA – (air bases), each of which under the FAP's system receives a digit for identification purposes. Each BA is formed into three Grupos (groups), one of which is Operativo (Operational) and responsible for the flying squadrons, airfield services, air traffic control, radar, communications, meteorology and fire-fighting/ambulance services. The second group is Material, whose purview is maintenance, weapons, electronics and supply, and the third is Apoyo (Support) which is in charge of caring for the base infrastructure. Under the direct command of the base CO there is also a services squadron.

BA 1 – Sintra

BA 1, near Sintra, houses the Air Force Academy and the FAP's Staff College, as well as four flying squadrons.

Esquadra 401 is equipped with six 'special mission' CASA C.212 Aviocars, two modified for photo survey roles with Wild ARC-10 mapping cameras, one functioning as an earth resources aircraft (with a tail-mounted MAD boom), one as a navigational trainer with five consoles for students and one for the instructor, and the final two as SAR/maritime patrol craft, with AN/APS-128 search radar in an extended nose radome. Two more Aviocars, this time the wingletted C.212-300 variant, powered by Garrett TPE331-10R-513C turboprops, were ordered in 1993. There aircraft are fitted with SLAR and IR/UV scanners and are intended for ECM training and geographical survey roles. After acceptance trials at OGMA during 1995, both aircraft joined Esq. 401.

Esquadra 502 is tasked with tactical and general purpose airlift roles and is equipped with eight CASA C.212 Aviocars, of which the air force acquired 24, replacing C-47s, between 1973 and 1974. The unit is also the declared operational transition unit for future Aviocar crews, which must undergo a minimum number of hours in the Spanish transport before posted to the Hercules squadron. Two of the Aviocars (C.212A-1s), similar to the Spanish TM.12D variant, form part of a semi-autonomous flight within Esq. 502 that undertakes electronic warfare tasks, both training and in the front line.

Esquadra 505, with 12 Cessna-Reims FTB-337G Miriroles on strength, is tasked for light transport, liaison, visual and photographic reconnaissance. The FAP received 32 Miriroles (to replace the survivors of 153 Do 27s), of which the first 16 were delivered armed, while eight were delivered with camera equipment along with a similar number of dual control aircraft, for training. Several years ago the COIN Cessnas were 'disarmed', and some were disposed of into the civil market. The FTB-337Gs are now used for transport, medevac and training

Esquadra 802 is equipped with a total of 10 sailplanes, replacing DHC-1 Chipmunks, though two were retained as tugs. Five Schleicher ASK.21s and three powered Aerostructure (Fournier) RF-10s provide initial air experience for the Academy cadets (who then progress to the primary syllabus in the Epsilons of Esquadra 101, which in 1993 moved to Beja in the south).

BA 2 – Ota

BA 2 at Ota has no air units assigned, although the required infrastructure has been provided by NATO to be activated in case of need. The CFMTA (AF Military & Technical Training Centre) is based at BA 2 and is in charge of providing the necessary qualifications to technical officers and NCOs.

BA 3 – Tancos

BA 3 at Tancos was recently deactivated and its squadrons transferred to Montijo and Beja. Until that time it had been home to the Alouette IIIs of Esq. 552 (including the 'Rotores de Portugal' helicopter display team), and the Aviocars of Esq. 502 and Esq. 111 which served as the Alouette and CASA Aviocar OCU. Tancos has been mooted as the new home of a future army aviation force, which has yet to be established.

BA 4 – Lajes

Lajes, in Terceira Island of the Azores archipelago, houses BA 4, which is a strategic staging airfield for Atlantic crossings and is used by the US Air Force and Navy plus other NATO members' air forces. Two FAP squadrons are based at Lajes: Esquadra 503 with eight C.212 Aviocars used for tactical and general-purpose transport and SAR work, and Esquadra 752 equipped with about half of the 10 surviving (of 12 acquired) SA 330 Pumas for SAR, logistic/troop transport and humanitarian tasks. The A-7 Corsairs from Esquadras 302 and 304 provide frequent detachments, while the Fighting Falcons of Esquadra 201 will do the same from late 1995.

BA 5 – Monte Real

There has been an air base at Monte Real since 1939 and today it is the Portuguese air force's main operational base.

The first A-7s were delivered to BA 5 in 1982, under a $198 million programme. Through the conversion of 28 ex-US Navy A-7As, 20 TF30-P-408-powered A-7Ps (with the A-7E avionics fit) and three spare airframes were delivered to Esq. 302 from December 1981. A single TA-7C was loaned to the FAP in 1982, for three years. Portugal's second batch of A-7s was ordered in September 1982, on completion of deliveries of the initial batch. A total of 42 ex-US Navy A-7s were transformed into 24 A-7Ps and six TA-7Ps. Deliveries of the A-7Ps, to newly-established Esq. 303, began in October 1984, followed by the TA-7Ps in May 1985. The A-7Ps can carry AIM-7P Sidewinders, but have also been the victims of a high attrition rate over the years. Spares support is provided by 20 non-flyable ex-US Navy A-7As, acquired for that purpose.

Esq. 302 and 304 now share the surviving 35 A-7Ps and five TA-7Ps. Their tasked missions cover tactical air support for maritime operations (TASMO), air interdiction (AI) and offensive/defensive air support (OAS/DAS) with a range of iron bombs and now AGM-65A Maverick ASMs. They can also perform as clear weather interceptors (CWI) with two AIM-9P3 Sidewinders and cannon. Portugal's single-seat Corsairs are unique in carrying a pair of Colt Browning Mk 12 20-mm cannon, as fitted to the original A-7A however, none of the two-seaters carries a gun. The A-7's interceptor role is being abandoned in favour of the Fighting Falcons. For defensive purposes, besides their RWR and chaff/flare dispensers, the aircraft have AN/ALQ-131 jamming pods.

Since their consignment in 1981 Portuguese Corsairs have provided sterling service but, after F-16 deliveries are completed, the FAP will begin to seek a replacement around 2001. The air force's preferred choice is the Eurofighter 2000. Portugal is not a partner nation in EFA development, and the type's high price could rule it out and force the acquisition of more Fighting Falcons (either new or second-hand). However, EFA acquisition would achieve commonality with Spain and allow for combined training, maintenance and logistics support.

The most important event to occur at Monte Real for many years was the commissioning in January 1994 of Esquadra 201 'Falcões' (Falcons) and its F-16s. The unit is equipped with a total of 17 new-build F-16A Block 15 OCUs (Operational Capability Upgrade) and three F-16B Block 15

Above: A single Esq. 401 Aviocar is fitted with a MAD boom along with survey cameras.

Below: This is one of Esq. 401's SLAR- and FLIR-equipped Aviocars, in use for fisheries protection missions.

Externally similar to the Spanish air force's TM.12D EW variant, this C.212 is one of a pair serving with an autonomous ECM training flight, as part of Esq. 502. These aircraft were previously flown by Esq. 401.

The latest type to enter service with Esq. 401 is the CASA C.212-300 Patrullero, which is a purpose-built maritime patrol aircraft, operated on behalf of the Fisheries Ministry.

The Alouette III is virtually the last African war veteran still in Portuguese service today. Well over 100 aircraft have seen FAP service over the years, but today the type is confined to a single unit – Esq. 552 based at BA 11, Beja – and numbers are dwindling.

The FAP's Dornier Do 27 STOL light transports are now virtually all museum aircraft. Both Dornier- and CASA-built aircraft were in use.

The Reims-Cessna FTB.337 is flown by a single unit, Esq. 505 based at BA 1 Sintra. The Miliroles have lost their weapons capability and are now used chiefly for transport and training tasks. This is a photo-recce version.

The Puma is now the backbone of the air force's SAR force, while also being responsible for army transport duties. All of Portugal's Pumas, which are divided between Esq. 751 and 752, are fitted with flotation gear and OMERA ORB-31 search radar.

The faithful Alouette III is no longer tasked with SAR as a prime mission, though some aircraft do retain emergency flotation gear.

OCUs. The first F-16A (15101) and F-16B (15118) were handed over on 18 February 1994 at Fort Worth and, on 8 July, two F-16As and two F-16Bs were delivered directly to Monte Real by USAF pilots. The aircraft were formally accepted into FAP service on 18 July and, by April 1995, all 20 aircraft (17 F-16As and three F-16Bs) were in service with Esquadra 201. The squadron's target strength is 30 pilots. It is intended that each aircraft logs 270 hours per year, while the desired in-commission rate is 80 per cent percent of the fleet. New construction has been undertaken at BA 5, including two hardened shelters for the two QRA aircraft, as well as maintenance hangars. Esq. 201 will also sustain detachments at Madeira and in the Azores

The F-16 programme

Portugal had originally requested 46 F-16s, in 1988, to be supplied under the MAP programme in return for continuing US use of facilities at Lajes. The US responded with an offer of second-hand Block 10 F-16s, but this was rejected in favour of new build Block 15 aircraft (originally referred to as Block 15S). The cost of the 20 aircraft finally agreed on, plus spares and support, amounted to $385 million, in 1990 US dollars.

The Portuguese F-16s are not standard Block 15 OCU aircraft as delivered to Thailand or Singapore (although this is their official designation). Instead, they closely resemble the early-model F-16A ADF (Air Defense Fighter) variant as delivered to the US Air National Guard. These capable aircraft, which were the first F-16 variant to have a BVR missile capability (AIM-7 Sparrow) had several external distinguishing features. They were fitted with distinctive finroot bulges (housing a relocated hydraulic accumulator) and Grimes identification light, on the port forward fuselage. The FAP F-16As do not, however, carry the four-bladed AN/APX-109 Mk IV IFF antenna arrays which were retrofitted to ANG F-16A ADFs, forward of the cockpit, above and below the nose. The Block 15 OCU designation has covered all new-build F-16A/Bs since 1988, all of which include strengthened airframes and updated avionics compared to earlier Block 15s. There are various differences, however, between OCU batches, depending on the customer. Thus, FAP aircraft have been modified to be Sparrow capable. Other OCU features include provision for laser ring gyros, ALR-69 RWR, ALQ-131 ECM pods and the Dash 220 engine. In FAP service, the aircrafts' primary mission will be all-weather interception armed with AIM-9P/L Sidewinders, AIM-7F Sparrows (but not AIM-120) and the M61 gun. It had been originally suggested that the aircraft would be delivered with Penguin AShMs, but this is not now the case.

BA 6 – Montijo

BA 6 at Montijo is the air force's main transport base and is home to four squadrons.

Esquadra 501 is equipped with the six C-130Hs originally delivered during 1977/78, two of which were recently (1991/92) converted to C-130H-30 standard, by the air force rework facility Oficinas Gerais de Material Aeronáutico (OGMA), at Alverca. The Hercules replaced the DC-6, Noratlas (and leased TAP Boeing 707s) in FAP service and, until the arrival of P-3Ps, conducted maritime patrol and SAR duties. Some

years after the C-130Hs entered service the air force attempted to acquire four stretched L-100-30s, but funding for this sizeable purchase was not approved. This situation was remedied somewhat by the two C-130H-30 conversions which began their careers flying UN supply missions to Angola in 1992. Plans are in hand to acquire two new C-130H-30s. The Hercules perform tactical and general airlift duties, including a regular shuttle service to the Azores and Madeira and they also act as emergency forest-fire fighters with add-on MAFFS kit.

Esquadra 504 has three Dassault Falcon 20s, acquired from Federal Express, in 1985. Two were converted for calibration and transport, by Flight Refuelling in the UK, and the third is dedicated to VIP roles, a task also undertaken by Esq. 504's two tri-jet Falcon 50s (delivered in 1990).

Esquadra 601 is equipped with six Lockheed P-3P Orions (ex-RAAF, No. 11 Sqn P-3Bs) and tasked with the maritime patrol mission, including anti-surface unit warfare (ASUW) and ASW. Since 1993 the squadron has detached one of its Orions to NAS Sigonella for Operation Sharp Guard over the Adriatic Sea, in two-month rotations. The Orions filled the gap left by the retirement of the FAP's last P-2E Neptunes in 1977. Several follow-on patrol aircraft were proposed, including the EMBRAER EMB-111 Patrulha, before the first of the P-3s arrived at OGMA, in 1987, for structural rework. A systems 'prototype' conversion was undertaken by Lockheed, in the US, in July 1988 and subsequently this work was transferred to OGMA also. The last example was delivered in 1990 to Esq. 601, which had been newly established to operate the type.

The P-3Ps have been refitted to a standard that approximates the US Navy's P-3C Update II standard. This replaces the analog systems of the P-3B with digital acoustic processor and display systems – AN/ASQ-114 and AN/AQA-7. It also adds a turret-mounted AN/AAS-36 FLIR, underwing Harpoon ASM capability and an improved sonobuoy monitoring and reference system. The Portuguese Orions all wear a unique striped two-tone grey scheme.

The final operational unit at Montijo is Esquadra 751 with five Pumas for SAR and tactical transport roles. All the FAP Pumas are equipped with the OMERA ORB-31 Hercules search radar and flotation gear. Portugal acquired 13 Pumas from 1972, and all were subsequently converted to AS 330L standard. Since then the survivors have been re-engined with Makila turboshafts, becoming the SA 330S, a virtual hybrid between the Puma and Super Puma.

BA 6 is also the home of the Training Centre for survival, NBC (Nuclear, Biological, Chemical) protection and explosive disposal teams.

BA 11 – Beja

BA 11 at Beja, in the Alentejo region of southern Portugal, is the FAP's most recent air base. It was commissioned in 1964 and until very recently was mainly used by the Luftwaffe for weapons training (the establishment was known as Deutsches Luftwaffe Ubungsplatzkommando Beja), and its construction was financed by Germany. Since 1980 the base had housed a permanent Alpha Jet detachment manned by JBG 49 instructors.

On 1 February 1987, Esquadra 103 with its T-33s and T-38s relocated from BA 5 Monte Real to BA 11 Beja. Known as Esquadra de Instruçao Complementar de Pilotagem de Aviones de Combate (EICPAC – fast jet training squadron), the unit retired its old T-Birds in October 1991, after a 38-year career in the FAP. By then, Esq. 103 was scheduled to re-equip with former German Alpha Jets, so it was uneconomical and unnecessary to maintain the small number of Talons in service. Shortly after the last class of new pilots graduated from the T-38s in June 1993, the Talons were finally retired, on 29 June.

FAP Alpha Jets

Towards the end of 1991 Esquadra 103 started to re-equip with Alpha Jet As, as did the recently relocated Esquadra 301. The end of the Cold War and German reunification forced the retirement of most Luftwaffe Alpha Jets and a deal was struck whereby they would be transferred to the FAP as G91/T-38 replacements. Luftwaffe operations at Beja concluded on 30 June 1993, and six months later the base was fully under FAP authority. Eighteen of the FAP's 'new' Alpha Jets had previously been based at Beja, on detachment from JBG 49. The balance was delivered from Germany between 6 October and 30 November, where initial Portuguese pilot training was undertaken by JBG 49. JBG 49 disestablished on 31 March 1994 and lost its wing status, and was renamed as the Fluglehrgruppe Fürstenfeldbruck (from 1 April 1994). Equipped with 36 machines, it is responsible for lead-in training for future Tornado pilots and has relocated to Fürstenfeldbruck. The Alpha Jets were the first FAP aircraft to carry the air force's new five-digit serials, which have now been universally adopted. Esq. 103 and 301 share 45 Alpha Jets (50 having been delivered, with five being used as spares sources). Recent reports indicate that only 11 of the FAP's Alpha Jets are actually airworthy and a sizeable number (10) have been withdrawn from use at Beja to act as a permanent spares source.

Esquadra 103 continues with its advanced training task. The length of a pupil's training depends on whether the student has come directly from Esquadra 101 or if he has completed Undergraduate Pilot Training with the USAF on the T-38 Talon.

Esquadra 103 soon will resurrect the FAP's flight demonstration team 'Asas de Portugal'. The team for many years used the T-37Cs of Esquadra 102 at Sintra as its mount, until premature fatigue cracks forced the aircraft's grounding late in 1990. Thirty T-37s were supplied by the US, and 24 remained in service at the time of their withdrawal. Esq. 102 was disbanded on 8 August 1992 and 12 of its T-37s are still held in storage at Sintra (along with several G91s).

Training syllabus

The Alpha Jets of Esquadra 301 have maintained the unit's previous missions of Battlefield Air Interdiction (BAI) and Offensive/Defensive Air Support (OAS/DAS). The Alpha Jet has a much better weapons capability than the old 'Gina', including Elettronica Spa ACE 2000 electronic warfare sets (carried in the empty rear cockpit), six of which have been acquired for aircraft of the 'Jaguares'. Esq. 301 has been a member of the NATO Tiger Squadron Association since the

Three Dassault Falcon 20Ds were acquired by Esq. 504, based at BA 6, Montijo. One is a dedicated VIP transport aircraft while the others were modified to convertible nav aid calibration/transport standard.

The smaller Falcon 20s were supplemented by three larger Falcon 50s, from 1990 onwards. The long-ranger Falcon 50s facilitate flights far beyond Portugal and the European Union.

Left: The Museu do Ar, at Alverca, maintains a large collection of former FAP aircraft, including several air worthy types, such as this T-6 Texan.

Right: The FAP's last Chipmunks survive as glider tugs, in the hands of Esq. 802, at Sintra. The Chipmunk was replaced by the Epsilon in the basic training role.

Esq. 802 has two rather unconventional types on strength for basic training and refresher flying. This is one of its German-built Schleicher ASK-21 sailplanes.

The second of Esq. 802's aircraft types (apart from the two Chipmunk glider tugs) is the French-built Aerostructure (Fournier) RF-10 powered sailplane.

The Portuguese air force's basic trainer is the Aérospatiale (SOCATA) TB-30 Epsilon. A total of 18 Epsilons was delivered to Esq. 104, at Sintra, between 1989 and 1990 and they are now operated by Beja-based Esq. 101.

KEY

- ✈ **Active airbase**
- ✈ Inactive airbase
- ✪ National capitol
- ● Towns & cities

The Azores

BA 4, Lajes

SPAIN

Atlantic Ocean

Viana do Castelo
Braga
Bragança
Porto
Vila Real
Aveiro
Viseu
Guarda
Coimbra
BA 5, Monte Real
Leiria
Castelo Branco
BA 3, Tancos
BA 2, Ota
Santarém
Portalegre
BA 1, Sintra
Alverca (OGMA)
Lisbon
Montijo
Évora
BA 11, Beja
Beja

PORTUGAL

Faro

| Map Scale | 100 km |
| 0 | 100 miles |

Gulf of Cadiz

The only type flown by the Portuguese navy is the Westland Lynx Mk 95, five of which are flown from the navy's three 'Vasco de Gama'-class frigates. The Lynxes are on charge with the Esquadrilha de Helicopteros de Marhina.

mid-1980s and its tiger-striped G91s were once a common sight.

Esq. 101 moved from Sintra to Beja in June 1993 and is equipped with 16 TB.30 Epsilons. Eighteen Epsilons were delivered, from a 1987 requirement for 24. In 1989 a single aircraft was delivered by Aérospatiale but the remainder were all assembled by OGMA, by mid-1990.

Esq. 101 is responsible for a student's first 120 hours of elementary flying training, a task in which the Epsilons replaced the DHC-1 Chipmunk and its 70-hour course. The pupil must next undergo 100-120 hours in the Alpha Jet with Esq. 103, or less if he is a graduate of the UPT. Esq. 103's syllabus is made of five different programmes, which comprise: a conversion course for students returning from the UPT in the United States; a jet training course for students who have completed the 120-hour primary course in the Epsilon; a refresher flying course for jet pilots on staff postings, to keep their aircraft commander qualifications; the Alpha Jet instructor course; and the weapons training course for graduating students.

Alouette survivors

The fourth unit at Beja is Esquadra 552, which is equipped with 24 Alouette IIIs and tasked with helicopter pilot training. This role was taken from the disbanded Esquadra 111, which together with 552 was previously based at Tancos. Other taskings include troop transport and SAR. Esq. 552's Alouettes are the last in Portuguese service, from a total of 144 of these utilitarian workhorses delivered since 1963. A similar number are in storage, and the remainder were lost either in accidents or during the African wars (in which they provided outstanding services), or simply disposed of. The FAP has a requirement for 30-40 medium-lift helicopters, either Black Hawks or Super Pumas/Cougars, to support army operations. Some confusion remains over whether the FAP will expand its helicopter fleet dedicated to the army, or whether the army itself will establish its own organic aviation arm. Several moves to do just that have been made in the past, but none have come to fruition.

The FAP has two reserve air bases, Aeródromo de Manobra (AM 1) at Ovar and AM 2 at San Jacinto. The former is a NATO infrastructure which is kept operational to receive detached forces in case of emergency or during exercises. The latter serves as a secondary airfield for Esquadra 505, and is also the headquarters of the Parachute Brigade.

Radar stations

The Air Defence System, activated in 1953, originally had two radar stations which reported to an Air Defence Operations Centre. One station was near Lisbon (Montejunto) and the other close to Oporto (Paço de Ferreira). This obsolete system, with only manual plotting capabilities, was entirely supplanted by the end of 1994 by the high-tech SICCAP (Sistema de Mando y Control Aéreo de Portugal/Portuguese Air Command and Control System), which features command and control operations centralised in a single Operations Centre. SICCAO has three three-dimensional radars, a COC at Montejunto, secure V/UHF communications and digital datalinks, as well as the possibility of connecting

with other ground-based early warning nets that include those of the Spanish (SADA) and French (STRIDA), AWACS and ships. In the near future, the Azores and Madeira Islands will have autonomous SICCAP cover. The Portuguese air force has a detachment of technicians and flying personnel attached to the NATO Early Warning Force, flying Boeing E-3 Sentries.

Comando Operacional de la Força Aérea Portuguesa

UNIT	TYPE	BASE
Grupo Operacional 12		
Esquadra 401	C.212 Aviocar	BA 1 Sintra
Esquadra 502	C.212 Aviocar	BA 1 Sintra
Esquadra 505	Cessna 337	BA 1 Sintra
Esquadra 802	RF-10, ASK.21, DHC-1	BA 1 Sintra
Grupo Operacional 41		
Esquadra 503	C.212 Aviocar	BA 4 Lajes
Esquadra 752	SA 330 Puma	BA 4 Lajes
Grupo Operacional 51		
Esquadra 201	F-16A/B Fighting Falcon	BA 5 Monte Real
Esquadra 302	A/TA-7P Corsair	BA 5 Monte Real
Esquadra 304	A/TA-7P Corsair	BA 5 Monte Real
Grupo Operacional 61		
Esquadra 501	C-130H/H-30 Hercules	BA 6 Montijo
Esquadra 504	Falcon 20/50	BA 6 Montijo
Esquadra 601	P-3P Orion	BA 6 Montijo
Esquadra 751	SA 330 Puma	BA 6 Montijo
Grupo Operacional 111		
Esquadra 101	TB-30 Epsilon, Cessna 337	BA 11 Beja
Esquadra 103	Alpha Jet	BA 11 Beja
Esquadra 301	Alpha Jet	BA 11 Beja
Esquadra 552	Alouette III	BA 11 Beja

Naval Aviation

Almost 50 years after it was merged with the Aeronáutica Militar to form the Força Aérea Portuguesa, the Aviaçao Naval was timidly reactivated in the early 1990s when five Westland Super Lynx Mk 95s were ordered. When the frigates were under construction, in 1988, Portugal approached the US to supply five Kaman SH-2 Seasprites, but chose the Lynx instead. An order was placed with Westland in 1989 and the first of these helicopters flew on 27 March 1992. The two initial examples were upgraded ex-Royal Navy machines (HAS.Mk 3S ZF559/ZH580 and HAS.Mk 3S ZF561/ZH581) while the remaining three have been built by Westland. The Super Lynx is an upgraded export variant of the naval HAS.Mk 8 with the designation Mk 95, and is

equipped with Doppler 91 and Racal RNS252 Super TANS navigation systems, Bendix/King RDR 1500 radar and an AN/AQS-18 dipping sonar. Their warload includes Mk 46 torpedoes or depth bombs.

The Lynx are operated from 'Vasco de Gama'-class (MEKO 200PM) frigates. The 'MEKO 200' class is a modern frigate design, built solely for export by a conglomeration of German ship yards. The Portuguese navy has three such vessels: *Vasco Da Gama* (launched in June 1989), *Alvares Cabral* (launched June 1990) and *Corte Real* (launched June 1990). Sixty per cent of their purchase cost was funded by NATO and they are the most potent vessels in the Portuguese fleet. They can each deploy up to two Lynx.

Marinha's aircrews were trained in basic helicopter operations first by Esquadra 111 and later by Esquadra 552, and then went to RNAS Portland to do the full Lynx course with UK's Fleet Air Arm. The first two aircraft were handed over on 29 July 1993 and delivered by a Heavylift Shorts Belfast on 24 August. The remaining aircraft were all delivered by 16 November. The aircraft are operated by the Esquadrilha de Helicopteros de Marhina.

During 1995 *Vasco De Gama* was deployed to the Adriatic in support of the United Nation's ongoing blockade of military supplies for the warring nations of the former Yugoslavia. Its onboard Lynx Mk 95 was used to survey suspect vessels in the area and land UN boarding parties, if required.

Army Aviation

Several attempts have been made to formally establish a Portuguese army aviation element, but so far without success. A requirement for 12 Agusta A 109s (including four BGM-71 TOW-armed examples) was issued in the mid-1980s. By 1986 this had been reduced to just the armed aircraft, but it was felt that the treasury could not support such a unit. The original F-16 deal, in 1989, was to have included up to 52 surplus UH-1s from US stocks, but this massive increase of the helicopter force has seemingly been abandoned. However, finding a replacement for the ageing air force Alouette IIIs is becoming increasingly pressing.

For air defence, the Portuguese army is equipped with a mix of ageing UK-supplied Short Blowpipe shoulder-launched SAMs and (from 1986) US-supplied MIM-72 Chaparral mobile SAMs (based around a version of the Sidewinder AAM). Portugal has a standing requirement for more modern MIM-23 Hawk and FIM-92 Stinger SAMs to replace both these systems.

National Republican Guard

Portugal's paramilitary Guarda Nacional Republicana (14,600 personnel) maintains a single small flying unit at Alverca, alongside the OGMA facility. This unit, the Brigada de Transito da Guarda Nacional Republicana (transport brigade), was established in 1984 and operates five SE.3130 Alouette IIs (which were themselves obtained

from German army surplus stocks in the 1960s). Seven helicopters were originally acquired, with a further four for spares use. The surviving Alouette IIs were flown with military serial numbers within the FAP's regular serial sequence, but they have now adopted civil registrations.

Salvador Mafé Huertas and Robert Hewson

Three G91s survive at Sintra; one is preserved outside the field, while these two can be found on the tarmac outside the Air Academy.

This pleasing air-to-air study harks back to the days when the G91 was the backbone of the Força Aérea Portuguesa. The 'Gina' was blooded in all three African wars and over 100 G91R3/R4s served in Portuguese markings, from 1965 until 1993.

The last T-38s were withdrawn from squadron service with Esq. 103 in June 1993. The unit had previously moved from Monte Real to Beja, and Esq. 103 is now one of the FAP's two Alpha Jet units. A small number of T-38s still appear to be active, however.

This 'Asas de Portugal' T-37 is on display outside the HQ of its former owner, Esq. 102, at Sintra. A second aircraft is also preserved there, as a gate guard.

The Museu do Ar has a large collection of FAP transport aircraft at Alverca, including two DC-6s, two Ju 52s and this Nord Noratlas.

A trio of F-86F Sabres still survives, in museum hands, on the ramp at Alverca. FAP Sabres were flown by Esq. 201, from Monte Real, and were a mix of ex-Luftwaffe Canadair Sabre Mk 6s and ex-Norwegian air force F-86Fs.

These dramatically posed G91s are on guard outside the air force HQ building, in Lisbon.

This C-47 is preserved at Sintra, along with several other FAP veterans including a North American T-6 Texan and Lockheed P-2 Neptune.

INDEX

158

Picture acknowledgments

Front cover: Warren Thompson. **4:** SIRPA-AIR (three). **5:** Michel Fournier (two). **6:** Bruno Cowet, M.J. Gerards, Michel Fournier. **7:** Kevin Wills, Régent Dansereau. **8:** Kevin Wills, Marco Amatimaggio, Jon Lake. **9:** E.A. Sloot (two). **10:** Richard Simon, Brane Lucovnik (three). **11:** Chris Ryan, Marcus Fulber. **12:** M.P. Attrill, Gerry Turner, Geoff Stockle. **13:** Tadao Iamizumi via Ted Carlson, Dylan Eklund, Jorge Padin. **14:** Régent Dansereau, Gary Bihary. **15:** Bob Archer. **16:** Renato E.F. Jones, Frank Smith. **17:** Gary Bihary, Schweizer. **18:** Nate Leong, Gary Bihary, Robert Hewson. **19:** Ted Carlson/Fotodynamics, Gilles Auliard. **20:** Jeremy Flack/API. **21:** Aldo Camoni (two). **22:** Jeremy Flack/API, Tim Ripley. **23:** Jeremy Flack/API (three), Peter R. Foster (two). **24:** Tim Ripley, Jeremy Flack/API. **25-26:** Jeremy Flack/API. **27:** Jeremy Flack/API (two), Tim Ripley. **28:** Jeremy Flack/API. **29:** Tim Ripley. **30:** Robert Hewson. **31:** Robert Hewson (two), Saab. **32:** Peter R. Foster (two), Ted Carlson/Fotodynamics. **33:** Peter R. Foster, Ted Carlson/Fotodynamics, Robert Hewson. **34:** Rockwell (two), MBB. **35:** Rockwell (two), NASA. **36:** Joe Cupido (two), Ted Carlson/Fotodynamics. **37:** Graham Robson. **38:** Joe Cupido, via Michael Stroud. **39:** Joe Cupido (four). **40:** Bob Burns (two). **41:** Rockwell. **42:** Rockwell (two). **43:** Rockwell. **44:** Rockwell. **45:** Rockwell, Joe Cupido. **46:** Rockwell (two). **47:** Jim Winchester, David Donald, Rockwell. **48-51:** Rockwell. **52-53:** Randy Jolly. **54:** US Air Force, Rockwell International (two), Rockwell International via Bruce Robertson. **56:** US Air Force (three). **57:** US Air Force, Rockwell International (two). **58-59:** Rockwell International. **61:** John Gourley, Randy Jolly. **69:** Randy Jolly, Warren Thompson (three), Jeremy Flack/API. **70-71:** US Air Force. **72:** Rockwell International, Tom Alexander via Warren Thompson. **73:** US Air Force. **74:** Rockwell International (two). **75:** Rockwell International (two). **76:** Rockwell International, General Electric. **77:** Rockwell International (two), US Air Force. **78-80:** Rockwell International. **81:** US Air Force, James Benson. **82:** Rockwell International (two), Warren Thompson. **83:** Rockwell International (two). **84:** Rockwell International, James Benson. **85:** US Air Force, Rockwell International. **86:** Rockwell International. **87:** Randy Jolly, Ted Carlson/Fotodynamics. **88:** Randy Jolly (two). **89:** Rockwell International. **90:** US Air Force. **91:** Randy Jolly (three). **92:** Rockwell International. **93:** Warren Thompson (three). **94:** Randy Jolly, David Donald. **95:** Ted Carlson/Fotodynamics. **96-97:** Randy Jolly. **98:** Warren Thompson. **99:** Ted Carlson/Fotodynamics, Randy Jolly. **100:** Randy Jolly. **101:** Randy Jolly, Ted Carlson/Fotodynamics. **102:** Randy Jolly (two). **103:** John N. Dale. **104:** Warren Thompson (two), Chris Ryan. **105:** Randy Jolly (eleven), Warren Thompson (six), Don Logan (two), Ted Carlson/Fotodynamics. **106:** Don Logan, Stephen Kill. **107:** John N. Dale, Don Logan (two), Warren Thompson (two). **108:** David Donald, Don Logan (two), Ted Carlson/Fotodynamics, Randy Jolly. **109:** Warren Thompson, Don Logan (two), Peter Wilson, Ted Carlson/Fotodynamics. **110:** Ted Carlson/Fotodynamics (two), Randy Jolly (four). **111:** D. Sorochan, David Donald, Ted Carlson/Fotodynamics. **112:** Warren Thompson, Don Logan (two). **113:** Ted Carlson/Fotodynamics (two), Don Logan. **114:** Piotr Butowski (two). **115:** Gordon Upton, Peter R. March (two), Piotr Butowski. **116:** Peter R. March (two), Chris Ryan, Piotr Butowski (two). **117:** Peter R. March, Gordon Upton, Piotr Butowski. **118:** Paul Jackson, Gordon Upton, Piotr Butowski, Peter R. March. **119:** Peter R. March (two), Piotr Butowski. **120:** Bruce Trombecky via Robert L. Lawson (two), Robert L. Lawson, LCdr Dave Baranek via Robert L. Lawson. **121:** Daniel Soulaine, Robert L. Lawson, Bryan Ward/Bogey Photography, NASA, Bob Burns, Henry B. Ham. **122:** Henry B. Ham, Tim Senior, Ton van Dreumel, Jeff Rankin-Lowe. **123:** Jeff Rankin-Lowe, Wolbers, Alan Key, Tim Senior, Austin J. Brown/APL, Neil Dunridge. **124:** A. Marden, Stephen Kill, Peter R. Foster (two), Stefan Degraef. **125:** RDAF, Stephen Kill, Tom Ross (two), Esk 726/RDAF, Tim Senior. **126:** Jeff Rankin-Lowe, Esk 727/RDAF, Mal Gault, Henry B. Ham. **127:** René van Woezik, Peter R. Foster (two), Henry B. Ham (two). **128:** IDF/AF, Henry B. Ham, Yehuda Borovik/BIAF Magazine. **129:** C. Lorch, Yves Debay, BIAF Magazine. **130:** KLu, M. Brouwer (two). **131:** KLu, Mike Reyno, Kees van der Mark, Jeff Rankin-Lowe KLu via G. Kromhout, Tieme Festner. **132:** B. Fischer, Peter R. Foster (two), Federico Anselmino, Alan Key, Jeff Rankin-Lowe. **133:** B. Fischer, Jeff Rankin-Lowe, G. Kromhout, Alan Key, Peter R. Foster. **134:** Jeff Rankin-Lowe, D. Adams, M. Baumann. **135:** Jeff Rankin-Lowe, Ian Black, Peter R. Foster. **136:** Henry B. Ham, Peter R. Foster. **137:** Henry B. Ham, Alan Key, Lockheed Martin TAS. **138:** Henry B. Ham, Lockheed Martin TAS (two), Jeremy Flack/API. **139:** M.P. Attrill, Peter Steinemann, Lockheed Martin TAS, Peter R. Foster. **140-147:** Georg Mader. **149:** Gary Best, Hans Nijhuis (two), M.J. Gerards, Gary Best. **151:** Hendrik J. van Broekhuizen, Gerd Kromhout, E.A. Sloot, Hans Nijhuis (three), Gary Best (two). **153:** Alan Key (two), René van Woezik, M.J. Gerards (two), Gary Best, Hans Nijhuis (two), M. Attrill. **155:** Hans Nijhuis (six), Gary Best, Westland. **157:** Gary Best (four), Bowers (two).